ECONOMIC SANCTIONS IN EU PRIVATE INTERNATIONAL LAW

Economic sanctions are instruments of foreign policy. However, they can also affect legal relations between private parties – principally in contract. In such cases, the court or arbitration tribunal seized must decide whether to give effect to the economic sanction in question.

Private international law functions as a 'filter', transmitting economic sanctions that originate in public law to the realm of private law. The aim of this book is to examine how private international law rules can influence the enforcement of economic sanctions and their related foreign policy objectives.

A coherent EU foreign policy position – in addition to promoting legal certainty and predictability – would presuppose a uniform approach not only concerning the economic sanctions of the EU, but also with regard to the restrictive measures imposed by third countries. However, if we examine in detail the application of economic sanctions by Member States' courts and arbitral tribunals, we find a somewhat different picture. This book argues that this can be explained in part by the divergence of private international law approaches in the Member States.

Volume 25 in the series Studies in Private International Law

Studies in Private International Law
Recent titles in the series

International Surrogacy Arrangements: Legal Regulation at the International Level
Edited by Katarina Trimmings and Paul Beaumont

The Hague Child Abduction Convention: A Critical Analysis
Rhona Schuz

Interregional Recognition and Enforcement of Civil and Commercial Judgments: Lessons for China from the US and EU Law
Jie Huang

The Recovery of Maintenance in the EU and Worldwide
Paul Beaumont, Burkhard Hess, Lara Walker and Stefanie Spancken

Australian Private International Law for the 21st Century: Facing Outwards
Edited by Andrew Dickinson, Thomas John and Mary Keyes

Maintenance and Child Support in Private International Law
Lara Walker

The Choice of Law Contract
Maria Hook

The Nature and Enforcement of Choice of Court Agreements: A Comparative Study
Mukarrum Ahmed

Cross-Border Litigation in Europe
Edited by Paul Beaumont, Mihail Danov, Katarina Trimmings and Burcu Yuksel

Forum (Non) Conveniens in England: Past, Present, and Future
Ardavan Arzandeh

Commercial Issues in Private International Law: A Common Law Perspective
Edited by Vivienne Bath, Andrew Dickinson, Michael Douglas and Mary Keyes

Jurisdiction and Cross-Border Collective Redress: A European Private International Law Perspective
Alexia Pato

Rethinking Judicial Jurisdiction in Private International Law
Milana Karayanidi

Economic Sanctions in EU Private International Law

Tamás Szabados

•HART•
OXFORD • LONDON • NEW YORK • NEW DELHI • SYDNEY

HART PUBLISHING

Bloomsbury Publishing Plc

Kemp House, Chawley Park, Cumnor Hill, Oxford, OX2 9PH, UK

HART PUBLISHING, the Hart/Stag logo, BLOOMSBURY and the Diana logo are trademarks of Bloomsbury Publishing Plc

First published in Great Britain 2019

A catalogue record for this book is available from the British Library.

A catalogue record for this book is available from the Library of Congress.

ISBN: HB: 978-1-50993-351-8
ePDF: 978-1-50993-353-2
ePub: 978-1-50993-352-5

Typeset by Compuscript Ltd, Shannon
Printed and bound in Great Britain by CPI Group (UK) Ltd, Croydon CR0 4YY

MIX
Paper from responsible sources
FSC® C013604

To find out more about our authors and books visit www.hartpublishing.co.uk. Here you will find extracts, author information, details of forthcoming events and the option to sign up for our newsletters.

Supported through the New National Excellence Program of the Ministry of Human Capacities

SERIES EDITOR'S PREFACE

Although this book primarily has an EU perspective it is of interest to readers outside the EU (including readers in the UK if Brexit goes ahead). The author gives detailed analysis of the private international law (and some substantive) case law concerning economic sanctions in England, France and Germany, much of which pre-dates the current EU regime in the Rome I Regulation. He also takes full account of the approach of arbitral tribunals to cases where economic sanctions have a bearing on the performance of a contract. Arbitral tribunals are in a different position to courts. The latter have a law of the forum which can make economic sanctions overriding mandatory norms that its courts must follow even when a foreign law is the governing law whereas the former have the law of the arbitral seat but do its overriding mandatory norms have any bearing on the arbitral tribunal when that law is not the law governing the contract?

One of the excellent contributions that this book makes (particularly in chapter four) is to bring to non-German readers a very helpful explanation of the different theories in German literature about overriding mandatory norms of the forum, of the applicable law, and of the law of any other State. It also helpfully considers German theory and practice on using a foreign law that is not the law applicable to the contract as a relevant piece of data as an element in deciding the substantive dispute. This use of a law other than the governing law at the substantive law stage is permitted by the Court of Justice of the European Union in the *Nikiforidis* case (C-135/15) when it is not possible to use that law as an overriding mandatory norm under Article 9(3) of Rome I because it is not the law of the place of performance of the relevant obligation under the contract. The Court of Justice said at paragraph 51 that:

> Article 9 of the Rome I Regulation does not preclude overriding mandatory provisions of a State other than the State of the forum or the State where the obligations arising out of the contract have to be or have been performed from being taken into account as a matter of fact, in so far as this is provided for by a substantive rule of the law that is applicable to the contract pursuant to the regulation.

How another law can be taken into account as a matter of "fact" is easier for a non-German speaking reader to understand after reading this book.

The author has very interesting ideas about how the EU courts should use Article 9(3) of Rome I in cases involving non-EU economic sanctions. He builds on the ideas of Andreas Köhler to encourage EU courts to only apply non-EU economic sanctions where the interests of the EU as a whole are upheld by giving effect to the illegality under the law of the place of performance in a non-EU State.

Although the UK will continue to apply Rome I for the foreseeable future even if Brexit goes ahead (with or without a deal) it seems unlikely that the UK courts will consider whether the illegality under the law of the place of performance should be applied only where it upholds the interests of the EU as a whole. Given the background to the UK only opting in to Rome I after the Regulation was adopted and the compromise in Article 9(3) had been reached (see Paul Beaumont and Peter McEleavy, *Anton's Private International Law* (3rd edn, SULI/W Green, 2011) paras 10.292 to 10.304) the UK courts are likely to apply Article 9(3) strictly without attempting the difficult task of speculating as to when giving effect to illegality under the law of the place of performance serves the interests of the EU as a whole.

I commend the book as a completely original contribution to Hart Studies in Private International Law and as a thorough and thoughtful examination of important issues of global, regional and national public policy (economic sanctions and blocking statutes trying to limit their effects) in the context of private international law.

Paul Beaumont FRSE,
Professor of Private International Law,
University of Stirling

CONTENTS

LIST OF ABBREVIATIONS

AFDI	*Annuaire français de droit international*
AJIL	*American Journal of International Law*
BGH	Bundesgerichtshof
CFSP	Common Foreign Security Policy
CJEU	Court of Justice of the European Union
CML Rev	*Common Market Law Review*
EC	European Community
EEC	European Economic Community
EFAR	*European Foreign Affairs Review*
EU	European Union
GATT	General Agreement on Tariffs and Trade
ICJ	International Court of Justice
ICLQ	*International & Comparative Law Quarterly*
ILM	International Legal Materials
IPRax	*Praxis des Internationalen Privat- und Verfahrensrechts*
JDI	*Journal du droit international*
LG	Landgericht
NJW	*Neue Juristische Wochenschrift*
OLG	Oberlandesgericht
RabelsZ	*Rabels Zeitschrift für ausländisches und internationales Privatrecht*
RCDIP	*Revue critique de droit international privé*
RBDI	*Revue belge de droit international*
RDAI/IBLJ	*Revue de droit des affaires internationales/International Business Law Journal*
RGDIP	*Revue générale de droit international public*

RIW	*Recht der Internationalen Wirtschaft*
SchiedsVZ	*Zeitschrift für Schiedsverfahren*
TEU	Treaty on European Union
TFEU	Treaty on the Functioning of the European Union
UN	United Nations
UNSC	United Nations Security Council
ZVglRWiss	*Zeitschrift für Vergleichende Rechtswissenschaft*

TABLE OF LEGAL SOURCES

UN legal sources

Treaties

Resolutions of the UN General Assembly

Resolutions of the UNSC

Judgments of the International Court of Justice

Legal sources of the EU

Treaties

Judgments of the CJEU

EU legislation

Other EU sources

Acts of other international organisations

NATIONAL LEGISLATION AND OTHER INSTRUMENTS OF NATIONAL LAW

Switzerland

UK

US

National case law

Canada

France

Germany

Italy

Netherlands

Switzerland

UK

USA

Legal sources of arbitration

Arbitral awards

Arbitration rules

1

Introduction

I. Economic Sanctions in Private International Law

Economic sanctions are 'anomalies' in the logic of free trade. Basedow described economic sanctions as a 'stroke of fate' for the companies affected.[1] Racine calls embargoes the most restrictive rules for international commerce and he depicts an embargo as an islet of resistance against the liberty characterising global commerce and an attack against the freedom of economic exchange.[2]

In addition to their intrusive nature disturbing the free flow of commerce, economic sanctions are surrounded by general scepticism. Many authors call their effectiveness into question. Speaking about the sanctions imposed by the European Union (EU), the positions seem to be quite polarised. EU sanction policy or a particular sanction regime was found by some authors to be successful,[3] effective or 'a relevant foreign policy tool'.[4] However, doubts also encompass the effectiveness of the economic sanctions imposed by the EU. The EU has been the subject of criticisms that its sanctions pursuing foreign policy objectives are 'generally ineffective'[5] and they are applied inconsistently.[6] In 1982, the European Parliament itself found in a resolution[7] that:

(b) economic sanctions have a history of failure,

(c) economic sanctions have proved to be thoroughly unsatisfactory as a means of achieving foreign policy objectives, although they may be appropriate to complement other forms of action,

[1] Jürgen Basedow, 'Entscheidung – Das Amerikanische Pipeline-Embargo vor Gericht. Niederlande: Pres. Rb. Den Haag 17. 9. 1982. (Fall Sensor)' (1983) 47 *RabelsZ* 141, 157.

[2] Jean-Baptiste Racine, 'L'arbitrage commercial international et les mesures d'embargo. À propos de l'arrêt de la Cour d'appel du Québec du 31 mars 2003' (2004) 134 *Journal du droit international* 89, 90.

[3] Concerning the sanctions against Russia, see NATO Review Magazine, 'Sanctions after Crimea: Have They Worked?', www.nato.int/docu/review/2015/Russia/sanctions-after-crimea-have-they-worked/EN/index.htm.

[4] Leander Leenders, 'EU Sanctions: A Relevant Foreign Policy Tool?' College of Europe, EU Diplomacy Papers 3/2014, 9 and 27, https://www.coleurope.eu/system/files_force/research-paper/edp_3_2014_leenders_0.pdf?download=1.

[5] Clara Portela, *European Union Sanctions and Foreign Policy* (Routledge, 2010) 101.

[6] Klaus Brummer, 'Imposing Sanctions: The Not So "Normative Power Europe"' (2009) 14 *European Foreign Affairs Review* 191.

[7] Resolution on the significance of economic sanctions, particularly trade embargoes and boycotts, and their consequences for the EEC's relations with third countries, Minutes of the sitting of Monday, 11 October 1982 [1982] OJ C292/13.

(d) hardly any state can be induced by economic pressure to make radical changes in its policies. Such pressure is much more likely to result in the hardening of political attitudes, while the national economies of the state imposing sanctions and of third countries not directly involved are very often as seriously affected and badly damaged as the national economy of the state on which sanctions have been imposed,

(e) there are many ways of circumventing and undermining economic sanctions. However stringently they are policed, it is impossible to guarantee that they are implemented absolutely consistently and without exception, at least in peace-time.

Taking the above into account, the European Parliament urged 'the Commission and Council not to associate themselves with any general sanctions which are manifestly unenforceable'[8] and to use economic sanctions only sparingly.[9] As Gherari points out, the total success of sanctions is as rare as their complete failure.[10] This also holds for the sanctions imposed by the EU.

In spite of their anomalous nature and all doubts, economic sanctions are ubiquitous. It suffices to refer here to the sanctions imposed against Russia or Iran, which feature almost every day on the front pages of newspapers. Irrespective of the question of the effectiveness of economic sanctions, they are present in international trade and affect the legal relationships between private parties. If we take a glance at the economic sanctions adopted by the EU, the multiplication of economic sanctions is remarkable. As the number of trade restrictions grows, so the number of cases involving economic sanctions increases.[11] The current network of economic sanctions has a widespread effect on the contractual relationship of private parties, primarily on the relationship between a private party from the target state and other private parties, but economic sanctions may also have repercussions on relationships between private entities which are not directly related to the target state.

Economic sanctions may be examined from many angles. Political science, international economics[12] and the study of international relations often examine the effectiveness of economic sanctions. Here, the focus is on whether or not the target state yields due to the economic sanction and changes its policy considered to be harmful. Public international law examines the legality of sanctions. Administrative law establishes the detailed rules of export and import, together with the possibility of exemptions. And even criminal law plays a role in establishing the penalties for violating economic sanctions. Economic sanctions are an instrument

[8] ibid para 1.

[9] ibid para 4.

[10] Habib Gherari, 'La mise en oeuvre des sanctions' in Habib Gherari and Sandra Szurek (eds), *Sanctions unilatérales, mondialisation du commerce et ordre juridique international* (Montchrestien, 1998) 53, 74.

[11] See Norbert Knüppel, *Zwingendes materielles Recht und internationale Schuldverträge* (Bonn, 1988) 2.

[12] See Gary Clyde Hufbauer, Jeffrey J Schott and Kimberly Ann Elliott, *Economic Sanctions Reconsidered: History and Current Policy* (Institute for International Economics, 1985).

of foreign policy. This is also the case with the EU, where economic sanctions are an important component of the Common Foreign and Security Policy (CFSP) and the EU has competence to impose restrictive measures in pursuit of specific CFSP objectives. From a human rights point of view, a further commonly asked question is whether the economic sanctions imposed by the EU comply with human rights standards, and the Court of Justice of the European Union (CJEU) has sometimes established – as in the famous *Kadi* judgment[13] – that certain measures did not meet these standards. It is thus obvious that economic sanctions may be found at the intersections of various branches and areas of law.

However, this book takes a different point of departure, and this is the perspective of private international law. Export and import regulation, including economic sanctions, provides a fertile ground for conflict lawyers, since commercial relations affected by economic sanctions concern more than one state by their nature.[14] Economic sanctions not only interlace economic relations between states, but also those between private parties. In fact, the court seised has to decide in a legal dispute between private parties involving the application of an economic sanction, the origin of which may be traced back to a conflict between two or more states,[15] usually between the state of the forum and another state, but it may equally be the case that the conflict involves two foreign states. The same issue may arise in proceedings before arbitral tribunals which do not even have a forum state.

The sanctions ordered to be applied by diplomats and the legislature must be applied to concrete cases by courts and arbitral tribunals. It may sometimes be difficult to decide whether to give effect to a sanction in a given legal relationship. For the courts of the Member States of the EU, it is unproblematic when they have to apply EU sanctions, but many times the question is whether a sanction imposed by a third country is applicable. Although EU private international law provides some rules for such cases, the courts of the Member States still have considerable leeway.

One can assert that there are only two options: to give effect or not to an economic sanction. The binarity of the logic of application/non-application of economic sanctions has an enormous significance for private parties; first, at the phase of transaction planning, when they intend to prevent the application of an economic sanction to their legal relation or conform their conduct to an economic sanction; and, later, in the event of a legal dispute. At both stages, the significance for the legal relationship of the parties of the predictability of the application or non-application of an economic sanction cannot be overstated. Behind the binarity

[13] Joined Cases C-402/05 P and C-415/05 P *Yassin Abdullah Kadi and Al Barakaat International Foundation v Council of the European Union and Commission of the European Communities* [2008] ECR I-6351.

[14] Bernhard Großfeld and Abbo Junker, *Das CoCom im internationalen Wirtschaftsrecht* (Mohr Siebeck, 1991) 10.

[15] François Gianviti, 'Le blocage des avoirs officiels iraniens par les Etats-Unis (executive order du 14 novembre 1979)' (1980) 69 *Revue critique de droit international privé* 279, 296.

of the application/non-application of economic sanctions, various adjudicatory techniques appear. It will be demonstrated that the conduct of the parties and institutions (primarily courts and arbitral tribunals) concerned and the outcome of such cases is largely influenced by the operation and interpretation of private international law rules.

II. The Aim of this Book

This book intends to present how the courts of the Member States and arbitral tribunals decide cases involving economic sanctions along with the rules of private international law. It will be demonstrated that private international law has a decisive role in determining the impact of economic sanctions on private law relationships. Private international law norms decide to a large extent whether an economic sanction must be applied or taken into account with regard to a contract entered into by private parties. Furthermore, it will be pointed out that the parties may develop techniques by which they can avoid the application of economic sanctions.[16] These include the choice of a foreign court or arbitral tribunal for the adjudication of the legal dispute in order to prevent the application of an economic sanction. Hence, it needs to be examined whether EU sanctions may be 'deactivated' by such techniques. Additionally, it will be also shown that the decisions of the courts of the Member States of the EU involving the application of economic sanctions sometimes rely on foreign policy arguments, which seems (at least at first sight) to be at odds with the traditionally apolitical nature of private international law and may give rise to a decentralised European judicial foreign policy.

Economic sanctions are a popular subject for public international law analysis. Despite the proliferation of economic sanctions and their impact on a number of planned or existing contractual relationships, their examination by private lawyers has been rather limited, usually focusing on a particular economic sanction regime or decisions rendered by courts or arbitral tribunals. The growing number of such articles and case notes on the application of economic sanctions in court and arbitration practice demonstrates that this is a rapidly evolving area. Despite its practical relevance, surprisingly few comprehensive books have been written on the private international law aspects of economic sanctions.[17] On many occasions, they have been touched upon in the broader context of overriding mandatory provisions, devoting less attention to the particularities of economic sanctions.

[16] Mary Keyes, 'Statutes, Choice of Law, and the Role of Forum Choice' (2008) 4 *Journal of Private International Law* 1, 9–10.

[17] Mercédeh Azeredo da Silveira, *Trade Sanctions and International Sales* (Kluwer, 2014); Nicola C Neumann, *Internationale Handelsembargos und privatrechtliche Verträge* (Nomos, 2000); Francisco J Garcimartín Alférez, *Contratación internacional y medidas de coerción económica* (Beramar, 1993).

III. Methodology and the Scope of the Work

This book relies on the traditional doctrinal method. It provides answers to the questions posed based on domestic, EU and international legal sources. The focus here is on private international law. Although private international law issues are strongly intertwined with the rules of substantive contract law when applying economic sanctions, this book does not intend to give a comprehensive analysis of the substantive consequences of economic sanctions upon contractual relations. The assessment of economic sanctions from the perspective of substantive law will be addressed only insofar as substantive contract law may imply a way to 'circumvent' private international law rules to effectuate foreign economic sanctions. The focus of this book is on private international law and it primarily aims to present how private international law rules influence the application of economic sanctions and the realisation of foreign policy objectives, and how foreign policy considerations appear in private international law decision making.

The legal analysis of economic sanctions may take place from the perspective of public and private law. Without denying the significance of the public international law and administrative law implications of economic sanctions, this book will address the private law, and more specifically the private international law, aspects of economic sanctions. For this reason, the analysis does not include the legality of economic sanctions (which are often questioned because of their extra-territorial application), any review of economic sanctions in light of the safeguard of fundamental rights, and the responsibility of the state or the EU for imposing economic sanctions.

The book is based on the analysis of national and EU legal sources, and primarily on the decisions of the courts of the Member States and the awards of arbitral tribunals. Nevertheless, a qualification must be made. Interestingly, there are not too many judicial decisions or arbitral awards on economic sanctions. The scant number of decisions does not prevent the analysis of the approach of the courts of the Member States and the arbitrators. These relatively few decisions and arbitral awards were in fact broadly discussed by legal scholars. The position of the courts of different Member States may be compared with each other, as well as with that of different arbitral tribunals.

IV. The Object of the Analysis: Economic Sanctions

A. Historical Introduction

Economic sanctions percolate the history of Europe.[18] It is often recalled that Athens introduced an import prohibition against Megara, an ally of Sparta, shortly

[18] On the history of economic sanctions, see Neumann (n 17) 27–28; Robert Charvin, 'Les mesures d'embargo: La part du droit' (1996) 29 *Revue belge de droit international* 5.

before the Peloponnesian War in 432 BCE.[19] Romans had similar recourse to this measure against uncooperative barbarians.[20] The Pope imposed economic coercive measures against some Italian cities during the war between the Guelphs and the Ghibellines. Similarly, the Hanseatic cities relied on economic coercion against Flanders. In the nineteenth century, Napoleonic France initiated an embargo against Britain with the backing of countries dependent on France. Further instances can be easily found in European history.

The weapon of economic coercion has been exported from Europe. The US responded to the violation of its neutrality during the Napoleonic Wars between Britain and France with the Embargo Act of 1807. Later, it applied embargoes against various countries.[21] As the comparative economic power of the US has grown, it took recourse to economic sanctions more often.

Nonetheless, the big era of economic sanctions began in the twentieth century, when economic sanctions started to be broadly used by different states and organisations, and this is also the age when the recourse to economic sanctions became regulated to a certain extent. Thus, the Covenant of the League of Nations allowed economic sanctions to be imposed in its Article 16, provided that one of the members of the League had resorted to war. This provision enabled the members of the League of Nations to impose economic sanctions against Italy after the invasion of Ethiopia in 1935, although without much success. The League of Nations threatened Greece with sanctions under Article 16 for having invaded Bulgaria in 1925 and Greece withdrew its troops and agreed to pay compensation. The subsequent evolution of the multilateral regulation of imposing sanctions will be discussed later, with special regard to the United Nations (UN), the General Agreement on Tariffs and Trade (GATT) and the EU regimes.

B. Definition of 'Economic Sanctions'

Economic sanctions are the object of this work. The term 'economic sanction' is not defined in legal sources. It has been defined in various ways by the representatives of different disciplines.[22]

Economic sanctions are measures of an economic nature restricting commercial or financial exchange adopted unilaterally or collectively by states or

[19] Hufbauer, Schott and Elliott (n 12) 4.

[20] EA Thompson, *Romans and Barbarians: The Decline of the Western Empire* (University of Wisconsin Press, 2002) 10–12.

[21] On the history of the application of economic sanctions by the US, see Meredith Rathbone, Peter Jeydel and Amy Lentz, 'Sanctions, Sanctions Everywhere: Forging a Path through Complex Transnational Sanctions Laws' (2013) 44 *Georgetown Journal of International Law* 1055, 1063–75.

[22] See in particular Andreas F Lowenfeld, *International Economic Law*, 2nd edn (Oxford University Press, 2008) 850; Barry E Carter, 'Economic Sanctions' in Rüdiger Wolfrum (ed), *The Max Planck Encyclopedia of Public International Law*, vol 3 (Max-Planck-Gesellschaft/Oxford University Press, 2012) 323, 323; Neumann (n 17) 28; Hossein G Askari, John Forrer, Hildy Teegen and Jiawen Yang, *Economic Sanctions* (Praeger, 2003) 76–84; Portela (n 5) 21.

(international or regional) organisations, primarily in order to bring a state, other entities and individuals to pursue a policy deemed desirable or not to pursue a policy deemed non-desirable by the entity adopting the measure. Most of the time, economic sanctions are adopted as an instrument of foreign policy to trigger a change in a given policy of the target state, including acts of warfare, human rights and the development of weapons of mass destruction. Nevertheless, economic sanctions may also pursue other objectives and it is sometimes difficult to reveal what is the main intended purpose of a sanction. It happened that an economic sanction was maintained, even after the occurrence of the change sought by the sanction, essentially as a punishment for a conduct in the past.[23] Other objectives may be also pursued by economic sanctions. For instance, freezing assets may serve as protective measures concerning the assets of a state concerned, as happened with the assets of the Kuwaiti government and its entities during the Gulf War.[24] Economic sanctions may also be used simply to attain internal political goals without envisaging a real change in the conduct of the target state.[25] Economic means are in this way used to achieve various political goals,[26] but our enquiry will focus on the foreign policy teleology of economic sanctions in private law relationships.

Economic sanctions have diverse forms, such as embargoes, freezing assets, the restriction of financial transactions, communication channels, and air connections and travel bans for certain persons concerned. The notion of embargo stems from the Spanish (*embargar*) and was originally used for seizing foreign vessels to put pressure on the state under whose flag the vessel sailed.[27] With the decreasing significance of carriage of goods by sea, the term 'embargo' started to connote a trade restriction in a more general sense.[28] In a broader sense, 'embargo' embraces the prohibition of both exportation and importation of goods,[29] while some authors uses it in a narrower sense, according to which the term refers exclusively to a ban of exports from a country.[30] In the widest sense, the term 'embargo' even covers

[23] See, for example, UNSC Resolution 660 (1990) of 2 August 1990, S/RES/660 (1990); Bernard Grelon and Charles-Etienne Gudin, 'Contrats et crise du Golfe' (1991) 118 *Journal du droit international* 633, 655.

[24] UNSC Resolution 661 (1990) of 6 August 1990, S/RES/661 (1990), para 9 (a); Kern Alexander, *Economic Sanctions – Law and Public Policy* (Palgrave Macmillan, 2009) 25, fn 37; Geneviève Burdeau, 'Le gel d'avoirs étrangers' (1997) 124 *Journal du droit international* 5, 11.

[25] Gherari (n 10) 71.

[26] Bart van Vooren and Ramses A Wessel, *EU External Relations Law* (Cambridge University Press, 2014) 395.

[27] Louis Dubouis, 'L'embargo dans la pratique contemporaine' (1967) 13 *Annuaire français de droit international* 99, 99–100; Jobst Joachim Neuss, *Handelsembargos zwischen Völkerrecht und IPR* (VVF, 1989) 17–18; Bernd Lindemeyer, 'Das Handelsembargo als wirtschaftliches Zwangsmittel der staatlichen Außenpolitik' (1981) 27 *Recht der Intemationalen Wirtschaft* 10, 10.

[28] Neuss (n 27) 18.

[29] Aurore Marchand, *L'embargo en droit du commerce international* (Larcier, 2012) 33; Lindemeyer (n 27) 10–11.

[30] Dubouis (n 27) 101; Racine (n 2) 90; Gherari (n 10) 56; Régis Chemain, 'Sanctions économiques: contre-mesures, boycott, embargo, blocus' in *Encyclopédie Dalloz du droit international, Répertoire de droit international* (May 2017), paras 151–55.

financial restrictions, such as asset freezing, imposed on individuals[31] or, going further, any partial or total interruption of economic relations. In this sense, it is referred to in Article 41 of the UN Charter as incorporating all forms of embargo (without using the term itself), when it circumscribes the measures which may be adopted by the United Nations Security Council (UNSC) as 'complete or partial interruption of economic relations and of rail, sea, air, postal, telegraphic, radio, and other means of communication'.[32] The word 'embargo' is used in this broadest sense by some authors,[33] which already coincides with the concept of 'economic sanction'.

'Economic sanction' is a broader concept than 'embargo' used in the sense of prohibition of exports or imports since, in addition to the interruption of commercial relations, transport and communication channels, it also embraces freezing the assets of states, organisations and individuals.[34] The often-used travel bans may equally have an economic impact if they are used against the political or economic leaders of the target state or companies thereof.

Finally, the term 'boycott' also often appears in relation to economic sanctions. The term may be applied in both a domestic and an international context. This latter is of interest for our purposes. Sometimes, 'boycott' is used as the interruption of commercial relations with states or entities;[35] sometimes its meaning is limited to the prohibition of imports to a state, contrasting it with embargoes prohibiting exports.[36] 'Boycott' is sometimes distinguished from 'embargo' or other economic sanctions on the grounds that a boycott is initiated and maintained by private entities against a foreign state or entity.[37] The origin of the concept of 'boycott' itself traces back to an action of private persons. In 1879, at the initiative of the Irish Land League, employees of the estate of Lord Erne, whose land agent was Charles Cunningham Boycott, a former British officer, decided to refuse to work and other private persons also refrained from providing services on behalf of the estate or Mr Boycott. Accordingly, Bismuth defines 'boycott' as the voluntary abstention from legal relationships with a given natural or legal person of private or public

[31] Sophie Mathäß, *Die Auswirkungen staaten- und personenbezogener Embargomaßnahmen auf Privatrechtsverhältnisse* (Nomos, 2016) 26–27.

[32] Geneviève Burdeau, 'Les conséquences de la crise sur les relations économiques privées' in Brigitte Stern (ed), *Les aspects juridiques de la crise et de la guerre du Golfe* (Monthcrestien, 1991) 415, 437–438.

[33] Neumann (n 17) 28–29; Lambert Matray, 'L'embargo national et international dans l'arbitrage' (1997) 74 *Revue de droit international et de droit comparé* 7.

[34] In this sense, see Francisco Garcimartín Alférez, 'Embargo' in Jürgen Basedow, Giesela Rühl, Franco Ferrari and Pedro de Miguel Asensio (eds), *Encyclopedia of Private International Law* (Edward Elgar, 2017) 599, 600.

[35] Charles Rousseau, 'Le boycottage dans les rapports internationaux' (1958) 62 *Revue générale de droit international public* 5, 5–6.

[36] Dubouis (n 27) 101; Burdeau (n 32) 438–39; Racine (n 2) 90.

[37] J Laferrière, 'Le boycott et le droit international' (1910) 17 *Revue générale de droit international public* 288, 291; Neumann (n 17) 30 and 38–40; Laurent Lucchini, 'Le boycottage in Société française pour le droit international' in Prosper Weil (ed), *Colloque d'Orléans, Aspects du droit international économique* (Pedone, 1972) 67, 69 referring to this original meaning; Louis Cavaré, 'L'idée de sanction et sa mise en oeuvre en droit international public' (1937) 44 *Revue générale de droit international public* 385, 416; Neuss (n 27) 19.

law in the field of the production and commerce of goods.[38] Private initiative led to the restriction of commercial relations in China against the US, the UK and Japan during the first decades of the twentieth century.[39] After the annexation of Bosnia-Herzegovina by the Austro-Hungarian Empire in 1908, goods originating from the monarchy were boycotted in Turkey.[40] Notwithstanding this, interrupting economic relations at the initiative of states or international organisations – by organising or at least encouraging it – is sometimes included in the concept of 'boycott'.[41] As one of the most famous illustrations of this, the boycott by the Arab League against Israel is usually referred to: according to this, each state of the Arab League prohibited trade with Israeli natural and legal persons for its citizens and companies, and some of the participating states put foreign companies doing business in or with Israel or Israeli entities on a black list.[42] Trade with blacklisted companies was also prohibited. These measures constituted a de facto embargo.[43] If the term 'boycott' is interpreted broadly, extending it also to actions of states and international organisations (eg, to the economic sanctions of the UN or the League of Nations),[44] the borderline between 'embargo' and 'boycott' becomes blurred.

The terms 'coercive measures' and 'economic coercion' are also used when speaking about economic sanctions. Coercive measures do not simply involve measures of an economic nature, but also other types of sanctions, including military intervention and diplomatic sanctions, which are beyond the scope of this volume. Similarly, the use of the term 'economic coercion' would go too far since it would embrace, for example, increases in tariffs or the withdrawal of certain economic benefits.

In this book, I will use the term 'economic sanction', partly because this term seems to be broader than the concepts of 'embargo' or 'boycott' and comprises a variety of coercive measures which may have an impact on the private law relationships of parties not necessarily covered by the other two terms, and partly because the boundary between the terms 'embargo' and 'boycott' seems to be blurred. Moreover, economic sanctions do not necessarily automatically prohibit transactions, but, for example, it may subject them to a declaration obligation or an authorisation procedure.[45] The transaction may be carried out if permission is given by the authorities of the state imposing the sanction.

[38] Jean-Louis Bismuth, *Le boycottage dans les échanges économiques internationaux au regard du droit* (Economica, 1980) 6.

[39] Laferrière (n 37) 291–301; Rousseau (n 35) 8–9.

[40] Laferrière (n 37) 301–11.

[41] Rousseau (n 35) 6.

[42] Andreas Behr, *Deutsche Unternehmen und der Israel-Boykott* (Verlag Recht und Wissenschaft, 1994).

[43] ibid 57.

[44] For such a broad interpretation, see Rousseau (n 35) 6; Lucchini (n 37) 77–80.

[45] See, for example, the Control of Gold, Securities, Payments and Credits (Kuwait) Directions 1990 adopted by the UK Treasury (SI 1990/1591); in Spain Orden de 6 de agosto de 1990 del Ministerio de Economía y Hacienda, BOE núm 188, 7 agosto 1990, 19202, p 23080, analysed by Francisco J Garcimartín Alférez, 'Medidas adoptadas por España ante la invasión iraquí' (1990) 42 *Revista española*

The enquiry of this book covers only those economic sanctions which primarily pursue a foreign policy objective. Those measures motivated primarily by security interests, for example, sanctions imposed against terrorists or terrorist groups, such as freezing assets or restrictions of financial transactions related to them, will not be examined in detail. The objective of these economic sanctions is the economic isolation of persons and groups involved in terrorism that appear in the terrorist lists issued by the UN,[46] the EU[47] or particular states. This limitation is explained by the book's focus on the presence of foreign policy considerations in private international law. However, it is not always easy to differentiate sanctions according to these two objectives, since it may be the case that a sanction pursues both objectives (eg, sanctions against 'state-sponsored terrorism').

A particular type of economic sanction may be applied separately or in combination with others, which is most often the case in practice. Economic sanctions may be full or partial. It seldom happens that an economic sanction extends to the trade in all products related to the target state (eg, the destination or origin of the product, or the nationality of the seller or buyer). This was the case concerning the sanctions against Iraq in the Gulf War and the harsh consequences of these sanctions on the Iraqi people are well known.[48] Currently, partial sanctions tend to be applied, focusing, for instance, on the trade of arms, dual-use goods, strategically important products and certain services. Economic sanctions may also include the prohibition of financial transactions and the seizure or freezing of assets owned by the target state or its citizens or by the target organisation and its members.[49] These more tailored sanctions have become known as 'smart sanctions'.

Economic sanctions are adopted unilaterally or multilaterally at three different levels: (1) by a state unilaterally; (2) by a regional organisation (such as the EU, the multilateral framework of which is the subject of particular scrutiny in the present analysis); (3) or the UN as a global international organisation. However, multilateral sanctions may also be adopted informally outside the framework of an institution. Trade restrictions were introduced by the Coordinating Committee for East-West Trade Policy (COCOM) outside a formal institutional framework to reduce the military force of the Soviet Union and its allies by restricting their

de derecho internacional 693, 695; concerning Swiss law, see Elliott Geisinger, Philippe Bärtsch, Julie Raneda and Solomon Ebere, 'Les conséquences des sanctions économiques sur les obligations contractuelles et sur l'arbitrage commercial international' (2012) *Revue de droit des affaires internationales/International Business Law Journal* 405, 407.

[46] See UNSC Resolution 1267 (1999) of 15 October, 1999S/RES/1267 (1999); UNSC Resolution 1390 (2002) of 28 January, 2002S/RES/1390 (2002).

[47] See Council Implementing Regulation (EU) 2018/281 of 26 February 2018 implementing Regulation (EU) 2016/1686 imposing additional measures directed against ISIL (Da'esh) and Al-Qaeda and natural and legal persons, entities or bodies associated with them [2018] OJ L541/1.

[48] Resolution 661 (1990) of 6 August 1990.

[49] On the topic of freezing assets, see Sophie Wernert, 'Le gel d'avoirs étrangers: Aspects de droit international public et de droit international privé' (dissertation, Université Paris II Panthéon-Assas, 2001).

supply of strategic goods which may have a military purpose.[50] The restrictions adopted by the COCOM gained legally binding force when member countries incorporated them into their national law. However, differences were not ruled out entirely by this informal agreement; members were not prevented from going beyond the agreed COCOM lists.

V. Foreign Policy and Private International Law

The relation between foreign policy and private international law fits into the broader question of politics and private international law. Private international law is usually seen as blind or neutral towards various policy considerations and values. Traditionally, private international law has been designed to exclude changing political considerations and value judgements, including foreign policy considerations.[51] This leads back to the idea that private international law covers only the legal relations of private parties and extends to the legal relations of the state only to the extent that it does not act as a sovereign. Consequently, at first sight, we could assume that private international law does not have anything to do with foreign policy considerations. However, such a conclusion would be premature.

One of the biggest myths of the traditional approach of private international law is that it is apolitical. As Schurig stated, the concept of an apolitical private law is merely a brilliant, witty legend (*geistvolle Legende*),[52] but nothing more than this. This thought may be perfectly transferred to private international law.[53] Undoubtedly, today's private international law is to a large extent exposed to various state interests and policies.[54] Regulation is often used to achieve foreign policy objectives[55] and private international law may not remain immune from legislation that has political purposes.

Private international law norms are not so distant from the acts of foreign states as one might immediately think. In private international law cases, the courts decide on the governing law and even apply foreign law, ie, the acts of a foreign state resulting from exercising its sovereign power, if so provided by the conflict-of-laws rules.[56] As a general rule, foreign law applies irrespective of its content.

[50] For a detailed analysis, see Großfeld and Junker (n 14).

[51] Campbell McLachlan, *Foreign Relations Law* (Cambridge University Press, 2014) 18.

[52] Klaus Schurig, *Kollisionsnorm und Sachrecht* (Duncker & Humblot, 1981) 272.

[53] See Dagmar Coester-Waltjen, '"Totgesagte leben länger" – gilt auch für das klassische internationale Privatrecht?' in Susanne Lilian Gössl (ed), *Politik und Internationales Privatrecht* (Mohr Siebeck, 2017) 1, 4.

[54] See Horatia Muir Watt, 'Aspects économique du droit international privé' in *Collected Courses of the Hague Academy of International Law*, vol 307 (Martinus Nijhoff, 2005) 307, 356–57.

[55] Anne Joyce, 'Libyan Arab Foreign Bank v. Bankers Trust: Common Law Meets its Limits?' (1988) 29 *Harvard International Law Journal* 451, 468.

[56] McLachlan (n 51) 527.

However, the judge in such cases even has the possibility of making a judgment on the substance of the foreign law and may occasionally reject the application of the designated foreign law if, for instance, it violates the *ordre public* of the forum.[57] Furthermore, there are some clear connection points between foreign policy and private international law. These include issues relating to foreign state immunity, the act of state doctrine and comity.

Recently, eminent private law and private international law scholars have not refrained from queries crossing the borderline between EU external policy and private law. Mills points out that: 'It must also be asked what external policy goals could or should the EU aim to achieve through the external effects of its internal rules of private international law?'[58] Similarly, in their thought-provoking book, Cremona and Micklitz have departed from the assumption that EU external policy and private law are 'increasingly interconnected' and ask: 'In what ways might European private law be a tool to achieve EU external policy objectives?'[59]

In order to give an answer, these questions have been addressed by the above authors and other academics dealing with similar issues from different points of view. The relation between private international law and the external action of the EU has been discussed mainly from two perspectives.

First, the EU appears in international relations as a party to international treaties related to private international law. The participation of the EU and its Member States in concluding (multilateral, regional or bilateral) international treaties has received considerable attention.[60] International treaties may help the EU to enforce certain policy considerations in an external dimension.

[57] ibid 524.

[58] Alex Mills, 'Private International Law and EU External Relations: Think Local Act Global, or Think Global Act Local?' (2016) 65 *ICLQ* 541, 543.

[59] Marise Cremona and Hans-W.Micklitz, 'Introduction' in Marise Cremona and Hans-W.Micklitz (eds), *Private Law in the External Relations of the EU* (Oxford University Press, 2016) 1.

[60] Mills (n 58) 543–61; Alberto Malatesta, 'The *Lugano* Opinion and its Consequences in Family and Succession Matters' in Alberto Malatesta, Stefania Bariatti and Fausto Pocar (eds), *The External Dimension of EC Private International Law in Family and Succession Matters* (CEDAM, 2008) 19; Andrea Santini, 'The Doctrine of Implied External Powers and Private International Law Concerning Family and Succession Matters' in Alberto Malatesta, Stefania Bariatti and Fausto Pocar (eds), *The External Dimension of EC Private International Law in Family and Succession Matters* (CEDAM, 2008) 31; David McClean, 'Bilateral Agreements with Non-Member States after the *Lugano* Opinion' in Alberto Malatesta, Stefania Bariatti and Fausto Pocar (eds), *The External Dimension of EC Private International Law in Family and Succession Matters* (CEDAM, 2008) 55; Stefania Bariatti, 'Bilateral Agreements with Non-Member States after the *Lugano* Opinion: Some Procedural Issues' in Alberto Malatesta, Stefania Bariatti and Fausto Pocar (eds), *The External Dimension of EC Private International Law in Family and Succession Matters* (CEDAM, 2008) 77; Marise Cremona, 'A Triple Braid – Interactions between International Law, EU Law, and Private Law' in Marise Cremona and Hans-W Micklitz (eds), *Private Law in the External Relations of the EU* (Oxford University Press, 2016) 33; Christiaan Timmermans, 'The Specificity of Private Law in EU External Relations: The Area of Freedom, Security and Justice' in Marise Cremona and Hans-W Micklitz (eds), *Private Law in the External Relations of the EU* (Oxford University Press, 2016) 59; Michael Wilderspin and Anne-Marie Rouchaud-Joët, 'La compétence externe de la Communauté européenne en droit international privé' (2004) 93 *Revue critique de droit international privé* 1.

Second, the legal literature equally focused on the contours of the external reach of EU private law and private international law. These writings mainly describe the extent to which EU private international law contributes to the enforcement of certain substantive policy objectives and values in external relations.[61] This involves in particular the enforcement of human rights standards or the level of consumer protection existing in the EU, extending the value judgements shared by the EU Member States to certain external relations. Such a case occurs, for example, when one of the parties to the legal relationship is from outside the EU. This facet thus essentially concerns how EU substantive rules may be enforced in a context beyond the EU in international relations. Research into this issue is based on a distinction between 'EU internal' and 'foreign' situations, and examines the differences in private international law regulation concerning the two sorts of situations.

These highly interesting enquiries led me to the examination of the relation between private international law and foreign policy. How external policy objectives may be enforced through private international law rules has rarely been considered in the relevant literature. There is an obvious point which was beyond the horizon of the above studies on EU external policy and private international law, namely the application of economic sanctions in private international law. My analysis will focus on this single connection point between foreign policy and private international law.

In my view, economic sanctions are sufficiently illustrative to explain how the operation of private international law rules may influence the enforcement of foreign policy objectives. Economic sanctions are the instrument of foreign policy and they are applied to international contracts through private international law.

Economic sanctions are overriding mandatory provisions of a highly political nature. It may be natural that the court seised applies an economic sanction imposed by its own state. However, by giving effect to a foreign economic sanction, the court as well as the forum state may immerse itself in a conflict between two different countries. Moreover, this conflict should be addressed by a court acting in a private legal dispute. Hence, at a theoretical level, the simplest way to avoid such troubles linked to foreign policy would be to set aside the question of applicability of foreign economic sanctions and not to apply them at all. In this way, the court and the forum state could remain neutral.[62] However, denying decision making in such private law disputes would involve barring private parties from

[61] Mills (n 58) 561–78; Hans-W Micklitz, 'The Internal versus the External Dimension of European Private Law: A Conceptual Design and a Research Agenda' in Cremona and Micklitz (n 60) 9, 14; Stéphanie Francq, 'The External Dimension of Rome I and Rome II: Neutrality or Schizophrenia?' in Cremona and Micklitz (n 60) 71; Horatia Muir-Watt, 'The Role of Conflict of Laws in European Private Law' in Christian Twigg-Flesner (ed), *The Cambridge Companion to European Union Private Law* (Cambridge University Press, 2010) 44, 49–54.

[62] Pierre Mayer, 'Les lois de police' (1988) *Droit international privé: travaux du Comité français de droit international privé* 105, 112.

access to justice. Consequently, judicial practice cannot remain fully immune from political considerations when facing the application of economic sanctions in the contractual relationship between private parties, and this appears in the legal argumentation used by courts in cases involving economic sanctions.

VI. Adjudicative Rhetoric and Foreign Policy Considerations

The appearance of economic sanctions and foreign policy considerations in private law disputes has an impact on the rhetoric of the courts and arbitral tribunals seised. From the fact that it is private international law that is decisive in terms of the application of economic sanctions, it could be inferred that foreign policy considerations do not have any role, since this would be contrary to the neutral approach of private international law. As McLachlan – referring back to Mann – states, private international law norms 'provide the best guide to decision without resort to concepts of *raison d'état*'.[63] This statement is true in many cases when courts have to address economic sanctions in international contract law relationships.

Courts usually wish to avoid making statements on foreign policy; instead, they may try to adhere to the technical operation and automatisms of conflict-of-laws norms when deciding on the application of economic sanctions. By so proceeding, courts assessing the impact of economic sanctions on contractual relations can render decisions chiefly based on legal norms. In this way, a political conflict is channelled into the world of law; it is 'legalised'.

However, in many instances, courts do not distance themselves from foreign policy arguments. It must be noticed that court decisions rendered in cases involving the application of economic sanctions sometimes raise foreign policy arguments to justify their decisions. Foreign policy arguments may be explicitly or implicitly present in the decisions involving economic sanctions. Although courts are obliged to render decisions based on the rule of law, it will be demonstrated that conflict-of-laws rules and substantive law rules give some leeway to the courts to pay attention to political considerations. The foreign policy rhetoric of these decisions equally calls into question the neutrality of private international law. When discussing the relevant national case law on the application of economic sanctions, the intervention of political considerations will be highlighted. Additionally, it will be demonstrated that the room to manoeuvre enjoyed by the courts of the Member States in giving effect to economic sanctions of third countries results in a decentralised European judicial foreign policy.

[63] McLachlan (n 51) 20.

2

The Legal Framework for Imposing Economic Sanctions

States are not obliged to trade with other countries.[1] The International Court of Justice (ICJ) stated that: 'A State is not bound to continue particular trade relations longer than it sees fit to do so, in the absence of a treaty commitment or other specific legal obligation.'[2] The principle of the UN Charter that 'All Members shall refrain in their international relations from the threat or use of force against the territorial integrity or political independence of any state' is construed as referring only to military force, but not to economic coercion.[3] Economic sanctions are therefore not generally considered to be unacceptable means under public international law. However, all states have to observe their bilateral or multilateral treaty obligations.[4]

The widespread application of economic sanctions made the necessity of regulation a clear priority. This took place by the League of Nations and later the UN at a global level. Moreover, several bilateral and multilateral treaties equally address economic sanctions specifically or, at least, contain provisions affecting the adoption of economic sanctions.

I. The UN Sanctions Regime

Under certain circumstances, the UN Charter explicitly authorises the UNSC to impose or recommend the adoption of economic sanctions. Article 39 of the UN Charter empowers the UNSC 'to determine the existence of any threat to the peace, breach of the peace, or act of aggression and shall make recommendations, or decide what measures shall be taken in accordance with Articles 41 and 42, to maintain or restore international peace and security'.

[1] Bernd Lindemeyer, 'Das Handelsembargo als wirtschaftliches Zwangsmittel der staatlichen Außenpolitik' (1981) 27 *Recht der Intemationalen Wirtschaft* 10, 16.

[2] *Case Concerning Military and Paramilitary Activities in and against Nicaragua (Nicaragua v United States of America)*, Merits, Judgment, ICJ Rep 1986 (27 June), p 14, para 276.

[3] Lindemeyer (n 1) 16.

[4] For a detailed account on bilateral treaties and economic sanctions, see Hans van Houtte, 'Treaty Protection Against Economic Sanctions' (1984–85) 18 *Revue Belge de Droit International* 34.

According to Article 41 of the Charter:

> The Security Council may decide what measures not involving the use of armed force are to be employed to give effect to its decisions, and it may call upon the Members of the United Nations to apply such measures. These may include complete or partial interruption of economic relations and of rail, sea, air, postal, telegraphic, radio, and other means of communication, and the severance of diplomatic relations.

These provisions enable the UNSC to adopt recommendations or impose an obligation on Member States to implement economic sanctions against a state, other entities and individuals. The measures adopted under Article 41 bind Member States and those decisions must be carried out by the Members in accordance with Articles 25 and 48 of the UN Charter. Articles 39 and 41 constituted the legal basis for adopting recommended or obligatory economic sanctions in numerous cases. Beyond these powers of the UNSC, the UN General Assembly may also adopt recommendations proposing economic sanctions, mostly when consensus is missing in the UNSC, as was the case regarding the sanctions imposed against China and North Korea after the outbreak of the Korean War.[5]

It is well known that, during the Cold War, the UNSC applied economic sanctions only against Rhodesia following its unilateral declaration of independence[6] and South Africa because of its apartheid regime. After the Cold War, economic sanctions were broadly applied by the UNSC to exercise economic pressure on state actors, other entities and individuals.

II. Economic Sanctions in Bilateral and Multilateral Treaties

Sometimes the provisions of bilateral treaties may affect the possibility of imposing economic sanctions (most-favoured-nation treatment and prohibition of discrimination); sometimes they have even excluded the application of economic sanctions in the mutual relationship of the states parties. Multilateral treaties may equally contain provisions related to economic sanctions. Article 20 of the Charter of the Organization of American States provides that: 'No State may use or encourage the use of coercive measures of an economic or political character in order to force the sovereign will of another State and obtain from it advantages of any kind.'

[5] UN Charter, arts 10–11. See, for example, General Assembly Resolution 500 (V) of 18 May 1951.

[6] UNSC Resolution 232 (1966) of 16 December 1966, S/RES/232 (1966); UNSC Resolution 253 (1968) of 29 May 1968, S/RES/253 (1968); UNSC Resolution 277 (1970) of 18 March 1970, S/RES/277 (1970).

Within the World Trade Organization (WTO) system, the GATT allows for the adoption of economic sanctions under very narrow circumstances. According to Article XXI of the GATT:

> Nothing in this Agreement shall be construed …
>
> (b) to prevent any contracting party from taking any action which it considers necessary for the protection of its essential security interests
>
> (i) relating to fissionable materials or the materials from which they are derived;
>
> (ii) relating to the traffic in arms, ammunition and implements of war and to such traffic in other goods and materials as is carried on directly or indirectly for the purpose of supplying a military establishment;
>
> (iii) taken in time of war or other emergency in international relations; or
>
> (c) to prevent any contracting party from taking any action in pursuance of its obligations under the United Nations Charter for the maintenance of international peace and security.[7]

Article XXI formed the legal basis of the export restrictions introduced by the COCOM regarding trade of goods with the countries of the Communist Bloc.

Irrespective of any other treaty obligation, UNSC sanctions must be implemented by all UN Member States.[8] Pursuant to Article 103, in the event of a conflict between the obligations of the UN Member States under the UN Charter and their obligations under any other international agreement, their obligations under the UN Charter prevail.

Economic sanctions, and in particular their legality under public international law, will not be examined in more detail in this book. Instead, we turn to the economic sanctions imposed by the EU in the framework of the CFSP. The following section will discuss the power of the EU to adopt sanctions and the peculiar features of the EU sanction regimes.

III. Economic Sanctions in EU Law

The EU has influence on international relations through the CFSP. The EU has competence to adopt economic sanctions which are part of the toolbox of the EU in shaping foreign affairs. It implements UNSC sanctions into EU law and it may also adopt autonomous sanctions unilaterally.

The EU is not directly bound by the economic sanctions imposed by the UN, since it is not a member of the UN, even though all Member States of the EU are

[7] On the interpretation of art XXI of the GATT in the context of the sanctions imposed by the EU on Russia, see Balázs Horváthy, 'Az Európai Unió Oroszországi Föderációval szemben bevezetett gazdasági szankciói és a Kereskedelmi Világszervezet joga' (2015) 59 *Külgazdaság* 172.

[8] UN Charter, art 25.

members of the UN. Article 48(2) of the UN Charter provides that the decisions of the UNSC must 'be carried out by the Members of the United Nations directly and through their action in the appropriate international agencies of which they are members'. In practice, it is the EU that implements the sanctions of the UNSC by regulations. Regarding the implementation of UNSC sanctions, in *Kadi* the CJEU stated that it may review EU acts transposing a UNSC resolution to ensure the respect of fundamental rights.[9]

Although most of the sanctions imposed by the EU follow a UNSC resolution, the EU also imposed unilateral sanctions even in the absence of the intervention of the UNSC, for instance, against Belarus,[10] Moldova,[11] Myanmar,[12] Uzbekistan[13] and Zimbabwe.[14] Following the annexation of Crimea by Russia, in the absence of a UNSC resolution due to Russia's presence on the UNSC, economic sanctions against Russia have been adopted unilaterally by both the EU and the US. The EU often goes beyond the UNSC sanctions, complementing them with unilateral measures, such as recently in the case of North Korea. The extension of UN sanctions unilaterally may involve adding further persons to a sanction list or providing for additional more comprehensive commercial restrictions.[15] Sometimes, the EU unilaterally prolongs the sanctions, even after the UNSC has lifted them. For instance, Council Regulation (EEC) No 3541/92 prohibiting the satisfying of Iraqi claims with regard to contracts and transactions, the performance of which was affected by UNSC Resolution 661 (1990) and related resolutions, has not been repealed by the EU, though the UNSC did so with a resolution.[16] Autonomous EU sanctions may prove necessary if the threshold for a UNSC sanction set out in Article 39 of the UN Charter – the existence of any threat to the peace, breach of the peace or act of aggression to maintain or restore international peace and security – is not reached.[17] The EU may adopt autonomous sanctions to enforce its own values, including democracy and the rule of law.

[9] Joined Cases C-402/05 P and C-415/05 P *Yassin Abdullah Kadi and Al Barakaat International Foundation v Council of the European Union and Commission of the European Communities* [2008] ECR I-6351, paras 280–86.

[10] Council Regulation (EC) No 765/2006 of 18 May 2006 concerning restrictive measures against President Lukashenko and certain officials of Belarus [2006] OJ L134/1.

[11] Council Decision 2010/573/CFSP of 27 September 2010 concerning restrictive measures against the leadership of the Transnistrian region of the Republic of Moldova [2010] OJ L253/54.

[12] Council Regulation (EU) No 401/2013 of 2 May 2013 concerning restrictive measures in respect of Myanmar/Burma and repealing Regulation (EC) No 194/2008 [2013] OJ L121/1.

[13] Council Regulation (EC) No 1859/2005 of 14 November 2005 imposing certain restrictive measures in respect of Uzbekistan [2005] OJ L299/23.

[14] Council Regulation (EC) No 314/2004 of 19 February 2004 concerning certain restrictive measures in respect of Zimbabwe [2004] OJ L55/1.

[15] Mirko Sossai, 'UN Sanctions and Regional Organizations: An Analytical Framework' in Larissa van den Herik, *Research Handbook on UN Sanctions and International Law* (Edward Elgar, 2017) 395, 407.

[16] UNSC Resolution 1483 (2003) of 22 May 2003, S/RES/1483 (2003).

[17] Klaus Brummer, 'Imposing Sanctions: The Not So "Normative Power Europe"' (2009) 14 *European Foreign Affairs Review* 191, 197.

Historically, the legal bases enabling the EU to adopt restrictive measures went through fundamental changes.[18] At the outset of the history of EU sanctions, no express competence was provided by the EEC Treaty to adopt economic sanctions and Member States seemed to have retained their exclusive competence to have recourse to economic sanctions as part of their competence in foreign policy.[19] They implemented the UNSC resolutions themselves and could equally introduce economic sanctions unilaterally. This was based on Article 224 of the EEC Treaty (the current Article 347 of the Treaty on the Functioning of the European Union (TFEU)).[20] This required the Member States only to consult each other:

> [W]ith a view to taking together the steps needed to prevent the functioning of the common market being affected by measures which a Member State may be called upon to take … in the event of war, serious international tension constituting a threat of war, or in order to carry out obligations it has accepted for the purpose of maintaining peace and international security.[21]

Sanctions imposed by the UNSC against Rhodesia were accordingly implemented based on Article 224 of the EEC Treaty without any intervention by the Community. The recognition of the competence of the Member States was labelled from this point onwards as the Rhodesia doctrine.[22] Article 224 of the EEC Treaty was also used to impose sanctions by the Member States following consultation against Iran in the aftermath of the hostage crisis in 1980.[23] However, this form of proceedings resulted in differences in the implementation of the UNSC resolutions concerned by the Member States.[24]

It therefore arose that the EEC could rely on its commercial competence based on Article 113 of the EEC Treaty (the current Article 207 TFEU) to impose economic sanctions. Accordingly, the measures against the Soviet Union after the invasion of Afghanistan (1980) and following the introduction of martial law in Poland in 1982 had already been implemented using EEC regulations and the

[18] For a historical account on the EU power to impose sanctions, see in particular: Kern Alexander, *Economic Sanctions – Law and Public Policy* (Palgrave Macmillan, 2009) 128–32; Clara Portela, *European Union Sanctions and Foreign Policy* (Routledge, 2010) 19–25; Panos Koutrakos, *EU International Relations Law* (Hart Publishing, 2006) 428–33; Panos Koutrakos, *Trade, Foreign Policy and Defence under the Law of the EU* (Hart Publishing, 2001) 58–66; Marc Vaucher, 'L'évolution récente de la pratique des sanctions communautaires à l'encontre des Etats tiers' (1993) 29 *Revue trimestrielle de droit européen* 39.

[19] Treaty Establishing the European Economic Community 1957.

[20] Consolidated version of the Treaty on the Functioning of the European Union [2016] OJ C202/47.

[21] See Jean-Louis Dewost, 'La Communauté, les Dix et les "sanctions" contre l'Argentine – De la crise iranienne à la crise des Malouines' (1982) 28 *Annuaire français de droit international* 215, 218; Lucette Defalque and David Luff, 'L'embargo et l'Union européenne' in *L'embargo, International Symposium, European Society for Banking and Financial Law* (Bruylant, 1996) 87, 100–02.

[22] On the reasons of the development of the Rhodesia doctrine, see Koutrakos, *Trade, Foreign Policy and Defence* (n 18) 58–59.

[23] Dewost (n 21) 219.

[24] Portela (n 18) 19–20; Koutrakos, *Trade, Foreign Policy and Defence* (n 18) 58.

latter explicitly referred to Article 113 of the EEC Treaty.[25] However, the relation between Article 113 and 224 of the EEC Treaty was hotly debated,[26] in particular in terms of whether commercial competence is appropriate in itself to issue economic sanctions of a political nature which pursue foreign policy objectives.[27] The reliance on Article 113 of the EEC Treaty clearly showed the use of commercial means for political purposes.[28]

As a compromise solution, Article 224 and Article 113 of the EEC Treaty were used successively in practice.[29] When introducing import restrictions against Argentina during the Falklands War, the relevant EEC regulation already relied on both Article 224 of the EEC Treaty and Article 113 of the EEC Treaty.[30] To avoid disparities in implementation, a two-stage process had been applied. First, an intergovernmental agreement was made in the framework of the European Political Cooperation (in accordance with Article 224 of the EEC Treaty), which was outside the ambit of the Community. Second, this was followed by an implementing regulation adopted under Article 113 of the EEC Treaty as an instrument of the common commercial policy.[31] In addition, to ensure uniformity in implementing UNSC sanctions, this way of procedure equally provided a legal mechanism to adopt autonomous EC sanctions.[32] Other provisions of the EEC Treaty were also used to impose sanctions, including Article 235 (the current Article 352 TFEU) for prohibiting satisfying or taking any step to satisfy a claim related to a contract or transaction the performance of which was affected by the UNSC resolution determining sanctions against Iraq.[33]

The Maastricht Treaty introduced Article 301 of the EC Treaty,[34] which was the predecessor of the current Article 215 TFEU, which makes clear that the EU has competence to adopt restrictive economic measures. At present, the EU has the power under Article 215 TFEU to adopt measures on the interruption or reduction, in part or completely, of economic and financial relations with one or more third countries. The new provision has largely detached economic sanctions from commercial policy.

[25] Council Regulation (EEC) No 596/82 of 15 March 1982 amending the import arrangements for certain products originating in the USSR [1982] OJ L72/15, preamble.

[26] Dewost (n 21) 227–29.

[27] Koutrakos, *EU International Relations Law* (n 18) 429; Aurore Marchand, *L'embargo en droit du commerce international* (Larcier, 2012) 469–70.

[28] Ramses A Wessel, 'The Inside Looking out: Consistency and Delimitation in EU External Relations' (2000) 37 *CML Rev* 1135, 1157.

[29] Dewost (n 21) 226; Defalque and Luff (n 21) 102.

[30] Angus Johnston, 'Other Exception Clauses' in Peter Oliver (ed), *Oliver on Free Movement of Goods in the European Union*, 5th edn (Hart Publishing, 2010) 370, 393; Dewost (n 21) 224; Council Regulation (EEC) No 877/82 of 16 April 1982 suspending imports of all products originating in Argentina [1982] OJ L102/1, 16 April, 1–2.

[31] Portela (n 18) 20.

[32] ibid 24.

[33] Council Regulation (EEC) No 3541/92 of 7 December 1992 prohibiting the satisfying of Iraqi claims with regard to contracts and transactions, the performance of which was affected by United Nations Security Council Resolution 661 (1990) and related resolutions OJ L361/1.

[34] Treaty Establishing the European Community (Consolidated version 1992) [1992] OJ C224/1.

Pursuant to Article 215 TFEU:

1. Where a decision, adopted in accordance with Chapter 2 of Title V of the Treaty on European Union, provides for the interruption or reduction, in part or completely, of economic and financial relations with one or more third countries, the Council, acting by a qualified majority on a joint proposal from the High Representative of the Union for Foreign Affairs and Security Policy and the Commission, shall adopt the necessary measures. It shall inform the European Parliament thereof.
2. Where a decision adopted in accordance with Chapter 2 of Title V of the Treaty on European Union so provides, the Council may adopt restrictive measures under the procedure referred to in paragraph 1 against natural or legal persons and groups or non-State entities.
3. The acts referred to in this Article shall include necessary provisions on legal safeguards.

Article 215 TFEU is contained in Part V of the TFEU bearing the title 'The Union's External Action'. 'A decision, adopted in accordance with Chapter 2 of Title V' of the Treaty on European Union (EU) refers to decisions adopted in the framework of the CFSP.[35] Accordingly, a CFSP decision is a precondition for adopting a measure which imposes economic sanctions. The CFSP decision presupposes unanimity.[36] This implies that the power to decide whether a sanction is necessary and to choose the appropriate measures is retained by the Member States. In the absence of an agreement necessary for a CFSP decision, Member States may take unilateral measures, though always respecting EU law.[37] Measures imposing economic sanctions are adopted in the form of regulations which are binding in their entirety and directly applicable in all Member States.[38] In this way, the two-stage procedure already known before the Maastricht Treaty was formally codified by it and confirmed by the TFEU. This in fact involved the incorporation of the successive application of Articles 224 and 113 of the EEC Treaty prior to the Treaty of Maastricht into a single provision.[39] First, a decision must be passed laying down the objective of the economic sanction under the CFSP (like before, within the framework of the European Political Cooperation), then a regulation determines the details of the economic sanction pursuant to Article 215 TFEU. A novelty brought about by the Treaty of Lisbon is that Article 215 allows sanctions to be adopted not only against states, but also against natural or legal persons and groups or non-state entities.

Article 215 TFEU is suitable for implementing the economic sanctions imposed by the UNSC, as well as establishing stricter measures than them or for adopting totally autonomous EU sanctions. Article 215 TFEU allows the adoption

[35] Consolidated version of the Treaty on European Union [2016] OJ C202/13.

[36] TEU, art 31(1).

[37] Marchand (n 27) 487.

[38] TFEU, art 288.

[39] Defalque and Luff (n 21) 106; Gudrun Monika Zagel, 'Economic Sanctions of the European Community: A Commentary on Art 301 TEC' 1, 5, https://papers.ssrn.com/sol3/papers.cfm?abstract_id=862024.

of 'measures', which in practice take the form of regulations directly applicable in the Member States. The choice of this legal source ensures the consistent enforcement of restrictive economic measures by the courts of the Member States.[40] A clear advantage of the two-stage process is that it eliminates differences in national implementing measures and may ensure a quicker course of procedure in comparison to separate actions by national legislation.[41] Consequently, the sanctions imposed by the UNSC and implemented through the EU and those adopted unilaterally by the EU are both in principle enforced uniformly in the Member States.

Article 215 TFEU vests the EU with the power to adopt sanctions; however, the nature of this competence is debated.[42] The CFSP is not listed as belonging either to the exclusive or the shared competences.[43] Although Article 3 TFEU does not list the CFSP or economic sanctions among the areas belonging to the exclusive competence of the EU, the dominant view seems to be that the EU has – at least in practical terms – exclusive competence in adopting autonomous economic sanctions and in the implementation of UN sanctions.[44] This means that the Member States cannot adopt economic sanctions without the authorisation of the EU.[45] De Vries and Hazelzet point out, without specifying the exact nature of the competence of the EU, that the Member States 'can hardly impose unilateral sanctions towards third countries', but 'the requirement of unanimity gives each Member State tremendous influence over whether or not sanctions are imposed, and if so, what type and against whom'.[46] Other authors reject the existence of such exclusive competence.[47] Shared competence is deduced from the fact that a qualified majority decision based on Article 215 TFEU is always preceded by the procedure under Chapter 2 of Title V of the TEU and accordingly it presupposes a unanimous decision in the Council.[48] Eckes qualifies the EU CFSP competence, including Article 215 TFEU, as neither shared nor exclusive.[49] Pursuant to Article 24(3) TEU:

> The Member States shall support the Union's external and security policy actively and unreservedly in a spirit of loyalty and mutual solidarity and shall comply with

[40] Zagel (n 39) 2.

[41] Anthonius W de Vries and Hadewych Hazelzet, 'The EU as a New Actor on the Sanctions Scene' in Peter Wallensteen and Carina Staibano (eds), *International Sanctions: Between Words and Wars in the Global System* (Frank Cass, 2005) 95, 96.

[42] See Robert Schütze, 'On "Middle Ground": The European Union and Public International Law' in *Foreign Affairs and the EU Constitution* (Cambridge University Press, 2014) 47, 64–65.

[43] Finn Laursen, *The EU's Lisbon Treaty: Institutional Choices and Implementation* (Ashgate, 2012) 8.

[44] Sophie Mathäß, *Die Auswirkungen staaten- und personenbezogener Embargomaßnahmen auf Privatrechtsverhältnisse* (Nomos, 2016) 52; Koen Lenaerts and Eddy de Smijter, 'The United Nations and the European Union: Living Apart Together' in Karel Wellens, *International Law: Theory and Practice – Essays in Honour of Eric Suy* (Martinus Nijhoff, 1998) 439, 454; Zagel (n 39) 5.

[45] TFEU, art 2(1).

[46] De Vries and Hazelzet (n 41) 98.

[47] See Johnston (n 30) 396.

[48] Robert Schütze, 'External Union Policies: A Substantive Overview' in *Foreign Affairs and the EU Constitution* (Cambridge University Press, 2014) 407, 458.

[49] Christina Eckes, 'Controlling the Most Dangerous Branch from Afar: Multilayered Counter-Terrorist Policies and the European Judiciary' (2011) 2 *European Journal of Risk Regulation* 505, 515.

> the Union's action in this area ... They shall refrain from any action which is contrary to the interests of the Union or likely to impair its effectiveness as a cohesive force in international relations.

Accordingly, after a CFSP decision has been adopted, the Member States cannot introduce any measure contrary to the purpose of that decision.[50] Nevertheless, if a CFSP decision cannot be adopted, Member States retain their competence to adopt national restrictive measures unilaterally.[51] Eeckhout also points out that, as they are not listed in Article 3 TFEU, economic sanctions may not belong to the exclusive competence of the EU.[52] Due to the prerequisite of the prior CFSP decision, the exercise of the competence of the EU is conditional. This implies that in the absence of a CFSP decision – for example, because no unanimity could be reached – Member States retain their power to adopt sanctions. Still regarding the former Article 224 and Article 113 of the EEC Treaty, Vaucher contended that, in the absence of unanimity on the part of the Member States, the Community did not possess any competence. Several authors argue that Article 207 TFEU (the former Article 113 of the EEC Treaty and Article 133 of the EC Treaty) may continue to provide a legal basis for economic sanctions having a commercial nature, in particular when no unanimous CFSP decision could be adopted to apply Article 215 TFEU.[53] Contrary to this view, Vaucher argued that the Community could not even exercise its commercial competence for adopting economic sanctions.[54] As he notes, the Community can avail itself only of the power of initiative for encouraging Member States to impose sanctions.[55] However, trade restrictions (eg, a trade embargo) imposed unilaterally by the Member States do not fall outside the realm of the common commercial policy simply because they also pursue foreign policy objectives.[56] The unilateral trade restrictions imposed by a Member State can be justified on public security grounds, an exception recognised by several EU instruments on trade with third countries.[57]

In addition to Article 301 of the EC Treaty, the Maastricht Treaty also introduced Article 73g, which empowered the Council to restrict movement of capital and payments with third countries for CFSP purposes. This was a crucial change, since financial sanctions fell beyond the scope of the common commercial policy, and relevant EU measures could only be adopted based on Article 235 of the EEC Treaty.

In practical terms, it is the EU that exercises its competence imposing economic sanctions. The Member States have undoubtedly some, though narrow,

[50] ibid 515.

[51] ibid.

[52] Piet Eeckhout, *External Relations of the European Union* (Oxford University Press, 2011) 541.

[53] Wessel (n 28) 1161; Zagel (n 39) 22–23.

[54] Vaucher (n 18) 55.

[55] ibid 55.

[56] Case C-70/94 *Fritz Werner Industrie-Ausrüstungen GmbH v Federal Republic of Germany* [1995] ECR I-3189, para 10.

[57] Eeckhout (n 52) 541–42. *Werner* (n 56) paras 6–29; Case C-83/94 *Criminal Proceedings against Peter Leifer, Reinhold Otto Krauskopf and Otto Holzer* [1995] ECR I-3231, para 30.

leeway. First, Article 346(1)(b) TFEU provides that it is not precluded that 'any Member State may take such measures as it considers necessary for the protection of the essential interests of its security which are connected with the production of or trade in arms, munitions and war material'. This provision is limited to arms embargoes, which accordingly fall within the competence of the Member States.[58] Second, the Member States are free to take restrictive measures independently under the circumstances mentioned in Article 347 TFEU (formerly Article 297 of the EC Treaty and Article 224 of the EEC Treaty), provided they consulted the other Member States.[59] Article 347 TFEU refers to measures necessary in order to carry out obligations of the Member State 'it has accepted for the purpose of maintaining peace and international security' that embrace UNSC resolutions determining sanctions.[60] Thus, if no sanction could be adopted under Article 215 TFEU, Member States can take measures to implement a UNSC sanction to avoid a breach of their international obligations.[61] The application of Article 347 goes well beyond the arms embargoes specified in Article 346(1)(b) TFEU and extends to a wide range of trade restrictions (including an embargo) on any sort of goods.[62] However, Article 347 remains a residual mechanism, applicable only exceptionally when the Member State cannot have recourse to any more specific provisions of the TFEU that may justify restrictive measures.[63] Although it has rarely happened, some Member States unilaterally adopted sanctions independently of the EU mechanism. Most notably, Greece imposed unilateral sanctions against the Former Yugoslav Republic of Macedonia in the dispute over the name of Macedonia.[64] Regarding the current Article 347, the CJEU established that it concerns a wholly exceptional situation.[65] It must be noted that both Articles 346 and 347 TFEU are subject to Article 348 TFEU. This introduces an obligation on the Commission, together with the Member State concerned, to examine how the measures adopted under Articles 346 and 347 TFEU may be adjusted to the rules laid down in the Treaties if those measures have a distorting effect on the conditions of competition in the internal market. Furthermore, either the Commission or any Member State may bring the matter directly before the CJEU if it considers that a Member State is making improper use of the powers provided for in Articles 346 and 347. Article 348 TFEU refers to 'powers provided for in Articles 346 and 347', from which it follows that the TFEU recognises their

[58] Koutrakos, *Trade, Foreign Policy and Defence* (n 18) 182–220.

[59] Defalque and Luff (n 21) 107–08. For a detailed analysis of the current art 347 TFEU, see Panos Koutrakos, 'Is Article 297 EC a "Reserve of Sovereignty"?' (2000) 37 *CML Rev* 1339.

[60] Johnston (n 30) 391.

[61] Wessel (n 28) 1166; Zagel (n 39) 24.

[62] Johnston (n 30) 390.

[63] ibid 391–92.

[64] ibid 395; Vaucher (n 18) 54. See Case C-120/94 *Commission of the European Communities v Hellenic Republic* [1996] ECR I-1513.

[65] Case 222/84 *Marguerite Johnston v Chief Constable of the Royal Ulster Constabulary* [1986] ECR 1651, para 27.

competence and, regarding Article 347, does not simply impose an obligation to consult on the Member States, but they are given the right to adopt restrictive measures, though under exceptional circumstances only.[66] Third, based on Article 65(1)(b) TFEU, the free movement of capital and payments may also be restricted by the Member States concerning third countries on the grounds of public policy and public security.[67] Fourth, travel bans and visa restrictions are implemented by the law of the Member States, even if introduced within the framework of the CFSP. Fifth, EU regulations may require Member States to take appropriate measures.[68] As the EU does not have a general competence in the field of criminal law, criminal law sanctions foreseen for breaches of economic sanctions are determined by the law of the Member States. EU sanctions regulations often call upon the Member States to establish penalties for non-compliance with the particular sanction regime.[69] Private law consequences of the application of sanctions are most often determined equally by national law.

Other legal bases equally allow the adoption of sanctions or restrictive measures. It suffices to refer here to Article 75 TFEU, which, as a *lex specialis*[70] promoting security policy objectives, permits sanctions against natural or legal persons, groups or non-state entities to fight terrorism by restricting capital movements and freezing assets. While Article 215 TFEU provides for sanctions against states and persons in their capacities linking them to a certain state, Article 75 embodies a legal basis for counter-terrorist measures.[71]

To sum up, the EU has competence to impose economic sanctions. In practice, economic sanctions are adopted at the EU level in a two-stage procedure. First, a CFSP decision is adopted, which is then followed by an EU regulation. Irrespective of the nature of the competence of the EU to impose economic sanctions, the room for manoeuvre of the Member States is limited. In particular, arms embargoes (now Article 346(1)(b) TFEU) and travel bans allow action by Member States.[72] The analysis below will demonstrate that the courts of the Member States apply economic sanctions imposed by the EU relying on its competence. Private international law rules do facilitate it. What is more uncertain is whether a court in the EU will apply an economic sanction which has not been imposed by the EU, but by a third state.

[66] Johnston (n 30) 390.
[67] Eeckhout (n 52) 542.
[68] Mathäß (n 44) 51.
[69] ibid 52. See Council Regulation (EC) No 329/2007 of 27 March 2007 concerning restrictive measures against the Democratic People's Republic of Korea [2007] OJ L88/1, art 14; Council Regulation (EU) No 833/2014 of 31 July 2014 concerning restrictive measures in view of Russia's actions destabilising the situation in Ukraine [2014] OJ L229/1, art 8.
[70] Marchand (n 27) 79.
[71] Andrés Delgado Casteleiro, 'The Implementation of Targeted Sanctions in the European Union' in Andrés Delgado Casteleiro and Martina Spernbauer (eds), *Security Aspects in EU External Policies*, EUI Working Papers, Department of Law 2009/1, 39, 48, http://cadmus.eui.eu/handle/1814/10288.
[72] Brummer (n 17) 195; Portela (n 18) 27–28; Eeckhout (n 52) 475.

3

Coherence and Legal Certainty in EU Law

In this chapter, EU private international law rules and the judicial practice of the Member States will be analysed based on two factors: coherence and legal certainty. This is necessary because the goal of this book is to scrutinise whether EU private international law rules contribute consistently to a uniform EU foreign policy approach and whether these two fit coherently. A further question is whether economic sanctions are applied in a predictable way in order to promote legal certainty. It is hypothesised here that the consistent application of private international law rules results in coherence between the EU policy of freedom, security and justice encompassing private international law and the EU CFSP. Consistency of the application of economic sanctions through private international law also promotes legal certainty. Coherence and legal certainty will be therefore briefly discussed in this chapter in light of EU law.

I. Coherence in the External Relations Law of the EU

Coherence is a crucial endeavour of the EU that should pervade the acts of the EU and its Member States that have effects on the international stage. Coherence may also pose a challenge within a single policy, but a further difficulty for the EU lies in creating coherence between the various EU policies (horizontal coherence) as well as regarding the action of the EU and its Member States (vertical coherence).[1] Coherence is often defined as an action free from contradictions (consistency) and a synergy emerging from the former in different policy areas.[2] In this sense, consistency is a component of coherence, but not the single one.[3]

[1] Christian Tietje, 'The Concept of Coherence in the Treaty on European Union and the Common Foreign and Security Policy' (1997) 2 *European Foreign Affairs Review* 211, 224.

[2] ibid 212; Pascal Gauttier, 'Horizontal Coherence and the External Competences of the European Union' (2004) 10 *European Law Journal* 23, 25–26; Carmen Gebhard, 'Coherence' in Christopher Hill and Michael Smith, *International Relations and the European Union*, 2nd edn (Oxford University Press, 2011) 101, 106. See also Panos Koutrakos, *Trade, Foreign Policy and Defence under the Law of the EU* (Hart Publishing, 2001) 39–40; Ramses A Wessel, 'The Inside Looking out: Consistency and Delimitation in EU External Relations' (2000) 37 *CML Rev* 1135, 1150.

[3] Tietje (n 1) 213. However, consistency is interpreted more broadly by other scholars: Christophe Hillion, 'Tous pour un, un pour tous! Coherence in the External Relations of the European Union'

The English version of the Treaties refers to the requirement of consistency generally and more specifically regarding the CFSP. Article 7 TFEU lays down that: 'The Union shall ensure consistency between its policies and activities, taking all of its objectives into account and in accordance with the principle of conferral of powers.' According to the English wording of Article 21(3) TEU: 'The Union shall ensure consistency between the different areas of its external action and between these and its other policies.' However, it must be noted that the French version of both Article 7 TFEU and Article 21(3) TEU mention 'cohérence' and this is supported by other language versions (*Kohärenz*, *coherencia*, *coerenza*), from which a general requirement for horizontal coherence may be deduced. Wessel points out that using the term 'coherence' better expresses the 'incremental approach' of the EU concerning the CFSP.[4]

Coherence not only imposes obligations on the EU and its institutions,[5] but also on the Member States. Under Article 24(3) TEU, the Member States shall support the EU's external and security policy actively and unreservedly, and shall refrain from any action which is likely to impair its effectiveness as a cohesive force in international relations. Coherence may be also conceived as a principle which must be taken into account when interpreting rules and other principles.[6]

Several other EU documents underline the role of coherence. Some of them relate generally to Europe's appearance on the international stage.[7] In addition, there are more specific documents concerning coherence in the external dimension of EU private international law.

Importantly for private international law, the brief external relations chapter of the Hague Programme of 2004 declared that: 'The European Council considers the development of a coherent external dimension of the Union policy of freedom, security and justice as a growing priority.' The Hague Programme also added that the EU should use its powers 'in an integrated and consistent way to establish the area of freedom, security and justice', taking into account inter alia the 'contribution to the general political objectives of the foreign policies of the Union'. Since the determination of private international rules also falls within the realm of the area of freedom, security and justice, coherence with foreign policy objectives is also a requirement there.

Accordingly, under the TFEU, not only must the different areas of external action operate coherently, but coherence is also required between EU external action and other policy fields. Consequently, coherence is indispensable

in Marise Cremona (ed), *Developments in EU External Relations Law* (Oxford University Press, 2008) 10, 12–17.

[4] Wessel (n 2) 1150.

[5] TEU, arts 13(1) and 26(2).

[6] Mauro Gatti, *European External Action Service: Promoting Coherence through Autonomy and Coordination* (Martinus Nijhoff, 2016) 38.

[7] See in particular Communication from the Commission to the European Council of June 2006 Europe in the World – Some Practical Proposals for Greater Coherence, Effectiveness and Visibility Brussels, 8 June 2006, COM(2006) 278 final.

in the relation between EU external policy and private international law. The consistent application of private international law rules on economic sanctions contributes to the coherence between the EU policy of freedom, security and justice embracing private international law and the CFSP.

Regarding the analysis of sanctions as a relevant foreign policy instrument, Leenders examines the coherence of the application of sanctions by the EU.[8] His macro-level query addressed whether the EU acts in a consistent way when applying sanctions, that is, in a similar manner in similar situations. This book similarly makes enquiries regarding the coherence of the application of sanctions, but at a micro-level. Coherence will be used in the same sense. However, the analysis does not scrutinise the conduct of EU institutions; it turns instead to the judicial practice of the courts of the Member States which apply economic sanctions in concrete cases with the help of private international law and substantive private law. What matters for the purposes of our analysis is whether the courts of the Member States of the EU act consistently when the application of economic sanctions, imposed either by the EU or by another state or organisation, is at issue. Such enquiry is crucial because the effectiveness of economic sanctions largely depends on their enforcement. Courts are among those institutions which take part in the enforcement of sanctions. As such, the practice of the courts of the Member States concerning the application of economic sanctions through private international law rules is highly relevant. If this judicial practice is consistent, it can contribute to coherence between EU private international law and EU foreign policy.

Several EU regulations imposing economic sanctions have been justified by the need for their uniform application[9] or implementation[10] throughout the EU.[11] Obviously, the claim in these EU regulations for a uniform application is limited to the application of the economic sanction imposed by the regulation concerned, ie, economic sanctions imposed by the EU. It is unequivocal that EU law endeavours to pursue a coherent approach towards the implementation of the UNSC sanctions as well as autonomous EU sanctions. However, the Treaties or other EU documents do not provide any guidance on the EU approach towards sanctions autonomously adopted by third countries.

A uniform approach towards third-country sanctions is lacking. The CFSP has not identified common interests and objectives regarding such sanctions, the sole exception being when Council Regulation (EC) No 2271/96 (hereinafter the EC

[8] Leander Leenders, 'EU Sanctions: A Relevant Foreign Policy Tool?' College of Europe, EU Diplomacy Papers 3/2014, 6, https://www.coleurope.eu/system/files_force/research-paper/edp_3_2014_leenders_0.pdf?download=1.

[9] Council Regulation (EU) No 833/2014 of 31 July 2014 concerning restrictive measures in view of Russia's actions destabilising the situation in Ukraine [2014] OJ L229/1, preamble (6).

[10] Council Regulation (EEC) No 2340/90 of 8 August 1990 preventing trade by the Community as regards Iraq and Kuwait [1990] OJ L213/1, preamble.

[11] Koutrakos (n 2) 64.

Blocking Regulation) was adopted against certain US sanctions (a topic to which we will return later).[12] The absence of a common policy towards foreign sanctions gives room to the enforcement of national interests and foreign policy objectives. Assuming a uniform EU external action, the approach towards the implementation of these restrictive measures should be equally uniform across the Member States. The same proposition is confirmed by the demands for a uniform area of justice, freedom and security, including judicial cooperation in civil matters.

Requiring a uniform EU position towards economic sanctions imposed by third countries may be rejected as involving the extension of EU competence and the deprivation of the Member States of their competence to determine their foreign policy approach towards such sanctions. However, it cannot be ignored that the EU sometimes reacts towards third-country sanctions, as happened with the EC Blocking Regulation, which excludes the application of certain US sanctions. The EC Blocking Regulation was adopted on the basis of Articles 73c (largely corresponding with Article 64 TFEU), 113 and 235 of the EC Treaty.

The fact remains that the absence of a common EU foreign policy approach to foreign sanctions shifts the decision on the applicability of these economic sanctions to the courts of the Member States. The courts of the Member States decide on the application of these economic sanctions with the help of uniform provisions, through the Rome I Regulation; however, due to its flexible wording, the practice of the national courts seems to be divergent and sometimes inconsistent.[13] National courts take national interests, values and foreign policy objectives into account instead of a common position. The lack of a common EU foreign policy approach and the inconsistent judicial practice of the Member States based on EU private international law rules further neither the vertical coherence of EU foreign policy with the foreign policy of the Member States nor the horizontal coherence between EU foreign policy and EU private international law.

II. Legal Certainty and EU Law

The principle of legal certainty is undoubtedly a component of the rule of law. This principle applies to both legislation and judicial practice. Citizens must be put in a position where they can foresee the rules applicable to them so that they can adapt their conduct appropriately to these rules. The necessity of this also arises for business actors which have to be aware of the governing rules with the certainty that enables the careful planning of business transactions and the reduction of transaction costs.

[12] Council Regulation (EC) No 2271/96 of 22 November 1996 protecting against the effects of the extra-territorial application of legislation adopted by a third country, and actions based thereon or resulting therefrom [1996] OJ L309/1.

[13] Regulation (EC) No 593/2008 of the European Parliament and of the Council of 17 June 2008 on the law applicable to contractual obligations (Rome I) [2008] OJ L177/6.

Legal certainty is a principle in both EU law[14] and the laws of the Member States, which requires foreseeability for private persons through clear, precise, certain and predictable rules.[15] As the CJEU laid down, EU legislation must be clear, certain and its application foreseeable for those subject to it.[16] It is of paramount importance that private persons can ascertain the rules applicable to them in advance in order to shape their conduct on the basis of such rules.[17]

The principle of legal certainty has been used by the CJEU primarily in interpreting EU law and it held that secondary EU law must preferably be interpreted in accordance with the principle of legal certainty.[18] At the same time, the CJEU also acknowledged that the principle of legal certainty is not applied in an absolute manner.[19]

The EU private international law regulations refer to the objective of legal certainty[20] or predictability.[21] Regarding the conflict of laws on contracts, the Rome I Regulation refers to legal certainty as a general objective of the regulation. According to the Rome I Regulation, 'legal certainty in the European judicial area, the conflict-of-law rules should be highly foreseeable'. It adds that: 'The courts

[14] On the principle of legal certainty in EU law, see: Takis Tridimas, *The General Principles of EU Law*, 2nd edn (Oxford University Press, 2006) 242; Jérémie van Meerbeeck, 'The Principle of Legal Certainty in the Case-Law of the European Court of Justice: From Certainty to Trust' (2016) 41 *European Law Review* 275; Hysni Ahmetaj, 'Legal Certainty and Legitimate Expectations in the EU Law' (2014) 1 *Interdisciplinary Journal of Research and Development* 20; Taha Ayhan, 'The Principle of Legal Certainty in EU Case Law' (2010) 4 *TODAIE's Review of Public Administration* 149; Paul Craig, *EU Administrative Law* (Oxford University Press, 2012) 549; Juha Raitio, 'Legal Certainty, Non-retroactivity and Periods of Limitation in EU Law' (2008) 2 *Legisprudence* 1; Juha Raitio, 'The Expectation of Legal Certainty and Horizontal Effect of EU Law' in Ulf Bernitz, Xavier Groussot, Felix Schulyok (eds), *General Principles of EU Law and European Private Law* (Kluwer, 2013) 199.

[15] Case C-301/97 *Kingdom of the Netherlands v Council of the European Union* [2001] ECR I-8853, para 43.

[16] Case C-325/91 *French Republic v Commission of the European Communities* [1993] ECR I-3283, para 26; Case 325/85 *Ireland v Commission of the European Communities* [1987] ECR 5041, para 18.

[17] Case C-345/06 *Handelsgesellschaft Heinrich Heine GmbH v Verbraucherzentrale Nordrhein-Westfalen eV* [2010] ECR I-3047, para 44; Case 169/80 *Administration des douanes v Société anonyme Gondrand Frères and Société anonyme Garancini* [1981] ECR 1931, para 17.

[18] Case C-1/02 *Privat-Molkerei Borgmann GmbH & Co KG v Hauptzollamt Dortmund* [2004] ECR I-3219, para 30.

[19] Joined Cases 42 and 49/59 *Société nouvelle des usines de Pontlieue – Aciéries du Temple (SNUPAT) v High Authority of the European Coal and Steel Community* [1961] ECR 101.

[20] Regulation (EC) No 864/2007 of the European Parliament and of the Council of 11 July 2007 on the law applicable to non-contractual obligations (Rome II) [2007] OJ L199/40, preamble (14) and (31); Council Regulation (EU) No 1259/2010 of 20 December 2010 implementing enhanced cooperation in the area of the law applicable to divorce and legal separation [2010] OJ L343/10, preamble (9), (15), (19), (21), (23) and (29); Council Regulation (EC) No 4/2009 of 18 December 2008 on jurisdiction, applicable law, recognition and enforcement of decisions and cooperation in matters relating to maintenance obligations [2009] OJ L7/1, preamble (19); Regulation (EU) No 650/2012 of the European Parliament and of the Council of 4 July 2012 on jurisdiction, applicable law, recognition and enforcement of decisions and acceptance and enforcement of authentic instruments in matters of succession and on the creation of a European Certificate of Succession [2012] OJ L201/107, preamble (37) and (48).

[21] Regulation (EU) No 1215/2012 of the European Parliament and of the Council of 12 December 2012 on jurisdiction and the recognition and enforcement of judgments in civil and commercial matters [2012] OJ L351/1, preamble (15).

should, however, retain a degree of discretion to determine the law that is most closely connected to the situation.' The Rome I Regulation wanted to strike in this way a fair balance between the need for legal certainty and flexibility.

Tridimas points out that the CJEU used the principle of legal certainty in its case law to maintain the coherence of the EU legal order.[22] Although the judgments cited by Tridimas concerned different issues, it should be underlined that the principle of legal certainty promotes consistency and thereby coherence.

Legal certainty is of paramount importance in international commerce, where the question of jurisdiction and applicable law arises.[23] This is an added difficulty in comparison to purely domestic transactions. Most often, the intervention of an economic sanction is not foreseeable for the parties to a contract affected by the economic sanction. Moreover, once the sanction has been imposed, it may be doubted whether business actors may always foresee with certainty whether an economic sanction will be given effect in their legal relationship by the courts of the Member States. It will be demonstrated that the application of economic sanctions by the courts of the Member States raises legal certainty concerns at the level of both legislation and judicial practice. First, the flexibly formulated Article 9 of the Rome I Regulation provides considerable leeway for courts in giving effect to economic sanctions which does not always render it foreseeable when a court will decide to apply an economic sanction. Second, the courts of the Member States have different approaches as to whether other economic sanctions may be taken into consideration in the same way as those referred to by Article 9 of the Rome I Regulation. This heterogeneity of court practice does not promote legal certainty and foreseeability, which are crucial for economic actors. Consistency and legal certainty are further jeopardised by the fact that both legislation and judicial practice give some room for foreign policy arguments in cases involving economic sanctions. The inclusion of foreign policy arguments in court decisions involves inherent uncertainty in such cases.

As discussed, EU sanctions regulations stressed the need for uniform implementation by Member States. More recently, it seems that the emphasis has shifted somewhat from the uniform implementation by the Member States to the uniform application of and compliance by economic operators with economic sanctions.[24] This leads us to the actual enforcement of economic sanctions in the Member States. The rules of private international law have a decisive role to play in terms of whether to apply or take into consideration an economic sanction or not. This will be the subject of the next chapter.

[22] Tridimas (n 14) 248.

[23] On legal certainty and international commerce, see Stefan Leible, 'Außenhandel und Rechtssicherheit' (1998) 97 *ZVglRWiss* 286.

[24] See Council Regulation (EC) No 765/2006 of 18 May 2006 concerning restrictive measures against President Lukashenko and certain officials of Belarus [2006] OJ L134/1, preamble (4); Council Regulation (EU) No 224/2014 of 10 March 2014 concerning restrictive measures in view of the situation in the Central African Republic [2014] OJ L70/1, preamble (2); Council Regulation (EU) No 270/2011 of 21 March 2011 concerning restrictive measures directed against certain persons, entities and bodies in view of the situation in Egypt [2011] OJ L76/4, preamble (2).

4

Economic Sanctions in Private International Law

I. Economic Sanctions: State Intervention in Private Law Relationships

It has been asserted many times that the goal of conflict-of-laws regulation has been to accommodate private interests when designating the law which has the strongest connection to the legal relation in the best possible way.[1] The traditional Savignian approach of private international law was based on value-neutrality. Accordingly, private international law norms should be immune from various policy considerations changing in place and time. This neutrality has only had to yield sometimes to the public interest. In private international law, public interest may be taken into account in various ways: through the *ordre public* clause or enforcing public interests in the form of overriding mandatory provisions.

Article 3(1) of the Code civil already referred to the *lois de police* which bind everybody living in the territory of France. In the Savignian model, strictly positive laws limited the free play of conflict-of-laws rules.[2] It must be noted that Savigny's concept of strictly positive rules, or as we call them overriding mandatory provisions, implied only the application of the overriding mandatory provisions of the forum state and not dealing with the strictly positive norms found in the law of other states.[3] Foreign public law provisions were not included in the idea of external decisional harmony (*äußerer Entscheidungseinklang*). In principle, taking other states' public interests into consideration could promote decisional harmony if all states would follow this approach.[4] However, this is far from reality. States are not obliged to take the interests of any other state into consideration, for example, by applying their economic sanctions. The Rome Convention[5] and the Rome I Regulation, at least, create the possibility of this under Article 7 and

[1] Karl F Kreuzer, 'Parteiautonomie und fremdes Außenwirtschaftsrecht' in Peter Schlechtriem and Hans G Leser (eds), *Zum Deutschen und Internationalen Schuldrecht* (Mohr Siebeck, 1983) 89, 89.

[2] Friedrich Karl von Savigny, *System des heutigen römischen Rechts*, vol 8 (Scientia, 1974) 32–37.

[3] Karl Kreuzer, *Ausländisches Wirtschaftsrecht vor deutschen Gerichten* (CF Müller, 1986) 8–9.

[4] Theodorus Martinus de Boer, 'Living Apart Together: The Relationship between Public and Private International Law' (2010) *Netherlands International Law Review* 183, 203.

[5] 80/934/EEC Convention on the law applicable to contractual obligations opened for signature in Rome on 19 June 1980 [1980] OJ L266/1.

Article 9, respectively, but this is not an obligation on the courts of the Member States. In economic sanction cases, if the norms of a foreign country are taken into account, this most frequently involves the interests of another state being sacrificed. An import prohibition clearly violates the interests of the exporting state.[6] The court of the exporting state and that of the importing state would probably not decide the case in the same manner and with the same outcome. Thus, decisional harmony is inherently limited in cases involving conflict-of-laws issues related to economic sanctions. Nevertheless, sometimes courts have to address the intervention of foreign state legislation.

Until the multiplication of state legislation regulating market conduct in domestic and international commerce, private international law was relatively untouched by public law legislation. From the twentieth century onwards, states have involved themselves more often in private relations by regulating markets.[7] The application of economic sanctions is one of these instances where states upset contractual relations for foreign policy reasons. The question arose as to how this intrusion into private – mainly contractual – relations, in particular by economic sanctions, should be treated in private international law.

In the private international law literature, the relationship between public and private international law has often been discussed, and their interaction[8] or confluence[9] has been studied in depth. The distinction between public and private international law is 'fading'.[10] Undoubtedly, private law relationships are often coloured by public international law norms. This is also the case for economic sanctions regulated largely by public international law.

Economic sanctions have a public law origin. They may still affect the legal – first of all contractual – relations between private parties; when, for example, one of the parties refuses to perform a contract because performance would violate an embargo or a financial restriction. In such a case, the court or arbitral tribunal seised has to decide whether to give effect to the economic sanction. It is private international law that functions as a 'filter' or a 'valve' which transmits economic sanctions having a public law origin to the realm of private law.

Economic sanctions not only raise concerns at the level of public international law, but also influence the legal relations between private parties and they are often subject to litigation.[11] Economic sanctions may affect contracts between states, contracts between states and private parties, and contracts between private

[6] Frank Vischer, 'Kollisionsrechtliche Parteiautonomie und dirigistische Wirtschaftsgesetzgebung' in *Juristische Fakultät der Universität Basel, Festgabe für Max Gerwig* (Helbing & Lichtenhahn, 1960) 167, 179.

[7] Kreuzer (n 1) 89–90.

[8] Ben Atkinson Wortley, *The Interaction of Public and Private International Law, Collected Courses of the Hague Academy of International Law*, vol 85 (Martinus Nijhoff, 1954).

[9] Alex Mills, *The Confluence of Public and Private International Law* (Cambridge University Press, 2009).

[10] De Boer (n 4) 195.

[11] See Aurore Marchand, 'Note – Cass com, 16 mars 2010, no 08-21.511' (2011) 138 *Journal du droit international* 99, 102.

parties. Contracts between states belong to the realm of public international law, so contracts between private persons and contracts between a state and private persons may be of interest to private international law.

We witness the multiplication of economic sanctions in their number and forms. Often, the UN, the EU, the US and other states adopt partly overlapping, partly diverging sanctions. Private international law faces economic sanctions in diverse settings and, accordingly, the solutions cannot be the same. The contracts potentially affected are also very diverse: sales, service and shipping contracts, technology transfer, licensing, insurance contracts and current account contracts. In addition, international commercial relationships usually embody a network of contracts and the economic sanction does not necessarily only affect the main contract, but may also have repercussions on other related contracts, such as shipping contracts, subcontracts and finance contracts.[12]

Périlleux described embargoes as half-public, half-private law measures and this also holds generally for economic sanctions.[13] He added that private international law accepts this reality with difficulty. In fact, economic sanctions use private parties as a means of achieving the foreign policy objectives of the imposing state.[14] As de Vauplane rightly explains, using market players to enforce economic sanctions involves publicising private relationships.[15] In this way, politics and diplomacy penetrate international commerce.[16] As commercial interconnections become stronger and stronger due to globalisation, this foreign policy weapon becomes increasingly effective.[17]

Economic sanctions are imposed against states, organisations and individuals. When imposing economic sanctions against a state or certain state entities, private parties' contractual relationships are also affected. These private parties cannot essentially do anything to have the sanction lifted and its negative impact prevented; only the state can do this. Therefore, even though economic sanctions are imposed against a state, private parties having commercial contracts with the target state are in fact equally punished due to the interruption of the normal course of business. Private parties are for this reason seen as hostages of such coercive measures.[18] They have to assess whether the sanction is applicable to their contractual relationship and, if so, they should comply with it.

[12] Geneviève Burdeau, 'Les conséquences de la crise sur les relations économiques privées' in Brigitte Stern (ed), *Les aspects juridiques de la crise et de la guerre du Golfe* (Monthcrestien, 1991) 454.

[13] Jacques Périlleux, 'L'embargo et le droit des obligations' in Association européenne pour le droit bancaire et financier' in *L'embargo* (Bruylant, 1996) 167, 181.

[14] Jürgen Basedow, *The Law of Open Societies: Private Ordering and Public Regulation of International Relations – General Course on Private International Law, Collected Courses of the Hague Academy of International Law*, vol 360 (Martinus Nijhoff, 2013) 294–95 and 306.

[15] Hubert de Vauplane, 'Une nouvelle géopolitique de la norme' in Antoine Garapon and Pierre Servan-Schreiber (eds), *Deals de justice* (Presses Universitaires de France, 2013) 23, 23.

[16] ibid 23.

[17] ibid 24; Antoine Garapon and Pierre Servan-Schreiben, 'Un changement de paradigme' in Antoine Garapon and Pierre Servan-Schreiben (eds), *Deals de justice* (PUF, 2013) 1, 14.

[18] Périlleux (n 13) 171.

Since the application of economic sanctions is largely dependent upon the rules of private international law, it must be examined how economic sanctions are treated in conflict of laws and how they fit into the logic of private international law.

II. Economic Sanctions as Overriding Mandatory Provisions

The freedom of contract in substantive law is coupled with the autonomy of the parties in conflict of laws. Private autonomy is a cornerstone of the private international law of contracts, and parties accordingly have the right to select the law for their contract which they find the most suitable. This is recognised in most national private international laws as well as in regional codifications. The possibility of choice of law has been also acknowledged by the Rome Convention and the Rome I Regulation.[19]

However, private autonomy is sometimes restricted in order to promote certain state interests and policy objectives.[20] These interests and objectives most often belong to the state of the forum or the interests of a foreign state. From a private international law perspective, they often take the form of overriding mandatory provisions. Overriding mandatory provisions may gain application because they have certain connections to the contract.

A contract may involve connections with several states. The traditional method of private international law is based on seeking the seat or centre of gravity of the legal relationship to determine the governing law by objective connecting factors. The parties may also specify this through their choice of law. In the vast majority of cases, the contract will be subject to one legal regime (apart from the case of *dépeçage*). However, this means that the links to the rest of the states concerned have been cut. Rules allowing the application of or giving effect to overriding mandatory provisions may allow the judge to have regard to certain norms of states which would otherwise be ignored under the normal operation of conflict-of-laws rules.

It is not disputed that the overriding mandatory provisions of the forum may be applied by the court, even if these are public law rules. The underlying reason may be that no judge can disregard those rules that are part of the public policy of his own state.[21]

[19] Rome Convention, art 3; Rome I Regulation, art 3. See in particular Helmut Heiss, 'Party Autonomy' in Franco Ferrari and Stefan Leible (eds), *Rome I Regulation* (Sellier, 2009) 1.

[20] Louis d'Avout, 'Le sort des règles impératives dans le règlement Rome I' (2008) 184 *Receuil Dalloz* 2165, 2165.

[21] Vischer (n 6) 171.

Several authors hold overriding mandatory provisions,[22] or at least those of the forum,[23] as unilateral conflict-of-laws rules. Overriding mandatory provisions show certain characteristics of unilateralism. For example, neither overriding mandatory provisions nor unilateral conflict-of-laws rules aim at designating a foreign law as governing law.[24] However, overriding mandatory provisions differ from unilateral conflict-of-laws rules.[25] Unilateral and bilateral conflict-of-laws provisions are at the same level; they designate the governing law. However, overriding mandatory provisions overwrite the law governing in accordance with conflict-of-laws rules and require application, irrespective of the otherwise applicable law, in order to enforce certain policy objectives and interests. The designation of the governing law is a precondition for the potential application of overriding mandatory provisions. If the governing law contains the same rules as the overriding mandatory provisions claiming application, there is no need for the intervention of the latter.

Taking economic sanctions in private international law into account counteracts the private autonomy of the parties. Most often, economic sanctions are outside the contractual agreement of the parties. They encumber from the outside the contractual relations of the parties, irrespective of the parties' intention. As Basedow notes, individual freedom is increasingly fettered by rules expressing a national economic or political order; private autonomy is taking on a nation-state character.[26] Thus, private autonomy is also defined in accordance with the divergent foreign policy considerations of states. It must also be added that the contours of private autonomy are determined not simply by national foreign policy considerations, but also by regional and international ones. Economic sanctions as a means of foreign policy intrude into the contract in accordance with the intention of the imposing state.

Economic sanctions are rules of a substantive nature.[27] They may be channelled into private international law as overriding mandatory provisions. The qualification of economic sanctions as overriding mandatory provisions in private international law is confirmed by the legal literature, which classifies economic sanctions,[28]

[22] Laurence Idot, 'Les conflits de lois en droit de la concurrence' (1995) 122 *Journal du droit international* 320, 324 and 327; Eric Wyler and Alain Papaux, 'Extraneité de valeurs et de systèmes en droit international privé et en droit international public' in Eric Wyler and Alain Papaux (eds), *L'éxtraneité ou le dépassement de l'ordre juridique étatique* (Pedone, 1999) 239, 262; Peter Nygh, *Autonomy in International Contracts* (Clarendon, 1999) 202.

[23] Moritz Renner, 'Article 9 Overriding Mandatory Provisions' in Gralf-Peter Calliess (ed), *Rome Regulations* (Kluwer, 2011) 195, 203.

[24] Pierre Mayer, 'Les lois de police étrangères' (1981) 108 *Journal du droit international* 277, 297.

[25] Mercédeh Azeredo da Silveira, *Trade Sanctions and International Sales* (Kluwer, 2014) 51–52.

[26] Jürgen Basedow, 'Wirtschaftskollisionsrecht' (1988) 52 *RabelsZ* 8, 19.

[27] Francisco J Garcimartín Alférez, *Contratación internacional y medidas de coerción económica* (Beramar, 1993) 38

[28] Mercédeh Azeredo da Silveira, 'Economic Sanctions and Contractual Disputes between Private Operators' in Larissa van den Herik (ed), *Research Handbook on UN Sanctions and International Law* (Edward Elgar, 2017) 330, 338 and 344.

embargoes,[29] import and export restrictions[30] or freezing assets[31] as overriding mandatory provisions. This means that the economic sanctions of the forum state are applied by the courts, irrespective of the governing law. In the context of the EU, where the EU sanctions policy has, to a large extent, replaced the autonomous sanctions of the Member States, the EU regulations imposing economic sanctions constitute supranational overriding mandatory norms.[32] Despite the supranational origin of the sanctions legislation, EU regulations are directly applied in the Member States as the domestic law of the forum.

A foreign overriding mandatory provision is applicable if the imposing state has the intention to apply it in international relations. Therefore, a preliminary question is whether the imposing state wishes to apply the economic sanction to the given transaction at all. The examination thereof also involves ascertaining the scope of application of the economic sanction. An economic sanction applies to the legal relation only if the case falls under its personal, territorial, temporal and material scope of application.[33] To ascertain whether a planned transaction is caught by economic sanctions is not always unequivocal. Considerable attention was devoted by academics and practitioners to circumscribe the scope of application of different economic sanctions.[34] However, the denomination of the overriding mandatory provisions is somewhat misleading. Although they claim application irrespective of the governing law, they may be applied or taken into

[29] Cyril Nourissat, 'Lois de police étrangères devant le juge français du contrat international: une première sous l'empire de la Convention de Rome et peut-être pas une dernière sous l'empire du règlement "Rome I"' (2010) 5 *Revue Lamy droit des affaires* 63, 64; Marchand (n 11) 101 and 103; Laurence Landy-Osman, 'L'embargo des Nations Unies contre l'Irak et l'exécution des contrats internationaux' (1991) 17 *Droit et Pratique du Commerce International* 597, 607; Michael Cremer, 'Embargovorschriften als Eingriffsnormen' (2016) 10 *Bucerius Law Journal* 18, 18; Mathäß 58; Francisco Garcimartín Alférez, 'Embargo' in Jürgen Basedow, Giesela Rühl, Franco Ferrari and Pedro de Miguel Asensio (eds), *Encyclopedia of Private International Law* (Edward Elgar, 2017) 603; Régis Chemain, 'Sanctions économiques: contre-mesures, boycott, embargo, blocus' in *Encyclopédie Dalloz du droit international, Répertoire de droit international* (May 2017), para 184; Chambre de commerce internationale, *L'apport de la jurisprudence arbitrale* (CCI Institut, 1986); Pierre Mayer, 'Mandatory Rules of Law in International Arbitration' (1986) 2 *Arbitration International* 274, 275.

[30] Ivana Kunda, *International Mandatory Rules of a Third Country in European Contract Conflict of Laws: The Rome Convention and the Proposed Rome I Regulation* (Rijeka Law Faculty, 2007) 132; Norbert Horn, 'Zwingendes Recht in der internationalen Schiedsgerichtsbarkeit' (2008) *SchiedsVZ* 209, 210; Nathalie Voser, 'Mandatory Rules of Law as a Limitation on the Law Applicable in International Commercial Arbitration' (1996) 7 *American Review of International Arbitration* 319, 325.

[31] Sophie Wernert, 'Le gel d'avoirs étrangers: Aspects de droit international public et de droit international privé' (PhD thesis, Université Paris II Panthéon-Assas, 2001) 91.

[32] See Kurt Siehr, 'Ausländische Eingriffsnormen im inländischen Wirtschaftskollisiomsrecht' (1988) 52 *RabelsZ* 41, 63–64.

[33] Da Silveira (n 25) 25–28.

[34] Concerning the Russian sanctions, see Ivan Aladyev, 'Die EU-autonomen "smart sanctions" gegen die Russische Föderation – Rechtsgrundlage, Rechtsmäßigkeit und Rechtsschutz' (2015) 56 *Jahrbuch für Ostrecht* 21; Matthias Geurts, 'Rechtsfragen der Embargo-Maßnahmen durch die EU am Beispiel des Konfliktes mit der Russischen Föderation' (2015) 61 *Recht der Internationalen Wirtschaft* 32. Concerning the Russian and Iran sanctions, see Bastian Mehle and Volkmar Mehle, 'Die notwendige Einhaltung von EU-Embargo-Regelungen durch Unternehmen mit Sitz in Drittstaaten' (2015) 61 *Recht der Internationalen Wirtschaft* 397.

account only to the extent that the law of the forum state permits this. This is in particular the case with foreign overriding mandatory provisions, where the courts usually have some discretion when deciding whether to give them any effect.

Overriding mandatory provisions are apt to project substantive policy considerations onto private relations in an external dimension. This may be illustrated by the *Ingmar* judgment of the CJEU.[35] The interest in protecting commercial agents was enforced even in an EU–US agent-principal relationship. Kühne describes the impact of overriding mandatory norms as the materialisation (*Materialisierung*) of private international law.[36] The same is clearly applicable to economic sanctions. The inclusion of the prohibitions set by economic sanctions in the interplay of conflict-of-laws rules undoubtedly contributes to this materialisation process. By applying the economic sanctions imposed by the EU as overriding mandatory norms, the courts of the Member States enforce CFSP objectives in an international dimension.

Overriding mandatory provisions may be private or public law norms. Since economic sanctions belong to the latter category, it must be examined how the theory and practice of private international law approach the application of public law norms. The application of the overriding mandatory norms of the forum state does not usually raise concerns. However, divergent views evolved as regards the application of foreign public law. This is discussed in the next section.

III. The Treatment of Foreign Public Law in Private Law Litigation

The view that foreign public law norms may not be applied was predominant over a relatively long period. This position could be contrasted with the requirement of international decisional harmony, which argues for a broad application of foreign overriding mandatory norms:[37] if foreign overriding mandatory norms are applied by the courts, judicial decisions will lead to the same outcome everywhere. As a general rule, this approach favours giving priority to the interests and political considerations of foreign states over the localisation of the legal relationship.[38] The principle of the general non-application of foreign public law has been mostly overcome in today's private international law. However, the question still remains of the extent to which foreign public law norms may be applied or taken into account.

[35] Case C-381/98 *Ingmar GB Ltd v Eaton Leonard Technologies Inc* [2000] ECR I-9305.

[36] Gunther Kühne, 'Methodeneinheit und Methodenvielfalt im internationalen Privatrecht – Eine Generation nach "Kollisionsnorm und Sahrecht"' in Ralf Michaels and Dennis Solomon (eds), *Liber Amicorum Klaus Schurig* (Sellier, 2012) 129, 138.

[37] Pierre Mayer and Vincent Heuzé, *Droit international privé*, 11th edn (LGDJ, 2014) 104; Sandrine Sana-Chaille de Nere, 'Transport maritime et lois de police étrangères' (2010) *Droit maritime français* 367, 371.

[38] Mayer and Heuzé (n 37) 103–04.

As to how foreign public law norms may be taken into account in private law litigation, two approaches evolved. The first one is the application of foreign overriding mandatory provisions through the conflict-of-laws rules, while the second is their consideration at the level of substantive law.

A. The Application of Foreign Public Law Norms through Conflict-of-Laws Rules

Conflict-of-laws theories are divided as to the extent of the application of foreign overriding mandatory norms through the conflict-of-laws norms. These differences are expressed by the *Einheitsanknüpfunsgtheorie*, the *Sonderanknüpfungstheorie* and the theory combining the two.

The underlying difference between these theories lies in the fact that private international law scholars have been divided on whether or not the reference to a foreign law includes the public law norms of the state concerned.

i. Einheitsanknüpfungstheorie

Some authors opine that the reference to a foreign law includes all norms of that legal system, both private and public law rules, that are relevant for the decision.[39] This has been described in the German legal literature as *Einheitsanknüpfungstheorie, Schuldstatutstheorie* or *privatrechtliche Theorie* and is also called *lex causae* theory.[40] Following this approach, in addition to the public law norms of the forum, the public law rules of the *lex causae* must also be applied. The application of the public law norms of the *lex causae* may only be set aside on the grounds of the violation of the *ordre public*.[41] However, a public law norm of a third country cannot be applied.[42] The application of the law of a third country would be against the will of the parties. The only way in which public law norms of third countries may be taken into account is their inclusion at the stage of the substantive law assessment of the case.[43] According to this theory, foreign state interests may be

[39] Rudolf Heiz, *Das fremde öffentliche Recht im internationalen Kollisionsrecht* (Polygraphischer Verlag, 1959); Vischer (n 6) 171; Anton Heini, 'Ausländische Staatsinteressen und internationales Privatrecht' (1981) 100 *Zeitschrift für Schweizerisches Recht* 65, 66 and 77; Anton Heini, 'Die Anwendung wirtschaftlicher Zwangsmaßnahmen im internationalen Privatrecht' in Wilhelm A Kewenig and Anton Heini, *Die Anwendung wirtschaftlicher Zwangsmaßnahmen im Völkerrecht und im internationalen Privatrecht* (CF Müller, 1982) 43; Frederick Alexander Mann, 'Eingriffsgesetze und Internationales Privatrecht' in Klaus Müller and Hermann Soell, *Festschrift für Eduard Wahl* (Carl Winter/Universitätsverlag, 1973) 139, 146.

[40] Basedow (n 14) 327–29.

[41] Heiz (n 39) 135; Vischer (n 6) 171.

[42] Vischer (n 6) 172; Heini, 'Ausländische Staatsinteressen und internationales Privatrecht' (n 39) 77; Heini, 'Die Anwendung wirtschaftlicher Zwangsmaßnahmen im internationalen Privatrecht' (n 39) 43.

[43] Rolf C Radtke, 'Schuldstatut und Eingriffsrecht' (1985) 84 *ZVglRWiss* 325, 345–49.

safeguarded by international conventions instead of conflict-of-laws norms. The theory has clear advantages. First of all, it overcomes the problem of the distinction between private and public law.[44] It promotes the unity of the governing law and thereby legal certainty. Furthermore, it contributes to the idea of international decisional harmony being realised.[45] This approach is also in line with the resolution of the Institute of International Law on the Application of Foreign Public Law, which lays down that: 'The public law character attributed to a provision of foreign law which is designated by the rule of conflict of laws shall not prevent the application of that provision, subject however to the fundamental reservation of public policy.' The *Einheitsanknüpfungstheorie* also gained confirmation by the Swiss private international law legislation. Article 13 of the Swiss Private International Law Act provides that the reference to a foreign law involves all provisions of the designated law applicable to the situation. Accordingly, the applicability of a provision of the governing foreign law is not excluded only on the grounds that a public law character is attributed to it.

However, the *Einheitsanknüpfungstheorie* has been the subject of much criticism.[46] First, it is often argued that conflict-of-laws rules accommodate the interests of private parties without the involvement of the public interest. Public law norms may be included only if they ensure the balance of the parties' position; for example, in rules protecting consumers or other protective measures.[47] It has therefore been argued that a reference to foreign law is to be construed narrowly, limited to private law provisions and with the exclusion of foreign norms having a public law origin.[48] Second, the reason for this approach is the belief that the *lex causae* is closely related to the legal situation. This is true if the governing law is designated by an objective connecting factor. However, in the event of choice of law of the parties, a close connection between the selected law and the facts of the case does not necessarily exist.[49] The parties rarely consider the application of the public law norms of the law chosen by them when entering into a choice of law agreement.[50] When the parties choose the governing law – which is

[44] Bettina Rentsch, 'Krisenbewältigung durch konstitutionalisiertes Kollisionsrecht, oder: Eingriffsrecht als integraler Bestandteil des europäischen IPR' in Jonathan Bauerschmidt, Bardo Fassbender, Michael Wolfgang Müller, Angelika Siehr and Christopher Unseld (eds), *Konstitutionalisierung in Zeiten globaler Krisen* (Nomos, 2015) 255, 279.

[45] ibid 279–80.

[46] Sebastian von Allwörden, *US-Terrorlisten im deutschen Privatrecht: zur kollisions- und sachrechtlichen Problematik drittstaatlicher Sperrlisten mit extraterritorialer Wirkung* (Mohr Siebeck, 2014) 67–68.

[47] Frank Vischer, *General Course on Private International Law, Collected Courses of the Hague Academy of International Law*, vol 232 (Brill, 1992) 9, 180.

[48] Andreas Köhler, 'Die Berücksichtigung ausländischer Eingriffsnormen im Europäischen Internationalen Vertragsrecht' in Kathrin Binder and Florian Eichel, *Internationale Dimensionen des Wirtschaftsrechts* (Nomos, 2013) 199, 200 and 206.

[49] Robert Freitag, 'Einfach und international zwingende Normen' in Stefan Leible (ed), *Das Grünbuch zum Internationalen Vertragsrecht* (Sellier, 2004) 167, 184.

[50] Robert Freitag, 'Eingriffsnormen (international zwingende Bestimmungen), Berücksichtigung ausländischer Devisenvorschriften, Formvorschriften' in Christoph Reithmann and Dieter Martiny, *Internationales Vertragsrecht*, 8th edn (Otto Schmidt, 2015) 349, 366.

sometimes a law that is neutral to them – they certainly do not intend to choose the application of a public law norm which constitutes part of the *lex causae* and which, for example, prohibits the underlying agreement.[51] Hence, it is not justified to apply the public law norms of the *lex causae* in the case of choice of law. Moreover, the *Einheitsanknüpfungstheorie* excludes the application of overriding mandatory provisions of any other foreign state, although they may also show a close relation to the legal situation.[52] The overriding mandatory provisions of third states are 'discriminated' against in favour of the similar provisions of the *lex causae*, although the public law norms of third states may equally have a close connection to the situation. For one reason or another, the majority view in German literature rejects the application of the theory of *Einheitsanknüpfung*.[53]

ii. Sonderanknüpfungstheorie

From another perspective, conflict-of-laws rules refer exclusively to the private law norms of the law of the state governing the contract. This is because the vocation of private international law is seen to be settling the interests of private persons. A foreign public law rule must be applied, provided that it has some special connection to the legal dispute – in the German literature called *Sonderanknüpfung* – and therefore a special conflict-of-laws rule orders its application in a given case. It does not matter whether the norm may be found in the *lex causae* or in the law of a third country: any rule belonging to one or the other category has to show a special connection to be applied. In addition to a close connection between the norm and the legal relationship, it is further required that the norm itself intends to be applied to the situation and that the applicable norm shall be in accordance with the legal order of the state of the forum. Even if a special connection exists, the foreign law does not apply if it violates the *ordre public* of the forum.[54]

Nevertheless, the representatives of this theory have different responses as to what this special connection, which is required for the application of foreign public law provisions, must be.[55] The application of foreign public law norms may be based on a close connection expressed in a general way or more concretely (through the connecting factor of citizenship, residence, seat of the parties, the place of performance or location of property).[56] The close connection criterion

[51] Vischer (n 47) 180; Basedow (n 14) 328.

[52] Freitag (n 49) 184.

[53] Daniel Zimmer, 'Ausländisches Wirtschaftsrecht vor deutschen Zivilgerichten: Zur Unterscheidung zwischen einer normativen Berücksichtigung fremder zwingender Normen und einer bloßen Beachtung ihrer tatsächlichen Folgen' (1993) 13 *IPRax* 65; Köhler (n 48) 200 and 206; Basedow (n 14) 327–29.

[54] These preconditions were formulated first by Wilhelm Wengler, 'Die Anknüpfung des zwingenden Schuldrechts im internationalen Privatrecht' (1941) 54 *ZvglRW* 168.

[55] See Kreuzer (n 3) 62–64; Radtke (n 43) 335–38.

[56] Stephan Göthel, 'Grenzüberschreitende Reichweite ausländischen Kapitalmarktrechts' (2001) 21 *IPRax* 411, 418.

elaborated by Wengler was criticised by Zweigert as being too imprecise as to the sufficient or insufficient nature of the connection. Instead, he suggested examining, in addition to the claim of a foreign prohibition to be applied, whether the internationally typical interests of the forum (going beyond merely national interests) do not exclude applying a foreign law.[57] Other factors may be examined, such as the identity or similarity of the interests of the forum state and those behind the foreign norm which demands application. It may be required that the application of the foreign norm shall serve the interests of the state of the forum or the international community, or, at least, that it is not contrary to those of the forum state.[58] Pursuant to the shared values approach, the forum applies a foreign overriding mandatory norm, provided that the values represented by the norm are also shared by the forum state.[59] Foreign overriding mandatory norms are applied following an 'examination of sympathy', provided that the content of the foreign norm is compatible with the interests and values of the forum state.[60] Such norms are applicable if the forum state adopted similar provisions which equally restrict private autonomy. The point of departure is that there is a categorical imperative to apply those foreign rules with which the domestic legal order sympathises through comparable provisions. This view also finds support in the need for value coherence between substantive and conflict-of-laws justice. Moreover, the requirement on the coincidence of the interests and values can be explained by the circumstance that the forum state does not otherwise have an original interest in applying a foreign overriding mandatory norm.[61]

It must be noted that the establishment of the lack of the existence of these required preconditions is easier for the courts than to reach the conclusion that the application of the foreign norm violates the *ordre public*.[62] However, even if it is stated that a foreign overriding mandatory provision does not comply with these conditions, it may be taken into account at the level of substantive law.

The territoriality principle represents a specific expression of the *Sonderanknüpfungstheorie*. In the view of some authors, the application of foreign overriding mandatory provisions was accordingly justified by certain territorial links.[63] The underlying idea behind this theory is that each state is entitled to regulate acts taking place and assets located on its territory.[64] Overriding mandatory

[57] Konrad Zweigert, 'Nichterfüllung auf Grund ausländischer Leistungsverbote' (1942) 14 *Zeitschrift für ausländisches und internationales Privatrecht* 283, 289–91.

[58] Göthel (n 56) 418 represents the latter view.

[59] Bernhard Grossfeld and C Paul Rogers, 'A Shared Value Approach to Jurisditional Conflicts in International Economic Law' (1983) 32 *International & Comparative Law Quarterly* 931, 939.

[60] Köhler (n 48) 214.

[61] Stefan Leible, 'Außenhandel und Rechtssicherheit' (1998) 97 *ZVglRWiss* 286, 300.

[62] Andreas Behr, *Deutsche Unternehmen und der Israel-Boykott* (Verlag Recht und Wissenschaft, 1994) 90.

[63] Franz Bydlinski, 'Anmerkung zur Entscheidung des OGH. 24. Juni 1959, 6 Ob 204/59.' (1961) 2 *Zeitschrift für Rechtsvergleichung* 18, 26–28.

[64] ibid 26–27.

provisions must be applied if they concern assets or acts performed (eg, when the place of performance is located) in the territory of the foreign state. This territorial link constitutes a special connecting factor between the legal relationship and the territory of the foreign state. Recognising the sovereignty of the foreign state in its own territory justifies the application of its norms, even if these are public law norms.[65] The application of a foreign mandatory rule may of course be rejected in the given case if it breaches the *ordre public* of the forum.[66] The flaw in this approach is that a connection other than a territorial one may give rise to a close link between the situation and the foreign public law norm.

However, the *Sonderanknüpfungstheorie* is not free from flaws. First, it leads to the application of various laws to the contract and thus to splitting the contractual relationship in terms of the applicable law. Vischer argues that the substantive unity and harmony of the legal relation is sacrificed on the altar of decisional harmony.[67] Second, there is no uniformity in legal scholarship on the question of the appropriate connecting factor, expressing a special connection between the facts of the case and the applicable foreign law. In the absence of a precise connecting factor, the court should, in theory, have regard to all of the legal systems and the overriding mandatory provisions thereof, all of which may potentially claim application based on a close connection.[68] Finally, the requirement on the examination of the interests and values behind the foreign law and their evaluation already involves a substantive review of the foreign law before its application, which seems to be contrary to the traditional neutral function of conflict of laws.[69]

iii. Kumulationslehre

A third approach combines the two above approaches and has been called cumulation theory (*Kumulationslehre*). The reference to the governing law is construed broadly so as to include the public law provisions of the *lex causae*. In this sense, the approach of *Einheitsanknüpfung* is followed. However, this is supplemented by giving effect to the overriding mandatory provisions of a third state if this is justified by a special connection to the legal dispute. This supplement characterises the *Sonderanknüpfungstheorie*. Yet, it is questionable whether it is possible to reconcile the fundamental differences of the *Einheitsanknüpfung* and the *Sonderanknüpfung*,[70] and whether it is theoretically sound to link these two conflicting doctrines.

[65] ibid 26–28.
[66] ibid 28.
[67] Vischer (n 6) 177–78.
[68] ibid 177.
[69] Mathias Kuckein, *Die 'Berücksichtigung' von Eingriffsnormen im deutschen und englischen internationalen Vertragsrecht* (Mohr Siebeck, 2008) 96.
[70] Radtke (n 43) 351.

B. The Substantive Law Approach

Another way to include foreign overriding mandatory provisions having a public law origin in the decision of the court is at the level of substantive law. The foreign norm will be accommodated within the governing substantive law, which also implies that the governing substantive law must contain provisions through which the foreign law can exert effect on the decision of the case.[71] The 'consideration' of foreign norms at the level of substantive law (also called as 'indirect application')[72] is distinguished from the (direct) 'application' of such norms. In the case of the application of a foreign norm, the private law consequences are determined by that foreign law, while in the case of considering a foreign norm through substantive law, the preconditions and the private law consequences thereof are determined by the *lex causae* and not by the foreign law itself.[73] In comparison to 'consideration' by integration into the governing law, 'application' also involves the recognition of the content of a foreign norm fully, together with its scope and its legal consequences.[74] The difference between application and considering foreign law at the level of substantive law is that the law applied decides the case directly, whereas the law considered does not itself decide the case,[75] but only contributes to it as an element to be taken into account.

Consideration may take place due to the factual effects of a foreign overriding mandatory provision. These factual effects are those which interfere with a legal relationship, irrespective of the position of the forum towards the foreign overriding mandatory norm. Factual effects may not be disregarded, for example, in the case of the seizure of goods by the authorities of the imposing state, even if the forum state rejects the underlying foreign norm. The factual effects of a foreign norm may be given effect through substantive law, even if it is contrary to the *ordre public* of the forum and as such could not be applied as a legal norm.[76] These factual effects are taken into account in the governing contract law, for example, as a ground for the impossibility of performance. At the same time, even in the absence of any factual impact, a court may consider a foreign overriding mandatory provision, while taking the normative content of the norm into account. If the normative content of the norm is compatible with the interests and values of the forum state, the court will give effect to the norm. This again takes place through a substantive law provision of the law of the forum, such as a provision prohibiting contracts breaching good morals, provided that there would be moral condemnation of the violation of the foreign overriding mandatory norm, even by the courts of the forum state.

[71] Kuckein (n 69) 116.
[72] ibid 51.
[73] Patrick Kinsch, *Le fait du prince étranger* (LGDJ, 1994) 383.
[74] Kuckein (n 69) 52.
[75] Estelle Fohrer-Dedeurwaerder, *La prise en considération des normes étrangères* (LGDJ, 2008) 43.
[76] Kinsch (n 73) 330 and 350.

This method may be necessary for various reasons. First, under the concept that the vocation of private international law is to balance private interests, the frame of reference of conflict-of-laws rules covers private law norms only. Foreign overriding mandatory norms having a public law nature may not be applied by virtue of conflict-of-laws rules directly because the latter exclusively concern the application of private law norms.[77] Even so, public law norms may be considered at the level of substantive law. The approach that gave effect to foreign public law norms but did not apply them directly proved to be particularly useful at a time when the theory of the non-application of foreign public law dominated, because the latter remained intact.[78] Second, even if foreign public law norms may be applied to a certain extent within the limits of the *Einheitsanknüpfungs* or the *Sonderanknüpfungstheorie*, a public law norm excluded under the private international law assessment of the case may be still considered as a next step at the level of substantive law. Foreign public law norms may be taken into consideration at the level of substantive law after the court has designated the law governing the contract. The first step is thus the determination of the applicable law through the conflict-of-laws rules of the forum, which is followed by the selection of a rule of substantive law in the *lex causae* that makes it possible to take foreign norms into consideration. Those norms which are taken into account at the level of substantive law are overriding mandatory provisions.[79] To be given effect, a foreign overriding mandatory provision must claim application internationally and specifically for the given case. However, the claim for application does not suffice. Overriding mandatory norms are applied by virtue of the law of the forum and to the extent that the law of the forum permits this. Giving effect to foreign overriding mandatory norms takes place through general clauses of contract law of the forum, such as the prohibition of contracts breaching law, good morals and public policy, the impossibility of the performance of the contract, the basis of the transaction ceasing to exist or frustration of the contract.

It is often asserted that consideration at the level of substantive law requires the correspondence of the interests or values behind the foreign norm and those of the forum. However, this is not a necessity. In relation to the shared values approach, it has been noted that even if the foreign law may not be applied in the absence of shared values, the forum may give effect to the foreign law as a fact that renders performance impossible.[80] If the foreign law does not render performance impossible, but only more burdensome (for example, by threatening penalties), it is acknowledged that the test is more subjective.[81] The court has to ascertain

[77] Christian Forwick, *Extraterritoriale US-amerikanische Exportkontrollen. Folgen für die Vertragsgestaltung* (Verlag Recht und Wirtschaft, 1993) 127.

[78] George van Hecke, 'Foreign Public Law in the Courts' (1969) 1 *Revue belge de droit international* 63, 65.

[79] Kinsch (n 73) 347.

[80] Grossfeld and Rogers (n 59) 945.

[81] ibid 945.

the chances of the foreign state waiving the penalties because of the conflicts of obligation the party faces.[82] In the event that the party knowingly gets into the position that he should comply with conflicting obligations, he has to bear the burden of them, while if the foreign legislation intervened subsequently, the forum has to decide on the risk allocation between the foreign state and the private party concerned.[83]

Contrary to a conflict-of-laws approach, the purpose of substantive justice may be served by considering foreign overriding mandatory norms at the level of substantive law, and this method may contribute to finding a just equilibrium between the interests of the parties by the court.[84]

Some national laws, such as the Swiss Private International Law Act,[85] make it possible to give effect to the overriding mandatory provisions of third states. This is also rendered possible by the Rome Convention and the Rome I Regulation, though the precise content of these provisions is debated.

This method has been subject to criticism by several authors. Mayer asserted that, in most cases, the same outcome could be achieved by the application of the foreign law.[86] In addition, it is not predictable for the parties in a given case when a court considers foreign overriding mandatory norms at the level of substantive law and, as such, it does not promote legal certainty. Often, political considerations play a role when deciding whether to give effect to a foreign overriding mandatory norm that results in the politicisation of court decisions.[87] This may be well illustrated by the cases involving economic sanctions, and the pertinence of this argument will be confirmed in the following chapters.

The substantive law consideration of foreign overriding mandatory norms is explained again by more specific theories, such as the datum theory and the *Machttheorie*.[88]

i. Datum Theory

The consideration of foreign law at the level of the substantive assessment of the case has been often discussed in the context of the datum theory. The datum theory is a method of taking foreign norms into consideration at the level of substantive law, irrespective of the governing law.[89] The datum theory, as first elaborated by

[82] ibid 945–56.
[83] ibid 946.
[84] Kuckein (n 69) 116.
[85] Bundesgesetz über das Internationale Privatrecht (IPRG) vom 18 Dezember 1987, art 19.
[86] Mayer (n 24) 309.
[87] Meiko Zeppenfeld, *Die allseitige Anknüpfung von Eingriffsnormen im Internationalen Wirtschaftsrecht* (Duncker & Humblot, 2001) 60–61.
[88] Bernhard Großfeld and Abbo Junker, *Das CoCom im internationalen Wirtschaftsrecht* (Mohr Siebeck, 1991) 105; Eberhard Vetter, 'Kollisionsrechtliche Fragen bei grenzüberschreitenden Subunternehmensverträgen im Industrieanlagenbau' (1988) 87 *ZVglRWiss* 248, 272.
[89] Kinsch (n 73) 332–46.

Currie, distinguished between foreign law operating as a rule of decision and as datum.[90] Accordingly, the vocation of conflict of laws is 'to find the appropriate rule of decision' by designating the applicable law, but a foreign rule may also constitute a datum that is significant in deciding a case, even if the foreign rule is not part of the governing law.[91] As Jayme formulates it, the application of certain foreign rules does not require any theoretical reflection; their application is self-evident.[92] The legal situation is so strongly linked to the foreign legal rule that the court cannot ignore it.[93] In other words, if the facts of the case take place abroad, the rules of the state concerned cannot be entirely disregarded.[94] Accordingly, foreign data could be taken into account in applying domestic substantive rules, most often through certain general clauses.[95] Foreign rules not only come into play if they are referred to by the conflict-of-laws provisions of the forum, but they also might be taken into consideration as local data by the forum. Even if the legal situation is governed by the *lex fori*, this does not exclude the consideration of foreign norms at the level of the substantive assessment of the case. Foreign public law rules can also be considered local data.[96] The necessity of such a solution has also been justified by the rigidity of conflict-of-laws rules.[97] Foreign law as a datum fulfils a corrective function against the 'blindness' of conflict-of-laws provisions.[98]

Ehrenzweig made a distinction between local[99] and moral data.[100] Local data are, in the words of Jayme, locally bounded rules which are one of the facts of the case.[101] The often-mentioned example of local data are the traffic and safety rules prevailing in the state of the accident. As opposed to Ehrenzweig, Jayme argued that even foreign moral data (and not only domestic moral data) could be taken into consideration in the substantive assessment of the case.[102] Moral data express certain important values of a state, including equity, 'natural law', moral values and customs.[103] In Ehrenzweig's proposition, the moral data must be primarily evaluated in accordance with the standards of the forum, irrespective of the otherwise

[90] Erik Jayme, 'Ausländische Rechtsregeln und Tatbestand inländischer Sachnormen – Betrachtungen zu Ehrenzweigs Datum-Theorie' in Erik Jayme and Gerhard Kegel (eds), *Gedächtnisschrift für Albert Ehrenzweig* (CF Müller, 1976) 35, 40.

[91] Brainerd Currie, 'On the Displacement of the Law of the Forum' in Brainerd Currie, *Selected Essays on the Conflict of Laws* (Duke University Press, 1963) 3, 66–67.

[92] Jayme (n 90) 39.

[93] Götz Schulze, 'Datum-Theorie und narrative Norm – Zu einem Privatrecht für die multikulturelle Gesellschaft' in Erik Jayme (ed), *Kulturelle Identität und Internationales Privatrecht* (CF Müller, 2003) 155, 157.

[94] Peter O Mülbert, 'Ausländische Eingriffsnormen als Datum' (1986) 6 *IPRax* 140.

[95] Jayme (n 90) 39.

[96] ibid 49.

[97] ibid.

[98] Schulze (n 93) 158.

[99] Albert A Ehrenzweig, *Private International Law – General Part* (Sijthoff, 1967) 83–85.

[100] ibid 77.

[101] Jayme (n 90) 39.

[102] ibid 49.

[103] Ehrenzweig (n 99) 77.

applicable law.[104] Elsewhere, however, he added that under certain circumstances, even foreign moral standards may be applicable.[105] Foreign moral data may be relevant when domestic provisions have become obsolete and foreign rules related to the legal dispute better reflect social changes.[106] Such a situation may induce taking a foreign rule into account as a datum.[107] However, it must be noted that in these cases, the inclusion of foreign moral data in the assessment of the case mostly coincides with the domestic value system. In fact, there is no difference between foreign and domestic values.

The process of the application of the datum theory, as well as the related criticisms, is broadly similar to the approach of the substantive law consideration of foreign overriding mandatory provisions. The method has been described as a flexible means to consider the impact of a foreign norm without qualifying it as applicable,[108] which also means that the foreign rule does not itself determine the legal consequences.[109] In a strict sense, the foreign norm is not a datum in itself that should be given effect merely because of its existence.[110] Whether effect will be given to the foreign norm and in what way (direct application as a legal norm or by consideration at the level of substantive law) depends exclusively on the law of the forum.[111] If a foreign datum is taken into consideration through the substantive rules of the *lex causae*, it presupposes the existence of a general clause in that law which admits to give some legal effect to foreign data.[112]

The datum theory has been linked to a two-pronged private international law process.[113] First, the applicable law must be designated based on conflict-of-laws rules. Second, it must be examined whether any norm of the supplanted foreign laws should be given effect within the framework of the applicable law, primarily through general clauses of substantive law of the *lex causae*, because the foreign norm presents a certain link to the situation. It needs to be examined whether the foreign law may be subsumed under the hypothesis of the relevant substantive norm. This implies that the governing law must be adapted to or modified in light of the situation. In this sense, the datum theory is similar to the 'Substitution' or 'Anpassung'. The first stage, the designation of the applicable law, serves conflict

[104] Albert A Ehrenzweig, 'Local and Moral Data in the Conflict of Laws: Terra Incognita' (1966) 16 *Buffalo Law Review* 55, 56. See also Jayme (n 90) 39.

[105] Ehrenzweig (n 99) 81.

[106] Jayme (n 90) 46.

[107] Albert A Ehrenzweig and Erik Jayme, *Private International Law Vol III – Special Part* (Sijthoff, 1967) 11.

[108] Vetter (n 88) 272.

[109] Mülbert (n 94) 141.

[110] Siehr (n 32) 80.

[111] ibid 81.

[112] Rentsch (n 44) 283.

[113] Marc-Philippe Weller, 'Die neue Mobilitätsanknüpfung im Internationalen Familienrecht – Abfederung des Personalstatutenwechsels über die Datumtheorie' (2014) 34 *IPRax* 225, 229; Hans-Joachim Hessler, 'Datum-Theorie und Zweistufigkeit des internationalen Privatrechts' in Rolf Serick, Hubert Niederländer and Erik Jayme (eds), *Albert A Ehrenzweig und das internationale Privatrecht* (Carl Winter/Universitätsverlag, 1986) 137.

justice – ie, to find the spatially best solution – whereas the second step may contribute to the realisation of substantive justice.[114] Taking a foreign norm into consideration as a datum in deciding a case implies observing the equal treatment principle.[115] Cross-border situations may not all be treated as purely domestic situations. The law designated by conflict-of-laws rules is tailored to decide purely domestic situations. The recognition of this difference justifies taking foreign norms into account as data in deciding legal disputes. However, it should be added that giving effect to foreign law through the datum theory is subject to the *ordre public* exception.[116]

The introduction of such a two-stage method in private international law is often considered to be flawed. The theory may not be described as one of private international law, because private international law is limited to the first stage, the designation of the applicable law, while the second stage belongs to the realm of substantive law.[117] Merging the two would expand the notion of private international law, as used generally, to include the settlement of international private legal relationships either directly (the substantive law method) or indirectly (the conflict-of-laws method).[118] However, this is not to say that foreign law may not be given effect through the application and interpretation of the substantive law, even if the foreign law does not govern the legal situation. The criticism is limited to establish that the private international law and the substantive law analysis of the case cannot be confused.

Other criticisms have also been raised against the datum theory. It has been argued that taking foreign rules into consideration already inherently involves an element of the conflict-of-laws method. Schurig opines that considering and applying local rules in a self-evident way as local data necessarily involves a conflict-of-laws decision.[119] Similarly, Pfeiffer asserts that, to the extent that these local rules are considered, a reference is made to them.[120] In this sense, the distinction between conflict-of-laws and substantive law norms is an artificial one that pulls the rug out from under the datum theory. Another argument against the datum theory is that it is not clear when a foreign rule is to be taken into consideration as a datum and in what way.[121]

[114] Weller (n 113) 231.

[115] ibid.

[116] ibid 232.

[117] Jan von Hein, 'Einleitung zum IPR' in F Säcker, R Rixecker and H Oetker (eds), *Münchener Kommentar zum Bürgerlichen Gesetzbuch, Band 10, Internationales Privatrecht I*, 6th edn (Beck, 2015) 1, 111.

[118] ibid 111.

[119] Klaus Schurig, *Kollisionsnorm und Sachrecht* (Duncker & Humblot, 1981) 312–13.

[120] Thomas Pfeiffer, 'Datumtheorie un "local data" in der Rom II-VO – am Beispiel von Straßenverkehrsunfällen' in Ralf Michaels and Dennis Solomon (eds), *Liber Amicorum Klaus Schurig* (Sellier, 2012) 229, 234.

[121] Schulze (n 93) 163; Ulrich Magnus, 'Art 9 Rom I-VO Eingriffsnormen' in Ulrich Magnus (ed), *J. von Staudingers Kommentar zum Bürgerlichen Gesetzbuch mit Einführungsgesetz und Nebengesetzen* (Sellier/De Gruyter, 2011) 637, 679.

In the context of economic sanctions, the question may be posed as to whether a foreign economic sanction may be given effect as a foreign datum. In this way, even if a foreign economic sanction (not pertaining to the *lex causae*) could not be recognised and applied as a legal norm, it can be taken into consideration as a datum. This may be a solution when the sanctioning state has the capacity to enforce the economic sanction which has an impact on the conduct of at least one of the parties to the contract.[122] The party may be hindered in performing the contract or may be exposed to penalties envisaged in the event of non-compliance with the economic sanction. This may induce economic players to observe the economic sanction and not to perform the contract as agreed before if this is prohibited by the economic sanction. Foreign economic sanctions may be considered as local or moral data. As a moral datum, an economic sanction may embody values that are also worthy of protection by the courts of the forum state,[123] so it should be examined whether there is a community of values between the forum and the sanctioning state.[124] This requires the court to establish whether the values and interests between the states concerned are shared, but it also necessitates the evaluation of the interests which link the forum to the state targeted by the sanction.

Professor Basedow highlighted that the datum theory was developed first of all concerning technical norms, such as traffic rules, and other situations taking place in the state of the foreign legislator.[125] Local as well as moral data are to be considered, since they determine the social life in the foreign state. However, an embargo does not reflect a social consensus, but instead is a norm of highly political nature which interferes with the contractual relation of the parties and expresses the intention of the imposing foreign state to enforce restrictions – often extraterritorially – in accordance with its changing political objectives. Therefore, concerning the US pipeline embargo, Professor Basedow argued that an embargo is not to be considered as a datum for a court in another state. Instead, a foreign embargo may be applied only if this is so provided by conflict-of-laws rules.[126]

Even if the datum theory is followed, it is difficult to decide whether economic sanctions may be treated as local or moral data. They may have a moral content, such as the embargo against the apartheid regime in South Africa, but they often pursue merely political purposes and may be treated at most as local data.

ii. Machttheorie

The *Machttheorie* may be also used to justify giving effect to economic sanctions imposed by third countries. It explains the application of or giving effect to foreign

[122] Da Silveira (n 25) 36.
[123] Garcimartín Alférez (n 27) 62.
[124] ibid 140.
[125] Jürgen Basedow, 'Entscheidung – Das Amerikanische Pipeline-Embargo vor Gericht. Niederlande: Pres. Rb. Den Haag 17. 9. 1982. (Fall Sensor)' (1983) 47 *RabelsZ* 141, 156–57.
[126] ibid 157.

public law provisions by the power of the foreign state to enforce its mandatory rules in international legal relationships. A foreign state may have the power to exercise an impact on the performance of a contract. It can hinder performance, or at least impose penalties in the event of the performance of the contract, with the aim of exerting a deterrent effect.

Even if the forum state does not share the interests and values of the imposing foreign state, the overriding mandatory norms of that foreign state may be recognised on the basis that it can enforce the economic sanction due to the location of products or the residence of the parties. The state imposing the economic sanction can enforce it with administrative and criminal penalties, such as the withdrawal of export and import licences, seizures, fines, prison sentences etc. Taking enforcing power strictly, overriding mandatory provisions, which are in fact enforced, are to be considered, while overriding mandatory provisions which may be potentially but not necessarily enforced should be disregarded. To consider overriding mandatory provisions which simply have the potential to be enforced would give rise to speculation on the part of the court, and giving effect to such foreign norms would give an advantage to the party who intends to escape from his obligations,[127] and these should be avoided.

The theory is opposed on the grounds that the power of designating the law which determines the outcome of the case is actually exercised by the forum based on its own law and not by the foreign state.[128] The (substantive) law of the forum ultimately decides whether to give effect to a foreign norm due to the enforcement capacity of the imposing state. The domestic impact of the foreign law is recognised by the law of the forum. Additionally, it may be difficult for a court to predict whether a foreign state will enforce its overriding mandatory provisions or not. Moreover, if applying this theory, even a prohibitive foreign overriding mandatory norm (which may be even approved by the state of the forum), such as the prohibition of an anti-bribery rule or a restriction on the trade of cultural heritage, could not be given effect by the forum if the state adopting these provisions cannot enforce it.[129] It may be argued that power itself cannot create law and it does not serve justice.[130] Furthermore, the content of that norm (compatibility with public international law) and the competence of the foreign state to adopt it may not be simply ignored.[131] This is true, but the factual consequences of enforcing a foreign law sometimes may not be avoided by the parties, even if the foreign law is unlawful or condemned by the forum state, for example, in the event of the seizure of property by the imposing state. German courts sometimes made an allusion to the *Machttheorie*, which may be illustrated by the *Solzhenitsyn* judgment of the BGH, where the BGH stated that a court must have regard for and enforce the Soviet

[127] Großfeld and Junker (n 88) 106–07.
[128] Von Allwörden (n 46) 68.
[129] Magnus (n 121) 667.
[130] Mann (n 39) 155.
[131] Großfeld and Junker (n 88) 107.

Union's state monopoly on foreign trade, provided that the Soviet authorities were in a position to enforce it.[132]

Großfeld and Junker state that the datum theory and the *Machttheorie* do not essentially differ. They consider the *Machttheorie* to be a variety of the datum theory. This statement is true to the extent that both theories consider the factual consequences of foreign public law norms. As far as economic sanctions are concerned, Großfeld and Junker's view can be accepted: that no essential difference exists between the datum theory and the *Machttheorie* from the perspective of the result, provided that an economic sanction is in fact enforced by the imposing state. The approach that the foreign law constitutes a datum which cannot be avoided by the forum does not differ from the idea that only those foreign sanctions which are effectively enforced by the imposing state are given effect. At the same time, the differences may not be ignored. For instance, the classical illustration of the datum theory, road and safety rules are considered as data, but not necessarily because of the enforcement capacity of the foreign state. Traffic rules are violated by drivers every day without sanctions. Local traffic rules are added to the substantive assessment of the case because this is required to give the appropriate solution: a driver causing an accident should expect to be bound by local traffic rules. Moreover, the *Machttheorie* does not say anything about cases when a foreign norm is given effect because the forum approves the moral values behind it (moral data).

Economic sanctions may be applied by state courts and arbitral tribunals. Their effectiveness may differ depending on whether a court or an arbitral tribunal is seised with the matter involving an economic sanction.[133] For this reason, first we examine the application of economic sanctions by the courts of the EU Member States, and economic sanctions in arbitral practice will be analysed afterwards.

IV. Conclusion

Economic sanctions embody state intervention for foreign policy purposes. Economic sanctions belong to the realm of public law, but may still affect the legal (primarily contractual) relationships of private parties. Private international law has a decisive role in terms of the application of foreign economic sanctions in private law relationships.

Economic sanctions qualify as overriding mandatory rules in private international law. In this sense, they interfere with the parties' autonomy. It is not debated that a court can apply the overriding mandatory norms of its own state, even if these have a public law origin. The extent to which foreign public law norms can gain application in private law litigation is more contentious. The answer is dependent upon conceptualising, at a more general level, how public law is to

[132] BGH, Urteil vom 16.4.1975 – I ZR 40/73, NJW 1975, 1220. See Großfeld and Junker (n 88) 114–16.
[133] Mayer (n 24) 108.

be treated in private law and in particular in conflict of laws. This is crucial for economic sanctions, which have an inherent public law nature.

Several conflict-of-laws theories have been elaborated on the application of foreign public law norms. The *Einheitsanknüpfungstheorie* makes it possible to apply the public law norms of the forum, as well as those of the *lex causae*, while the *Sonderanknüpfungstheorie* permits the application of foreign public law rules if a special connection is present between the foreign rule and the case. However, this special connection is formulated differently by various authors. Beyond conflict-of-laws, foreign public law rules may also be considered through the governing substantive law.

Understanding the theoretical foundations for applying or taking foreign public law norms, including economic sanctions, into consideration is indispensable, because the provisions of the currently applicable Rome I Regulation on overriding mandatory rules and the surrounding theoretical and practical issues may be grasped only in the light of these theories. The courts of the Member States are bound to apply the Rome I Regulation and this involves the first way to apply economic sanctions in international legal disputes. Additionally, national courts can take overriding mandatory provisions, including economic sanctions, beyond the reach of the Rome I Regulation into consideration at the level of the governing substantive law. The relevant provisions of the Rome I Regulation and the coexistence between the conflict-of-laws and the substantive law approaches will be explored in the following chapter.

5

Economic Sanctions as Overriding Mandatory Provisions in EU Private International Law

In current EU private international law, Article 9 of the Rome I Regulation determines the application of overriding mandatory provisions regarding contracts. Article 9 of the Rome I Regulation is the amended version of its predecessor, Article 7 of the Rome Convention, and concerns overriding mandatory provisions in the following structure: Article 9(1) defines the notion of overriding mandatory provisions; Article 9(2) allows the overriding mandatory provisions of the forum to be applied; and a court may also give effect to the overriding mandatory norms of the state of the place of performance pursuant to Article 9(3).

In the legal literature, it has been disputed whether Article 9 is a conflict-of-laws rule at all. On the one hand, it has been argued that Article 9 (or Article 7 of the Rome Convention) does not constitute a connecting factor[1] or a conflict-of-laws rule because it does not contain in itself an order to apply a norm.[2] Article 9(3) has also been described as an inchoate (*unfertig*)[3] or empty[4] (*Leerformel*) clause. Nevertheless, the majority view considers Article 9(3) of the Rome I Regulation to be a conflict-of-laws norm. The main argument behind this that the possibility of giving effect to a foreign law also includes a choice between legal systems;[5] therefore, Article 9(3) fulfils the same function as any other conflict-of-laws norm. It is also seen as a conflict-of-laws rule hidden in a substantive law provision.[6]

As a novelty, the Rome I Regulation defines overriding mandatory provisions in accordance with the definition given by the CJEU in the *Arblade* judgment,[7]

[1] Oliver Remien, 'Art 9 ROM I' in Hanns Prütting, Gerhard Wegen and Gerd Weinreich (eds), *BGB Kommentar*, 11th edn (Luchterhand, 2016) 3324, 3326 concerning art 9 of the Rome I Regulation.

[2] Ansgar Staudinger, 'Art. 9 Eingriffsnormen' in Franco Ferrari, Peter Mankowski, Eva-Maria Kieninger, Karsten Otte, Ingo Saenger, Götz Schulze and Ansgar Staudinger (eds), *Internationales Vertragsrecht* (Beck, 2012) 241, 244–45.

[3] Andreas Köhler, 'Die Berücksichtigung ausländischer Eingriffsnormen im Europäischen Internationalen Vertragsrecht' in Kathrin Binder and Florian Eichel, *Internationale Dimensionen des Wirtschaftsrechts* (Nomos, 2013) 205.

[4] ibid 201.

[5] ibid 204.

[6] ibid.

[7] Joined Cases C–369/96 and C–376/96 *Criminal Proceedings against Jean-Claude Arblade and Arblade & Fils SARL and Bernard Leloup, Serge Leloup and Sofrage SARL* [1999] ECR I–8453, para 30.

which was interestingly given not in the context of private international law, but in relation to the freedom to provide services. The formulation in *Arblade* in turn can be traced back to the definition given by Francescakis.[8]

According to Article 9(1):

> Overriding mandatory provisions are provisions the respect for which is regarded as crucial by a country for safeguarding its public interests, such as its political, social or economic organisation, to such an extent that they are applicable to any situation falling within their scope, irrespective of the law otherwise applicable to the contract under this Regulation.

The definition clarifies the difference between simple mandatory rules and overriding mandatory provisions that was lacking in the Rome Convention. In interpreting the Rome I Regulation, overriding mandatory provisions must be construed restrictively[9] and this has also been confirmed by the CJEU in *Unamar*.[10] This approach can be explained by the fact that the intervention of the overriding mandatory rules impairs the predictable operation of conflict-of-laws rules and thus legal certainty.[11] In addition, overriding mandatory provisions also interfere with the autonomy of the parties. Nevertheless, there is no doubt that economic sanctions fall into the category of overriding mandatory provisions within the meaning of the Rome I Regulation and, as we have already explained, the legal literature is unanimous in this respect.

As a consequence, economic sanctions may be applied as overriding mandatory norms in EU law. We have seen that the EU has the power to adopt economic sanctions. The reliance of the EU on its competence to adopt various economic sanctions also implies successive waves of overriding mandatory provisions. It suffices to mention the more recent series of sanctions that have been adopted against Russia, Crimea and Sevastopol, and certain persons involved in the occupation of Crimea[12] or the sanctions against North Korea which attracted

[8] Phocion Francescakis, 'Quelques précisions sur les 'lois d'application immédiate' et leurs rapports avec les règles sur les conflits de lois' (1966) 55 *Revue critique de droit international privé* 1.

[9] Rome I Regulation, preamble (37).

[10] Case C–184/12 *United Antwerp Maritime Agencies (Unamar) NV v Navigation Maritime Bulgare* ECLI:EU:C:2013:663, para 49.

[11] Robert Freitag, 'Eingriffsnormen (international zwingende Bestimmungen), Berücksichtigung ausländischer Devisenvorschriften, Formvorschriften' in Christoph Reithmann and Dieter Martiny, *Internationales Vertragsrecht*, 8th edn (Otto Schmidt, 2015) 361.

[12] See in particular Council Decision 2014/145/CFSP of 31 July 2014 concerning restrictive measures in view of Russia's actions destabilising the situation in Ukraine [2014] OJ L78/16; Council Regulation (EU) No 269/2014 of 17 March 2014 concerning restrictive measures in respect of actions undermining or threatening the territorial integrity, sovereignty and independence of Ukraine [2014] OJ L78/6; Council Implementing Regulation (EU) No 284/2014 of 21 March 2014 implementing Regulation (EU) No 269/2014 concerning restrictive measures in respect of actions undermining or threatening the territorial integrity, sovereignty and independence of Ukraine [2014] OJ L86/27; Council Implementing Regulation (EU) No 433/2014 of 28 April 2014 implementing Regulation (EU) No 269/2014 concerning restrictive measures in respect of actions undermining or threatening the territorial integrity, sovereignty and independence of Ukraine [2014] OJ L126/48; Council Implementing Regulation (EU) No 477/2014 of 12 May 2014 implementing Regulation (EU) No 269/2014 concerning restrictive

the attention of the public. The application of EU sanctions by the courts of the Member States is usually not problematic because the courts of the Member States apply the economic sanctions imposed by the EU as part of the law of the forum.

The courts of the Member States have varying approaches towards foreign economic sanctions, notwithstanding the existence of common conflict-of-laws rules on contractual relationships. In Europe, the applicability of foreign overriding mandatory provisions was very different under the law of various countries. This changed to a certain extent following the adoption of the Rome Convention. However, several states made reservations to the provision of the Rome Convention on mandatory rules and continued to apply their own conflict-of-laws approach. The Rome I Regulation, nonetheless, excluded reservations and created a uniform system for the Member States. In spite of the existence of uniform conflict-of-laws rules on contractual obligations, the Rome I Regulation allows different interpretations regarding foreign overriding mandatory provisions. These differences are not even eliminated by the case law of the CJEU. The CJEU practice on overriding mandatory provisions under the Rome Convention or the Rome I Regulation is scant and, concerning economic sanctions in particular, it is missing. The CJEU had to address overriding mandatory provisions in very few cases, such as *Ingmar*, *Unamar* and *Nikiforidis*,[13] but none of these decisions concerned economic sanctions. The rulings of the CJEU rendered up to now instead gave guidance on determining the scope of application of certain economic sanctions[14] and on ascertaining whether a sanction is in conformity with fundamental rights (rights of defence, in particular the right to be heard, the

measures in respect of actions undermining or threatening the territorial integrity, sovereignty and independence of Ukraine [2014] OJ L137/3; Council Implementing Regulation (EU) No 826/2014 of 30 July 2014 implementing Regulation (EU) No 269/2014 concerning restrictive measures in respect of actions undermining or threatening the territorial integrity, sovereignty and independence of Ukraine [2014] OJ L226/16; Council Decision 2014/512/CFSP of 31 July 2014 concerning restrictive measures in view of Russia's actions destabilising the situation in Ukraine [2014] OJ L229/13; Council Regulation (EU) No 833/2014 of 31 July 2014 concerning restrictive measures in view of Russia's actions destabilising the situation in Ukraine [2014] OJ L229/1; Council Regulation (EU) No 692/2014 of 23 June 2014 concerning restrictions on the import into the Union of goods originating in Crimea or Sevastopol, in response to the illegal annexation of Crimea and Sevastopol [2014] OJ L183/9; Council Implementing Regulation (EU) No 961/2014 of 8 September 2014 implementing Regulation (EU) No 269/2014 concerning restrictive measures in respect of actions undermining or threatening the territorial integrity, sovereignty and independence of Ukraine [2014] OJ L183/70; Council Decision 2014/386/CFSP of 23 June 2014 concerning restrictive measures in response to the illegal annexation of Crimea and Sevastopol [2014] OJ L183/70; Council Implementing Regulation (EU) No 810/2014 of 25 July 2014 implementing Regulation (EU) No 269/2014 concerning restrictive measures in respect of actions undermining or threatening the territorial integrity, sovereignty and independence of Ukraine [2014] OJ L221/1; Council Regulation (EU) No 960/2014 of 8 September 2014 amending Regulation (EU) No 833/2014 concerning restrictive measures in view of Russia's actions destabilising the situation in Ukraine [2014] OJ L271/3.

[13] Case C-135/15 *Republik Griechenland v Grigorios Nikiforidis* ECLI:EU:C:2016:774.

[14] Case C-84/95 *Bosphorus Hava Yollari Turizm ve Ticaret AS v Minister for Transport, Energy and Communications and others* [1996] ECR I-3953; Case C-177/95 *Ebony Maritime SA and Loten Navigation Co Ltd v Prefetto della Provincia di Brindisi and Others* [1997] ECR I-1111; Case C-371/03 *Siegfried Aulinger v Bundesrepublik Deutschland* [2006] ECR I-2207; Case C-117/06 *Gerda Möllendorf and Christiane Möllendorf-Niehuus* [2007] ECR I-8361.

right to an effective legal remedy and the right to property).[15] Given that the CJEU has not so far addressed the private international law aspects of economic sanctions, the examination of national court practice in applying economic sanctions is particularly interesting.

Overriding mandatory provisions, and thus economic sanctions, may be present in the *lex fori*, the *lex causae* or in the law of a third country. Magnus calls this the Bermuda triangle of international contract law.[16] The following sections demonstrate how EU private international law legislation contributes to differences in applying economic sanctions.

I. Economic Sanctions Imposed by the Law of the Forum State

The application of the economic sanctions of the forum seems to be straightforward. The forum is free to apply sanctions imposed by its own state. This possibility is expressly anchored in the Rome Convention as well as in the Rome I Regulation.

Article 7(2) of the Rome Convention provides:

> Nothing in this Convention shall restrict the application of the rules of the law of the forum in a situation where they are mandatory irrespective of the law otherwise applicable to the contract.

Article 7(2) of the Rome Convention was inserted at a relatively late phase of the codification process. The overriding mandatory provisions of the forum could already have been applied on the grounds of paragraph 1 of the same Article, which permits giving effect to overriding mandatory provisions of laws with which the situation manifests a close connection. However, paragraph 2 exempts courts from examining the conditions mentioned in paragraph 1.[17]

Article 9(2) of the Rome I Regulation declares that:

> Nothing in this Regulation shall restrict the application of the overriding mandatory provisions of the law of the forum.

This and the analogous provision in the Rome Convention have been interpreted by most authors as an order for the courts to apply an overriding mandatory

[15] See Joined Cases C-402/05 P and C-415/05 P *Yassin Abdullah Kadi and Al Barakaat International Foundation v Council of the European Union and Commission of the European Communities* [2008] ECR I-6351.

[16] Ulrich Magnus, 'Art 9 Rom I-VO Eingriffsnormen' in Ulrich Magnus (ed), *J. von Staudingers Kommentar zum Bürgerlichen Gesetzbuch mit Einführungsgesetz und Nebengesetzen* (Sellier/De Gruyter, 2011) 644.

[17] Allan Philip, 'Mandatory Rules, Public Law (Political Rules) and Choice of Law in the EEC Convention on the Law Applicable to Contractual Obligations' in Peter M North (ed), *Contract Conflicts* (North-Holland Publishing Company, 1982) 81, 101.

provision, under which they are obliged to act accordingly.[18] Indeed, courts are bound to apply the law of the state as an organ of which they are operating. The court is obliged to apply its law whenever it requires application. Once it is established that the case concerns an overriding mandatory norm within the meaning of Article 9(1) of the Rome I Regulation, the single question is to examine whether the domestic rule claims application as regards the legal relationship.[19] Hence, it rarely happens that a court refrains from applying an overriding mandatory rule of the forum state.[20] However, the wording of Article 9(2) of the Rome I Regulation and Article 7(2) of the Rome Convention only provides a possibility.[21] It may happen that the norm does not claim application in the given case (for example, an obsolete provision still formally in force), hence it is not necessary to apply it.

Therefore, 'mandatory rules' and 'overriding mandatory provisions' of the forum, as set out in the Rome Convention and the Rome I Regulation respectively, may be applied by the court seised. The application of the overriding mandatory rules of the forum is not subject to further conditions, such as those of third states.

Several representatives of the legal literature claim there must be a close connection between the case and the forum state for the application of its overriding mandatory norms, notwithstanding the fact that this requirement is not set by the Rome I Regulation or the Rome Convention.[22] This view seems to find confirmation in the *Ingmar* judgment, where the Court established that overriding mandatory provisions are to 'be applied where the situation is closely connected with the Community'.[23] The close connection may include the place of performance, the (habitual) residence or the seat or main place of business of the parties.[24] According to other authors, national legislation may surrender a close connection requirement and apply its overriding mandatory provisions at face value.[25] In my opinion, the close connection exists in most of the cases where the jurisdiction is based on an objective jurisdictional ground.[26] The necessity of

[18] Louis d'Avout and Dominique Bureau, 'Lois de police étrangères devant le juge français du contrat international' (2010) 84 *La Semaine Juridique – Entreprise et Affaires* 18, 18–19, 23, 25; Sandrine Sana-Chaille de Nere, 'Transport maritime et lois de police étrangères' (2010) *Droit maritime français* 367, 369; Francisco Garcimartín Alférez, 'Embargo' in Jürgen Basedow, Giesela Rühl, Franco Ferrari and Pedro de Miguel Asensio (eds), *Encyclopedia of Private International Law* (Edward Elgar, 2017) 603; Christopher George John Morse, 'The EEC Convention on the Law Applicable to Contractual Obligations' in Francis Geoffrey Jacobs (ed), *Yearbook of European Law (1982)* (Clarendon, 1983) 107, 144.

[19] Rolf C Radtke, 'Schuldstatut und Eingriffsrecht' (1985) 84 *ZVglRWiss* 325, 329; Paul Hauser, *Eingriffsnormen in der Rom I-Verordnung* (Mohr Siebeck, 2012) 43.

[20] Wolf-Georg Ringe, 'Art 9 Rom I-VO Eingriffsnormen' in Ingo Ludwig (ed), *JurisPraxis Kommentar BGB, Band 6, Internationales Privatrecht*, 5th edn (Juris, 2011) 1119, 1122.

[21] Moritz Renner, 'Article 9 Overriding Mandatory Provisions' in Gralf-Peter Calliess (ed), *Rome Regulations* (Kluwer, 2011) 203; Dietmar Czernich, 'Die Rom I-VO als Grundlage für die Anwendung von Eingriffsnormen durch Schiedsgerichte' (2016) 62 *Recht der Internationalen Wirtschaft* 701, 702.

[22] Freitag (n 11) 380; Staudinger (n 2) 248; Magnus (n 16) 663–64.

[23] Case C–381/98 *Ingmar GB Ltd v Eaton Leonard Technologies Inc* [2000] ECR I–9305, para 25.

[24] Renner (n 21) 206.

[25] Mathias Kuckein, *Die 'Berücksichtigung' von Eingriffsnormen im deutschen und englischen internationalen Vertragsrecht* (Mohr Siebeck, 2008) 71.

[26] See also Staudinger (n 2) 248.

the existence of a connection to the forum may only involve an additional requirement when the jurisdiction is based on the choice of the parties, who intend to stipulate a neutral forum.

The Rome I Regulation enables the courts of the Member States to apply the overriding mandatory provisions of the forum. This implies the protection of the interests of both the individual Member States as well as the EU.[27] The courts of the Member States must apply overriding mandatory provisions determined by EU law.[28] The overriding mandatory provisions of the EU constitute part of the law of the Member States, either by directly applicable regulations or through domestic provisions implementing directives. In the case of economic sanctions, it is immaterial that the legal source specifying the sanction is an EU regulation. EU regulations are directly applicable in the Member States and constitute part of the law of the Member States. In the case of economic sanctions adopted by the UNSC and implemented by the EU or adopted unilaterally by the EU in the form of a regulation, the courts of the Member States are obliged to apply these economic sanctions. An economic sanction of the law of the forum state is applied unless it violates the constitution of that state or international law.[29]

By applying the rules of the forum, the economic sanctions of the EU and thus the relevant foreign policy objectives of the EU are enforced. We can find instances from the case of the jurisdictions examined in this book for the application of various EU sanctions regulations.[30] Although conflict-of-laws analysis has often been neglected in these cases, it does not alter the fact that the sanctions imposed by the EU were actually applied. A legal basis for their application could have been found in the Rome I Regulation or the Rome Convention or, prior to the adoption of these EU legal sources, in national law. The application of the overriding mandatory provisions of the *lex causae* and those of third states is more problematic and will be discussed in the following sections.

II. Economic Sanctions of the *Lex Causae*

A. Overriding Mandatory Provisions of the *Lex Causae*

Neither the Rome Convention nor the Rome I Regulation contains an express provision on the applicability of the overriding mandatory rules of the *lex causae*.

[27] See Renner (n 21) 195.

[28] Freitag (n 11) 371.

[29] Bernardo Cortese, 'International Economic Sanctions as a Component of Public Policy for Conflict-of-Laws Purposes' in Laura Picchio Forlati and Linos-Alexander Sicilianos (eds), *Economic Sanctions in International Law/Les sanctions économiques en droit international, Hague Academy of International Law, The Law Books of the Academy*, vol 23 (Nijhoff, 2004) 717, 724.

[30] See in particular in France: Cour d'appel de Paris, Chambre 1, section B, 23 juin 1995 (1997) JDI 441; Cour de cassation, Chambre civile 1, 24 February 1998, JDI (1998) 963. In England, see: *DVB Bank SE and Others v Shere Shipping Company Ltd and Others* [2013] EWHC 2321 (Comm).

If the *lex causae* and the *lex fori* coincide, no particular concern arises. The *lex causae* that is identical to the law of the forum may be applied based on Article 7(2) of the Rome Convention and Article 9(2) of the Rome I Regulation. The situation is less clear when the *lex causae* differs from the *lex fori.*

Several authors opine that the reference to a foreign law also embraces public law[31] or the overriding mandatory provisions[32] of the designated law in the context of the Rome Convention and the Rome I Regulation. This view has been seen as dominant by the study of the Max Planck Institute on the Conversion of the Rome Convention into a Community Instrument.[33] The application of foreign norms designated by the conflict-of-laws rules is only subject to the *ordre public* exception. This view is confirmed by the fact that the private and public law distinction became elusive[34] and public law rules increasingly permeate private law.[35] Moreover, some legal systems do not even know this distinction. UK[36] and US[37] court practice applied foreign overriding mandatory rules as part of the *lex causae.* This has also been accepted in Article 13 of the Swiss Private International Law Act. French court practice also tends to apply foreign overriding mandatory norms as part of

[31] Marie-Laure Niboyet and Géraud de Geouffre de la Pradelle, *Droit international privé*, 5th edn (LGDJ, 2015) 142–43; Henri Batiffol and Paul Lagarde, *Traité de droit international privé*, vol 1, 8th edn (LGDJ, 1993) 416–417; Annie Toubiana, *Le domaine de la loi du contrat en droit international privé* (Dalloz, 1972) 174–79.

[32] Pierre Mayer, 'Les lois de police étrangères' (1981) 108 *Journal du droit international* 277, 313 and 330; Pierre Mayer and Vincent Heuzé, *Droit international privé*, 11th edn (LGDJ, 2014) 103; Bernard Audit and Louis d'Avout, *Droit international privé*, 7th edn (Economica, 2013) 169; Catherine Kessedjian, *Droit du commerce international* (Thémis, 2013) 52; Sana-Chaille de Nere (n 18) 370 fn 12; Ole Lando and Peter Arnt Nielsen, 'The Rome I Regulation' (2008) *CML Rev* 1687, 1719; Andrea Bonomi, 'Quelques observations sur le règlement Rome I sur la loi applicable aux obligations contractuelles' in *Regards comparatistes sur le phénomène contractuel* (PUAM, 2009) 225, 239 fn 49; Garcimartín Alférez (n 18) 605; Wulf-Henning Roth, 'Europäische Kollisionsrechtsvereinheitlichung: Überblick – Kompetenz – Grundfragen' in Eva-Maria Kieninger and Oliver Remien (eds), *Europäische Kollisionsrechtsvereinheitlichung* (Nomos, 2012) 11, 35; Xavier Dieux, 'Questions relatives aux effets de la contrainte étatique sur les contrats économiques internationaux – un point de vue belge' (1987) 20 *Revue belge de droit international* 184, 188; Ole Lando, 'Party Autonomy in the EC Convention on the Law Applicable to Contractual Obligations' in François Rigaux, *L'influence des Communautés européennes sur le droit international privé des Etats members* (Larcier, 1981) 191, 205; Ivana Kunda, *International Mandatory Rules of a Third Country in European Contract Conflict of Laws: The Rome Convention and the Proposed Rome I Regulation* (Rijeka Law Faculty, 2007) 170, 196–203, 211; Stefan Leible, 'Außenhandel und Rechtssicherheit' (1998) 97 *ZVglRWiss* 286, 299 concerning the Rome Convention.

[33] Max Planck Institute for Foreign Private and Private International Law, *Comments on the European Commission's Green Paper on the Conversion of the Rome Convention of 1980 on the Law Applicable to Contractual Obligations into a Community Instrument and its Modernization* 74.

[34] Niboyet and de la Pradelle (n 31) 143; Toubiana (n 31) 176–79; David Jackson, 'Mandatory Rules and Rules of "Ordre Public"' in Peter M North, *Contract Conflicts* (North-Holland Publishing Company, 1982) 59, 64.

[35] Toubiana (n 31) 176; Jackson (n 34) 64.

[36] *R v International Trustee for the Protection of Bondholders Aktiengesellschaft* [1937] AC 500; *Kahler v Midland Bank* [1950] AC 24, 42. See ch 6, section III.B.

[37] *Perutz v Bohemian Discount Bank in Liquidation* 304 NY 533 (NY 1953).

the *lex causae*.[38] By its resolution adopted in 1975, the International Law Institute set aside the principle of the a priori inapplicability of foreign public law and took the position that 'the public law character attributed to a provision of foreign law which is designated by the rule of conflict of laws shall not prevent the application of that provision, subject however to the fundamental reservation of public policy'.[39] Accordingly, public law provisions of the *lex causae*, such as economic sanctions, should be applied.[40]

The Rome Convention is mute as to the application of the overriding mandatory provisions of the *lex causae*. Article 7(1) of the Rome Convention is also interpreted as referring to the overriding mandatory provisions of the *lex causae*. The wording '*When applying under this Convention the law of a country*, effect may be given to the mandatory rules of *the law of another country* with which the situation has a close connection' (emphasis added) may suggest giving effect to overriding mandatory provisions of *another country* in addition to those of the *lex causae*. As a consequence, it may be inferred that the overriding mandatory norms of the *lex causae* always apply.[41] Compliance with the conditions set out in Article 7(1) of the Rome Convention or Article 9(3) of the Rome I Regulation is thus unnecessary. Article 7(1) suggests that the public law norms of the *lex contractus* are always applicable, whereas those of a third party are so only if they have a close connection with the situation, and this is justified by the nature and objective of the norms and the consequences of their application or non-application. The Giuliano-Lagarde Report is also called upon to support this position, since it considered the possibility of giving effect to the mandatory provisions of third countries in addition to those of the *lex causae* to be self-evident:[42]

> The principle that national courts can give effect under certain conditions to mandatory provisions other than those applicable to the contract by virtue of the choice of the parties or by virtue of a subsidiary connecting factor, has been recognized for several years both in legal writings and in practice in certain of our countries and elsewhere.[43]

Knüppel departs from the system of the legislation: first, the provisions determining the law governing the contract are determined in Articles 3–6 of the Rome Convention and, only subsequent to this, Article 7 adds that mandatory norms

[38] See ch 6, section I.A on the relevant French judicial practice; Tribunal de grande instance de Paris (9e ch.), 8 and 12 March 1985 (1985) Dalloz, Informations Rapides 500.

[39] Institute of International Law, Session of Wiesbaden – 1975, The Application of Foreign Public Law.

[40] Hans van Houtte, 'Les effets des sanctions économiques sur les contrats transnationaux' in Association européenne pour le droit bancaire et financier, *L'embargo* (Bruylant, 1996) 189, 193.

[41] Wulf-Henning Roth, 'Savigny, Eingriffsnormen und die Rom I-Verordnung' in Jürgen F Baur, Otto Sandrock, Boris Scholtka and Amos Shapira (eds), *Festsschrift für Gunther Kühne* (Verlag Recht und Wirtschaft 2009) 859, 870.

[42] ibid 870–71.

[43] Mario Giuliano and Paul Lagarde, Report on the Convention on the law applicable to contractual obligations [1980] OJ C282/1, 26 (hereinafter Giuliano-Lagarde Report).

of another state may be taken into consideration. Accordingly, 'another state' is different from the one whose law governs the contractual relationship.[44]

Furthermore, it is also pointed out that Article 3(3) of the Rome Convention allows the application of the mandatory rules of the otherwise applicable law. These must include overriding mandatory norms, which suggests that they apply as part of the governing law in other cases too.[45] The same is deduced from the fact that it would be surprising to treat overriding mandatory provisions of third states more generously than those of the *lex causae*. No less significance may be given to the law designated by an objective connecting factor or the law chosen by the parties than to the law of a country with which the situation otherwise shows a close connection under Article 7(1) of the Rome Convention.[46] Objective connecting factors specified by the Rome Convention equally presuppose a close connection and concretise it. This view leads accordingly to the *Kumulationslösung*: overriding mandatory provisions of the *lex causae* shall apply as well as those of third countries when a close connection is present.

The Proposal of the Max Planck Institute on the Conversion of the Rome Convention into a Community Instrument found 'consequent and desirable' to include a rule on the application of the internationally mandatory norms of the proper law of the contract in the Community Instrument replacing the Rome Convention.[47] However, this proposal was not endorsed by EU legislation. Like the Rome Convention, the Rome I Regulation does not explicitly provide for the application of the overriding mandatory provisions of the *lex causae*. The arguments related to the interpretation of the Rome Convention may be transferred to the Rome I Regulation, despite its somewhat different wording as regards giving effect to the overriding mandatory provisions of third states. Roth argues that, from the change in the wording, it may be inferred that only the definition of the overriding mandatory provisions and the consideration of overriding mandatory provisions of third countries were in question during the negotiations; the approach towards the overriding mandatory provisions of the *lex causae* was not affected.[48] The conclusion is consequently that the Rome I Regulation follows the *Schuldstatutstheorie* concerning the scope of the *lex causae* and also grants the possibility for courts to give effect to the overriding mandatory norms of the law of the place of performance on a cumulative basis.[49] The application of the overriding mandatory norms of the *lex causae* based on Article 9 may even thereby be supported, in that neither the parties (in the case of choice of law) nor the legislator (when laying down objective connecting factors) distinguish between

[44] Norbert Knüppel, *Zwingendes materielles Recht und internationale Schuldverträge* (Bonn, 1988) 84–85.

[45] Roth (n 41) 871.

[46] Kunda (n 32) 203.

[47] Max Planck Institute for Foreign Private and Private International Law (n 33) 76 and 81.

[48] Roth (n 41) 873.

[49] ibid 873.

dispositive and mandatory norms, but they consider their application together.[50] One remark must be made in relation to this argument: the parties would probably set aside (at least) some of the mandatory norms exercising their freedom if they have a choice and know about those rules – this limitation does not exist with regard to objective conflict-of-laws rules.

The application of the overriding mandatory provisions of the *lex causae* is strongly linked to whether it is the task of private international law to accommodate public interests manifesting in the rules of public law in a private law dispute. Hence, if the *lex causae* contains an overriding mandatory provision of public law origin, such as an economic sanction, it is questionable whether it is applicable automatically as a public law provision of the governing law or whether it must satisfy additional conditions, such as those set out in Article 7(1) of the Rome Convention or Article 9(3) of the Rome I Regulation. The first approach would mean that the reference to a foreign law also embraces foreign overriding mandatory norms, including public law norms. In the context of the *Einheitsanknüpfung*, it is not relevant whether a particular norm is overriding or not, or public or not; if it constitutes part of the *lex causae*, it applies automatically. Deinert argues that the restriction contained in Article 9(3) of the Rome I Regulation concerns only overriding mandatory provisions of third countries; however, it does not limit the application of other overriding mandatory rules.[51] From this, he draws the conclusion that the overriding mandatory norms of the *lex causae* shall apply.

Roth explains that deviations from the otherwise applicable law are exceptional under Article 9 of the Rome I Regulation in order to promote party autonomy and legal certainty.[52] However, as he notes, the parties can foresee the application of the overriding mandatory provisions of the *lex causae*. Unlike the overriding mandatory provisions of the forum or third countries, this does not result in the cumulation of various applicable laws. As the *Schuldstatuttheorie* is broadly applied in the Member States, EU legislation should have made a clear statement if it had intended to disregard it.[53] He therefore concludes that the overriding mandatory provisions of the *lex causae* are to be applied.[54]

Magnus finds that the overriding mandatory provisions of the governing law are not automatically applicable, though Article 9(3) gives too little room to give them effect.[55] This provision allows effect to be given only to the overriding mandatory provisions of the place of performance. The governing law designated by the choice of law of the parties or an objective factor shows a close connection between the facts of the case and the overriding mandatory provisions in itself,

[50] Ringe (n 20) 1125.
[51] Olaf Deinert, *Internationales Arbeitsrecht* (Mohr Siebeck, 2013) 257–58.
[52] Wulf-Henning Roth, 'Drittstaatliche Eingriffsnormen und Rom I-Verordnung' (2018) 38 *IPRax* 177, 182.
[53] ibid 183.
[54] ibid 182.
[55] Magnus (n 16) 677.

even if the *lex causae* is not the law of the state of performance.[56] For this reason, Magnus argued for the application of the overriding mandatory provisions of the *lex causae* subject to the priority of the overriding mandatory provisions and the *ordre public* of the forum.

According to the second and strictest view, from the silence of the Rome Convention and the Rome I Regulation regarding the application of the overriding mandatory norms of the *lex causae*, it can be inferred that they simply may not be applied. Overriding mandatory provisions other than those contained in the law of the forum and the state of the place of performance cannot be applied, including the overriding mandatory provisions of the *lex causae*.[57]

A third approach, even though it does not recognise the automatic application of the overriding mandatory provisions of the *lex causae*, still permits their application provided that they comply with the requirements of Article 9(3). Accordingly, it is argued that, by analogy, the public law norms of the *lex causae* may be applied under the same conditions as those of third states.[58] This approach represents a restrictive view, according to which the reference concerns only private law norms, while foreign public law rules must comply with additional requirements. Article 7(1) of the Rome Convention could be construed as making it possible to take the public law provisions of a third country as well as those of the *lex contractus* into account.[59] Garcimartín Alférez argues that the public law provisions of both the *lex contractus* and of a third country may only be applied if they meet the requirements set out in Article 7(1), ie, if a close connection exists.[60] This is because, in both cases, it concerns the intervention of foreign state interests. Others similarly opine that the overriding mandatory provisions of the *lex causae* must comply with the same conditions as those of third countries[61] and find the omission of reference to the *lex causae* in the Rome Convention and the Rome I Regulation to be intentional.[62] If the Rome I Regulation does not provide for the overriding mandatory provisions of the *lex causae*, then it is not coincidence, but a conscious choice by the EU legislator.[63] Accordingly, the overriding mandatory provisions of the *lex causae* apply only if they meet the requirements set out in Article 9(3) of

[56] ibid 677–78.

[57] Peter Mankowski, 'Die Rom I-Verordnung – Änderungen im europäischen IPR für Schuldverträge' (2008) 8 *Internationales Handelsrecht* 133, 148; Peter Mankowski, *Interessenpolitik und europäisches Kollisionsrecht* (Nomos, 2011) 56.

[58] Frank Vischer, *General Course on Private International Law, Collected Courses of the Hague Academy of International Law*, vol 232 (Brill, 1992) 181; Jette Beulker, *Die Eingriffsnormenproblematik in internationalen Schiedsverfahren* (Mohr Siebeck, 2005) 118.

[59] Francisco J Garcimartín Alférez, *Contratación internacional y medidas de coerción económica* (Beramar, 1993) 123.

[60] ibid 122–30.

[61] Robert Freitag, 'Einfach und international zwingende Normen' in Stefan Leible (ed), *Das Grünbuch zum Internationalen Vertragsrecht* (Sellier, 2004) 183; Michael Cremer, 'Embargovorschriften als Eingriffsnormen' (2016) 10 *Bucerius Law Journal* 18, 20.

[62] Freitag (n 11) 365–66; Cremer (n 61) 20.

[63] Cremer (n 61) 20.

the Rome I Regulation, and in particular the overriding mandatory provisions of the *lex causae* may only be applied if this is the law of the place of performance.[64]

This view relies on the arguments brought forward against the *Einheitsanknüpfung* and it is not necessary to reiterate them in detail here. Most notably, there may be overriding mandatory norms in the law other than the *lex causae*, which may be more closely connected to the case. The wording of the Rome I Regulation also reinforces this position. It refers to the overriding mandatory provisions of the forum and those of the state of the place of performance. There is no further option.[65] Moreover, the reference to a foreign law cannot be construed in a broad sense to embrace foreign public law; it is argued that, based on Article 1(1), the application of public law rules is excluded from the scope of the Rome I Regulation.[66] Pursuant to paragraph (37) of the preamble of the Rome I Regulation: 'Considerations of public interest justify giving the courts of the Member States the possibility, in exceptional circumstances, of applying exceptions based on … overriding mandatory provisions.' This exceptional character implies that, as a general rule, the overriding mandatory provisions of the *lex causae* will not be automatically applied, but only if they meet the criteria set out in Article 9(3).[67]

It could also be argued that, as the Rome I Regulation determines its scope as concerning civil and commercial matters, the public law norms of the *lex causae* are excluded. This limitation is not convincing in itself, since the underlying contractual relationship affected by an economic sanction is undoubtedly a private law relationship. The intervention of public law rules does not alter the private law nature of the legal relationship. Taxes, customs and administrative legal relationships are excluded from the scope of the Rome I Regulation. Moreover, the public law norms of the forum and potentially those of the place of performance may intervene, despite the private law character of the Rome I Regulation.

It has also been argued that, with regard to choice of law, the parties do not consider the application of the overriding mandatory provisions of the selected law, in particular when they opt for the application of a neutral law, and therefore the overriding mandatory norms of the *lex causae* should not be applied automatically.[68] As Magnus explains, in the context of the Rome I Regulation, the parties cannot abrogate the overriding mandatory provisions of the *lex fori* or of a third state that is the place of performance. Consequently, it does not seem to be justified to disregard the overriding mandatory provisions of the *lex causae*.[69] The application of such overriding mandatory provisions may be foreseen by the parties choosing the governing law in the same way as they can with those of the forum.

[64] Freitag (n 11) 359.
[65] ibid 365–66.
[66] ibid 366.
[67] Hauser (n 19) 127–28.
[68] Oliver Remien, 'Außenwirtschaftsrecht in kollisionsrechtlicher Sicht' (1990) 54 *RabelsZ* 431, 461–63.
[69] Magnus (n 16) 678.

Based on the wording of the Rome Convention, it would follow that the overriding mandatory provisions of the *lex causae* are not to be applied.[70] It cannot be said that, if foreign public law norms may be applied under Article 7(1) of the Rome Convention, a fortiori the public law norms of the *lex causae* must be applied. Article 7(1) only grants an option for the court to give effect to foreign overriding mandatory rules. As opposed to this, the application of the overriding mandatory norms of the *lex causae* would involve the obligatory application of public law norms.[71] However, this is not to say that the laws of the Member States could not decide in favour of the application of the public law norms of the *lex causae*;[72] they have the option, but not an obligation to do so.

Philip stated that the Rome Convention is limited to the application of foreign private law norms as part of the *lex causae* and excluding public law norms, save those of the forum.[73] A deviation in favour of the public law norms of the *lex causae* should have been made unequivocal.[74] He interpreted the judgment in the *Boll* case of the ICJ as limiting the reference of conflict-of-laws rules of the Hague Guardianship Convention to private law norms, excluding the rules relating to protective measures of a public law nature.[75] More specifically, he explained that the Rome Convention constituted a private international law source and as such does not concern public law norms. As an answer in relation to the Rome Convention, Jackson argues that the appropriate distinction lies between (overriding) mandatory and non-(overriding) mandatory rules instead of differentiating between private law and public law norms to the exclusion of the latter, and (overriding) mandatory rules may be applied pursuant to the Rome Convention, irrespective of their origin.[76] There is no reason why the norms of the *lex causae* that are not internationally mandatory should apply, while the overriding mandatory rules of the *lex causae* do not apply at all, based simply on the 'overriding' nature of the latter.[77]

The *Nikiforidis* judgment may be seen as a clarification. In this judgment, to which we will return later, the CJEU established that:

> 49 It follows from the foregoing that the list, in Article 9 of the Rome I Regulation, of the overriding mandatory provisions to which the court of the forum may give effect is exhaustive.
>
> 50 Article 9 of the Rome I Regulation must therefore be interpreted as precluding the court of the forum from applying, as legal rules, overriding mandatory provisions other than those of the State of the forum or of the State where the obligations arising out of the contract have to be or have been performed.

[70] Philip (n 17) 87–88.
[71] ibid 106.
[72] ibid 88.
[73] ibid 85.
[74] ibid 87.
[75] ibid 86; Case Concerning the Application of the Convention of 1902 Governing the Guardianship of Infants (*The Netherlands v Sweden*), Judgment, ICJ Reports 1958 (28 November), 55; Hague Convention of 1902 relating to the settlement of guardianship of minors.
[76] Jackson (n 34) 64.
[77] Mercédeh Azeredo da Silveira, *Trade Sanctions and International Sales* (Kluwer, 2014) 74.

From these paragraphs, it may be inferred that only the overriding mandatory provisions of the forum and the place of performance may be applied or given effect by the courts of the Member States, excluding the overriding mandatory provisions of the *lex causae*. The court could have mentioned the overriding mandatory provisions of the *lex causae* or could have chosen a less rigid formulation, but it did not do so. Such an interpretation may be objected to on the grounds that the CJEU did not have to address the overriding mandatory provisions of the *lex causae* in *Nikiforidis* and perhaps found their application to be self-evident.

The Rome Convention and the Rome I Regulation do not give express guidance on the applicability of the overriding mandatory provisions of the *lex causae*. Pursuant to a first approach, which essentially represents the *Einheitsanknüpfung* theory and the traditions of some Member States, foreign public law norms apply as part of the *lex causae*. With regard to the Rome I Regulation, Dicey, Morris and Collins state: 'Mandatory provisions of the law which governs the contract under the Regulation of course apply by virtue of the general principle of the conflict of laws that a statute forming part of the governing law of the contract will normally be applied.'[78] In his commentary on the Rome I Regulation, McParland notes in a footnote that: 'When, of course, any overriding provisions will fall to be applied as part of the governing law of the contract.'[79] Accordingly, the reference to a legal system through a conflict-of-laws norm covers overriding mandatory norms, including those of a public law nature. However, the theory of *Einheitsanknüpfung* has received only limited support in German scholarship and court practice, and it seems that the majority view excludes the automatic application of public law norms from the scope of the *lex causae*.[80] The same view is supported in other Member States.[81] This difference in the approach of the Member States probably resulted in the silence on the application of the overriding mandatory provisions of the *lex causae* in the Rome Convention and this muteness has also been retained in the Rome I Regulation.[82] If so, the silence of these legal sources may be construed as a compromise solution, neither providing for nor prohibiting the application of the overriding mandatory provisions of the *lex causae*, and Member States are accordingly left to follow their own approach.[83] This uncertainty stemming from the formulation of the Rome I Regulation could be resolved by making clear through EU legislation whether the overriding mandatory provisions of the *lex causae*, including public law norms, are covered by the reference to foreign law. This issue could be addressed by legislation, as urged earlier by the Proposal of the Max Planck Institute on the Conversion of the Rome Convention into a Community Instrument.

[78] Lawrence Collins (ed), *Dicey, Morris & Collins on the Conflict of Laws*, vol 2, 15th edn (Sweet & Maxwell, 2012) 1840.

[79] Michael McParland, *The Rome I Regulation on the Law Applicable to Contractual Obligations* (Oxford University Press, 2015) 705 fn 140.

[80] Remien (n 1) 3329; Freitag (n 11) 365; Freitag (n 61) 182.

[81] Philip (n 17) 85.

[82] Freitag (n 61) 182.

[83] Kuckein (n 25) 69.

B. Economic Sanctions of the *Lex Causae*

Economic sanctions may also be found in the *lex causae*. No problem arises if the *lex fori* and the *lex causae* contain essentially the same economic sanction.[84] The court has to make a comparison between the sanction provisions of the *lex fori* and the *lex causae* and to ascertain whether they pursue the same functional objective.[85] If this is the case, the *lex causae* identical to the *lex fori* can be applied. The single exception may be the recourse to the *ordre public* exception if the economic sanction of the *lex causae* violates the *ordre public* of the forum.[86] In the latter case, however, there is no functional equivalence between the rules. If the *lex causae* does not contain an economic sanction comparable to the measures provided by the *lex fori*, the court can apply its own rules, imposing an economic sanction as an overriding mandatory provision.[87]

It is more questionable what happens if the *lex causae* imposes an economic sanction not provided by the forum state. According to a first approach, they are automatically applicable as the component of the law governing the contract as long as it does not infringe the *ordre public* of the forum.[88] The *ordre public* exception will probably be applied where the economic sanction imposed by the *lex causae* was condemned by the UN Assembly General or targets the forum state, or the forum adopted a blocking statute regarding the sanction or the sanction violates public international law and in particular human rights.[89] Following the more restrictive view, the economic sanctions of the *lex causae* would be applicable only if they meet the preconditions set out in Article 9(3) of the Rome I Regulation.

A further question related to the application of the economic sanctions of the *lex causae* is whether the parties can subject their contract to foreign rules imposing economic sanctions. This usually takes place through contract clauses referring to an obligation to comply with a given economic sanction. This question arose in particular regarding the US pipeline embargo, which will be discussed later, where in contracts on the sale of American technology between American sellers and European buyers, the buyers had to undertake to comply with the US export regulations on not re-exporting US technology to the Soviet Union. Similarly, during Arab League boycott of Israel, parties entering into contracts with Arab entities had to undertake not to maintain trade relations with Israeli entities.

Such submission clauses may be examined from the perspective of both public and private international law.[90] It has been argued that, in light of public

[84] Cortese (n 29) 724.
[85] ibid 725.
[86] ibid.
[87] ibid 726.
[88] ibid 726–27.
[89] Da Silveira (n 77) 189–90.
[90] AV Lowe, 'Public International Law and the Conflict of Laws: The European Response to the United States Export Administration Regulations' (1984) 33 *International & Comparative Law Quarterly* 515, 518.

international law, such submission clauses are not acceptable to the extent that they extend the jurisdiction of the sanctioning state through private parties, despite the limits on exercising jurisdiction under public international law.[91] Indeed, submission clauses require compliance with a prohibition on the sale or use of goods located outside the territory of the imposing state by persons outside its jurisdiction. The European Communities stated, concerning the submission clauses encouraged by US authorities concerning the pipeline project, that: 'If a Government in law and in fact systematically encourages the inclusion of such submission clauses in private contracts, the freedom of contract is misused in order to circumvent the limits imposed on national jurisdiction by international law.'[92] These submission clauses are sometimes seen as the circumvention of the rules of public international law using the 'language' of private law[93] and accordingly should not be recognised as valid contractual clauses.[94] At the same time, some authors consider that such clauses are not invalid simply because they extend public law rules to areas regarding which state legislature does not see itself as competent under public international law.[95] Generally speaking, the *ordre public* clause involves a limit for such a choice of law. Private autonomy is obviously also subject to limitations in this respect, for example, when the law of the forum excludes the application of the trade restriction by a blocking statute or if the trade restriction is not compatible with public international law.[96] However, it cannot be ignored that the extent to which the extraterritorial application of domestic law, including economic sanctions, is contrary to public international law is strongly debated.

From the angle of private international law, such clauses may be considered to be valid based on the autonomy of the parties and in particular their freedom to determine the law applicable to the contract. It must be noted that the autonomy of the parties, in terms of choice of trade restrictions, has also been contested from a private international law perspective. Accordingly, private autonomy ensures that the parties can determine the rules governing their contractual relationship and deviate from the otherwise applicable private law rules, but not from public law norms. Otherwise, they could modify the economic constitution of the state concerned.[97] It should also be added that it is usually not the parties' aim to subject their contract to a trade restriction by agreement because they really wish to see its application, but because they want to comply with the interests of the state imposing the economic sanction.[98]

[91] Alexander Georgieff, *Kollisonen durch extraterritoriale staatliche Regelungen im internationalen Wirtschaftsrecht* (Carl Heymanns Verlag, 1989) 38–39.
[92] European Communities, Comments on the US Regulations Concerning the Trade with the USSR (1982) 21 ILM 891, 896.
[93] Lowe (n 90) 525.
[94] A Vaughan Lowe, 'Extraterritorial Jurisdiction – British Practice' (1988) 52 *RabelsZ* 157, 197.
[95] Remien (n 68) 473.
[96] ibid 473–74.
[97] Christian Forwick, *Extraterritoriale US-amerikanische Exportkontrollen. Folgen für die Vertragsgestaltung* (Verlag Recht und Wirtschaft, 1993) 158–59.
[98] ibid 159.

As a conclusion, the uncertainty regarding the application of overriding mandatory provisions of the *lex causae* under the Rome I Regulation may also influence the application of the economic sanctions of the governing law. One view is that the overriding mandatory provisions, such as economic sanctions, of the *lex causae* are automatically applicable irrespective of their public law nature. Others opine that the overriding mandatory norms of the *lex causae* do not apply at all, or apply only if they meet the requirements laid down in Article 9(3) of the Rome I Regulation. Although we are not aware of any case concerning the application of economic sanctions of a foreign *lex causae*, it must be underlined here that the court practice of the Member States may differ in this respect, in particular as to the application of the law of non-EU Member States. The assessment of contractual clauses stipulating the application of economic sanctions is not free from uncertainties either. The following section will demonstrate that even more uncertainties surround the overriding mandatory provisions of third countries.

III. Economic Sanctions in the Law of a Third State Other than the *Lex Causae*

Economic sanctions of a third state may also have an impact on the contractual relations between the parties. Generally speaking, the law of a third state is construed as the law which is neither the *lex fori* nor the *lex causae*. This terminology is not correct if the *lex fori* and the *lex causae* coincide and the applicability of the overriding mandatory norms, including economic sanctions, of the law of another country is at stake.[99] In such a case, the foreign economic sanction imposed by this country is a sanction imposed not by a third state, but simply by another state. Overriding mandatory norms, and thus economic sanctions, are seen to belong to the law of a third country if they constitute neither a part of the *lex fori* nor of the *lex causae*. Since from the perspective of any EU forum, the *lex fori* contains EU economic sanctions, here we discuss only cases where the question of the application of an economic sanction imposed by a non-EU Member State arises and the law of this state is not the *lex causae*.

Giving effect to foreign overriding mandatory norms has been advocated for various reasons, such as decisional harmony, international cooperation, mutual legal assistance and comity.[100] Even before the adoption of the Rome Convention

[99] Kirsten Anderegg, *Ausländische Eingriffsnormen im internationalen Vertragsrecht* (Mohr Siebeck, 1989) 5; Bernhard Großfeld and Abbo Junker, *Das CoCom im internationalen Wirtschaftsrecht* (Mohr Siebeck, 1991) 97; Hauser (n 19) 52; Kuckein (n 25) 13.

[100] Anton Heini, 'Ausländische Staatsinteressen und internationales Privatrecht' (1981) 100 *Zeitschrift für Schweizerisches Recht* 65, 67; Anton Heini, 'Die Anwendung wirtschaftlicher Zwangsmaßnahmen im internationalen Privatrecht' in Wilhelm A Kewenig and Anton Heini, *Die Anwendung wirtschaftlicher Zwangsmaßnahmen im Völkerrecht und im internationalen Privatrecht* (CF Müller, 1982) 38.

and the Rome I Regulation, the law of the Member States developed various approaches to address the intervention of foreign public law rules. Under certain circumstances, they made it possible to give effect to overriding mandatory rules of third countries.

A. Court Practice before the Rome Convention

Even before the adoption of the Rome Convention and the Rome I Regulation, the courts of the Member States sometimes had to consider the application of foreign overriding mandatory provisions. The solutions of the courts differed, relying either on a conflict-of-laws or a substantive law approach. The latter approach implied that instead of applying foreign norms, they might be given effect within the scope of the applicable law. In this way, first the governing law was designated and, as a second step, a foreign economic sanction could be given effect through the rules of the applicable substantive contract law. A foreign overriding mandatory provision, including an economic sanction, could be given effect within the governing law, for instance, as grounds of impossibility of performance, *force majeure* or immorality of the contract. This way of proceeding also made it possible to give effect to the provisions of countries, the legislation of which could not be applied as law because its legality was questioned under public international law or due to hostility between the two countries.

i. Alnati

This may be illustrated by the well-known *Alnati* judgment of the Dutch Hoge Raad and, concerning economic sanctions, by the *Sensor* judgment. As early as 1966, in the *Alnati* judgment, the Dutch Hoge Raad held that it may be the case that the court can set aside the law selected by the parties by giving priority to a foreign law if the observance of certain provisions of that law, even outside the territory of that state, involves such important interests for the foreign state that the Dutch court has to take them into account.[101] In the given case, however, the Hoge Raad did not give priority to Belgian mandatory law regarding the carriers' liability over the parties' choice in favour of Dutch law. Although in the given case the possibility of giving effect to the law other than the *lex fori* and the *lex contractus* arose over a choice-of-law clause, commentators added that the same possibility would have been equally available if the governing law had been determined based on

[101] Cour de cassation des Pays-Bas (Hoge Raad) – 13 May 1966 (1967) 56 *Revue critique de droit international privé* 522 with the comment of AVM Struycken at 523; JEJT Deelen, 'Carriage of Goods by Sea: Party Autonomy – Supreme Court, May 13, 1966, N.J. 1967, no. 3 ("Alnati"-case)' (1968) 15 *Netherlands International Law Review* 82; Jan C Schultsz, 'Dutch Antecedents and Parallels to Article 7 of the EEC Contracts Convention of 1980' (1983) 47 *RabelsZ* 267, 273.

objective connecting factors.[102] The judgment was also deemed to be a resurgence of a new theory of comity.[103]

ii. Sensor

The *Sensor* decision was a remarkable court judgment in relation to the gas pipeline deal between West European countries and the Soviet Union which took shape at the end of the 1970s and the beginning of the 1980s. The pipeline business and the related legal issues attracted considerable attention in the legal literature.[104] The US sanctions related to the pipeline project raised several important legal issues, such as the compatibility of the extraterritorial application of the sanctions with public international law.[105] The analysis below focuses purely on the private international law aspects of the case. The deal aimed at the construction of a gas pipeline from Siberia to Czechoslovakia, from where the gas could be forwarded through the existing West European pipeline. The deal consisted of a network of agreements: the sale of equipment and pipes to the Soviet Union by West European companies, financing these transactions by West European banks, and the supply of gas through the pipeline from the Soviet Union to West European countries as consideration for the equipment and pipes. Through the project, European states intended to decrease their dependency on Arab petrol producer countries, thereby increasing the diversity of energy resources and a means of creating jobs after the European economic recession that resulted in redundancies in the steel industry. The US opposed this transaction from the outset because it meant that European dependency on Russian gas exports would increase and it was presumed

[102] Deelen (n 101) 92.

[103] ibid.

[104] Jürgen Basedow, 'Entscheidung – Das Amerikanische Pipeline-Embargo vor Gericht. Niederlande: Pres. Rb. Den Haag 17. 9. 1982. (Fall Sensor)' (1983) 47 *RabelsZ* 141, 147–53; Jobst Joachim Neuss, *Handelsembargos zwischen Völkerrecht und IPR* (VVF, 1989); Bernard Audit, 'Extra-territorialité et commerce international. L'affaire du gazoduc sibérien' (1983) *Revue critique de droit international privé* 401; Georgieff (n 91) 7–43; Großfeld and Junker (n 99) 78–83; Klaus Bockslaff, 'The Pipeline Affair of 1981/82: A Case History' in Jost Delbrück, Rainer Hofmann and Andreas Zimmermann (eds), *German Yearbook of International Law*, vol 27 (Duncker & Humblot, 1985) 28; Detlev F. Vagts, 'The Pipeline Controversy: An American Viewpoint' in Jost Delbrück, Rainer Hofmann and Andreas Zimmermann (eds), *German Yearbook of International Law*, vol 27 (Duncker & Humblot, 1985) 38; AV Lowe, 'International Law Issues Arising in the "Pipeline" Dispute: The British Position' in Jost Delbrück, Rainer Hofmann and Andreas Zimmermann (eds), *German Yearbook of International Law*, vol 27 (Duncker & Humblot, 1985) 54; Pieter Jan Kuyper, 'The European Community and the US Pipeline Embargo: Comments on Comments' in Jost Delbrück, Rainer Hofmann and Andreas Zimmermann (eds), *German Yearbook of International Law*, vol 27 (Duncker & Humblot, 1985) 72; Karl M Meessen, 'Extraterritoriality of Export Control: A German Lawyer's Analysis of the Pipeline Case' in Jost Delbrück, Rainer Hofmann and Andreas Zimmermann (eds), *German Yearbook of International Law*, vol 27 (Duncker & Humblot, 1985) 97; Massimo V Benedettelli, 'Sull' applicazione extraterritoriale delle misure di embargo degli stati uniti relative al "gasodotto siberiano"' (1984) 67 *Rivista di diritto internazionale* 529.

[105] See Georgieff (n 91) 20–43.

that the European financial resources would be used to strengthen the military capacity of Russia. The Export Administration Act of 1979 granted power to the President to restrict or prohibit any export of goods and technology subject to the jurisdiction of the US or exported by any person subject to the jurisdiction of the US for the protection of national security and foreign policy interests, and to prevent the drain of scarce materials.[106] The Export Administration Act rendered the export of oil and gas exploration and production equipment and technical data related to oil and gas exploration and production subject to licence. In Poland, starting with the strikes of the shipyard workers in Gdansk in 1980, the power of the Communist Party was challenged and the Solidarity trade union called for a referendum that challenged the legitimacy of the governing party. In 1981, in reaction to this, General Jaruzelski proclaimed a state of emergency and Polish tanks appeared on the streets of Warsaw, which temporarily halted the process of liberalisation. President Reagan condemned the proclamation of the state of emergency and severed the already restricted US trade with the Soviet Union, with the presumption that General Jaruzelski was simply implementing the orders of the Soviet Union (although Jaruzelski actually intended to prevent a Soviet invasion by demonstrating force and neither the Soviet Union nor the troops of the Warsaw Pact took part in the military action). By the Americans' legislative amendments, which came into force on 30 December 1981, the controls were extended to the exportation of goods and technical data related to the refinement of petrol and natural gas to the Soviet Union for use or transmission.[107] The relevant technical data could be exported from the US only if the addressee assumed an obligation not to re-export these data or the products resulting from these data directly or indirectly to the Soviet Union. President Reagan also ordered the processing of all licensing procedures regarding exports to the Soviet Union to be suspended. This embargo was limited to US persons. With an additional amendment, which was effective from 22 June 1982, further restrictions were introduced.[108] First, the prohibition on exports of relevant equipment and technical data of foreign origin to the Soviet Union was to be applied not only to US citizens, residents and corporations registered in the US, like the previous restrictions, but also for US-owned or controlled companies (eg, subsidiaries). Second, the export restrictions were extended to relevant equipment produced abroad based on a US licence. One of the companies concerned, Dresser, claimed for injunctive relief from the application of the sanctions and the withdrawal of its export privileges before a US court

[106] Export Administration Act (EAA) of 1979 (PL 96–72), (1979) ILM 1508. On the regulatory framework of the US regime of that time, see John L. Ellicot, 'Trends in Export Regulation' (1983) 38 *Business Lawyer* 533; Werner von Hein, 'Recht und Praxis der Ahndungsvorschriften des US-Export Administration Act' (1986) 32 *Recht der Internationalen Wirtschaft* 496; László Burián, 'A jogi személyek honossága különös tekintettel az amerikai embargó extraterritoriális hatályára' (1984) *Jogtudományi Közlöny* 199.

[107] Foreign Policy Export Controls (1982) ILM 853, 855.

[108] ibid 864.

without success.[109] The district judge held that 'the United States has a grave interest in its ability to enforce these regulations which are, in its view, essential to the accomplishment of important foreign policy objectives' and concluded that 'the public interest does not lie with a grant of the injunction requested by plaintiffs'.

The EEC claimed that the US restrictions were unlawful under public international law and considered them to be an unacceptable interference with the independent EEC commercial policy.[110] It made its position clear:

> The practical impact of the Amendments to the Export Administration Regulations is that E.C. companies are pressed into service to carry out U.S. trade policy towards the U.S.S.R., even though these companies are incorporated and have their registered office within the Community which has its own trade policy towards the U.S.S.R.[111]

While the EEC adopted its own sanctions following the Polish crisis,[112] the US wanted to compel the EEC to match US trade policy interests and the US sanctions regime, irrespective of the independent trade interests of the EEC.[113] The EEC instead called upon the US to withdraw the extraterritorial economic sanctions.

Despite the US prohibition, other European companies performed deliveries to the USSR of their own will or due to an obligation imposed on them by their government.[114] The UK government rejected the application of the US restrictions based on the Protection of Trading Interests Act 1980.[115] As a blocking statute, the Protection of Trading Interests Act 1980 enabled the Secretary of State to order persons not to comply with foreign orders breaching British interests. The Secretary of State established, based on the Protection of Trading Interests (US Reexport Control) Order of 30 June 1982, that the US pipeline embargo violated the trading interests of the UK. Later, four UK companies were ordered not to comply with the US sanctions and to perform their obligations under their contracts related to the pipeline project. In France, the government obliged companies seated in France to perform the contracts affected by the US embargo, relying on an ordinance of 1959 which rendered possible the seizure of goods for the public interest.[116] Accordingly, the equipment required for the pipeline project was seized and sent to the

[109] *Dresser Industries v Baldridge* 549 F Supp 108 (1982); David Z Vance, 'Export Controls: Challenge to the Validity of Department of Commerce Regulations Restricting the Export of Oil and Gas Equipment and Technology to the Soviet Union-Temporary Restraining Order Denied. *Dresser Industries v. Baldridge*, No. 82-2385 (D. D.C. filed Aug. 23, 1982)' (1983) 18 *Texas International Law Journal* 203; Ann dePender Zeigler, 'The Siberian Pipeline Dispute and the Export Administration Act: What's Left of Extraterritorial Limits and the Act of State Doctrine?' (1983) 6 *Houston Journal of International Law* 63; Homer O Blair, 'Toward a Workable System of Controls on the Export of Technology – Export Controls on Nonmilitary Goods and Technology: Are We Penalizing the Soviets or Ourselves?' 21 (1986) *Texas International Law Journal* 363, 368–70.

[110] European Communities (n 92) 904.

[111] ibid 895, also cited by Großfeld and Junker (n 99) 80.

[112] Regulation (EEC) No 596/82.

[113] See Kuyper (n 104) 83.

[114] See Großfeld and Junker (n 99) 81–83.

[115] See Lowe (n 94) 182–90.

[116] Ordonnance n°59–63 du 6 janvier 1959 relative aux réquisitions de biens et de services.

Soviet Union. The US authorities blacklisted these companies and refused them to grant an export licence in response. Without legislative intervention, the German authorities reminded the companies concerned to perform their contracts.[117] The extensive embargo was lifted by President Reagan following a political compromise between the US government and the Western European states. Accordingly, the controls imposed on exports to the USSR on 30 December 1981 and 22 June 1982 were removed in November 1982.[118]

The *Sensor* case fits into this chain of events. It concerned the contractual relationship between the Dutch Sensor company and Compagnie Européenne des Pétroles, a company which had its seat in France.[119] Sensor was a 100 per cent subsidiary of a Dutch company, Geosource International (Nederland), which was in turn a fully owned subsidiary of Geosource Inc, a US company. The French company undertook to deliver strings of geophones to Sensor with an ultimate destination in the USSR. Later, Sensor informed Compagnie Européenne des Pétroles that, as a subsidiary of a US company, it could not perform the contract due to the export prohibition ordered by the US President. The export prohibition also covered corporations owned or controlled by corporations organised in the US, irrespective of their place of organisation or business. The Hague District Court held that, in the absence of a choice of law by the parties, based on the Rome Convention (which had been signed by the Netherlands, but had not yet entered into force at that time), the law governing the contract was Dutch law. Regarding the extent to which the trade restrictions of US law must be considered, the court declared that the US sanction might not be taken into account. First, the court drew the conclusion that the extraterritorial reach of the export prohibition was not in accordance with public international law. At the same time, the court remarked that it would be conceivable to apply such a rule of jurisdiction, for example, if US citizens would have liked to circumvent the export prohibition by setting up a company outside the US. However, no such intention was found in the case. Second, the Hague District Court recognised that, under certain circumstances, the overriding mandatory provisions of a foreign law may be given priority over Dutch law governing the contract. Yet, the application of foreign overriding mandatory provisions necessitates the existence of sufficient connection between the contract and the foreign country. This precondition was not met in the given case. Consequently, the court obliged Sensor to perform the contract. It has been stressed that the addition of the *Sensor* judgment was to acknowledge the applicability of foreign overriding mandatory norms not only over the law selected by the parties, as in *Alnati*, but also over the law designated by objective conflict-of-laws rules.[120] A close connection was required for the application of the overriding

[117] Knüppel (n 44) 148–49.

[118] 15 CFR Parts 379, 385, 390, and 399 – Revision of Export Controls Affecting the USSR and Poland, Federal Register, Vol 47, No 223, 18 November 1982, 51858.

[119] Based on the German translation of the text provided by Basedow (n 104) 141; Schultsz (n 101) 279.

[120] Kunda (n 32) 73.

mandatory norm of a third state. The investment in a company by a foreign (here US) company does not suffice to establish this close connection.[121]

The interests in the application or non-application of the US sanctions of the government of the US and the Member States of the EEC, as well as of the European Commission, were well articulated in the case.[122] The US intended to punish the Soviet Union for its intervention in Poland, while the EEC Member States pursued their economic interests in building the pipeline. The outcome of the *Sensor* judgment is not surprising: it seems to be a specific expression of the opposition of the European governments concerned against the extensive US sanctions.[123] However, the judgment did not address the interests concerned, but rather was based on the compatibility of the US measures with public international law and the lack of sufficiently close connection between the contract and the foreign economic sanction in terms of private international law. Accordingly, based on the judgment, Kunda distinguishes between overriding mandatory rules 'whose purpose is justified (such as security or solvency) and those whose extraterritorial effects are inadmissible'.[124]

In their comment on the *Sensor* judgment, de Boer and Kotting claimed that the judgment was not well-founded, since the US embargo should have been applied as fact.[125] An economic sanction is to be given effect if it factually renders the performance of the contract impossible. Sensor was accordingly in a hostage-like situation: it would have had to perform or obey the sanctions due to the threatening penalties, including criminal sanctions, under US law.[126] The two authors argued that the fact that the sanction violated the *ordre public* of the forum because of the breach of public international law did not exclude the point that it resulted in a factual impossibility of performance. They stated that the reason for impossibility is the existence of the threat of punishment. Such a fact may not be disregarded, even in the case of the violation of *ordre public* or the norms of international law. This view could also be seen as the expression of the datum theory. However, it was questionable in the given case whether the Dutch supplier was factually deprived of the possibility of performing the contract.[127]

iii. Beverly Overseas SA v Privredna Bank Zagreb

Foreign economic sanctions are also given effect at the level of substantive law in countries outside the EU and the regime of the Rome Convention when considering

[121] Basedow (n 104) 159.
[122] Audit (n 104) 418–19.
[123] Knüppel (n 44) 149.
[124] Kunda (n 32) 72.
[125] TM de Boer and R. Kotting, 'Der niederländische Richter und das US-Gasröhren-Embargo' (1984) *IPRax* 108, 110.
[126] ibid 110.
[127] Eberhard Vetter, 'Kollisionsrechtliche Fragen bei grenzüberschreitenden Subunternehmensverträgen im Industrieanlagenbau' (1988) 87 *ZVglRWiss* 248, 275.

the violation of a foreign economic sanction as a breach of good morals. In spite of the governing Swiss law, the Swiss Federal Court took into account the UN embargo against Yugoslavia regarding a contract on the sale of arms between a Lebanese seller and a Croatian buyer during the Yugoslavian war.[128] As Switzerland was not a member of the UN at that time, the UN arms embargo against Yugoslavia could not be applied directly. The Swiss Federal Court established that the contract on the supply of arms violated good morals under Article 20 (1) of the Swiss Law of Obligations and was null and void, even though the contract was not connected to Switzerland, let alone the choice of the Swiss law and the jurisdiction of the court. The worldwide arms embargo imposed by the UNSC constituted part of the universal public policy that coincided with Swiss public policy and there was no reason to deprive this comprehensive arms embargo of its effects unilaterally. The court differentiated foreign policy considerations and Swiss good morals, by which it was not primarily foreign policy objectives that justified giving effect to the embargo. Instead, giving effect to the UN embargo was based on its nature of constituting international public policy and its universal moral significance, which was also respected by Switzerland.

B. Giving Effect to the Mandatory Rules of Third Countries under the Rome Convention

The Rome Convention enabled the courts of the Member States of the EU to give effect to foreign overriding mandatory provisions, such as economic sanctions. In fact, the Rome Convention did not imply a big change in comparison to the previous practice of the courts of some Member States.[129] The courts could have already taken foreign overriding mandatory norms, including economic sanctions, into account before. The Rome Convention made this possibility explicit.

According to Article 7(1) of the Rome Convention:

> When applying under this Convention the law of a country, effect may be given to the mandatory rules of the law of another country with which the situation has a close connection, if and in so far as, under the law of the latter country, those rules must be applied whatever the law applicable to the contract. In considering whether to give effect to these mandatory rules, regard shall be had to their nature and purpose and to the consequences of their application or non-application.

Foreign overriding mandatory provisions could therefore be given effect under the Rome Convention if the case had a close connection to the law of this state. Under Article 4(1) of the Rome Convention, 'the contract shall be governed by the law of the country with which it is most closely connected' in the absence of choice of law.

[128] *Beverly Overseas SA v Privnedna Bank Zagreb*, Bundesgericht, 28 March 2001.

[129] Jacques Périlleux, 'L'embargo et le droit des obligations' in Association européenne pour le droit bancaire et financier' in *L'embargo* (Bruylant, 1996) 167, 182–85.

The close connection requirement appears in both provisions, with the difference that Article 4(1) refers to the closest connection and not simply a close connection. In this sense, the court enjoys a somewhat broader leeway in applying the mandatory rules other than those which may be found in the *lex fori*. Consequently, not only the rules applicable in the absence of choice of law, but also other laws showing a close (but not necessarily the closest) connection may be given effect.[130] The Giuliano-Lagarde Report interpreted the close connection as a genuine connection based on, for example, the place of performance, the residence or the main place of business of any of the parties.[131] Further factors establishing a close connection may be the nationality or domicile of the parties, the location of a property or the location of the market affected.[132] Consequently, the court can give effect to economic sanctions contained in a law other than the *lex fori* or *lex causae*. The court has the discretion to give effect to a foreign sanction.[133] When deciding on their application, it has to take various circumstances into account, including the nature and purpose of the economic sanction, and the consequences of its application or non-application. The economic sanction of a third state will probably not be given effect if the forum state pursues different foreign policy objectives[134] or if it finds that the sanction violates domestic or international law. However, it should be noted that Article 7(1) of the Rome Convention creates the possibility for the judge to observe the interests of foreign states that are even contrary to the interests of the parties. In reality, this depends on the discretion of the court, which is empowered to limit party autonomy by foreign mandatory provisions.

This wording may be interpreted as a legal basis for both the application and the substantive law consideration of foreign mandatory rules.[135] The legal consequences of giving effect to foreign mandatory rules are determined by the *lex contractus*. Pursuant to Article 10(1), the applicable law governs, inter alia, the consequences of breach, the various ways of extinguishing obligations and the consequences of nullity of the contract.

The solution of the Rome Convention was welcomed for various reasons. In theory, it could contribute to a decisional harmony that would limit forum shopping.[136] Article 7(1) permits taking foreign state interests into account, which facilitates the free movement of judgments.[137] However, it was acknowledged that it shifts the task of balancing the interests of various states to judicial organs.

[130] Da Silveira (n 77) 143.

[131] Giuliano-Lagarde Report (n 43) 27.

[132] Michael Hellner, 'Third Country Overriding Mandatory Rules in the Rome I Regulation: Old Wine in New Bottles?' (2009) 5 *Journal of Private International Law* 447, 464.

[133] Peter Mankowski, 'Drittstaatliche Embargonormen, Außenpolitik im IPR, Berücksichtigung von Fakten statt Normen: Art. 9 Abs. 3 Rom I-VO im praktischen Fall (zu Cour d'appel de Paris, 25.2.2015 – 12/23757)' (2016) 36 *IPRax* 485, 488.

[134] Cortese (n 29) 728.

[135] Patrick Kinsch, *Le fait du prince étranger* (LGDJ, 1994) 466.

[136] Gaetan Escudey, 'Les lois de police étrangères en matière contractuelle: application ou prise en considération? Commentaire de l'affaire Nikiforidis' (Réseau universitaire européen droit de l'espace de liberté, sécurité & justice) 5, www.academia.edu/33290129/Les_lois_de_police_etrangeres_en_mati%C3%A8re_contractuelle_-_note_sous_CJUE_18_octobre_2016_Nikiforidis_Aff._C-135_15.

[137] ibid 5.

It must be noted that the Rome Convention did not create uniformity. This is because the Rome Convention allowed reservations to be made to the application of Article 7(1).[138] Germany, Ireland,[139] Latvia, Luxembourg, Portugal, Slovenia and the UK[140] availed themselves of such a reservation.[141] The reasons behind the reservations lay in the rejection of the wide discretion of courts and the legal uncertainty incidental to it.[142] A further concern was the prolongation of court proceedings due to the difficulties related to establishing and proving the content of foreign public law.[143]

Differences might have emerged even in those jurisdictions where Article 7 was applicable due to the broad discretion enjoyed by the courts. Did this situation change with the adoption of the Rome I Regulation? As we will see, although the Rome I Regulation eliminated the possibility of reservations, the open-textured nature of Article 9 of the Rome I Regulations may still give rise to differences in its application. In this sense, most of the issues related to the Rome Convention survived in the Rome I Regulation.

C. Giving Effect to the Mandatory Rules of Third Countries under the Rome I Regulation

The conversion of the Rome Convention into a regulation was preceded by a Green Paper[144] and the Commission proposal for the Rome I Regulation. Both documents discussed norms – what we call now overriding mandatory provisions. The Commission proposal for the Rome I Regulation by and large followed Article 7(1) of the Rome Convention.[145] Pursuant to Article 8 of the Proposal for the Rome I Regulation:

> 1. Mandatory rules are rules the respect for which is regarded as crucial by a country for safeguarding its political, social or economic organisation to such an extent that they are applicable to any situation falling within their scope, irrespective of the law otherwise applicable to the contract under this Regulation.

[138] Rome Convention, art 22(1)a).

[139] Treaty Series 2009 N° 21 Convention on the law applicable to contractual obligations and Ireland's reservation to Article 7(1) of the Convention, Done at Rome on 19 June 1980, signed on behalf of Ireland on 19 June 1980.

[140] Contracts (Applicable Law) Act 1990, art (2), s 2.

[141] See www.consilium.europa.eu/en/documents-publications/treaties-agreements/agreement/?id=1988024&DocLanguage=en.

[142] Magnus (n 16) 646; Sebastian von Allwörden, *US-Terrorlisten im deutschen Privatrecht: zur kollisions- und sachrechtlichen Problematik drittstaatlicher Sperrlisten mit extraterritorialer Wirkung* (Mohr Siebeck, 2014) 65–66.

[143] Von Allwörden (n 142) 66.

[144] Commission, Green Paper on the conversion of the Rome Convention of 1980 on the law applicable to contractual obligations into a Community instrument and its modernisation COM(2002) 654.

[145] Proposal for a Regulation of the European Parliament and the Council on the law applicable to contractual obligations (Rome I) Brussels, 15 December 2005 COM(2005) 650 final.

2. Nothing in this Regulation shall restrict the application of the rules of the law of the forum in a situation where they are mandatory.
3. Effect may be given to the mandatory rules of the law of another country with which the situation has a close connection. In considering whether to give effect to these mandatory rules, courts shall have regard to their nature and purpose in accordance with the definition in paragraph 1 and to the consequences of their application or non-application for the objective pursued by the relevant mandatory rules and for the parties.

The Commission's commentary to the Proposal explains the need for giving effect to mandatory provisions alien to the forum by mitigating the effect of forum shopping caused by the alternative grounds of jurisdiction determined by the Brussels I Regulation by considering the relevant mandatory rules of other Member States.[146] Article 8(3) of the Proposal for the Rome I Regulation would in fact have allowed effect to be given to the mandatory rules of the law of any other country with which the situation has a close connection.[147] This was rejected by the UK as giving too broad a discretion to the court seised and became a significant ground for the UK not wishing to opt in to the Rome I Regulation. The attitude of the UK government, as well as the fervid criticisms expressed by English legal scholars, were explained by the uncertainties, confusion, expense and delay caused by the proposed provision for the pre-contractual negotiations of the parties and in the application of this rule and ultimately the fear of the move of business from London to New York.[148]

Later on, a compromise was born, which resulted in the current wording of Article 9(3) of the Rome I Regulation. This restricts the applicability of foreign overriding mandatory norms limiting intervention to the autonomy of the parties. It is often stated that the present text reflects to a large extent English court practice prior to the Rome I Regulation, in particular *Ralli Bros*,[149] *Foster v Driscoll*[150] and *Regazzoni v Sethia*.[151] Article 9(3) of the Rome I Regulation is even considered to be a provision that re-establishes *Ralli Bros*.[152] In accordance with the *Ralli Bros* decision of the Court of Appeal, only the overriding mandatory provisions

[146] ibid.

[147] ibid 8.

[148] Stuart Dutson, 'The Law Applicable to Contracts: Amendments to Undermine Common Sense and the Attractiveness of European Courts' (2006) 7 *Journal of International Banking and Financial Law* 300; Andrew Dickinson, 'Third-Country Mandatory Rules in the Law Applicable to Contractual Obligations: So Long, Farewell, Auf Wiedersehen, Adieu?' (2007) 3 *Journal of Private International Law* 53; von Allwörden (n 142) 72–73; Hauser (n 19) 61–67.

[149] *Ralli Bros v Compania Naviera Sota y Aznar* [1920] 2 KB 287.

[150] *Foster v Driscoll* [1929] 1 KB 470.

[151] *Regazzoni v Sethia* [1958] AC 301 (HL).

Paul Lagarde and Aline Tenenbaum, 'De la convention du Rome au règlement Rome I' (2008) 97 *Revue critique de droit international privé* 727, 778; Jonathan Harris, 'Mandatory Rules and Public Policy under the Rome I Regulation' in Franco Ferrari and Stefan Leible (eds), *Rome I Regulation* (Sellier, 2009) 269, 269; Hauser (n 19) 66–67.

[152] Adrian Briggs, 'When in Rome, Choose as the Romans Choose' (2009) 125 *Law Quarterly Review* 191, 192.

of the place of performance may be taken into consideration and only if these norms rendered the performance unlawful. Notwithstanding this similarity to the solution applied by English law, Article 9(3) requires an autonomous EU law interpretation.[153]

This change also meant that the possibility of giving effect to foreign overriding mandatory provisions was considerably limited in comparison to the Rome Convention. As Thorn remarks, the final wording of Article 9(3) leaves almost no room for manoeuvre for the application of foreign overriding mandatory norms.[154] It is therefore no coincidence that there are very few cases where the courts of the Member States had to decide on giving effect to foreign overriding mandatory provisions including economic sanctions.

In the current EU private international law, the Rome I Regulation provides for an explicit legal basis to take foreign economic sanctions into account. Pursuant to Article 9(3):

> Effect may be given to the overriding mandatory provisions of the law of the country where the obligations arising out of the contract have to be or have been performed, in so far as those overriding mandatory provisions render the performance of the contract unlawful. In considering whether to give effect to those provisions, regard shall be had to their nature and purpose and to the consequences of their application or non-application.

Article 7 of the Rome Convention and Article 9 of Rome I Regulation are often compared.[155] While Article 22 of the Rome Convention allowed state parties to make a reservation to the application of Article 7(1), reservations are excluded under the Rome I Regulation, since regulations are directly applicable in the Member States. The denomination changed from mandatory rules to overriding mandatory provisions, although this does not affect the nature of rules covered by the two provisions. The order of the rules was reversed: the Rome Convention provided first for giving effect to the mandatory rules of third states, which was followed by the application of the mandatory provisions of the forum, whereas the Rome I Regulation first established the courts' freedom to apply the overriding mandatory norms of their own state in Article 9(2) and foreign overriding mandatory provisions may be given effect under Article 9(3). The connecting factors are different. Article 9(3) of the Rome I Regulation exclusively permits the application of the overriding mandatory provisions of the state of the place of performance, while Article 7(1) of the Rome Convention refers to the mandatory rules of the law of any other country with which the situation has a close connection. The Rome I

[153] Robert Freitag, 'Die kollisionsrechtliche Behandlung ausländischer Eingriffsnormen nach Art. 9 Abs. 3 Rom I-VO' (2009) 29 IPRax 109, 111; von Allwörden (n 142) 74; Hauser (n 19) 67.

[154] Karsten Thorn, 'Artikel 9: Eingriffsnormen' in Thomas Rauscher (ed), *Europäisches Zivilprozess- und Kollisionsrecht*, vol 3 (Otto Schmidt, 2016) 432, 433.

[155] Jürgen Basedow, *The Law of Open Societies: Private Ordering and Public Regulation of International Relations – General Course on Private International Law, Collected Courses of the Hague Academy of International Law*, vol 360 (Martinus Nijhoff, 2013) 332–33.

Regulation thus requires the existence of a clear territorial connection to the dispute: effect may be given exclusively to the overriding mandatory provisions of the law of the country where the obligations arising out of the contract have to be or have been performed.

It is questionable whether the switch from the close connection to the place of performance promotes legal certainty and predictability. The Rome Convention gives wider leeway to the court to apply foreign mandatory rules, while the Rome I Regulation limits giving effect to foreign overriding mandatory norms to the overriding mandatory provisions of the state of the place of performance in favour of predictability and certainty.[156] In fact, it can be said that this does not involve a significant change. The place of performance often coincides with other connecting factors,[157] such as the nationality or habitual residence of the parties. However, a consequence of the change is that the replacement of the more extensive close connection test by the place of performance limits the overriding mandatory provisions which may be given effect, though sometimes it may seem necessary to give effect to the overriding mandatory provisions of countries other than the place of performance.[158] Although predictability is somewhat better ensured by Article 9(3), Basedow points out that the narrow construction of Article 9 may not always be sufficient to guarantee material justice in the legal relationship between the parties.[159] This may give an impetus for the courts to give effect to such overriding mandatory norms through substantive contract law, thus circumventing conflict-of-laws rules determined by the Rome I Regulation. Thus, it is even less predictable when a court has recourse to the substantive law consideration or sticks to Article 9 of the Rome I Regulation; the conclusion is correct that the endeavour to bring more certainty may turn into less predictable outcomes.

The wording of the second sentence of Article 7(1) of the Rome Convention and Article 9(3) of the Rome I Regulation are almost entirely the same. Article 9(3) of the Rome I Regulation provides that, in considering whether to give effect to those provisions, regard shall be had to their nature and purpose and to the consequences of their application or non-application. The single but negligible difference is that the Rome Convention mentions 'mandatory rules' instead of 'those provisions' which also allude to overriding mandatory provisions.

After this introduction on Article 9(3) of the Rome I Regulation, each precondition of its application must be examined generally and in the particular context of the possibility to give effect to foreign economic sanctions. Following the examination of these conditions, the question of whether Article 9 excludes the application or giving effect to overriding mandatory provisions of states not referred to in Article 9, ie, whether Article 9 has an exhaustive nature, will be analysed.

[156] Mankowski (n 133) 487.
[157] Hellner (n 132) 467.
[158] ibid 470.
[159] Basedow (n 155) 333–34.

i. Place of Performance

In comparison to the Rome Convention, foreign overriding mandatory provisions are given effect in a more limited way. Only overriding mandatory provisions of the place of performance may be given effect. Thus, the 'close connection' mentioned in the Rome Convention is limited by the Rome I Regulation to the place of performance. Although this restriction limits the laws which might potentially gain application, the place of performance may be examined for each obligation arising out of the contract, which may lead to a plurality of places of performance.[160] In this way, various laws may be given effect under Article 9(3) depending on the obligation at issue.[161] In certain cases, there is not a single place of performance and this multiplies those legal systems, the overriding mandatory provisions of which may be taken into consideration by the court.

A particular problem is whether the breach of an export prohibition realises the violation of the place of performance if goods must be delivered to a country which does not prohibit their import.[162] In a narrow sense, the place of performance is the state of destination which does not deem the performance as unlawful. However, in a broader sense, the obligation to supply the goods consists of various part obligations, and performance also embraces exportation. Consequently, the breach of the export prohibition is to be considered to be a violation of the law of the place of performance.

Some authors include the application of the *Machttheorie* into the interpretation of the place of performance. Accordingly, only those overriding mandatory provisions of those places of performance must be given effect, which would factually exclude or hinder performance due to the effective enforcement of the overriding mandatory norm.[163] Nevertheless, pursuant to the *Machttheorie*, overriding mandatory provisions other than those of the state of the place of performance could be given effect too. This is because countries which are not the place of performance may also be in a position to enforce their norms through various sanctions. However, the wording of the Rome I Regulation does not refer to the enforcement capacity of the state of the place of performance as a connection factor. Moreover, this would not provide for a predictable connecting factor,[164] although predictability and legal certainty are mentioned among the goals of the Rome I Regulation.[165] Irrespective of the enforcement capacity of the imposing state, the forum may give effect to an overriding mandatory provision of the state of the place of performance, taking the factors mentioned in Article 9(3) into account. The enforcement capacity of the imposing state is simply a factor to

[160] Renner (n 21) 207.
[161] Harris (n 151) 316.
[162] ibid 317.
[163] Thorn (n 154) 460–61; Cremer (n 61) 19.
[164] Ringe (n 20) 1123.
[165] Preamble (6) and (16) of the Rome I Regulation.

be taken into account when deciding whether to give effect to a foreign overriding mandatory norm.

ii. Unlawfulness under the Law of the Place of Performance

It is often said that the wording of the Rome I Regulation, and in particular the reference to unlawfulness, are based on the earlier English judicial practice. It is considered that this was the price of appeasing those countries which made a reservation to the Rome Convention and especially of avoiding an opt-out by the UK. Under English law, illegality involves the breach of a prohibition.[166] In English conflict of laws, if a contract is illegal under the law of the state of the place of performance, the recognition and enforcement of such a contract would violate not only the values of that state, but also the interests of England in maintaining friendly relations with the state concerned, and thus the contract will qualify as contrary to public policy under English law.[167] Consequently, in English conflict of laws, the protection of its own and foreign public policy is in this way intertwined.

It is suggested that unlawfulness must be construed in a broad sense, including cases when performance triggers either a civil or a criminal law sanction. A criminal sanction is not a necessary precondition; it suffices if the contract is rendered invalid by the foreign law[168] or cannot be enforced.[169] Regarding obligations establishing a maximum price or amount of goods, it may be said that the performance above the maximum is unlawful and, as Article 9(3) of the Rome I Regulation does not specify whether the performance should be fully or partially rendered unlawful, rules setting such a maximum concerning the performance are also caught by Article 9(3).[170] In terms of applying Article 9(3), it is immaterial whether the foreign provision renders the contract unlawful after the conclusion of the contract or unlawfulness exists *ab initio*.[171]

It is questionable what happens when the economic sanction does not impose illegality, but, for example, only an obligation to declare and non-compliance with this gives rise to (eg, financial) penalties. Certain authors interpret the term 'unlawful' in a broad sense, extending the scope of application of Article 9(3) to norms that do not render the contract invalid or unenforceable, but imposing another sanction or simply giving rise to the modification of the contract.[172] Others limit unlawfulness to norms which render a contract invalid. Accordingly, Article 9(3) does not cover cases where the law of the foreign state does not

[166] Hauser (n 19) 71.
[167] Magnus (n 16) 672.
[168] Freitag (n 153) 112; Andreas Köhler, *Eingriffsnormen – Der „unfertige Teil" des europäischen IPR* (Mohr Siebeck, 2013) 212.
[169] McParland (n 79) 708.
[170] Köhler (n 168) 212.
[171] Freitag (n 153) 113; Hauser (n 19) 79–80.
[172] Renner (n 21) 207; Freitag (n 153) 112–13.

prohibit performance.[173] Ancillary obligations imposed by foreign overriding mandatory norms are not relevant (information obligations).[174] Under this approach, an obligation to declare would not fall under the concept of unlawfulness.

iii. Nature and Purpose

The examination of the factors mentioned in the second sentence of Article 9(3) of the Rome I Regulation – the nature and purpose of the overriding mandatory provision, the consequences of its application or non-application – is obligatory and may be subject to review.[175] Therefore, these factors limit the discretion of the court and direct the justification of any court decision.[176] These factors must therefore be analysed here, starting with the nature and purpose of the overriding mandatory rule.

The court has to ascertain the exact purpose of and the legislative intent behind the overriding mandatory provision concerned. Regarding economic sanctions, it is not always an easy task and places the judge(s) in the role of a political or foreign affairs analyst. This is because economic sanctions may serve various purposes, whether truly foreign policy objectives, or political, economic or symbolic ones. Sometimes, it might be difficult to reveal the real motive(s) behind a sanction.

It is often stressed that the purpose must be lawful: it must be in accordance with the laws of the forum and the law of organisations to which the forum state belongs, as well as international law. The sanctions imposed by the UNSC rarely raise problems of legality.[177] Similarly, if a sanction is recommended by the UNSC or the UN General Assembly and a state or regional organisation follows such a recommendation, the lawfulness of the purpose of the sanction is rarely called into question. Conversely, a unilateral restricting measure condemned by the UN is usually not treated as lawful. Likewise, the court of a state which is the subject of an economic sanction or that of a state issuing a blocking statute will most probably not consider the economic sanction to be legal.

However, the assessment of the purpose goes beyond the examination of the legality. There are varying arguments behind the exercise of the discretion of the court to give effect to overriding mandatory rules of third countries. This idea is not new and is not linked to Article 9 of the Rome I Regulation or the Rome Convention. These approaches have been elaborated in order to facilitate deciding whether to give effect to foreign overriding mandatory norms at the level of substantive law. Nevertheless, these approaches fit well into the analysis of the purpose of the overriding mandatory norm under the Rome I Regulation. It may be questioned whether the purpose of the legislation is shared by the international

173 Czernich (n 21) 705.
174 Ringe (n 20) 1124; Freitag (n 153) 113.
175 Roth (n 52) 181.
176 ibid 181.
177 Da Silveira (n 77) 154–55.

legal community.[178] It covers its compatibility with the fundamental interests and values of the forum, the EU and the international community. The examination of the interests concerned gives a very practical and flexible means to judges to decide whether to give effect to foreign economic sanctions.[179] The coincidence of the interests of the states concerned may also be deemed necessary to give effect to the overriding mandatory rules of a third state. Certain authors limit the assessment to the promotion of the interests of the forum,[180] while others depart from a broader range of interests. The question of whether to give effect to a foreign overriding mandatory norm or not is justified either by a coincidence with the interests of the state of the forum or by the coincidence with the interests of the international community.[181] Of course, the interests of the state of the forum and the international community may also coincide. Widely recognised interests may also serve as a basis to give effect to foreign overriding mandatory norms.[182] Effect is given to a foreign overriding mandatory norm if it contributes at least indirectly to the interests of the state of the forum, or at least does not harm them. It is also asserted that the relevant public interests may be strengthened if they represent the interests of one of the parties.[183] Others find that the private interests protected by the foreign overriding mandatory norm may also be considered independently from public interests.[184]

The shared values approach requires giving effect to those foreign overriding mandatory rules which express values that are fundamentally identical in the forum state. The court applies a foreign overriding mandatory provision only if it finds that the values behind the foreign norm are acceptable to it.[185] It is noted that, under Article 9(3) of the Rome I Regulation, it should not suffice that the forum does not reject the values expressed by the foreign regulation; it should positively recognise them.[186] This approach is very close to looking at the common interests of the states concerned,[187] but the two are to be treated separately. The analysis of the values represented by the foreign legislation and its coincidence with the value system of the forum is seen as a first step, which is followed by the examination of the interests concerned.[188] If the values behind the legislation are not shared, there is no need to scrutinise the interests.

[178] Ringe (n 20) 1124.

[179] Ulrich Drobnig, 'Die Beachtung von ausländischen Eingriffsgesetzen – eine Interessenanalyse' in Werner Barfuß, Bernard Dutoit, Hans Forkel, Ulrich Immenga and Ferenc Majoros (eds), *Festschrift für Karl H Neumayer* (Nomos, 1985) 159, 174.

[180] Karl Kreuzer, *Ausländisches Wirtschaftsrecht vor deutschen Gerichten* (CF Müller, 1986) 92–94.

[181] Drobnig (n 179) 174.

[182] Pascal Deumier, Jean-Baptiste Racine and Édouard Treppoz, 'La loi de police étrangère: une possibilité que le juge a l'obligation d'envisager' (2010) *Revue des contrats* 1385, 1388.

[183] Drobnig (n 179) 174.

[184] Sana-Chaille de Nere (n 18) 374.

[185] See Freitag (n 11) 411; van Houtte (n 40) 197; Ringe (n 20) 1124.

[186] Freitag (n 153) 111.

[187] Dominique Bureau and Horatia Muir Watt, *Droit international privé – Tome 1* (PUF, 2010) 606; Deumier, Racine and Treppoz (n 182) 1388.

[188] Großfeld and Junker (n 99) 133.

In addition, it was also claimed that the advantages stemming from giving effect reciprocally to overriding mandatory norms in the cooperation between two states may also be a decisive factor.[189] The purpose must be in accordance with the policy objectives of the forum. A court will examine in essence whether the foreign policy objective of the issuing state is in accordance with the foreign policy of the forum.[190] It is highly improbable that a forum would give effect to an economic sanction that is at odds with the foreign policy objectives of the forum state. Another potential precondition is requiring the closeness of the policy objectives pursued by the third country and the forum state. According to the most lenient approach, any overriding mandatory provision of a third state is to be applied unless its application violates the *ordre public* clause. The evaluation of the purpose involves a preliminary assessment from the point of view of the *ordre public*.[191] If the purpose of the measure is against the forum's *ordre public*, the court will disregard it. Such an analysis makes any later application of the *ordre public* clause under Article 21 of Rome I Regulation redundant.

Nevertheless, it should be noted that there are instances when the review of the purpose, including its lawfulness, and the evaluation of interests, values and policy objectives behind the overriding mandatory norm are held back by the facts of the case and therefore these factors cannot be exclusive. In the often-mentioned example of the seizure of goods by the authorities of the state imposing the economic sanction, even if the forum establishes the illegality of the measure or its incompatibility with the interests, values and policy objectives of the forum state, the foreign economic sanction rendering performance impossible may be given effect.

It is pointed out that the obligation of the examination of the purpose of legislation by courts in fact involves the admission of the governmental interest analysis promoted in the US conflict of laws.[192] This is not altered by the other factors to be considered, such as the consequences of the application or non-application of the norm. Morse points out that balancing the (political) interests concerned without much guidance places the courts of the EU Member States in a situation where they are forced to carry out a governmental interest analysis.[193] Interestingly, the private international law of European countries and the EU resisted this American theory in terms of the determination of the applicable law. Nevertheless, Article 9(3) and its predecessors may be seen as the incarnation of the governmental interest analysis fervidly opposed by European private international law scholarship.

[189] Bonomi (n 32) 240; Sana-Chaille de Nere (n 18) 373–74.

[190] Garcimartín Alférez (n 18) 605.

[191] Thorn (n 154) 463.

[192] Adeline Chong, 'The Public Policy and Mandatory Rules of Third Countries in International Contracts' (2006) 2 *Journal of Private International Law* 27, 36; Dickinson (n 148) 57–59.

[193] Morse (n 18) 146.

iv. The Consequences of their Application and Non-application

It is asserted that the consequences of the application and non-application of economic sanctions may be examined from the point of view of the parties' interests[194] and the interests of the states concerned.[195] In my opinion, considering private interests is rarely helpful. The economic sanction hinders the performance of the contract. If both parties are willing to perform, the economic sanction harms the interests of both parties. If one of the parties does not wish to perform but the other would adhere to performance, one of the parties is worse off due to the intervention of the economic sanction. It is therefore hardly possible to see situations where both parties would be interested in applying an economic sanction. As economic sanctions are external to the parties' legal relationship and are beyond the original interests of the parties, I tend to think that most of the time, the analysis of the parties' interests cannot be helpful in deciding whether to give effect to an economic sanction or not.

It has been asserted that when assessing the consequences of the application or non-application of overriding mandatory provisions, courts have to carry out a balancing exercise.[196] Balancing also includes taking political interests (foreign policy considerations) into account. Even so, the decision of the court will largely be determined by the interests and values of the forum state which prevail over those of any other state concerned. It has also been added that, by weighing up the above factors, the solution must result in an appropriate balance between the interests of the parties concerned,[197] but, as has been explained above, this is rarely helpful.

The court has to have regard for the penalties and their severity as foreseen in the event of non-compliance with the economic sanction.[198] Blocking statutes and the legal consequences envisaged by it for observing the economic sanction must also be taken into consideration. Penalties and the consequences of non-performance may be neutralised by states through clawback statutes, which must also be considered when deciding whether to give effect to an economic sanction.[199] Furthermore, other factors, such as the possible recognition and enforceability of the decision, may also be taken into account in determining the consequences of the application or non-application of the sanction.

It has also been asserted that the analysis of the consequences should also concentrate on whether the issuing state has the power to enforce the overriding mandatory provision – for example, an economic sanction.[200] This view represents

[194] Thorn (n 154) 463; Garcimartín Alférez (n 18) 605.
[195] McParland (n 79) 712.
[196] Kunda (n 32) 234.
[197] Von Allwörden (n 142) 125.
[198] Da Silveira (n 77) 146 and 162; Mercédeh Azeredo da Silveira, 'Economic Sanctions and Contractual Disputes between Private Operators' in Larissa van den Herik (ed), *Research Handbook on UN Sanctions and International Law* (Edward Elgar, 2017) 351.
[199] Da Silveira (n 77) 178; da Silveira (n 198) 351.
[200] Da Silveira (n 77) 146 and 162; da Silveira (n 198) 351.

in principle the *Machttheorie*. If the court decides not to give effect to a foreign economic sanction, it cannot be excluded in advance that the parties will not be penalised for complying with such a judgment or award. This puts parties at risk and may induce a court to give effect to the sanction. If it can factually hinder performance (eg, by the seizure of goods), the overriding mandatory norm should be given effect.[201] However, the case is not so unequivocal when performance is theoretically possible but the performing party would be subject to serious criminal or administrative sanctions.

A practical illustration from the French case law for taking into account the consequences of the application or non-application of a foreign economic sanction is the *Fruehauf* case, which will be discussed in Chapter 6. In this case, the Cour d'appel de Paris did not apply or give effect to a US sanction against China because of the disastrous consequences of potential non-performance on the business of the company:[202] its financial situation would have been undermined due to the payment of a high amount of damages in the case of non-performance because of the US embargo and non-performance would also have caused the loss of the moral credit of the company. This could have resulted in the disappearance of the company from the market, with the consequence of the potential dismissal of its employees.

v. *Giving Effect*

Foreign overriding mandatory provision may intervene in two ways.[203] First, the foreign mandatory norm may be applied as a legal norm that takes place through a special connection (*Sonderanknüpfung*). In this case, the foreign norms will apply per se. Application implies applying a norm together with its legal consequences and, to this extent, the foreign norm would replace the otherwise governing law. Second, foreign mandatory norms may be taken into consideration at the level of the substantive assessment of the case. The forum is not obliged to 'apply' a foreign overriding mandatory provision; instead, it may give effect to it at the level of the substantive law of the *lex causae*. Consideration at the level of substantive law means that the *lex causae* remains intact, but the impact of the foreign norm is recognised through a substantive law provision of the governing law, such as a rule on the impossibility of performance or the prohibition of contracts breaching good morals. This often enables the court to modify the legal consequences of the foreign overriding mandatory norms and determine the legal consequences in accordance with the law of the forum if it coincides with the *lex causae*.

Article 7(1) of the Rome Convention used the wording 'give effect' regarding the mandatory rules of third countries. Article 9(3) of the Rome I Regulation

[201] Kunda (n 32) 236.
[202] Cour d'appel de Paris, Chambre 14, 22 mai 1965, Gazette du Palais (1965) 86.
[203] Freitag (n 11) 412.

equally uses the expression 'give effect' to foreign overriding mandatory norms, as opposed to the 'application' of the forum rules as set out in Article 9(2). The question arises as to what 'giving effect' actually means. The wording is unclear and it is debated in the literature whether this means that overriding mandatory provisions of third countries may apply as law or whether they may be taken into account only through the governing substantive law. Most of the language versions distinguish between the language of Article 9(2) and that of Article 9(3), but other language versions speak about application in both cases.[204] Moreover, pursuant to Article 9(3), when deciding whether to give effect to foreign overriding mandatory norms, 'regard shall be had to their nature and purpose and to the consequences of their application or non-application', ie, giving effect is contrasted with application, even in the same paragraph.[205]

The question is whether Article 9(3) gives rise to a special conflict-of-laws rule providing for the application of foreign overriding mandatory norms (*Sonderanküpfung*) or whether it allows foreign overriding mandatory provisions to be taken into consideration at the level of the substantive law assessment of the case.[206] The Rome Convention and the Rome I Regulation are assessed differently by scholars. A part of the literature deems that Article 7(1) of the Rome Convention[207] and Article 9(3) of the Rome I Regulation[208] express a *Sonderanknüpfung* rule, while others find them to be an authorisation for courts to give effect to foreign overriding mandatory norms at the level of substantive law. Article 9(3) may be interpreted in both ways.[209] Those arguing for the approach of *Sonderanknüpfung* point out that in most countries, the former prevailing doctrine of non-application of foreign public law has been broken down; there is no obstacle to applying foreign public law rules and to breaking away from the approach that foreign public law is taken into account simply as a fact.[210] Putting this into a historical context, d'Avout and Bureau argue that, at the time that the Rome Convention was conceived, the application of foreign public law was not accepted and taking it into consideration was already a novelty.[211] However, the time became ripe for change and when the application of foreign overriding norms, together with all its legal consequences, is viable and appropriate, that law is to be applied.[212] It is also added that the equal

[204] Mankowski (n 133) 487–88.

[205] ibid 488; Hauser (n 19) 67.

[206] Thorn (n 154) 464.

[207] Meiko Zeppenfeld, *Die allseitige Anknüpfung von Eingriffsnormen im Internationalen Wirtschaftsrecht* (Duncker & Humblot, 2001) 98; Forwick (n 97) 128 fn 49; Ringe (n 20) 1122; Leible (n 32) 299, adding that the self-evident application of the mandatory provisions of the *lex causae* (*Schuldstatutstheorie*) and the *Sonderanknüpfung* in the Rome Convention represents a theory combining them (*Kombinations-* oder *Kumulationstheorie*); Beulker (n 58) 124.

[208] Mankowski (n 57) 148; Ringe (n 20) 1123 and 1125.

[209] Staudinger (n 2) 263; Magnus (n 16) 674.

[210] Freitag (n 61) 185.

[211] D'Avout and Bureau (n 18) 25.

[212] ibid 25.

treatment of the legal orders of the Member States[213] and international decisional harmony also require this.[214] Those who argue for the real application of foreign norms point out that taking them into consideration at the level of substantive law may simply disguise an actual application by wrapping one norm in another (*emboîtement*).[215]

The CJEU noted in *Nikiforidis* that: 'Article 9 of the Rome I Regulation must therefore be interpreted as precluding the court of the forum from applying, as legal rules, overriding mandatory provisions other than those of the State of the forum or of the State where the obligations arising out of the contract have to be or have been performed.'[216] As Escudey points out, an *a contrario* argumentation leads to the result that the overriding mandatory provisions of the state of the forum or of the state where the obligations arising out of the contract have to be or have been performed apply as legal rules.[217] Following this language, the judgment provides for the application of the overriding mandatory provisions of third countries and not simply taking them into account at the level of substantive law. From this perspective, giving effect amounts to application as a legal norm.

According to the other interpretation, giving effect under Article 9(3) is to be identified as a substantive law consideration. Concerning Article 7(1) of the Rome Convention, the Giuliano-Lagarde Report stated 'that the words "effect may be given" impose on the court the extremely delicate task of combining the mandatory provisions with the law normally applicable to the contract in the particular situation in question'.[218] The necessity of the combination of the foreign mandatory provisions and the governing law points to a substantive law approach.[219]

The wording of Article 7 of the Rome Convention and Article 9 of the Rome Regulation do not exclude a priori either of the two solutions.[220] Giving effect may be interpreted broadly as granting freedom to the judge, ranging from considering a foreign overriding mandatory norm at the level of substantive law to fully applying it.[221] The use of the expression of giving effect is usually explained as a compromise. The provision has been interpreted as granting a choice for the court.[222] It can apply the foreign overriding mandatory norm as the imposing state

[213] Freitag (n 61) 185.
[214] Thorn (n 154) 466.
[215] Louis d'Avout, 'Case note on Cour de cassation (Ch. soc.) – 24 février 2004' (2005) 94 *Revue critique de droit international privé* 62, 70; d'Avout and Bureau (n 18) 25.
[216] *Nikiforidis* (n 13) para 50.
[217] Escudey (n 136) 6.
[218] Giuliano-Lagarde Report (n 43) 27–28.
[219] Freitag (n 153) 115.
[220] Deumier, Racine and Treppoz (n 182) 1389.
[221] See ibid 1389; Ringe (n 20) 1125; Hans-Joachiem Prieß and Martin Schaper, 'Erfüllung oder Nichterfüllung – Zur Durchsetzbarkeit vertraglicher Ansprüche bei entgegenstehendem ausländischen Embargorecht' in Dirk Ehlers and Hans-Michael Wolffgang (eds), *Recht der Exportkontrolle: Bestandsaufnahme und Perspektiven; Handbuch zum Exportkontrollrecht – Festschrift für Dr Arnold Wallraff* (Fachmedien Recht & Wirtschaft, 2015) 267, 273.
[222] Freitag (n 11) 412.

does or it can modify its effects in accordance with its own legal rules.[223] The choice should depend on the circumstances of the case and the legal provisions that may be relevant in deciding the case. One explanation is that this solution solves the problem of the principle of the non-application of foreign public law followed by certain Member States, since the provision does not compel these states to apply foreign public law norms.[224]

Magnus infers from the wording 'effect may be given' that it is at the discretion of the judge whether to apply foreign overriding mandatory provisions through *Sonderanknüpfung* or to take them into account in the substantive assessment of the case. In the case of *Sonderanknüpfung*, the legal consequences are determined by the law designated through the *Sonderanknüpfung*, whereas, at the substantive law level, foreign overriding mandatory provisions may be handled within the framework of the law governing the contract, for instance, as a ground for impossibility.[225] In terms of legal consequences, the substantive law method authorises the court to combine various sets of rules, primarily those of the place of performance and the *lex causae*, as well as exceptionally the *lex fori* (eg, if it also intervenes by an overriding mandatory norm).[226] If the foreign norms of the imposing state do not provide for a legal consequence, the governing law will determine it.[227] However, it is not expected to apply a stricter sanction than those foreseen by the foreign law.[228] Even if the foreign law provides for the legal consequences, it may be conceivable that the court does not apply a stricter sanction than the one provided by the law of forum state: a penal sanction may be set aside in favour of a civil law consequence (nullity) or a stricter civil law sanction (nullity of the entire contract) may be replaced by a less strict legal consequence (nullity of the contractual provision in question).

For Magnus, even though the inclusion of foreign overriding mandatory provisions into the substantive assessment of the case is allowed, the *Sonderanknüpfung* method must be given priority in order to ensure the coherence between the preconditions and the legal consequences of the overriding mandatory provision.[229] Similarly, recognising the possibility of the choice of the court seised, Freitag argues that, in the event of doubt, the *Sonderaknüpfung* approach must be preferred.[230]

The possibility of application in addition to the substantive law consideration is further explained by two interrelated reasons.[231] First, it would be strange to

[223] ibid 411.
[224] Kunda (n 32) 246.
[225] Magnus (n 16) 674.
[226] Harris (n 151) 312–13.
[227] Großfeld and Junker (n 99) 136.
[228] ibid.
[229] Magnus (n 16) 675.
[230] Freitag (n 153) 115.
[231] Radtke (n 19) 350.

regulate exclusively substantive law consideration in a set of rules (convention or regulation) the aim of which is the unification of conflict-of-laws rules. Second, the extent of substantive law consideration through the national rules of contract law depends on the choices and solutions of national law. This is available even without providing for it in a conflict-of-laws convention or regulation. Therefore, an EU convention or regulation should provide something more than substantive law consideration and this is the application by virtue of conflict of laws.

vi. Discretion of the Court

In applying Article 9(3), national courts are not obliged to give effect to foreign overriding mandatory norms; they clearly enjoy discretion. In relation to the Rome Convention, this made it possible to give effect to the mandatory rules of foreign countries with which the situation shows a close connection; Fawcett noted that although the freedom of the court in doing so leads to some uncertainty, the alternative – the application of giving effect to foreign overriding norms instead – would result in compelling the forum to apply foreign overriding mandatory norms that are contrary to the interests of the forum state.[232]

Sometimes, the extensiveness of this discretion is stressed; sometimes, on the contrary, its limited nature. Clearly, the court is obliged to have regard to the criteria set out in the second sentence of this paragraph, namely the nature and purpose of the overriding mandatory norm and the consequences of its application or non-application. The French *Moller Maersk* judgment, which will be discussed later, shows that the consideration of these factors may not be ignored: such an omission may result in the annulment of the judgment. This course of action is supposed to exclude any arbitrariness.[233] Judgments must be justified; the court has to state the reasons explaining the application or non-application of a given overriding mandatory norm.[234] The consideration of the above-mentioned criteria and the justification of a judgment is, in principle, a legal question and as such may be normally subject to review by a higher court.[235]

However, if we focus on the application of economic sanctions, the situation is more difficult. Even if the court considers the nature and purpose of an economic sanction imposed by a third state and the consequences of its application or non-application and the decision to be well supported by formal legal reasons, courts often also take foreign policy considerations into account. Foreign policy arguments may hardly be subject to review, since a higher-level court is not more competent on political questions than a lower-level court. Theoretically, political arguments could be fully excluded from the scope of a judicial decision, but if we

[232] James J Fawcett, 'Evasion of Law and Mandatory Rules in Private International Law' (1990) 49 *CLJ* 44, 61.

[233] Kunda (n 32) 243.

[234] ibid 244.

[235] ibid.

look at the decisions on economic sanctions, we can notice that even supreme or higher-level courts rely on foreign policy arguments when deciding on the applicability of economic sanctions.

vii. The Exhaustive Nature of Article 9 of the Rome I Regulation

In the legal literature, the question arose as to whether any overriding mandatory norm of countries other than those referred to in Article 9 (those of the forum and the place of performance) may be given effect. The question has been posed as to whether Article 9 also excludes the consideration of foreign economic sanctions at the level of substantive law in addition to the prohibition of the conflict-of-laws application of overriding mandatory norms of other states.

Certain academics in the legal literature argued that Article 9 realises the full harmonisation of conflict-of-laws norms concerning overriding mandatory provisions and it is exhaustive in nature towards the conflict-of-laws application of other overriding mandatory rules, but not necessarily their inclusion through substantive law consideration.[236] Some authors argued in favour of the fully exhaustive nature of Article 9 and even against the substantive law consideration of foreign overriding mandatory provisions other than those referred to in Article 9.[237] Giving effect to other foreign economic sanctions by national courts endangers the unification of conflict-of-laws rules, which was an objective of the Rome Convention and the Rome I Regulation.[238] It has also been argued that the exhaustive nature of Article 9(3) allows substantive law consideration only subject to the conditions of that provision.[239] The exclusive nature of Article 9 is also confirmed by the codification history of Article 9(3), ie, the deviation of the wording of the Rome Convention and the purpose of thereby limiting the applicability of foreign overriding mandatory norms.[240] In comparison to Article 7(1) of the Rome Convention, the more restrictive nature of Article 9(3) was intended to promote legal certainty that precludes giving effect to foreign overriding mandatory provisions other than the *lex loci solutionis*.[241] When Article 9(3) is seen as a means of substantive law consideration, it would be odd to allow any substantive law consideration outside the scope of Article 9. Giving effect to other foreign overriding mandatory norms at the level of substantive law would clearly imply the circumvention of Article 9. In order not to ignore cases where the imposing state can factually hinder performance, as an exception to the exhaustive character of Article 9, Cremer

[236] Mankowski (n 133) 486–87 and 489–92.
[237] Harris (n 151) 332–34.
[238] Hans Jürgen Sonnenberger, 'Die Eingriffsnorm: ein internationalprivatrechtliches σκανδαλον? Beobachtungen und Betrachtungen' in Bernhard Großfeld, Rolf Sack, Thomas MJ Möllers, Josef Drexl and Andreas Heinemann (eds), *Festschrift für Wolfgang Fikentscher* (Mohr Siebeck, 1998) 283, 290.
[239] Hauser (n 19) 114–17.
[240] Harris (n 151) 332; Mankowski (n 133) 486–87.
[241] Harris (n 151) 332.

suggested considering them as facts (and not legal norms to be considered under Article 9(3)) that may be given effect under the *lex causae*.[242]

The dominant view of the legal literature has found that Article 9 does not exclude other foreign overriding mandatory norms from being taken into consideration at the level of substantive law.[243] This position takes as a point of departure that the Rome I Regulation only aims at conflict-of-laws harmonisation, but not the unification of substantive contract law. National substantive contract laws can therefore decide what significance is to be attributed to relevant facts, such as economic sanctions, in terms of the performance of the contract. National contract law determines the scope of the principle of *pacta sunt servanda*, *clausula rebus sic stantibus*, frustration, *force majeure*, the loss of the contractual cause or the impossibility of performance.[244] International decisional harmony underlying the harmonisation of EU private international law may also justify giving effect to any foreign overriding mandatory provision,[245] though other authors reject this argument based on international decisional harmony as an outdated concept.[246]

Moreover, even conflict-of-laws arguments may support the possibility of giving effect to foreign overriding mandatory norms. Bonomi points out that the same reasons may explain giving effect to foreign overriding mandatory norms other than those of the place of performance, namely shared values and interests, which can also be present in the case of countries other than the *lex loci solutionis*.[247] Such an approach can contribute to reducing forum shopping and increasing the chances of the recognition and enforcement of the decision in the country imposing the foreign overriding mandatory norm.[248] It can also be added that the preference for the place of performance may be seen as arbitrary, as this connecting factor does not necessarily imply a closer connection to the case than other possible connecting factors (eg, the parties' habitual residence).[249]

This question seems to have been decided by the CJEU in its *Nikiforidis* judgment. In *Nikiforidis*, the CJEU held that Article 9 of the Rome I Regulation provides an exhaustive list of overriding mandatory provisions to which the court of the forum may give effect.[250] However, the Court noted that Article 9 does not preclude the court from taking into account the overriding mandatory norms of other states as a matter of fact, insofar as this is provided for by a substantive rule of

[242] Cremer (n 61) 21.

[243] Renner (n 21) 209; Chris Thomale, 'Österreichisches Arbeitsvertragsstatut und deutsches Betriebsverfassungsrecht – intertemporale Dimensionen ausländischer Eingriffsnormen' (2013) 33 *IPRax* 375, 379; Mankowski (n 133) 491; Bonomi (n 32) 240–41; Remien (n 1) 3331; Garcimartín Alférez (n 18) 605.

[244] See Mankowski (n 133) 491.

[245] Thomale (n 243) 379.

[246] Mankowski (n 133) 487.

[247] Bonomi (n 32) 240.

[248] ibid 241.

[249] ibid.

[250] *Nikiforidis* (n 13) para 49.

the law governing the contract.[251] The CJEU explained that the Rome I Regulation only harmonises conflict-of-laws rules, but not the substantive rules of contract law.[252] The case did not concern economic sanctions, but the determination of the law applicable to a labour contract. However, the logic of the decision may be transferred to economic sanctions.

The decision may seem somewhat surprising, given the fact that the CJEU stressed foreseeability and legal certainty when excluding the application of overriding mandatory norms imposed by states other than those referred to in Article 9 of the Rome I Regulation.[253] The same factors would point to the exclusion of the substantive law consideration of foreign overriding mandatory provisions. Nevertheless, *Nikiforidis* makes it possible to take foreign economic sanctions as facts at the level of the substantive assessment of the case. It is not a coincidence that this possibility arose regarding a case referred by a German court, since this approach is in line with earlier German judicial practice.

The solution provided by *Nikiforidis* was welcomed in the legal literature as contributing to material justice without violating the integrity of conflict of laws.[254] The substantive law consideration promotes the interests of the parties in the concrete case, in particular those of the debtor, when he is exempted from a contractual obligation the performance of which is impossible or when he should comply with conflicting obligations.[255] Consideration of foreign overriding mandatory norms is also possible when they could not be applicable as law because of their illegality or the opposing interests of the forum. The *Nikiforidis* judgment makes it possible to give effect to the overriding mandatory norms of countries other than those referred to in Article 9 as a matter of fact. However, there is no reason not to extend this interpretation to cases when the foreign overriding mandatory norm is not considered as a matter of fact, but in another way at the level of substantive law. A foreign overriding mandatory norm is not necessarily considered at the level of substantive law due to its factual effect, but because of its normative content approved by the forum state. For example, in the case of a contract violating a foreign overriding mandatory norm, such as a contract by which the parties endeavour to escape from the application of an economic sanction, the overriding mandatory norm may be considered because the contract breaches good morals and as such is prohibited under substantive contract law.

From the perspective of the sanctioning state, it is immaterial whether the forum applies or gives effect to its economic sanction.[256] The state imposing the sanction deems these norms to be applicable and will do everything to apply them.[257]

[251] ibid para 51.
[252] ibid para 52.
[253] Roth (n 52) 183.
[254] Escudey (n 136) 2.B.
[255] Roth (n 52) 183.
[256] Mankowski (n 133) 489.
[257] ibid.

The forum can give effect to foreign economic sanctions as facts, irrespective of Article 9 of the Rome I Regulation.

IV. Conclusion

Foreign overriding mandatory provisions may be applied or otherwise given effect if this is permitted by the law of the forum. The Rome Convention (as well as the Rome I Regulation) constitutes such a legal basis.

Economic sanctions qualify as overriding mandatory provisions in private international law, and they are most often applied as overriding mandatory provisions of the forum. In accordance with the express authorisation of Article 9(2) of the Rome I Regulation, the courts of the Member States do not hesitate to apply sanctions imposed by the EU as part of the law of the forum. There is no problem here: the courts of the Member States seem to apply EU sanctions uniformly.

Nevertheless, concerns arise if the economic sanction has been imposed by a law other than the *lex fori* if this different law is not the law of a Member State. This implies that the economic sanction may be located in the *lex causae* or in the law of another state. It would be desirable to have a common EU approach towards these sanctions. However, such a position is currently missing.

The applicability of overriding mandatory provisions – and thus economic sanctions – of the *lex causae* is debated. This is because the Rome I Regulation is silent as to the overriding mandatory provisions of the *lex causae*. Some of the legal literature and practice hold it self-evident that the governing law also embraces public law provisions. However, another group of legal scholars and court practice construe the reference to the designated law in a narrow sense, limiting the reference to foreign private law norms (in the absence of a special connection, a *Sonderaknüpfung*), thereby excluding the application of foreign overriding mandatory provisions that have a public law origin.

Even more serious uncertainties arise concerning economic sanctions imposed by a law other than that of the forum or the *lex causae*. Article 9(3) of the Rome I Regulation allows courts only to give effect to the overriding mandatory provisions 'of the country where the obligations arising out of the contract have to be or have been performed, in so far as those overriding mandatory provisions render the performance of the contract unlawful'. National courts have some discretion in terms of giving effect to the economic sanctions of third states. The courts of the Member States may exercise their discretion subject to the examination of the factors mentioned in Article 9(3). The decision of the court must be justified and indicate the reasons for the application or non-application of the economic sanction. At the same time, although Article 7(1) of the Rome Convention and Article 9(3) of the Rome I Regulation enumerate similar lists of factors to be considered before giving effect to an economic sanction, these do not really provide precise pointers for the court, and how they will be taken into account is not predictable from the point of view of the parties. This may already result in differences in applying non-EU economic sanctions. The criteria mentioned in the second sentence of Article 9(3) – the nature and purpose of the overriding mandatory provisions and the consequences of their application or non-application – provide a possibility for taking foreign policy considerations into account. It is broadly accepted in the legal literature that Article 9(3) requires the interests involved to be examined and balanced. This includes the examination of foreign policy interests; in most cases, the forum will only apply an economic sanction from a third country which is in accordance with the foreign policy interests of its own state.

The issue of the application of the overriding mandatory provisions, including economic sanctions, of the *lex causae* could be settled first by way of legislation. The Rome I Regulation should be amended so as to make clear whether the governing law also embraces its overriding mandatory provisions, including public law norms. As we have already discussed, the inclusion of such a rule in the Rome I Regulation was already suggested by the Max Planck Institute in its Proposal on the Conversion of the Rome Convention into a Community Instrument. Second, the CJEU could orientate court practice concerning the application of the overriding mandatory provisions of the *lex causae*, but a statement by the CJEU is dependent on a request for preliminary ruling in a concrete legal dispute.

The leeway enjoyed by the courts based on Article 9 of the Rome I Regulation does not prevent inconsistent decisions involving economic sanctions, which does not promote legal certainty and may call into question the coherence between private international law and EU foreign policy action. It can therefore be established that the first source of the lack of legal certainty and coherence related to the application of foreign economic sanctions is the open-textured EU legislation. Another problem is the differences in the judicial practice of the Member States when deciding on economic sanctions imposed by third countries. These problems, far from being purely theoretical ones, appear in reality, which becomes visible when we examine the judicial practice of the courts of the Member States.

6

The Judicial Practice of the Member States

After the presentation of Article 7 of the Rome Convention and Article 9 of the Rome I Regulation on overriding mandatory provisions, it is obvious that many uncertainties surround the application of these articles in general and particularly when the issue of the application of economic sanctions arises. Therefore, it is not surprising that the supple rules gave rise to divergent court practice in the Member States. This concerns in particular the application of overriding mandatory provisions, including economic sanctions, of the *lex causae*, and when the economic sanctions of third countries may be given effect.

This chapter concentrates on court decisions on the application of economic sanctions of three selected jurisdictions: France, Germany and England. The choice of these legal systems may be justified for various reasons. First, these legal systems represent different legal families. Second, and turning to economic sanctions, it will be demonstrated that we find instances in French judicial practice for excluding a priori economic sanctions of countries not referred to in Article 9 of the Rome I Regulation, while Germany is a country where there is a long tradition of taking foreign overriding mandatory provisions into account at the level of substantive law. English law previously relied on the concept of public policy to take foreign economic sanctions into account, but the issue of whether it took place as a conflict-of-laws rule or within the purview of domestic substantive law remained hazy. English law demonstrates well how EU unification of conflict of laws affected the application of economic sanctions and, due to the recent development, the question also arises as to how Brexit will influence the application of economic sanctions by English courts.

The analysis extends to the court practice of the relevant jurisdictions before the Rome Convention and the Rome I Regulation, because the approach towards the interpretation of these legal sources in the states examined can only be understood in its historical embedment.

The conclusions of this examination are somewhat limited as the number of cases in the practice of national courts where the application of economic sanctions arose in a private international law context is not too high. This may be due to various reasons. First, the parties may include into their contract more general or more specific clauses addressing the intervention of economic sanctions, which may prevent the need to have recourse to litigation. Second, the parties have the option of stipulating arbitration; in this way, cases involving economic sanctions eschew the state judicial system and many of them certainly do not come to light and are never published because of the confidentiality of arbitration. It may also be noticed that there are more court decisions in Germany than in England or France. This may perhaps be the result of the broader application of the above techniques in the latter states. To reveal the precise reasons would require an empirical analysis which is beyond the scope of this book. Our aim is simply to demonstrate that there are diverging tendencies in national court practice in the treatment of cases involving economic sanctions, which cause serious uncertainties for business actors and do not promote a uniform EU approach in particular as regards economic sanctions imposed by third countries. These decisions also prove that, in addition to formal legal arguments, the courts of the selected Member States are not afraid of using foreign policy arguments in their deliberation.

I. France

A. Foreign Economic Sanctions in French Judicial Practice

Formerly, French legal thinking also followed the idea that foreign public law rules cannot be applied[1] and we find examples in French judicial practice which supported this position. A Russian restriction on the export of the ruble was not applied by the Cour d'appel de Paris because of its political and penal nature, noting that the purpose of legislation was simply to protect the national legal tender.[2] It was therefore held that it has a territorial effect only. However, this resistance has subsequently disappeared.[3] It became the dominant view that the *lex causae* also embraces overriding mandatory provisions, including public law norms.[4] As to the French judicial practice, the *Royal Dutch* decisions are usually referred to as having made this turn clear.[5] In this case, the Cour de cassation recognised that a Dutch decree (applicable as part of the law governing the relationship between the company and the shareholder) requiring the validation of shares of Dutch companies by a declaration by shareholders wherever they stay is not incompatible with the French *ordre public*, even if failing to make the declaration within the deadline set by the decree resulted in the deprivation of the holders of the shares of their

[1] E Fohrer-Dedeurwaerder, *La prise en considération des normes étrangères* (LGDJ, 2008) 253–54.

[2] Cour d'appel de Paris, 30 June 1933 (1933) JDI 963, 968.

[3] Marie-Laure Niboyet and Géraud de Geouffre de la Pradelle, *Droit international privé*, 5th edn (LGDJ, 2015) 142–43.

[4] Sophie Wernert, 'Le gel d'avoirs étrangers: Aspects de droit international public et de droit international privé' (PhD thesis, Université Paris II Panthéon-Assas, 2001) 90–91; Patrick Kinsch, *Le fait du prince étranger* (LGDJ, 1994) 382.

[5] Cour de cassation, Chambre civile 1, 25 janvier 1966 and Cour de cassation, Chambre civile 1, 17 octobre 1972.

rights and the transfer of their rights to the Dutch state. Contracts were considered to be null and void by virtue of the application of foreign exchange control provisions constituting part of the *lex causae*.[6] Furthermore, even in cases where foreign overriding mandatory provisions were not part of the *lex causae*, French judicial practice gave effect to them through the provisions of French substantive contract law.[7] The former Articles 1108, 1131 and 1133 of the French Code civil, requiring a lawful cause for the validity of a contract, could serve as a basis for giving effect to foreign prohibitions challenging the validity of the contract. Article 6 continues to prohibit any derogation by contract from acts concerning public policy and good morals. Moreover, a foreign economic sanction may also be given effect as a ground of *force majeure* under Article 1218 of the Code civil.

In the *Massardy* decision rendered in 1965, the Cour d'appel de Paris permitted the French minority directors of Fruehauf-France, SA, a French company, to appoint a provisional administrator to execute a contract on the sale of trailers entered into with another French company, Automobiles Berliet, in violation of a US embargo against the People's Republic of China, as the goods had to be delivered to the latter country.[8] The French company was in the majority ownership of a group of US persons who intended to comply with the US sanction and refused to perform the contract with Berliet. This was opposed by a group of French minority shareholders because of the harsh consequences of the refusal of performance. Berliet was the largest and habitual customer of Fruehauf-France and delivery by Freuhauf was important in order for it to be able to perform a contract with its Chinese buyer. The non-performance of the contract would have exposed Fruehauf-France to severe consequences, primarily a damages action on the part of Berliet and the loss of future business. In the absence of a licence by the US Treasury Department, the performance of the contract was unlawful under US law and a licence could not be expected to be issued under the political circumstances. The negotiations with Berliet before a French court on the termination of the contract were unfruitful. For this reason, the French minority directors requested the appointment of a provisional administrator for the management of the company for a definite period of time, the execution of the contract and the general assembly of the company to be convened. This was granted and the Cour d'appel de Paris affirmed the order on the appointment of a temporary administrator made by the court of first instance. The Cour d'appel de Paris took into account in detail the consequences of the non-performance of the contract (the exposure to damages action and its impact on the financial situation, the moral credit and the employees

[6] Cour de cassation, Chambre civile 1, 6 février 1973, (1975) 102 JDI 66; Tribunal de grande instance de Paris, 8 et 12 mars 1985, (1985) Recueil Dalloz, Informations rapides 346 and 500.

[7] Cour d'appel de Paris, Chambre 1, 15 mai 1975, RCDIP 1976, 690.

[8] Cour d'appel de Paris, Chambre 14, 22 mai 1965, Gazette du Palais, 1965 II, 86–90; English summary (1966) ILM 476. William Laurence Craig, 'Application of the Trading with the Enemy Act to Foreign Corporations Owned by Americans: Reflections on Fruehauf v Massardy' (1969–70) 83 *Harvard Law Review* 579.

of the company). It noted that the judge must give preference to the interests of the company to those of certain shareholders, even if they are majority shareholders, and as a consequence did not apply the US economic sanction. It is interesting to note that the US authorities did not impose any penalty on the French company or its owners for not complying with the US sanctions.[9]

As was referred to earlier, French courts sometimes gave effect to foreign overriding mandatory provisions at the level of substantive law. The *Bank Markazi* case is seen by certain authors as an example of taking a foreign economic sanction into account, although it did not belong to the governing law. As a reaction to the Iranian hostage crisis, Executive Order No 12170 of 14 November 1979 issued by US President Carter 'blocked all property and interests in property of the Government of Iran, its instrumentalities and controlled entities and the Central Bank of Iran which are or become subject to the jurisdiction of the United States or which are in or come within the possession or control of persons subject to the jurisdiction of the United States'.[10] Bank Markazi Iran, the central bank of Iran, kept a deposit on the account of the City Bank Paris, the subsidiary of the American City Bank.[11] Bank Markazi claimed for the restitution of the deposited amount of $50 million or its value in French francs with interest. City Bank Paris recognised its obligation to pay, but refused to perform because of the executive order applicable to foreign entities controlled by US persons. The judge of expedited matters seised in the case established that a bank established and registered in France is bound to comply with its obligations stemming from a deposit contract in accordance with French law. The judge distinguished the obligation to reimburse the amount and its performance, and it noted that although the obligation to reimburse the amount could not be called into question, its performance and the modalities thereof raised difficulties which were deemed to be beyond the competence of the judge of the expedited matters seised in the case. The judge referred the parties in this question to the court deciding on the merits of the case. However, he indicated that American dollar was the currency of the deposit and the fact that City Bank Paris was a subsidiary of the US City Bank.

Wernert sees this case as taking the US sanction into consideration.[12] Analysing this case, Gianviti argued that the court deciding on the merits of the case should have applied French law in the absence of the choice of law by the parties and that even if US law could have been applied, it could have been established that it violated the French *ordre public*.[13] In his view, the US sanction could not have been taken into consideration as a fact at the level of substantive contract law as a

[9] Cedric Ryngaert, 'Extraterritorial Export Controls (Secondary Boycotts)' (2008) 7 *Chinese Journal of International Law* 625, 630.

[10] Executive Order No 12170, 14 November 1979, 44 FR 65729.

[11] Tribunal de grande instance de Paris, 21 décembre 1979 et 21 janvier 1980, with the case comment of Christian Gavalda, Gazette du Palais 1980, 13 mars 1980, 154.

[12] Wernert (n 4) 92.

[13] François Gianviti, 'Le blocage des avoirs officiels iraniens par les Etats-Unis (executive order du 14 novembre 1979)' (1980) 69 *Revue critique de droit international privé* 279, 296–301.

ground of *force majeure*, since it could not be concluded that the French bank was deprived of all means to satisfy the claim of the Iranian bank.[14]

B. Article 7(1) of the Rome Convention: *Moller Maersk*

Among the states examined in this book, only France did not make a reservation to Article 7(1) of the Rome Convention. This is why it is interesting to examine how the Cour de cassation interpreted Article 7(1) of the Rome Convention. The *Moller Maersk* case[15] concerned the application of this provision to a foreign import prohibition, which was based on public health reasons. However, the conclusions of the court apply without doubt to trade restrictions related to foreign policy. Here, Société Viol Frères, a seller of frozen meat, had charged Société Fauveder, a freight forwarder, with organising the transport of the goods from France to Ghana. The freight forwarder entrusted Moller Maersk, a Danish carrier, with transporting the goods to Ghana. However, Ghana introduced an embargo on meat of French origin during the 'mad cow' crisis. The carrier returned the perishable products to Viol and the goods were sold urgently. The seller claimed damages from the freight forwarder and the carrier for non-delivery of the goods. In its counterclaim, Moller Maersk relied on the nullity of the transport contract due to the unlawfulness of its cause under Articles 1131 and 1133 of the Code civil.[16] However, the fact that the adoption of the embargo by Ghana preceded the conclusion of the contracts between Viol and Fauveder, as well as the transport contract,[17] could weaken the position of Moller Maersk, since, as a professional carrier should have been aware of an existing embargo and should have refused to enter into the contract.[18]

[14] ibid 302–03.

[15] Cour de cassation, Chambre commerciale, financière et économique, Arrêt n° 330 du 16 mars 2010 (08-21.511). See the comments by Cyril Nourissat, 'Lois de police étrangères devant le juge français du contrat international : une première sous l'empire de la Convention de Rome et peut-être pas une dernière sous l'empire du règlement "Rome I"' (2010) 5 *Revue Lamy droit des affaires* 63, 63; Louis d'Avout and Dominique Bureau, 'Lois de police étrangères devant le juge français du contrat international' (2010) 84 *La Semaine Juridique – Entreprise et Affaires* 18, 23; Pascal Deumier, Jean-Baptiste Racine and Édouard Treppoz, 'La loi de police étrangère : une possibilité que le juge a l'obligation d'envisager' (2010) *Revue des contrats* 1385, 1385; See Aurore Marchand, 'Note – Cass com, 16 mars 2010, no 08-21.511' (2011) 138 *Journal du droit international* 99, 99; Philippe Delebecque, 'Transport maritime. Loi de police étrangère. Qualification. Effet (oui)' (2010) *Revue trimestrielle de droit commercial et de droit économique* 457; Jean-Pierre Mattout, 'Opérations internationales' in Jean-Pierre Mattout and André Prüm, 'Chronique – Droit bancaire, Janvier 2010 – juin 2010 : Clair-obscure' (2010) 195 *Droit & Patrimoine* 100, 109; Sylvain Bollée, 'Conflits des lois en matière de contrats' in Louis d'Avout and Sylvain Bollée, 'Panorama – Droit du commerce international (septembre 2009 – août 2010)' (2010) *Receuil Dalloz* 2323, 2329; Fabienne Jault-Seseke, 'Panorama – Droit internal privé (février 2010–février 2011)' (2011) *Receuil Dalloz* 1374, 1375.

[16] Report of M Potocki (extract), *Droit maritime français* (2010) 390, 398.

[17] ibid 398.

[18] Sandrine Sana-Chaille de Nere, 'Transport maritime et lois de police étrangères' (2010) *Droit maritime français* 367, 368.

The Cour d'appel d'Angers found that the embargo did not have an obligatory force concerning the freight forwarder and the carrier and established their responsibility. The law applicable was French law and thus the object of the transport contract was not unlawful under Article 1133 of the Code civil. The Cour d'appel reached this conclusion without having recourse to the Rome Convention.

The Cour de cassation annulled the judgment of the Cour d'appel d'Angers, which should have examined the potential effects of the embargo under Article 7 of the Rome Convention. Based on Article 7(1) of the Rome Convention, effect may be given to the mandatory rules of the law of another country with which the situation has a close connection, if and insofar as, under the law of the latter country, those rules must be applied whatever the law applicable to the contract. Even if the governing law was French law, the court had an obligation to apply the Rome Convention, and in particular Article 7, and consider the possibility of giving effect to a foreign overriding mandatory norm. The court statement did not oblige the court to apply foreign overriding mandatory norms, such as the embargo imposed by Ghana, but it must be construed as requiring the court, at least, to consider the applicability of a foreign overriding mandatory norm under Article 7(1) of the Rome Convention.[19] The Cour de cassation imposed this obligation on the court, even though the interests protected by the embargo were not in line with French interests.[20] The court did not take a position on the question of whether Article 7 of the Rome Convention implies the application or the consideration of a foreign overriding norm, enabling the pursuit of either of the two approaches,[21] and how a French court should give effect to a foreign mandatory rule.

After the decision of the Cour de cassation, the case was referred to the Cour d'appel de Poitiers. This court decided that effect must be given to the Ghanaian embargo.[22] The prohibition of importation of meat from France constituted an overriding mandatory norm to protect public health in relation to mad cow disease. The embargo showed up a close connection to the situation, because the recipient of the goods was located in Ghana. The embargo rendered exporting meat from France to Ghana impossible. The Cour d'appel de Poitiers concluded that the overriding mandatory provisions of Ghanaian law on the embargo must be given effect, which had the consequence that the transportation contract was declared null and void due to the impossible purpose, and it stated that Viol Frères could not render Moller Maersk responsible for the defaulted performance of the transport contract.

[19] ibid 372–73.

[20] Philippe Delebecque, 'L'acceuil des lois de police étrangères' (2010) *Revue de droit des transports* 15, 16; Sana-Chaille de Nere (n 18) 372.

[21] Deumier, Racine and Treppoz (n 15) 1389; Mattout (n 15) 110.

[22] Cour d'appel de Poitiers, Chambre civile, 29 novembre 2011, N° 10/03500.

C. Article 9(3) of the Rome I Regulation: *Giti*

Article 9(3) of the Rome I Regulation was interpreted by French courts in the specific context of economic sanctions. In the *Giti* case,[23] the Cour d'appel de Paris did not give effect to a US prohibition to export goods to Iran laid down by Article 560-204 of the Code of Federal Regulations[24] concerning a distribution contract entered into between a French subsidiary of an American company and an Iranian company. The French company undertook to supply HIV testing devices to the Iranian company. However, Bio-Rad SNC suspended the delivery of goods to its distributor, Giti Tajhiz Teb Co Ltd, on the grounds that it was the subsidiary of the American Bio-Rad Inc and thus was covered by the American embargo against Iran. The US embargo is very broadly tailored: it prohibits the exportation, re-exportation, sale or supply, directly or indirectly, from the US, or by a US person, wherever located, of any goods, technology, or services to Iran or the government of Iran.[25] 'A US person' also involved the foreign branches of entities organised under the laws of the US.[26] At first sight, it could have been inferred that the embargo did not apply to Bio-Rad SNC as it was a subsidiary and not a branch of the US parent company. However, due to the expansive interpretation by the Office of Foreign Assets Control (OFAC), even subsidiaries were exposed to penalties in the case of non-compliance.[27] Giti brought a damages action against the French company due to the breach of the contract by the latter. The place of performance was Iran and the governing law was French law. The court pointed out that, under Article 9 of the Rome I Regulation, no effect may be given to any foreign law other than that of the state of the place of performance when the performance of the contract is rendered illegal by the law of that state. US law could not be given effect as different from French (*lex fori*) or Iranian (place of performance) rules, the only rules applicable under Article 9. As a consequence, the French company was held responsible for the breach of the contract: it should have performed in spite of the existence of the US embargo.

The refusal to apply US law undoubtedly has advantages. The burden of the civil law consequences of the embargo imposed by a third state, the law of which was not applicable to the contract, was not shifted to the party intending to perform the contract and the country which was subject to the economic sanction, but falls upon the company that brought about the rupture of the commercial relationship.[28] Even if it is recognised that the US sanction could have been given

[23] Cour d'appel de Paris, 25 février 2015, n° 12/23757.

[24] 31 CFR Part 560 – Iranian Transactions and Sanctions Regulations.

[25] 31 CFR § 560.204 Prohibited exportation, re-exportation, sale, or supply of goods, technology, or services to Iran.

[26] 31 CFR 560.314 – United States person; US person.

[27] Matteo Winkler and Arnaud Lacombe, 'Mesures à vocation extraterritoriale et lois de police : un revers à l'hégémonie juridique outre-Atlantique?' (2015) 21 *Recueil Dalloz* 1260, 1262–63.

[28] Louis d'Avout, 'Opérations – L'extraterritorialité contrariée par la théorie des lois de police?' in Louis d'Avout and Sylvain Bollée (eds), 'Panorama – Droit du commerce international, août 2014–juillet 2015' (2015) *Recueil Dalloz* 2031.

effect through substantive French law as a ground for impossibility of the object of the contract or *force majeure*, the formal approach liberated the court to find legal reasons or perhaps foreign policy motives to justify the consideration of the economic sanction at the level of substantive law.[29]

The case could have been assessed differently if the EU had imposed comparable economic sanctions against Iran, since such sanctions could or should have been applied by the French court as part of the *lex fori*.[30] Following a formal approach, as the Cour d'appel de Paris did, sanctions other than those imposed by the state of the *lex fori* and the state of the place of performance (and potentially the *lex causae*) may not be given effect. It is asserted that a party potentially threatened by penalties for the non-compliance with an embargo must take care to insert a clause in the contract in advance which provides for the exemption from performance in the event of the intervention of an economic sanction.[31] This may be illustrated by the use of OFAC sanctions compliance clauses concerning US sanctions.[32] However, inserting such a clause into the contract is, of course, subject to the acceptance of the other party and we have already addressed the uncertainties concerning the admissibility of submission clauses.

Although recognising it as a legally well-justified decision, certain authors called into question the practical soundness of the *Giti* judgment.[33] Accordingly, a foreign overriding norm cannot be disregarded when it has an impact on the contractual relationship of the parties.[34] For example, if it actually impedes the performance of one of the parties, its effect must be recognised. The judgment essentially ignores the existence and potential force of economic sanctions adopted by third states, such as the US. Under US law, serious administrative (withdrawal of export licence or licence of operation, or exclusion of financial institutions from the US dollar clearing system) and criminal sanctions (fines and prison sentence) may be imposed on those who violate the US sanctions regime. Even if a court in an EU Member State dispenses with the application of a US economic sanction by correctly applying Article 9(3), the company is exposed to being penalised by US authorities. This is demonstrated by the sanctions imposed on various European banks that tried to avoid US sanctions. Most notably, authors usually refer to the

[29] ibid.

[30] Yann Beckers and Nicolas Demigneux, 'Les mesures d'embargo américaines édictées par l'OFAC sont-elles des lois de police étrangère applicables en France?' (2015) 141 *Actes pratiques et ingénierie sociétaire* 1.

[31] ibid 2.

[32] ibid.

[33] Winkler and Lacombe (n 27) 1262–63. Peter Mankowski, 'Drittstaatliche Embargonormen, Außenpolitik im IPR, Berücksichtigung von Fakten statt Normen: Art. 9 Abs. 3 Rom I-VO im praktischen Fall (zu Cour d'appel de Paris, 25.2.2015 – 12/23757)' (2016) 36 *IPRax* 485, 490 agrees on this point.

[34] See Sana-Chaille de Nere (n 18) 374–75 concerning the *Moller Maersk* case.

case of BNP Paribas SA. In order to prevent proceedings, the French bank entered a guilty plea with the Department of Justice and agreed to assume the obligation to pay an amount of nearly $9 billion for conducting financial transactions on behalf of Iranian, Cuban and Sudanese companies subject to US sanctions.[35] Moreover, BNP Paribas also agreed to be subject to monitoring to supervise the internal processes to be introduced for ensuring legality for the protection of state interests. The US authorities considered the acts of BNP Paribas to be a conspiracy to deliberately avoid US sanctions. The jurisdiction of US authorities was principally based on the fact that BNP Paribas acted as a financial intermediary for transactions in US dollars and the amounts went through the US clearing system. The establishment of the jurisdiction in this way was based on a weak link. Several authors call into question whether the US jurisdiction was well founded in this case, as it was based solely on the location of the clearing service and the use of US currency.[36] Although clearing took place in the US, this was an ancillary operation to a transaction taking place entirely outside the US, which does not suffice to establish territorial jurisdiction.[37] In addition, if the use of US dollars was sufficient to establish the competence of US authorities, the US would have practically universal jurisdiction.[38] The effects doctrine has also been rejected in such cases, as the foreign conduct does not have direct, substantial and foreseeable effects in US territory.[39] The application of the protective principle presupposing the need for the protection of the vital interests of the state asserting jurisdiction is also controversial, in extending sanctions legislation to entities incorporated in other countries but dealing with the target states.[40] On the contrary, d'Avout found it acceptable to establish US territorial competence if an order of payment is made with a US bank or a bank posting takes place in the US territory, and additionally noted that the documents related to the guilty plea of BNP Paribas did not indicate

[35] Department of Justice, 1 May 2015, BNP Paribas Sentenced for Conspiring to Violate the International Emergency Economic Powers Act and the Trading with the Enemy Act, www.justice.gov/opa/pr/bnp-paribas-sentenced-conspiring-violate-international-emergency-economic-powers-act-and; Winkler and Lacombe (n 27) 1263.

[36] Julien Bueb and Marion Geffrault, 'Un colosse chez les géants. Splendeur et déclin de la stratégie économique américaine' in Frédéric Charillon and Célia Belin (eds), *Les États-Unis dans le monde* (CNRS, 2016) 83, 99–100; Mathias Audit, 'Sanctions contre BNP Paribas : l'extraterritorialité du droit américain est-elle conforme au droit international?' *Les Echos*, 25 June 2014, http://archives.lesechos.fr/archives/cercle/2014/06/25/cercle_101744.htm. More generally, see Michael Gurson, 'The US Jurisdiction over Transfers of US Dollars between Foreigners and over Ownership of US Dollar Accounts in Foreign Banks' (2004) *Columbia Business Law Review* 721.

[37] Mathias Audit, Régis Bismuth and Astrid Mignon-Colombet, 'Sanctions et extraterritorialité du droit américain : quelles réponses pour les entreprises françaises?' (2015) 89 *La Semaine Juridique – Édition générale* 1–2, 64, 65.

[38] ibid 65.

[39] Susan Emenegger, 'Extraterritorial Economic Sanctions and Their Foundation in International Law' (2016) 33 *Arizona Journal of International & Comparative Law* 631, 656–57; Audit, Bismuth and Mignon-Colombet (n 37) 65.

[40] Emmenegger (n 39) 651–52 and 658–59.

that the use of US dollars alone would have established US jurisdiction.[41] BNP Paribas also assumed the obligation not to challenge the sanction imposed by the US authorities in any country, which indicates the global extent of the sanction.[42] Other European banks, such as Commerzbank, ING Bank and Deutsche Bank, were equally penalised by US authorities. As a matter of fact, none of these companies contested the jurisdiction of US authorities.[43]

Multinational companies may not risk being excluded from the US market. The force of US economic sanctions stems from the fact that, for multinational groups, the US market cannot be avoided, so they have to comply with the rules imposed by US law.[44] Companies tend to comply rather than taking the risk of being penalised. The risk is present, even if a court in an EU Member State does not require compliance. The infringement of a US sanction may be penalised by the withdrawal of export or other licences, the existence of which is in the vital interest of companies. In addition, companies denied export privileges are put on a public black list that endangers the reputation of the company concerned. Such cases prove the 'normative power' of the US.[45]

As a corollary of this socio-economic reality related to the enforcement of economic sanctions by US authorities, foreign undertakings are compelled to adapt themselves to the US sanction regime. In the case of the breach of US sanctions, instead of a prosecution, companies usually enter into an agreement – which may be a guilty plea, a deferred prosecution agreement or a non-prosecution agreement – with the US authorities, which suspend or abandon the prosecution.[46] A guilty plea is an agreement by which the company admits its culpability and the company may be subject to certain sanctions. BNP Paribas was subject to such a guilty plea. Within the framework of a deferred prosecution agreement, as its name suggests, the prosecution is deferred. Although it is initiated, it is then suspended immediately. The company has to recognise the facts and accept a financial sanction and launch a monitoring programme, often under the supervision of a monitor. Once these undertakings have been fulfilled over the duration of the agreement, the charges are withdrawn; if the company breaches the terms of the agreement, prosecution may be restarted. A non-prosecution agreement does not involve the start of a prosecution, but the prosecutor retains the possibility thereof if the company does not observe the agreement over its duration. A non-prosecution agreement does not necessarily presuppose the admission of a breach and the running of a

[41] Louis d'Avout, 'Sources – Entreprises mondiales, régulation locale' in Louis d'Avout and Sylvain Bollée (eds), 'Panorama – Droit du commerce international août – juillet 2014' (2014) 34 *Receuil Dalloz* 1967, 1968.

[42] Michel Menjucq, *Droit international et européen des sociétés*, 4th edn (LGDJ, 2016) 348.

[43] Antoine Garapon and Pierre Servan-Schreiben, 'Un changement de paradigme' in Antoine Garapon and Pierre Servan-Schreiben (eds), *Deals de justice* (Presses Universitaires de France, 2013) 2.

[44] Menjucq (n 42) 349; Michael Cremer, 'Embargovorschriften als Eingriffsnormen' (2016) 10 *Bucerius Law Journal* 18, 23.

[45] Bueb and Geffrault (n 36) 99.

[46] On the different forms of agreements, see Audit, Bismuth and Mignon-Colombet (n 37) 65.

monitoring programme. For this, the company undertakes to pay a fine, launch a compliance programme and accept the supervision by compliance officers.[47] The operation of the compliance programme may even require a significant reorganisation.[48] Continuously monitoring US export restrictions, which can change quickly, may be difficult and costly, particularly for smaller companies.[49]

Notwithstanding the current business practice of 'complying or paying', it has been asserted that the extraterritorial sanctions based on a narrow link could have been challenged before the ICJ on the basis of public international law, and in particular bilateral treaties, such as the Franco-American Convention of Establishment of 1959, which guarantees equal treatment for citizens and companies of the two countries, and recourse to the ICJ.[50] Such an argument could alternatively be used during negotiations at a political level with the US administration.[51]

D. Conclusion

French court practice has not excluded the application of the overriding mandatory provisions of the *lex causae* and instances involving the possibility of considering foreign overriding mandatory norms at the level of substantive law may also be found.

Giti, the single judgment interpreting Article 9 of the Rome I Regulation, adhered to the wording of this provision and was clear that the overriding mandatory provisions of states other than those referred to in Article 9 may not be applied or given effect. This approach attributes exhaustive character to Article 9 of the Rome I Regulation, even towards the substantive law consideration of economic sanctions.

This view is a legally correct one, but the reality is that the authorities of the state imposing an economic sanction can often find a way to enforce it by various penalties, such as in the US. Notwithstanding the formal approach of *Giti*, which is limited to the civil law consequences, it is not excluded that the US authorities could impose an administrative or criminal sanction on an entity that did not comply with the US sanctions regime.

Although foreign overriding mandatory norms other than those belonging to the place of performance are excluded under the Rome I Regulation, they can return in the form of certain substantive provisions of the governing law, such as those relating to the impossibility of performance or contracts breaching good

[47] Mathias Audit, 'Application extraterritoriale du droit américain : un enjeu pour les entreprises françaises' (2015) 104 *Echanges internationaux, Magazine du Comité Français de la Chambre de Commerce Internationale* 9; Bueb and Geffrault (n 36) 100.

[48] Audit (n 47) 9.

[49] Christian Forwick, *Extraterritoriale US-amerikanische Exportkontrollen. Folgen für die Vertragsgestaltung* (Verlag Recht und Wirtschaft, 1993) 65–66.

[50] Audit (n 36); Audit, Bismuth and Mignon-Colombet (n 37) 65.

[51] Audit (n 36).

morals.[52] Regarding the *Giti* judgment, d'Avout remarked that, although in the given case the court did not find it necessary to apply the US sanction through conflict of laws, it would not have been excluded to give effect to such rules by virtue of French substantive contract law.[53]

To handle foreign economic sanctions at the level of substantive law is not alien to other jurisdictions. German courts often approach cases in this way and this possibility has recently gained confirmation in the *Nikiforidis* judgment of the CJEU. As this approach differs considerably from the formal approach of the Cour d'appel de Paris in *Giti*, in the next section we discuss German judicial practice on economic sanctions.

II. Germany

A. Foreign Overriding Mandatory Provisions in German Law

There are countries where (and we would like to refer here primarily to Germany) there is a long tradition of giving effect to foreign overriding mandatory provisions, including economic sanctions, at the level of substantive law. The question of the extent to which a foreign economic sanction may be applied arose in German judicial practice well before the establishment of the EU and the adoption of common conflict-of-laws rules.

Some earlier German court judgments demonstrate that German courts applied foreign overriding mandatory norms as part of the *lex causae* subject to the *ordre public* clause. Concerning the sale of cattle, the Reichsgericht found that although it could have breached a Dutch export prohibition, this was not applied because of the *ordre public* clause of the original Article 30 EGBGB with respect to the difficulties in food supply existing in Germany caused by the blockade against Germany during the First World War.[54] This judgment is seen as the expression of the *Schuldstatutstheorie*.[55] Foreign exchange restrictions belonging to the *lex causae* were applied, such as Russian foreign exchange provisions by the Reichsgericht[56] or Austrian foreign exchange provisions to a loan agreement

[52] Louis d'Avout, 'Le sort des règles impératives dans le règlement Rome I' (2008) 184 *Receuil Dalloz* 2165, 2168.

[53] D'Avout (n 28) 2031.

[54] RG 21.10.1921, II. Zivilsenat, II 245/21, (1924) Niemeyers Zeitschrift für Internationales Recht 452.

[55] Bernhard Großfeld and Abbo Junker, *Das CoCom im internationalen Wirtschaftsrecht* (Mohr Siebeck, 1991) 112.

[56] RG Urteil vom 1.7.1930, VII 643/29. – WuR. 5 (1930), IPRspr. 1930, Nr 15, 49. See also other decisions by the Reichsgericht, RG, Urteil vom 28.5.1936 – IV 272/35, RabelsZ 10 (1936) 385, 387.

entered into between two Austrian citizens, which was governed by Austrian law.[57] However, it must be added that, in German legal literature, the dominant view has become the *Sonderanknüpfungstheorie*, barring the automatic application of foreign public law rules as part of the governing law.

Foreign trade restrictions were often taken into account through substantive contract law rules. The intervention of the First World War affected the performance of many contracts. During the First World War, due to the blockade of the UK against Germany under the Trading with the Enemy Act, goods in German vessels were sequestrated.[58] German courts rendered several judgments in such cases. The Trading with the Enemy Act could not be applied by German courts as law, but instead the factual consequences of the English regulation were taken into consideration. UK legislation was seen as colliding with the German *ordre public*. The Trading with the Enemy Act was seen as impeding the performance of the contract (*Leistungsstörung*) under German law (§ 275 BGB 1896) that otherwise governed the contract. This approach made clear that the foreign provision was not granted any normative power, but it allowed the recognition of the factual consequences of the foreign law which rendered performance impossible.[59] Zimmer explains that these cases well illustrate the fact that the substantive law consideration of foreign law does not necessarily depend on the interests of the states concerned or the values represented by the norm.[60] It had to be applied as a result of its factual consequences on the contractual relationship of the parties.[61] Zimmer argues that the question is therefore rather whether the norm requires application in the given case and whether the imposing state has the necessary power to enforce the provisions at issue.[62]

In another decision, the Reichsgericht found that a regulation of the governor of the Falkland Islands, which prohibited the export of whale oil and required it to be delivered to the UK, rendered performance impossible.[63] Thus, the Falkland Islands legislation was taken into account at the level of substantive German contract law. Regarding a contract of supply of quebracho extract between a German and an English company, the Reichsgericht accepted that the outbreak of the First World War rendered the performance of the contract impossible under

[57] Schleswig-Holsteinisches OLG, 2. ZS, Urteil vom 1.4.1954 – 3 U 7/53, IPRspr 1954 and 1955, Nr 163, 463, 464–66.

[58] See Mankowski (n 33) 490; P Mankowski, 'Deutscher Versischerer und das US-Embargo gegen Iran – ein kleines Lehrstück zu ausländischen Eingriffsnormen' (2015) *Recht der Internationalen Wirtschaft* 405, 406.

[59] Rolf Lehmann, *Zwingendes Recht dritter Staaten im internationalen Vertragsrecht* (Peter Lang, 1986) 59; Daniel Zimmer, 'Ausländisches Wirtschaftsrecht vor deutschen Zivilgerichten: Zur Unterscheidung zwischen einer normativen Berücksichtigung fremder zwingender Normen und einer bloßen Beachtung ihrer tatsächlichen Folgen' (1993) 13 *IPRax* 65, 67–68.

[60] Zimmer (n 59) 68.

[61] ibid.

[62] ibid.

[63] RG 13 November 1917, RGZ 91, 260.

German law.[64] The Reichsgericht referred back to the decision of the court of appeal in the given case, stating that English law, the Trading with the Enemy Act, was not applied (as law), but was taken into account as a hindrance of performance in the sense of German law, because it factually rendered performance impossible. As the court itself formulated, the court could and might not have kept its eyes closed when faced with the existence of the English act. In another case, linseed oil was not supplied in due time to the buyer because the goods were located in Sweden, which had issued an export prohibition after the conclusion of the contract.[65] Although the Reichsgericht found that the performance of the contract was no longer lawful, it noted that it violated neither good morals nor Article 134 BGB, which applies only to a prohibition laid down by German law. It stated that export prohibitions issued by foreign states during the war that are contrary to German interests are not to be protected by German courts. However, the seller was not expected to deliver the goods to Germany as a consequence of the Swedish export prohibition. The performance was considered impossible by the Reichsgericht in a case where the steamship transporting specific goods subject to the contract was redirected by English authorities and the goods were seized.[66] The court pointed out that the intervening English regulations had already been in force at the time of the conclusion of the contract and they were similar to an export prohibition. A Russian export prohibition on cereals that was not part of the governing German law was considered by the OLG Marienwerder at the level of substantive law as a ground impeding performance by the seller.[67]

These cases demonstrate that a foreign economic sanction violating the interests of the forum state may still be given effect because of the factual effects of the foreign restriction. Factual effects of foreign economic sanctions may not be ignored, even if they are contrary to the interests of the forum state, provided the goods concerned are located in the territory of the state imposing the sanction and it can enforce the prohibition (eg, by seizure).[68]

This approach, which permitted in principle the application of foreign public law as part of the *lex causae* subject to the *ordre public* clause, changed following a judgment of the BGH in 1959, in which the BGH established the principle of the non-application of foreign public law,[69] at least in cases where the foreign public law norm concerns the economic and political objectives of the issuing

[64] RG 28 June 1918, RGZ 93, 182, 185.

[65] RG, Urteil vom 22. Dezember 1916, II 265/16 (1917) 61 Beiträge zur Erläuterung des deutschen Rechts (Gruchot) 460.

[66] RG, Urteil vom 20.09.1918, II 137/18, (1918) Warneyers Jahrbuch der Entscheidungen Nr 217, 323.

[67] OLG Marienwerder, 14 October 1892 – *Rawitzki c Goldhaber* (1893) 20 Journal de droit international privé 908.

[68] Jürgen Basedow, 'Private Law Effects of Foreign Export Controls' (1984) 27 *German Yearbook of International Law* 109, 139.

[69] BGH Urteil vom 17.12.1959, Az: VII ZR 198/58, BGHZ 31, 367, 371. This change in the judicial practice is described by Andreas Behr, *Deutsche Unternehmen und der Israel-Boykott* (Verlag Recht und Wissenschaft, 1994) 92–93; Kirsten Anderegg, *Ausländische Eingriffsnormen im internationalen*

state and not the balancing of private interests deserving certain protection. This approach was deduced from the principle of territoriality. In a subsequent case, the exceptional applicability of foreign public law norms was extended somewhat by referring to cases where the issuing state has the actual power to enforce its own public law in addition to balancing private interests worthy of protection.[70] This solution essentially incorporated the *Machttheorie* into judicial practice. The judgment of the BGH rendered in 1959 set aside the *Schuldstatutstheorie*.[71] This restrictive judicial practice blocked the penetration of foreign overriding mandatory provisions having a public law nature into conflict of laws and laid down that a separate conflict-of-laws system exists for foreign public law norms.[72] Although further court judgments, even BGH decisions, declared the non-application of foreign public law provisions,[73] the German courts did not entirely ignore foreign public law norms, even if it did not apply them as law based on conflict-of-laws rules. The German courts were compelled to choose another way, and this is the substantive law consideration that had been already used by the Reichsgericht before. Foreign overriding mandatory rules were given effect through substantive provisions of contract law. This happened in principle in two ways:[74] first, the violation of the foreign law was seen as immoral under Article 138(1) BGB; and, second, the factual consequences of the foreign prohibition constituted a factual obstacle to performance (*Leistungshindernis*), resulting in impossibility (*Unmöglichkeit*) (Articles 275, 281, 307, 323 and 325 BGB) or frustration of purpose (*Wegfall der Geschäftsgrundlage*).[75] In the following, the focus is on cases involving economic sanctions.

B. Taking Foreign Economic Sanctions into Consideration through Substantive Law

In the *Borax* case,[76] the BGH took the US prohibition on sales to the Eastern Bloc into account through substantive contract law. The borax produced in Germany was made from a basic material, known as rasorite, which was imported from the

Vertragsrecht (Mohr Siebeck, 1989) 9–18; and Großfeld and Junker (n 55) 101. See also BGH, Urteil vom 19.4.1962 - VII ZR 162/60 IPRspr 1962/63. Nr 163, 523.

[70] BGH, Urteil vom 16.4.1975. - I ZR 40/73, BGHZ 64, 183, NJW 1975, 1220; see also BGH, Urteil vom 17.11.1994 - III ZR 70/93, DtZ 1995, 250.

[71] Daniel Busse, 'Die Berücksichtigung ausländischer "Eingriffsnormen" durch die deutsche Rechtsprechung' (1996) 95 *ZVgRWiss* 386, 409–10.

[72] See ibid 395.

[73] BGH, Urteil vom 28.01.1965 - Ia ZR 273/63; BGH Urteil vom 16.4.1975 - I ZR 40/73, BGHZ 64, 183, NJW 1975, 1220.

[74] Großfeld and Junker (n 55) 100–01.

[75] BGH, Urteil vom 08.02.1984 - VIII ZR 254/82, RabelsZ 1989, 146 with the comment by Haralb Baum, 'Anmerkung: Faktische und potentielle Eingriffsnormen' (1989) 53 *RabelsZ* 152.

[76] BGH, Urteil vom 21.12.1960 - VIII ZR 1/60, NJW 1961, 822.

US. The US authorities granted an export licence, provided that the rasorite would not be shipped to socialist countries. The goal of controlling the export of rasorite as well as the products made from this material was to limit the increase in the armament potential of the Eastern Bloc. The seller promised to transport borax to the buyer. Both the seller and the buyer were West German traders and the contract was governed by German law. Both parties were aware that the final destination of the borax would have been in East Germany, but they agreed to indicate Denmark as the destination in order to conceal their intention. The seller refused to supply the product; for this reason, the buyer claimed damages. The BGH rejected the claim since it found that the contract breached good morals, as the parties intended to circumvent the prohibition by fraud. It considered the contract to be null and void under Article 138 BGB. Here, the US export restriction was taken into consideration due to the immoral nature of the parties' conduct. The BGH did not rely on a conflict-of-laws approach, but rather on the immorality of the parties' conduct on the basis of the governing German law.[77]

The approach of the BGH was founded on the fact that the US and German interests coincided. Foreign policy arguments found their way into the BGH judgment. Even though German law did not explicitly take over the US export prohibition, immorality may be relied on in relation to a conduct directed against the community, in particular a conduct which infringes the interests of the community.[78] The objective of the US embargo was to limit the increase in the war potential of the Eastern Bloc with Western goods. The embargo thus served the maintenance of peace and the liberal order of the Western countries. The measures concerned not only promoted US interests, but also the interests of the entire liberal West, including those of the German Federal Republic. The embargo rules therefore served the vital interests of the community. Those who act against these interests by pursuing their self-interest through fraud act in an immoral way. Those who act fraudulently, securing financial advantages for themselves, ignore the demands of the community which serve freedom and peace. The BGH decision treated the foreign economic sanction at the level of substantive law and imposed the consequence of immorality under German substantive law. The judgment could also be interpreted in a way that, in reality, the BGH did not directly enforce the US sanction, but rather the public policy of the forum state.[79] After the Second World War, the US adhered to a broader reach of sanctions and tended to press, using various means, its European allies to observe US trade restrictions, while European countries argued for a more permissive approach. An interesting feature of this judgment, which gave effect to the US sanction, was that it overcame the debate between the US and its European partners on the necessity and extent

[77] Jürgen Basedow, *The Law of Open Societies: Private Ordering and Public Regulation of International Relations – General Course on Private International Law, Collected Courses of the Hague Academy of International Law*, vol 360 (Martinus Nijhoff, 2013) 329.

[78] BGH, Urteil vom 21.12.1960 – VIII ZR 1/60, NJW 1961, 823.

[79] Basedow (n 68) 123.

of the trade restrictions against the Eastern Bloc by recognising common interests and values.[80]

Not much later, in the *Borsäure* case, the BGH followed closely the Borax judgment under somewhat different circumstances. A US company and a German company entered into a contract for the sale of 500 tonnes of boric acid.[81] The transport of the goods from Los Angeles to Hamburg was covered by an insurance policy. However, borates were subject to US trade restrictions. The buyer declared for the US authorities that it would use the material in West Germany, although it aimed at forwarding the shipment to Poland. The US authorities therefore withdrew the export licence and sequestrated the goods. After this, the insurance company was sued for not paying the sum insured because of the loss of the goods due to the seizure. The BGH referred back to its previous *Borax* judgment and in fact reiterated its foreign policy arguments.[82] The US export restriction was aimed at preventing the increase of the armament potential of the Eastern Bloc. The embargo served the maintenance of peace and the liberal order of the West. Not only did US interests warrant the restrictions, but so too did those of Western European countries, including the German Federal Republic. The court pointed out that such an insurance contract is against the sense of decency of all who think fairly and justly, and repeated that individuals who circumvent the US embargo rules fraudulently to secure financial advantages ignore the demands of the community which serve freedom and peace. Additionally, it noted that in the meantime, the German legislator espoused the US embargo policy and enacted a corresponding prohibition and in it referred parenthetically to Article 134 BGB. The insurance contract aimed at decreasing the risk related to the US trade restrictions and the potential seizure of the products due to these. It was therefore found that the insurance contract had an immoral character. The sea transport insurance contract concerning the transport of strategic goods from the US in breach of the US embargo rules was null and void under Article 138(1) BGB if both parties were aware of the prohibition. Even if the insurer was not aware of the prohibition, the contract was invalid in the absence of an insurable interest. In the *Borax* case and *Borsäure*, the BGH did not apply the US embargo, but took it into account within the framework of the governing German law.[83] In the legal literature, Article 138 BGB was even seen as an implied conflict-of-laws rule which can allow the application of foreign law with the legal consequence of nullity.[84]

[80] Norbert Knüppel, *Zwingendes materielles Recht und internationale Schuldverträge* (Bonn, 1988) 143–44.

[81] BGH, Urteil vom 24.5.1962 – II ZR 199/60, NJW 1962, 1436.

[82] BGH, Urteil vom 24.5.1962 – II ZR 199/60, NJW 1962, 1437.

[83] Abbo Junker, 'Schadensersatzpflicht bei einem Verstoß gegen ein ausländisches Embargo – Zugleich eine Besprechung der Entscheidung des BGH vom 20. 11. 1990' (1991) 46 *JuristenZeitung* 699, 701.

[84] Lehmann (n 59) 47.

Immorality was also considered under Article 826 BGB, which provides for damages in the case of causing damage to someone else in a way that is contrary to good morals. The BGH acknowledged in essence that the owner of a vessel may claim damages under Article 826 BGB when a German charterer entered into a freight contract breaching the Thai embargo on steel against South Africa.[85] Although the real destination of the shipment was South Africa, the bill of lading indicated Hamburg as the port of loading. This resulted in the seizure of the vessel by the authorities. The BGH stated that the defendant was aware of the embargo and that the Thai authorities were deceived by altering the destination in the bill of lading. The court added that the application of Article 826 BGB was not a priori excluded by the fact that an embargo primarily seeks foreign and commercial policy objectives; on the contrary, a breach of embargo may be assessed under this provision. By intending to circumvent the embargo, the property of the claimant was consciously endangered. Negligence against others' property interests may qualify the damage as a breach of good morals. Junker points out that the EEC also imposed sanctions against South Africa, so the values behind the Thai prohibition were shared by the EEC and could justify giving effect to it by a German court.[86]

In fact, German court practice considered foreign public law norms (not belonging to the *lex causae*) at the level of the substantive assessment of the case and a breach thereof was treated as a ground for the immorality of the contract or the impossibility of performance. The advantage of the reliance on good morals is that even if the performance of the contract is factually not impossible, the violation of good morals may serve as an appropriate legal basis to justify non-performance. In this way, the German courts avoided the conflict-of-laws treatment of foreign economic sanctions and their direct application as foreign overriding mandatory provisions.[87] The qualification of the contract as immoral or rendering performance impossible brought the assessment of the case to the level of substantive law. The Rome Convention did not influence German judicial practice on foreign economic sanctions because of the German reservation made to Article 7(1) of the Rome Convention. Although the necessity for reservation was explained by the legal certainty concerns related to the wording of the Rome Convention and the courts' discretion,[88] it seems that German judicial practice does not exclude the room to manoeuvre of the courts when deciding on the substantive consideration of foreign overriding mandatory provisions. As such, German courts avoided

[85] BGH, Urteil vom 20.11.1990 – VI ZR 6/90, NJW 1991, 634. See also BGH, Urteil vom 20.10.1992 – VI ZR 361/91, NJW 1993, 194. Junker 699.

[86] Junker (n 83) 701–02.

[87] Sebastian von Allwörden, *US-Terrorlisten im deutschen Privatrecht: zur kollisions- und sachrechtlichen Problematik drittstaatlicher Sperrlisten mit extraterritorialer Wirkung* (Mohr Siebeck, 2014) 71; Eberhard Vetter, 'Kollisionsrechtliche Fragen bei grenzüberschreitenden Subunternehmensverträgen im Industrieanlagenbau' (1988) 87 *ZVglRWiss* 248, 271.

[88] Stellungnahme des Bundesrates zur Entwurf eines Gesetzes zur Neuregelung des Internationalen Privatrechts, 10/504, 20.10.83, 98, 100.

the conflict-of-laws treatment of foreign economic sanctions and their direct application as foreign overriding mandatory provisions.[89] The substantive law approach enjoyed an exclusive position in Germany until the starting date of the application of the Rome I Regulation.

C. Refusal to Take Foreign Economic Sanctions into Account through Substantive Law

Nevertheless, the consideration of foreign economic sanctions at the level of substantive law is not a necessity. A German decision concerned the US sanctions imposed against Iran following the Iranian hostage crises. In an unpublished, but still often mentioned, judgment of the LG Krefeld, a German subsidiary of a US company entered into a contract on supplying generator equipment with a buyer intending to deliver the goods to Iran.[90] Although the seller argued that, as a German subsidiary of a US company, it was subject to the US embargo against Iran, the court did not exempt the supplier from performance. The court established that the seller was a company under German law that could not rely on the US export prohibition. The US export restrictions were accordingly not taken into account. The approach of the court differed from that of the judgments of the BGH in *borax* and *Borsäure*.

The rejection of giving effect to foreign economic sanctions may also sometimes be strengthened by foreign policy considerations. This may be well illustrated by a decision of the LG Hamburg.[91] In the course of the transportation of 400 sacks of Iranian liquorice powder to Hamburg, the transported product was damaged. The shipment was insured with a German company, which in the meantime became part of a US concern. A claim was made against the insurance company for covering that damage. The insurance company recognised that the damage was covered by the insurance policy. However, before payment, it found it necessary to obtain the consent of US authorities as the contract concerned Iran, a country subject to US economic sanctions. The claimant argued that the sanction clause in the insurance policy was limited to the sanctions and embargoes of the EC, and that foreign prohibitions may not be given effect in the case of the given legal relationship, which was governed by German law. The defendant argued that it was an establishment of a US company and therefore was required to comply with US sanctions

[89] Von Allwörden (n 87) 71; Nicola C Neumann, *Internationale Handelsembargos und privatrechtliche Verträge* (Nomos, 2000) 213; Vetter (n 87) 271.

[90] LG Krefeld, Urteil vom 24.9.1980, 7 O 190/80; Knüppel (n 80) 62 and 140. The judgment is also referred to by Karl Kreuzer, *Ausländisches Wirtschaftsrecht vor deutschen Gerichten* (CF Müller, 1986) 27; Forwick (n 49) 125; Mankowski (n 58) 406.

[91] LG Hamburg, Urteil vom 3.12.2014 – 401 HKO 7/14, also reported in RIW Reichweite des EU-Embargos gegen den Iran – keine materiell-rechtlichen Auswirkungen des entsprechenden US-Embargos (2015) RIW 458. Commented on by Mankowski (n 58) 405.

related to the Iran embargo. It claimed that the contract should be adjusted to the effect that the payment to the policy holder should be made once this was authorised by the OFAC.

The LG Hamburg decided in favour of the claimant, finding that foreign laws do not have mandatory force in Germany and do not qualify as a prohibitive law within the meaning of Article 134 BGB. The breach of Article 138 BGB (immoral contracts) was not found either, because the contract concerned the transport of liquorice powder. The EC sanctions prohibited only the trade of dual-use goods related to the use of atomic energy and not food or other consumer products. The trade of the latter did not violate the values and principles of German law and the *ordre public*. However, the insurance company breached its accessory contractual obligation to inform the claimant that it had become member of a US concern and the possible consequences of this. The risk of integrating into a US group was to be borne by the insurance company and could not be shifted to the policy holder. The performance of the contractual obligation did not depend on the approval of the OFAC.

In this case, the governing law was German law and the ultimate place of performance was Hamburg. Therefore, the US sanction could not have been given effect under Article 9(3) of the Rome I Regulation as the place of performance was not the US. The applicability of the US sanctions was therefore examined at the level of substantive German contract law through Article 134 and Article 138 BGB. However, the application of these provisions was rejected by the German court. The final and legally binding judgment of the LG Hamburg was in line with the objective of the EU sanctions policy, which was to limit sanctions to certain sensitive products, such as dual-use goods, and not to interrupt fully the trade with Iran.

Sometimes, it happens that a court has to choose between parallel sanctions. In such a scenario, a decision of the OLG Frankfurt am Main did not give effect to US sanctions.[92] The court gave preference to the sanctions imposed by the EU insofar as it simply applied the *lex fori*. The plaintiff bank requested transfers of money in accordance with mandates from its client. The defendant bank, the German establishment of a US bank, blocked the payments through its branch in London, which acted as an intermediary within the TARGET2 payment system. The defendant claimed that, as an establishment of a US bank, it was obliged to block the amounts transferred in order to comply with an executive order of the US President imposed against Iran.[93] An action was brought for the reimbursement of the blocked amount.

The OLG Frankfurt held that, due to the domestic establishment of the US bank, German courts may assert jurisdiction. The applicable law was German law based on Article 28 EGBGB. Article 7(1) of the Rome Convention could not be

[92] OLG Frankfurt, Urteil vom 9.5.2011 – Az. 23 U 30/10, ZIP 2011, 1354.
[93] Executive Order 13382 of the US President of 28 June 2005.

applied since Germany had made a reservation to that provision. The court referred to the principle of territoriality followed by German judicial practice, according to which the application of foreign overriding mandatory norms is excluded; at most, they may be considered as facts. However, to give effect to foreign overriding mandatory norms in this way necessitates a domestic ground of justification, including the examination of whether the foreign overriding mandatory norms directly serve any German or any other relevant interests. The defendant referred to foreign policy arguments similar to those presented in the *borax* and *Borsäure* cases: the US embargo served the intention of ensuring peace and the limitation of the use of atomic power by Iran for military purposes, and this goal was in accordance with German values and policy objectives. The court took the primacy of EU law as a point of departure. According to the court, the transfer was subject only to the restrictions imposed by EU law against Iran, namely Regulation 423/2007/EC[94] and Regulation 961/2010/EU,[95] but not to the US embargo. In terms of general objectives, these EU regulations corresponded to the US embargo, but laid down an alternative system that independently determined which persons are covered by the sanctions and also determined the conditions of the release of the frozen amounts. The OLG Frankfurt found no reason why a differentiated and detailed system that is subject to procedural guarantees should be replaced by a regulation originating outside the EU. It rejected the defendant's argument that performance became legally impossible. The court pointed out that the US prohibition did not exclude performance. Then, somewhat oddly, it pointed to the several breaches of embargoes in practice through which the contractually agreed performance could be achieved. This conclusion was not altered by incidental penalties imposed by US authorities on the employees of the bank. The court limited itself to stating that US courts and authorities do not adhere to enforcing an extraterritorial US sanction, provided that the person concerned proves that compliance with it would result in the breach of a legal obligation under the law of his state of residence and could not obtain an exemption from this obligation.

Interestingly, the OLG Frankfurt referred to *Libyan Arab Foreign Bank v Bankers Trust Co* and *Libyan Arab Foreign Bank v Manufacturers Hanover Trust Co*, which were decided by English courts and to which we will return below. There are resemblances between the English cases and the case before the OLG Frankfurt. The similarity lies primarily in the fact that these cases all concerned the restriction of accounts. Moreover, the English cases where US sanctions were ignored could neatly confirm the German court's approach to rejecting a US sanction. The OLG Frankfurt used these two cases to demonstrate that the OFAC authorised payment of blocked amounts, notwithstanding the extraterritorial US sanctions. However, a qualification must be made. Unlike the case before the OLG Frankfurt,

[94] Council Regulation (EC) No 423/2007 of 19 April 2007 concerning restrictive measures against Iran [2007] OJ L103/1.

[95] Council Regulation (EU) No 961/2010 of 25 October 2010 on restrictive measures against Iran and repealing Regulation (EC) No 423/2007 [2010] OJ L281/1.

the English judgments were rendered on the basis of conflict-of-laws rules and the enquiry on giving effect to US sanctions did not move to the stage of the substantive law assessment of the case.

According to the judgment of the OLG Frankfurt, the establishment of a US bank located in the EU could not rely successfully on extraterritorial US sanctions for rejecting transfers within the EU. The court decided that the blocked amounts must be reimbursed to an account of the plaintiff held with the German Federal Bank, which was subject to the EU sanctions.

The significance of the case is that the OLG Frankfurt took as a departure point the primacy of EU law.[96] It deduced from this that foreign law is not to be applied or taken into consideration when EU law imposes parallel restrictions. Although the court was justified in drawing this conclusion, as we have already discussed and as has been demonstrated by cases in the European bank sector such as BNP Paribas, such rulings in fact do not leave the parties concerned immune from the wide range of penalties that may be imposed by US authorities.[97] German banks were not free from extraterritorial US sanctions either. Deutsche Bank paid $258 million for conducting transactions on behalf of Iranian, Libyan, Syrian, Burmese and Sudanese entities subject to US economic sanctions.[98]

The German court practice following the substantive law approach has not been significantly affected by the entry into force of the Rome I Regulation.[99] Foreign economic sanctions may be given effect either by virtue of Article 9(3) if they pertain to the law of the place of performance or under the substantive law rules of the law governing the contract. The criteria to be considered under Article 9(3) are in principle the same as those to be taken into account under the substantive law approach. They include the examination of whether giving effect to the norm is necessary for the protection of the interests and fundamental values of Germany.[100] In this respect, it must be mentioned that the decisions of the LG Hamburg and the OLG Frankfurt am Main considered EU foreign policy interests and objectives as well as European values (eg, referring to procedural

[96] Helge-Torsten Wöhlert, 'EU-Verordnungen genießen beim Einfrieren von Geldern gegenüber einer Exekutiv-Order des Präsidenten der USA Anwendungsvorrang' (2011) *Gesellschafts- und Wirtschaftsrecht* 340, 340.

[97] Bernd R Mayer and Michael Albrecht, 'Bankvertrag und Finanzsanktionen: Leistungsverweigerungsrecht bei drohendem Verstoß gegen US-Verordnungen?' (2015) 26 *Zeitschrift für Wirtschafts- und Bankrecht* 1226, 1229–30.

[98] New York State Department of Financial Services, 'NYDFS Announces Deutsche Bank to Pay $258 Million, Install Independent Monitor, Terminate Employees for Transactions on Behalf of Iran, Syria, Sudan, Other Sanctioned Entities', 4 November 2015.

[99] Hans-Joachiem Prieß and Martin Schaper, 'Erfüllung oder Nichterfüllung – Zur Durchsetzbarkeit vertraglicher Ansprüche bei entgegenstehendem ausländischen Embargorecht' in Dirk Ehlers and Hans-Michael Wolffgang (eds), *Recht der Exportkontrolle: Bestandsaufnahme und Perspektiven; Handbuch zum Exportkontrollrecht – Festschrift für Dr Arnold Wallraff* (Fachmedien Recht & Wirtschaft, 2015) 273.

[100] ibid.

safeguards in the EU regulations) when deciding whether to give effect to US sanctions. These judgments thus point towards an approach which does not focus exclusively on national interests and values. Both decisions expressed the autonomy of EU sanctions policy and the interests of EU foreign policy that could not be overridden by those of the US.

D. Conclusion

German judicial practice is illustrative for using substantive law to take foreign economic sanctions into account outside conflict-of-laws analysis. German courts usually did not approach cases from the point of view of private international law, but they directly turned to the substantive law assessment of the case.

The decisions of the German BGH in the *Borax* and *Borsäure* judgments demonstrate that foreign policy interests play a decisive role when deciding on giving effect to foreign economic sanctions. These cases represent an era hallmarked by the strong cooperation between Germany and the US within the framework of the COCOM.[101] During the Cold War period, they shared common foreign policy and security interests to stop Russian military and economic expansion. Fissures, such as the pipeline case (see Chapter 5), seldom arose in this cooperation. However, differences have emerged more and more often after the Cold War period. This is clear if we follow with attention the subsequent decisions of German courts, such as the LG Hamburg and the OLG Frankfurt, which refused to give effect to US sanctions. These decisions are illustrative in the respect that reliance on the objectives of EU sanctions policy can justify the refusal of giving effect to a foreign economic sanction. These cases prove that both the admission and the refusal of foreign economic sanctions may be supported by foreign policy considerations. The two decisions also confirm that, when deciding whether to give effect to a foreign economic sanction, not only are national interests and values decisive, but so too are interests and values shared at an EU level. Such common interests and values are naturally part of national interests and values, but the courts' focus was on the European dimension of these cases.

The courts of the Member States may give effect to the economic sanctions of the state of the place of performance under Article 9(3) of the Rome I Regulation or may take other foreign economic sanctions into account outside the purview of Article 9. In practice, however, German courts had recourse to the substantive law approach to decide whether a foreign economic sanction is applicable. This indicates an opposite tendency to the formal approach accepted by the Cour d'appel de Paris in the *Giti* judgment.

[101] Großfeld and Junker (n 55) 131.

III. England and Wales

A. The Concept of Public Policy in English Law

Before opting into the Rome I Regulation, English law followed its own path. Until the application of the Rome Convention and the Rome I Regulation, English courts applied English rules or had regard to foreign rules that we call today overriding mandatory provisions based on common law.

Unlike continental private international law, English private international law did not distinguish terminologically between the *ordre public* reservation and overriding mandatory provisions prior to the Rome Convention.[102] Both of them were covered by the concept of public policy.[103] In common law, the concept of public policy has been used in two senses.[104] English law traditionally allowed the operation of public policy to set aside the application of a foreign law and also to apply its own internationally overriding provisions.[105] The operation of public policy under English law thus accomplished both a negative and a positive function. Public policy implied any deviation from the law that was otherwise applicable.[106]

First, largely corresponding to the continental *ordre public* exception, the application of foreign law may be derogated on the ground of the public policy of the forum. Under English conflict-of-laws rules, an English court does not enforce or recognise a right or a legal relationship (eg, a contract) arising under the law of a foreign state if its enforcement or recognition in the given case would violate the fundamental public policy of England.[107] In *Kuwait Airways Corporation v Iraqi Airways Company and Others*, in the course of the invasion of Kuwait by the Iraqi army, the Revolutionary Command Council of Iraq ordered by a resolution the dissolution of Kuwait Airways and the transfer of all its property, including its aircraft, to Iraqi Airways, a company owned by the Iraqi state.[108] After the end of the Gulf War, Kuwait Airways claimed the return of its aircraft and damages from Iraqi Airways. The acquisition of property had to be assessed under the *lex situs* rule under English conflict of laws, ie, Iraqi law, but Kuwait Airways argued that Iraqi law should be disregarded as a matter of public policy. The House of Lords

[102] Jonathan Harris, 'Mandatory Rules and Public Policy under the Rome I Regulation' in Franco Ferrari and Stefan Leible (eds), *Rome I Regulation* (Sellier, 2009) 297.

[103] ibid 297–98.

[104] Adeline Chong, 'The Public Policy and Mandatory Rules of Third Countries in International Contracts' (2006) 2 *Journal of Private International Law* 27, 30.

[105] Ronald Harry Graveson, *Conflict of Laws*, 7th edn (Sweet & Maxwell, 1974) 163–64.

[106] Harris (n 102) 298.

[107] Lawrence Collins (ed), *Dicey, Morris & Collins on the Conflict of Laws*, vol 1, 15th edn (Sweet & Maxwell, 2012) Rule 2, 99; see also Rule 229, 1871–77.

[108] *Kuwait Airways Corporation v Iraqi Airways Company and Others* [2002] UKHL 19. See Adrian Briggs, 'Public Policy in the Conflict of Laws: A Sword and a Shield?' (2002) 6 *Singapore Journal of International & Comparative Law* 953.

refused to give effect to the resolution as a matter of English public policy due to the violation of the rules of international law by Iraq and the condemnation of its acts by the international community.

Second, public policy also embraced overriding mandatory norms, although this latter notion was not used in English private international law.[109] Public policy not only permitted setting aside a non-desired foreign law, but could equally result in the application of the law of the forum, ie, the application of the overriding mandatory provisions of English law, even if it was otherwise not applicable.[110] In *Ertel Bieber Co v Rio Tinto Co Ltd*, the English rules on trade with the enemy were in fact applied through the public policy, even though the governing law was German. Lord Parker of Waddington stated simply that 'no subject of the Crown can be allowed to evade the rule by entering into such a contract out of the jurisdiction and stipulating expressly or impliedly that the contract shall be governed by a foreign law'.[111] This is the expression of the positive side of the public policy.[112] Further examples may be brought forward regarding the mandatory application of currency control provisions.[113]

Public policy thus clearly permitted the enforcement of fundamental rules and values of English law by not applying the otherwise applicable foreign law or by applying the overriding mandatory rules of English law. Foreign overriding mandatory provisions were applied or given effect in two cases: as part of the proper law of the contract or the law of the place of performance, when the foreign provisions rendered performance illegal. These two cases are discussed in sections III.B and III.C below, because these permit the application of or giving effect to foreign economic sanctions. However, it should be noted that foreign overriding mandatory norms which did not belong to either of them has been ignored by English courts.[114]

B. Overriding Mandatory Provisions of the Proper Law of the Contract

The material validity of the contract has been determined by the law governing the contract: the proper law of the contract.[115] If English law governs a contract, this

[109] Harris (n 102) 298.

[110] Peter Stone, *EU Private International Law*, 3rd edn (Edward Elgar, 2014) 340; Trevor C Hartley, 'The Modern Approach to Private International Law: International Litigation and Transactions from a Common-Law Perspective' in *Collected Courses of the Hague Academy of International Law*, vol 319 (Nijhoff, 2006) 9, 193.

[111] *Ertel Bieber Co v Rio Tinto Co Ltd* [1918] AC 260, 302.

[112] Collins (n 107) vol 2, 1860.

[113] *Boissevain v Weil* [1950] AC 327, 434–44.

[114] *Kleinwort, Sons and Company v Ungarische Baumwolle Industrie Aktiengesellschaft and Another* [1939] 2 KB 678.

[115] Collins (n 107) vol 2, 1846–47.

of course implies the application of the 'overriding mandatory rules' of English law. In addition to applying the overriding mandatory norms of English law, foreign overriding mandatory provisions were equally applied if they constituted part of the law governing the contract.[116] Dicey, Morris and Collins call this a 'general principle of the conflict of laws'.[117] Briggs states that, regarding a provision of public policy which is part of the *lex causae*, 'there is no reason whatever for an English court to decline to give it effect'.[118] This approach also prevailed concerning economic sanctions.[119]

It should be noted that English courts did not refrain from applying the public law norms of the governing foreign law. Although the distinction between private and public law has not been traditionally applied in English law, foreign penal, tax and administrative law in principle had not been applied as an exception to the application of foreign law. A further exception, 'other foreign public law', is usually also added to this list. Such an exception is crucial in terms of the application of foreign economic sanctions. However, it seems that this does not involve the exclusion of foreign public law as a whole from the scope of the governing law. In *Attorney-General of New Zealand v Ortiz and Others*, Staughton J established that 'I cannot by process of inductive reasoning arrive at the conclusion that foreign public laws, as a whole, will not be enforced here'.[120] This may be illustrated by a decision where the Chancery Division of the High Court applied German foreign exchange provisions as part of the governing German law concerning a loan agreement.[121] The non-application of foreign public law seems to depend instead on the circumstances of the case and the need to exclude the application of a foreign public law norm on a special ground of public policy.[122] Even the strict approach excluding the application of foreign public law does not rule out the consideration of foreign public law at the level of substantive law.

C. Overriding Mandatory Provisions of Other Foreign Countries: Illegality under the Law of the Place of Performance

Foreign overriding mandatory provisions other than those belonging to the proper law of a contract were not to be applied;[123] however, they could be taken

[116] *R v International Trustee for the Protection of Bondholders Aktiengesellschaft* [1937] AC 500; *Kahler v Midland Bank* [1950] AC 24, 42; *British Nylon Spinners v Imperial Chemical Industries* [1955] Ch 37.

[117] Collins (n 107) vol 2, 1840.

[118] Adrian Briggs, *The Conflict of Laws*, 3rd edn (Oxford University Press, 2013).

[119] A Vaughan Lowe, 'Extraterritorial Jurisdiction – British Practice' (1988) 52 *RabelsZ* 157, 194–95.

[120] *Attorney-General of New Zealand v Ortiz and Others* [1982] QB 349.

[121] *In Re Claim by Helbert Wagg & Co Ltd* [1956] 2 WLR 183, [1956] Ch 323.

[122] Mathias Kuckein, *Die 'Berücksichtigung' von Eingriffsnormen im deutschen und englischen internationalen Vertragsrecht* (Mohr Siebeck, 2008) 207–08, referring to *Attorney-General of New Zealand v Ortiz and Others* (n 120) 371.

[123] *Kleinwort* (n 114).

into account exceptionally in the case of illegality. Illegality has been primarily examined under the law of the forum[124] and the proper law of the contract.[125] Illegality under another foreign law has been taken into account only where the rules of the law of the place of performance rendered the performance of the contract illegal. Accordingly, a contract (or a contractual term) was not valid and enforceable if it was illegal under the law of the place where the contract had to be performed. This is why Staughton J could state in *Euro-Diam Ltd v Bathurst* that: 'There are thus overlapping conflict rules on the topic of contractual illegality, producing three connecting factors, the forum, the proper law, and the place of performance.'[126]

English courts had to address illegality under the law of the place of performance under three seminal judgments. These judgments demonstrate that the law of the state of the place of performance rendering performance illegal could be given effect under English common law, which paved the way to giving effect to foreign economic sanctions. As we will see, English courts could not remain immune from foreign policy considerations either.

i. Ralli Bros

In *Ralli Bros*, an English charterer and a Spanish shipowner entered into a contract for the transportation of jute from India to Spain. In the course of the transportation, Spain adopted a decree which set a maximum for the price of the freight and the English charterer paid accordingly. As the price agreed previously exceeded this maximum, the Spanish shipowner company claimed the balance before the English court. All the judges in this case (Lord Sterndale MR, Warrington LJ and Scrutton LJ) referred to the second edition of *Dicey's Conflicts of Laws*, according to which: 'A contract … is, in general, invalid in so far as … the performance of it is unlawful by the law of the country where the contract is to be performed.'[127] The court found that the charterer could not be obliged to perform the payment of the freight above the maximum established by Spanish law if it has become illegal by the law of the place of performance. Scrutton LJ added that:

> [W]here a contract requires an act to be done in a foreign country, it is … an implied term of the continuing validity of such a provision that the act to be done in the foreign country shall not be illegal by the law of that country. This country should not in my opinion assist or sanction the breach of the laws of other independent States.[128]

[124] Trevor C Hartley, 'Mandatory Rules in International Contracts: The Common Law Approach' in *Collected Courses of the Hague Academy of International Law, Vol 266 – 1997* (Martinus Nijhoff, 1998) 337, 387–88.

[125] ibid 387.

[126] *Euro-Diam Ltd v Bathurst* [1987] 2 All ER 113, 125.

[127] Albert Venn Dicey, *A digest of the law of England with reference to the conflict of laws*, 2nd edn (Stevens and Sons, 1908) 553.

[128] *Ralli Bros v Compania Naviera Sota y Aznar* [1920] 2 KB 287, 304.

Divergent interpretations are attached to the *Ralli Bros* judgment. Certain authors see it as a specific conflict-of-laws norm, which makes the validity and enforceability of a contract subject to the *lex contractus* and the law of the place of performance, while others opine that this is a rule of English substantive contract law that expresses the discharge or suspension of contractual obligations due to supervening illegality under the law of the place of performance.[129] The substantive law approach is buttressed by the reference to the implied term in the judgment, while the conflict-of-laws nature of the rule is supported by the allusion to international comity.[130] *Ralli Bros* concerned a case where English law was the governing law. It remained questionable what happens if the applicable law is a foreign law and the contract must be performed in a country other than England. According to the substantive law approach, illegality under foreign law is simply a fact that has to be taken into account by an English court, which may lead to the frustration of the contract and to the discharge or suspension of the parties' contractual obligations as a result of supervening illegality. However, such a rule of contract law only applies if the contract is governed by English law. The consequence of this is that contracts governed by foreign law may be enforceable before English courts even if their performance would be unlawful under the law of the place of performance and their validity remains unaffected. The substantive law approach also gained confirmation in judicial practice[131] and shows undoubted similarities to the German court practice on giving effect to foreign overriding mandatory norms through substantive rules of contract law.[132] The other view considers the rule on the illegality under the place of performance as an English conflict-of-laws rule which permits the application of the provisions of the place of performance, provided that they render the performance illegal, regardless of the law otherwise governing the contract. Some court decisions confirmed this approach.[133] From this perspective, the case could also be seen as permitting the direct application of the Spanish rule on price maximisation as an overriding mandatory norm of the place of performance.[134]

[129] Interpreting it as a rule of substantive contract law: Frederick Alexander Mann, 'Proper Law and Illegality in Private International Law' in John Fischer Williams and AD McNair (eds) (1937) 18 *British Yearbook of International Law* 97, 110–113; Collins (n 107) vol 2, 1840; Simon James, 'Rome I: Shall We Dance?' (2008) 2 *Law and Financial Markets Review* 113, 117.

[130] Kinsch (n 4) 39–40.

[131] *Libyan Arab Foreign Bank v Bankers Trust* [1989] QB 728,. 749; *Empresa Exportadora de Azucar v Industria Azucarera Nacional (The 'Playa Larga' and 'Marble Islands')* 190 [1983] 2 Lloyd's Law Reports 171, 190; *Kursell v Timber Operators and Contractors* [1927] 1 KB 298, 313; *Kahler v Midland* [1950] AC 24, 48; *Ispahani v Bank Melli Iran* (1997) *The Times*, 29 December, [1997] Lexis Citation 4800, [1997] All ER (D) 124.

[132] Ivana Kunda, *International Mandatory Rules of a Third Country in European Contract Conflict of Laws: The Rome Convention and the Proposed Rome I Regulation* (Rijeka Law Faculty, 2007) 85.

[133] *Zinovstenska Banka National Corporation v Frankman* [1950] AC 57, 79. However, Lord Reid phrased the rule in a different way in a judgment delivered on the same day: *Kahler v Midland* [1950] AC 24, 48. See also *Sharif v Azad* [1967] 1 QB 605, 617; *Euro-Diam Ltd v Bathurst* [1987] 2 All ER 113, 124; Kinsch (n 4) 41. The conflict-of-laws approach is also supported by *Mackender v Feldia AG* [1967] 2 QB 590, 601.

[134] Harris (n 102) 304.

ii. Foster v Driscoll

In *Foster v Driscoll*, a contract on smuggling alcohol into the US while spirits were prohibited in that country was considered to be void and unenforceable before the English courts, although the contract was governed by English law. The intention of the contracting parties taking part in this enterprise was to sell whisky in the US, or alternatively, in Canada or on the high seas, from where it could have easily been smuggled into the US. The majority of the judges found that the object of the agreement was contrary to the public policy based on international comity. The court made its frequently cited statement that:

> An English contract should and will be held invalid on account of illegality if the real object and intention of the parties necessitates them joining in an endeavour to perform in a foreign and friendly country some act which is illegal by the law of such country notwithstanding the fact that there may be, in a certain event, alternative modes or places of performing which permit the contract to be performed legally.[135]

Scrutton LJ, dissenting, opined that the whisky could have been sold outside the US, in Canada or on the high seas under the contract without any breach of US law.

The Court of Appeal had regard to the foreign policy effects of the judgment. Lawrence LJ referred to international comity and foreign policy considerations as follows:

> I am clearly of opinion that a partnership formed for the main purpose of deriving profit from the commission of a criminal offence in a foreign and friendly country is illegal, even although the parties have not succeeded in carrying out their enterprise, and no such criminal offence has in fact been committed; and none the less so because the parties may have contemplated that if they could not successfully arrange to commit the offence themselves they would instigate or aid and abet some other person to commit it. The ground upon which I rest my judgment that such a partnership is illegal is that its recognition by our Courts would furnish a just cause for complaint by the United States Government against our Government (of which the partners are subjects), and would be contrary to our obligation of international comity as now understood and recognized, and therefore would offend against our notions of public morality.[136]

iii. Regazzoni v Sethia

The *Ralli Bros* and *Foster v Driscoll* line of case law was brought forward in *Regazzoni v Sethia*, where the court was equally concerned with foreign policy considerations. *Regazzoni v Sethia* deserves a thorough analysis since it addressed economic sanctions imposed by a foreign state.

[135] *Foster v Driscoll* [1929] 1 KB 470, 521–522.
[136] ibid, 470, 510.

In *Regazzoni v Sethia*, the parties agreed that the seller supplies jute bags from India to Genoa. However, it was clear that the parties' intention was to resell the products to South Africa.[137] In the fight against apartheid, the Indian government prohibited the export of jute from India to South Africa. The parties were aware of this prohibition. As there was a big demand for this type of product in South Africa, big profits could be achieved by evading the prohibition. The seller denied performance and the buyer sued it for damages. The law governing the contract was English law. However, the performance of the contract was illegal under the law of another state: India. The parties intended to circumvent the prohibition of Indian law. The ultimate place of performance in the contract at issue was Italy, but the seller could not perform the contract without making an illegal act in India. The House of Lords unanimously dismissed the claim and established that an English court will not enforce a contract, or award damages for its breach if its performance would involve doing an act in a foreign and friendly State which violates the law of that State. This principle is based on public policy and international comity.[138] As contracts are avoided based on public policy if they violate English law, public policy also avoids certain contracts which infringe foreign law 'because public policy demands that deference to international comity'.[139] Hence, the case seemed to have been decided primarily on public policy grounds.

It is interesting to look at how the judgment addressed foreign policy arguments. Lord Reid and Lord Keith of Avonholm attempted to isolate the judgment from foreign policy considerations. They asserted that any court judgment addresses the illegality of the contract under Indian law only, but not political considerations. According to Lord Reid:

> [I]t is quite impossible for a court in this country to set itself up as a judge of the rights and wrongs of a controversy between two friendly countries, we cannot judge the motives or the justifications of governments of other countries in these matters and, if we tried to do so, the consequences might seriously prejudice international relations. By recognizing this Indian law so that an agreement which involves a breach of that law within Indian territory is unenforceable we express no opinion whatever, either favourable or adverse, as to the policy which caused its enactment.[140]

Lord Keith of Avonholm also expressed an essentially similar view:

> The English courts cannot be called on to adjudicate upon political issues between India and South Africa. The Indian law is not a law repugnant to English conceptions of what may be regarded as within the ordinary field of legislation or administrative order even in this country. It is the illegality under the foreign law that is to be considered and not the effect of the foreign law on another country.[141]

[137] *Regazzoni v Sethia* [1958] AC 301 (HL).
[138] ibid 302.
[139] ibid 319 (Viscount Simonds).
[140] ibid 326.
[141] ibid 327.

At the same time, these statements cannot conceal that, as a matter of fact, the House of Lords had to pass a decision which affected international relations between two friendly states.[142] Giving effect to the Indian trade restriction implied infringing the interests of South Africa, a country with which the British government nourished an equally friendly relationship, while ignoring the Indian rules would have infringed the interests of the latter state. Indian law was given effect, primarily not because of the spatial proximity of the case to the foreign law (usually required in private international law), but based on political (foreign policy) considerations.[143]

iv. *Interpretations of* Foster v Driscoll *and* Regazzoni v Sethia

Divergent interpretations were attached to the *Foster v Driscoll* and *Regazzoni v Sethia* judgments. First, like in *Ralli Bros*, it is questionable whether the cases imply a substantive law or a conflict-of-laws rule. Second, their demarcation from *Ralli Bros* was also broadly discussed in the literature.

In *Foster v Driscoll* and *Regazzoni v Sethia*, the governing law was English law. Mann found that it is a rule of English municipal contract law that establishes the invalidity of a contract which involves performing an act that is illegal under the law of the place of performance.[144] Similarly, Nygh considered both *Ralli Bros* and *Regazzoni v Sethia* as the endorsement of a substantive rule of domestic law and accordingly the cases did not express a conflict-of-laws rule.[145] On the contrary, certain authors argued that the rule should apply even if the contract was governed by foreign law.[146]

Interpreting these judgments as a rule of conflict of laws relied in principle on two methods. The first way is by applying the rule of the foreign place of performance rendering performance illegal as a foreign overriding mandatory norm. In his comparative analysis, Enonchong points out that *Foster v Driscoll* does not exclude the application of a foreign law; on the contrary, it requires the court to 'include' it as dictated by international comity in the case of the breach of the law of the country where the contract must be performed.[147] This essentially corresponds to the positive function of public policy as described in the continental legal literature. As Enonchong notes, international comity counters the refusal

[142] Frederick Alexander Mann, 'Illegality and the Conflict of Laws' (1958) 21 *Modern Law Review* 180, 183.

[143] Kunda (n 132) 87.

[144] Frederick Alexander Mann, 'Conflict of Laws and Public Law' in *Collected Courses of the Hague Academy of International Law – 1971*, vol 132 (Sijthoff, 1971) 107, 158, without specifying cases.

[145] Peter Nygh, *Autonomy in International Contracts* (Clarendon, 1999) 224–25.

[146] Chong (n 104) 33; Peter Basil Carter, 'The Rôle of Public Policy in English Private International Law' (1993) 42 *ICLQ* 1, 4–5; AJE Jaffey, *Introduction to the Conflict of Laws* (Butterworths, 1988) 154; Hartley (n 110) concerning *Foster v Driscoll* (at 241–42) and *Sethia v Regazzoni* (at 243); Peter Basil Carter, 'Rejection of Foreign Law: Some Private International Law Inhibitions' in Ian Brownlie and DW Bowett (eds) (1984) 55 *British Yearbook of International Law* 111, 125; Richard Williams, 'The Impact of Sanctions on Charterparty Operations' (2013) 19 *Journal of International Maritime* Law 290, 292.

[147] Nelson Enonchong, 'Public Policy in the Conflict of Laws: A Chinese Wall around Little England?' (1996) 45 *ICLQ* 633, 649.

of the application of foreign law, while favouring its 'inclusion',[148] but also adds the caveat that the reliance on international comity promoting the application of foreign law and the maintenance of friendly relations between states may not go so far as to neutralise the public policy of the forum.[149] According to another line of reasoning, these cases in fact do not concern the application of foreign overriding mandatory provisions; instead, their unenforceability was the consequence of the violation of English public policy.[150] Public policy is used in its negative function (*ordre public*) here. This procedure does not involve the direct application of foreign overriding mandatory provisions, but instead makes it possible to give effect to them through the protection of English public policy. This corresponds to the assertion that a contract is against public policy and accordingly void if it breaches British interests of state or it threatens the friendly relations between the UK and other governments.[151] Chong pointed out in this sense that in *Regazzoni v Sethia*, the House of Lords used English public policy to give effect to a foreign prohibition.[152] The Indian prohibition was not applied directly, but instead it was taken into account by the House of Lords, since the contract going against the spirit of comity breached English public policy.[153] In the latter case, the application of foreign overriding mandatory norms would take place in the form of English public policy.[154] Nevertheless, Chong claimed that overriding mandatory norms of third countries should be directly applied instead and should not be treated only through English public policy.[155] Harris also favours the direct application of foreign overriding mandatory provisions, considering the foreign law as the 'trigger' for its own application, although the law of the forum is what ultimately decides on their application.[156]

Lalive offered a further interpretation.[157] He considered the judgment of the House of Lords in *Regazzoni v Sethia* as a manifestation of transnational public policy, since the court extended the protection of the public policy of the forum to the public policy of a foreign state. This was necessitated by disapproving of the South African apartheid legislation and safeguarding human rights.

The literature often separates two lines of case law. *Foster v Driscoll* and *Regazzoni* on the one hand, and *Ralli Bros* on the other. Clearly, *Foster v Driscoll* and *Regazzoni v Sethia* concerned contracts which were already illegal at the time of their conclusion (initial illegality), while in *Ralli Bros* the contract was entered into by the parties legally, but later became illegal (supervening illegality).[158]

[148] ibid 650.
[149] ibid 658.
[150] Collins (n 107) vol 1, 102.
[151] ibid 1875–76.
[152] Chong (n 104) 41.
[153] ibid 41.
[154] ibid 34.
[155] ibid 45–47.
[156] Harris (n 102) 301.
[157] Pierre Lalive, 'Transnational (or Truly International) Public Policy and International Arbitration' in Pieter Sanders (ed), *Comparative Arbitration Practice and Public Policy in Arbitration, ICCA Congress Series, 1986 New York*, vol 3 (Kluwer, 1987) 258, 279.
[158] Hartley (n 110) 243.

Foster v Driscoll and *Regazzoni v Sethia*, and *Ralli Bros* are also distinguished in a different way. *Ralli Bros* addresses a situation where the contract is to be performed in a country where performance is unlawful under the law of that country, while the two other judgments concern situations where 'the real object and intention of the parties necessitates them joining in an endeavour to perform in a foreign and friendly country some act which is illegal by the law of such country notwithstanding the fact that there may be, in a certain event, alternative modes or places of performing which permit the contract to be performed legally'.[159] It is thus required for the application of the *Ralli Bros* rule that the act must be an act necessary for the performance of the contract, while an action (eg, a preparatory step) that a party may take to be able to perform under the contract does not suffice.[160] As we have seen, *Foster v Driscoll* and *Regazzoni* were seen as cases which could be addressed under the public policy of the forum, since the contracts concerned interfered with Britain's maintenance of relations with friendly foreign countries as a result of entering into a contract with the objective of defeating the application of a foreign prohibition.[161] On the contrary, *Ralli Bros* could simply be interpreted as a rule concerning contracts that do not violate English public policy in the absence of endangering friendly relations with other countries, but are illegal under the law of the place of performance.[162]

Notwithstanding the above, the similarity between the two lines of case law cannot be denied. The Court of Appeal acknowledged that the two lines of case law – *Ralli Bros* on the one hand, and *Foster v Driscoll* and *Regazzoni v Sethia* on the other – have the same origin and that both of them concern illegality.[163] Briggs considers them together under the category of illegality under the law of the place of performance.[164] Differences clearly appear between the two lines of case law when we turn to the substantive contract law consequences. However, if we look at these decisions from a private international law point of view, they may be set together as cases concerning in principle the same problem, the applicability of the overriding mandatory provisions of the law of the place of performance. Putting the case in a private international law context, the question left unanswered by the English judicial practice is whether we can consider these cases as the direct application of the foreign norms or whether they are given effect simply through the public policy reservation of English conflict of laws.

v. The Libyan Arab Foreign Bank *Litigation*

Under English law, a foreign economic sanction was not automatically given effect and thus did not exempt a non-performing party, unless it was part of the proper

[159] *Foster v Driscoll* [1929] 1 KB 470, 521–22. See the distinction in *Ispahani v Bank Melli Iran* (n 131).
[160] Stone (n 110) 337.
[161] Collins (n 107) vol 2, 1837.
[162] ibid 1837.
[163] *Ispahani v Bank Melli Iran* (n 131).
[164] Adrian Briggs, *Private International Law in English Courts* (Oxford University Press, 2014) 615.

law of the contract or if it involved an act that was unlawful under the law of the place of performance.[165] In addition to *Regazzoni v Sethia*, the application of foreign economic sanctions was at issue in the *Libyan Arab Foreign Bank* litigation. As the cases were decided before the entry into force of the Rome Convention and the adoption of the Rome I Regulation, they also required the interpretation of the above-discussed English case law on the application of foreign prohibitions.

Freezing assets in US banks and in the foreign establishments of US banks as US-controlled entities raised concerns in relation to economic sanctions imposed by the US against foreign states, such as Iran[166] and Libya. The question arose as to whether European banks had to comply with the US sanctions. US sanctions, and in particular freezing assets kept in US accounts, were intended to be avoided by clients by moving assets to accounts of banks outside the US.[167] As the deposits were made in US dollars at the accounts of mainly European banks, as well as European subsidiaries or branches of American banks, these deposits were given the name 'eurodollars'. Even in this case, foreign branches of US banks faced a challenging situation as regards US sanctions: non-compliance with US sanctions could expose the banks to penalties under US law, while non-performance under the contract entered into with a client due to the freezing of its account could render the banks concerned liable to pay significant amounts of damages to clients and could also lead to a loss in the depositors' trust towards the bank.[168]

This was also the background to the *Libyan Arab Foreign Bank* cases. In these cases, the English courts carried out a purely conflict-of-laws approach and did not immerse themselves in the issue of whether the US sanctions could be considered at the level of English substantive law. In *Libyan Arab Foreign Bank v Bankers Trust Co*, Bankers Trust, an American bank, opened two accounts for Libyan Arab Foreign Bank, a Libyan bank, with its New York and London branches respectively, with a daily management of those accounts involving the transfer of any amount exceeding a certain level from the New York account to the London account and, in the event that the balance fell below that level, the missing amount being transferred from London to New York.[169] Both the London and the New York accounts

[165] Ross Cranston, 'The Libyan Arab Foreign Bank Case' (1987) *Journal of Business Law* 499, 499–500.

[166] Executive Order No 12170 of President Carter of 14 November 1979, 44 FR 65729. See Christian Gavalda, 'L'efficacité juridique en France de l'executive order du président Carter "gelant" les avoirs officiels iraniens?' (1979) Gazette du Palais 18 décembre 1979, 645.

[167] Geneviève Burdeau, 'Le gel d'avoirs étrangers' (1997) 124 *Journal du droit international* 5, 13.

[168] Corinne R Rutzke, 'The Libyan Asset Freeze and its Application to Foreign Government Deposits in Overseas Branches of United States Banks: *Libyan Arab Foreign Bank v Bankers Trust Co*' (1988) 3 *American University International Law Review* 241, 244.

[169] *Libyan Arab Foreign Bank v Bankers Trust Co* [1989] QB 728. See Joseph Gold, *The Fund Agreement in the Courts*, vol 4 (IMF, 1989) 156–78; AV Lowe, 'Freezing Foreign Bank Accounts – *Libyan Arab Foreign Bank v Bankers Trust Co*' (1988) *Lloyd's Maritime and Commercial Law Quarterly* 1; Rutzke (n 166) 241; Cranston (n 163) 499; Ross Cranston, 'The Libyan Assets Case: Limits to Extraterritorial Claims' (1987) 3 *Journal of International Banking Law* 177; Daniel Urech, 'Eurodollar Deposits and Freezing Orders: The Libyan Assets Case Revisited' (1988) *Journal of International Banking Law* 269.

were denominated in US dollars. This arrangement aimed at preventing the effects of a potential freeze of the US accounts due to the expected US sanctions.[170]

The transfer of money (as well as any payments) was denied by Bankers Trust from the account with its New York branch to the account of the client, Libyan Arab Foreign Bank, held with its London branch, when US President Reagan issued an executive order blocking all property of the Libyan government and its agencies, instrumentalities and controlled entities in the US or in the possession of or control of US persons, including the overseas branches of US persons.[171] The sanction imposed by the Executive Order of 8 January 1986 was an answer to the terrorist attack supported by the Libyan state and the refusal of Libya to extradite the perpetrators. After payment was demanded by the client, the American bank argued that it was illegal for it to make any transfer or payment on behalf of the Libyan bank due to the executive order. The London branch was an overseas branch of a US person, whereas Libyan Arab Foreign Bank, which was wholly owned by the Central Bank of Libya, was an agency, instrumentality or controlled entity by the Libyan government within the meaning of US law.

As far as foreign policy considerations are concerned, Staughton J gently detached such considerations from the assessment of the case and focused on private international law:

> The United Kingdom Parliament did not enact any similar legislation. No doubt there were reasons of high policy for that forbearance; but with them I am not concerned. It is sufficient to say that nothing in English domestic law prohibited such a transaction. So the main issues in this case are concerned with the rules of conflict of laws, which determine when and to what extent the law of New York is given effect in our courts, and with the contractual obligations of banks.[172]

At the same time, he acknowledged that political factors might influence the investors' choice where to deposit their money:

> Political risk must commonly be an important factor to those who deposit large sums of money with banks; the popularity of Swiss bank accounts with some people is due to the banking laws of the Cantons of Switzerland. And I have already found, on the evidence of Bankers Trust, that the Iranian crisis was at the back of everyone's mind in 1980. Whatever considerations did or did not influence the parties to this case, I believe that banks generally and their customers normally intend the local law to apply. So I would require solid grounds for holding that the general rule does not apply, and there do not appear to me to be such grounds in this case.[173]

The court found that a single contract existed between the parties concerning the two accounts, but made a split as to the applicable law. The contract was governed partly by English and partly by New York law in accordance with the law of the

[170] Burdeau (n 165) 52.
[171] Executive Order 12544 of 8 January 1986, FR 1235, 3 CFR, 1986 Comp, 183.
[172] *Libyan Arab Foreign Bank v Bankers Trust Co* [1989] QB 728, 733.
[173] ibid 747.

place where the account was kept respectively for the London and the New York accounts. The court held that, concerning the London account, the contract between the bank and the client was determined by the law of the place where the account was kept, ie, by English law. Under English law, the bank could have denied payment for the client only if the payment was illegal by the proper law of the contract or it involved doing an act which was unlawful in the place in which it was performed. The court distinguished the case from *Regazzoni v Sethia*, where the parties' object and intention was to perform an act in the territory of a foreign and friendly state which was deemed to be unlawful under the law of that state. In *Libyan Arab Foreign Bank v Bankers Trust Co*, the objective was not to perform an illegal act. Instead, the other principle (essentially reflecting *Ralli Bros*) could be applied according to which the performance is excused if it necessarily involves doing an act which is unlawful by the law of the place of performance. Staughton J stated that the payment could be performed without breaching New York law either, in cash in US dollars, from the London office after dispatching the required amount from the US to London, or it was also available for the bank to make payments for the client in cash in pounds sterling from the London account. Based on the above, the court decided in favour of the Libyan bank and did not take the US sanction into consideration.

The *Libyan Arab Foreign Bank v Manufacturers Hanover Trust Co* case was based on similar (but not identical) facts and had a similar outcome.[174] Libyan Arab Foreign Bank and Manufacturers Hanover Trust (MHT) entered into an agreement, according to which MHT opened on behalf of Libyan Arab Foreign Bank two bank accounts: one US dollar account with MHT London and another one with MHT New York. The accounts were subject to an automatic fund transfer agreement: sums exceeding a threshold were automatically transferred from the New York account to the London account on a daily basis and vice versa if the balance of the New York account fell below the threshold concerned. Following the Executive Order of President Reagan issued on 8 January 1986, MHT refused payment out of the London account of Libyan Arab Foreign Bank at the request of the latter. It argued that the agreement between the parties was a single composite agreement governed by New York law and, accordingly, that it was unlawful to perform payment under that proper law. The court decided that Libyan Arab Foreign Bank was entitled to recover its frozen funds despite the Executive Order. Under the executive order, it was illegal for the defendant bank to make any payment on behalf of its client, as the US sanction covered all property of the Libyan government in the possession of US persons, including their overseas branches. Unlike in *Libyan Arab Foreign Bank v Bankers Trust Co*, the court held that there were two separate contracts here concerning the accounts in London and New York.

[174] *Libyan Arab Foreign Bank v Manufacturers Hanover Trust Co*, QB (Com Ct) [1988] 2 Lloyd's Law Reports 494; *Libyan Arab Foreign Bank v Manufacturers Hanover Trust Co (No 2)*, QB (Com Ct) [1989] 1 Lloyd's Law Reports 608.

This was deduced from the fact that the parties intended to distance themselves and keep the two accounts separate. This could be best achieved through two contracts. The contract related to the New York account was governed by New York law, but the US sanction could not be applied to the account in London, since the proper law of this contract was English law, as England was the place where the account was kept. The extraterritorial US sanction was thus not applied in this case either.

The court decisions were based on a formal conflict-of-laws approach without any reliance on foreign policy considerations: English conflict-of-laws rules were applied without examining the possibility of giving effect to US law outside the conflict-of-laws analysis.[175] Illegality under the law of the state of the currency used did not result in illegality under English law.[176] Political considerations and values did not replace the normal operation of conflict-of-laws rules. This feature of the decisions has been considered as the accentuation of the significance of legal certainty for economic players and from the point of view of the London financial market.[177] The acceptance of the US sanctions regime would have deterred depositors from placing money in eurodollar accounts or would have resulted in a withdrawal of such funds.[178] However, this choice could be seen as a policy choice in favour of party interests instead of supporting the foreign policy objectives of other states, even in the fight against terrorism.[179]

Concerning the *Libyan Arab Foreign Bank v Bankers Trust Co* case, it is often recalled that the bank did not appeal against the judgment.[180] Furthermore, it was granted an authorisation from the US authorities for the payment to the client.[181] In this way, the US itself denounced the extraterritorial application of the sanctions against Libya. Rutzke interprets the *Libyan Arab Foreign Bank v Bankers Trust Co* judgment as demonstrating that the US needs the cooperation of other countries for the effective enforcement of its sanctions regime.[182]

D. *Iran Continental Shelf Oil Company v IRI International Corporation*

The Court of Appeal indirectly addressed economic sanctions in a case decided under the Rome Convention. In *Iran Continental Shelf Oil Company v IRI International Corporation*, Iranian companies brought an action against IRI, a company

[175] Angelika Fuchs, 'Freigabe libyschen Vermögens in England trotz US-Einfrierungsbeschluß' (1990) *IPRax* 260, 263.
[176] ibid 264.
[177] ibid.
[178] Rutzke (n 166) 280.
[179] Fuchs (n 173) 264.
[180] Cranston (n 163) 499; Rutzke (n 166) 281.
[181] Rutzke (n 166) 281–82.
[182] ibid 280–81.

incorporated in Delaware and having its principal place of business in Houston, Texas, but which at the same time had an office in the UK.[183] IRI undertook in a contract to supply certain parts and equipment for the refurbishment of an oil rig in the Persian Gulf owned by the Iranian companies and to send engineers to oversee their installation on the rig. However, IRI refused to send its engineers to carry out the work agreed because it argued that Executive Order 12959 of President Clinton prevented it from doing this. The Iranian companies thus had to engage others to do the work and claimed damages from IRI for breach of contract. The question in this case was whether English or Texas law governed the contract. As it was not possible to establish a choice of law of the parties, the governing law had to be determined in accordance with Article 4 of the Rome Convention. It seemed to be clear that the characteristic performance was effected by IRI. However, the outcome of the case turned upon the question requiring the interpretation of the second sentence of Article 4 (2) of the Rome Convention as to whether the characteristic performance under the contract was provided by the principal place of business of the company in Texas or instead by another place of business of the same company, such as the UK office of IRI. IRI claimed the former, in favour of Texas law, while the claimants argued for the latter resulting in the application of English law.

Clarke LJ held that the characteristic performance was effected by the UK office and accordingly that English law applied. The judge came to this conclusion from the circumstances of the case. All characteristic elements of the contractual performance were effected by the UK office and its personnel, including invoicing, the arrangement of the shipment and tendering the documents to the buyer. This conclusion was not altered by the fact that the contractual arrangements and the appearance of the UK office in the contractual relationship served to avoid the Iranian Prime Minister's Order prohibiting purchases by Iranian entities of goods from the US. The contractual documents between the parties were prepared carefully in a way that did not violate the Iranian prohibition, which did not extend to products purchased from non-US sellers, and this was the reason for IRI UK appearing in those documents.

Finally, the Court of Appeal stated that the application of English law could not be disregarded on the grounds that the characteristic performance cannot be determined or that the contract is more closely connected with another country under Article 4(5) of the Rome Convention. The fact that the materials were shipped in Houston and that the far greater part of the contracted price concerned the value of goods having a US origin did not result in the rebuttal of the presumption in favour of English law.

Although the Court of Appeal judgment was limited to establishing that English law applied, this also had an effect on the application of the sanction imposed by the US President, which was excluded as it did not constitute part

[183] *Iran Continental Shelf Oil Company v IRI International Corporation* [2002] EWCA Civ 1024.

of the governing law. Again, the approach of the English court was to focus on conflict-of-laws analysis without examining the possibility of giving effect to a foreign economic sanction falling outside the applicable law. The discussion of the court centred on Article 4 of the Rome Convention and did not extend to the question of the application of overriding mandatory provisions under Article 7, which the executive order clearly was. This may be explained by the reservation made by the UK to Article 7(1) of the Rome Convention.

E. The Rome Convention and the Rome I Regulation in England

In fact, the notion of mandatory rules was introduced into English law by the Rome Convention.[184] The Rome Convention was adopted by the UK,[185] but it made a reservation to Article 7(1).[186] In view of the reservation made by the UK to Article 7(1), from the time of the adoption of the Rome Convention, interference with the otherwise applicable law was possible based on the (overriding) mandatory provisions of English law as the law of the forum under Article 7(2) of the Rome Convention and on the grounds of the English *ordre public* (the public policy clause) pursuant to Article 16 of the Rome Convention.

However, it was questionable whether the *Ralli Bros* judgment, according to which a contract (or a contractual term) is invalid and cannot be enforced if its performance was unlawful under the law of the country of the place of performance, was still living law. If it is deemed to be a rule of conflict of laws, then it could not be applied under the Rome Convention and the Rome I Regulation because the EU-level private international law rules replaced English conflict-of-laws rules concerning the law applicable to contractual obligations. Yet, thanks to the Rome I Regulation, English courts would have more freedom to give effect to the rules of the place of performance. This is because Article 9(3) of the Rome I Regulation grants discretion to the courts to apply the rules of the place of performance, while under English common law, this was an obligation for the courts.[187] The reservation made to Article 7(1) of the Rome Convention led to the result that overriding mandatory norms of third states could not be applied or given effect by an English court. However, if *Ralli Bros* were to be construed as a rule of substantive law, there was no obstacle to applying it as a ground of frustration, provided that the contract could not be performed due to the legislation of the place of performance.[188] If it were a rule of substantive contract law, then it would not be affected by the

[184] Susanne Knöfel, 'Mandatory Rules and Choice of Law: A Comparative Approach to Article 7(2) of the Rome Convention' (1999) *Journal of Business Law* 239, 239; Hartley (n 124) 346 fn 4.

[185] Contracts (Applicable Law) Act 1990, s 2(1).

[186] ibid s 2(2).

[187] James (n 129) 117.

[188] Kinsch (n 4) 42.

Rome Convention or by the subsequent Rome I Regulation, but would apply only if the contract is governed by English law. In *Ispahani v Bank Melli Iran*,[189] the Court of Appeal stated that it seems that the principles laid down by *Ralli Bros* and *Foster v Driscoll* are 'part of the English law of contract (as opposed to part of the English law of conflict) and as such are unaffected by the Rome Convention'.[190] The Court of Appeal, however, added that it was 'unnecessary to express any final view on that point'.[191]

As we have seen, English case law has been burdened with some uncertainties as regards contracts which violated English public policy or breached the rules of the state of the place of performance. These uncertainties were not dispelled by the Rome Convention. The divergent interpretations outlined in section III.C.iv above suggest that serious legal certainty concerns arose in relation to English law, even if Article 7(1) of the Rome Convention was not adopted and the Proposal for the Rome I Regulation was contested by the UK.[192] The situation changed with the Rome I Regulation, which did not leave any room for manoeuvre for the Member States by permitting reservations. The Rome I Regulation created more certainty than the patchwork of English court decisions. Under the Rome I Regulation, only overriding mandatory provisions of the forum or the place of performance may be given effect. The Rome I Regulation has been phrased by taking common law practice into account. This was the precondition for the compromise which induced the UK to opt in to the Rome I Regulation. As discussed before, Article 9(3) essentially takes over the *Ralli Bros* rule and makes it clear that an English court may give effect to the law of the place of performance if it renders the performance of the contract unlawful, irrespective of whether the law governing the contract is English or not. The Rome I Regulation thus eliminated to a large extent the uncertainties and clarified the possibility of applying English overriding mandatory norms by English courts, and giving effect to those of foreign states where the contract is to be performed.[193]

Article 9(3) of the Rome I Regulation may be seen as rendering it possible to apply foreign overriding mandatory provisions in the aforementioned cases raised before English courts. McParland, considering *Foster v Driscoll* as a case based on English public policy preventing the enforcement of a contract that was against international comity, found that the case well demonstrates the overlap between Article 9(3) and Article 21 of the Rome I Regulation.[194] Analysing Article 21 of the Rome I Regulation, Stone remarks that under Article 16 of the Rome Convention, English courts could deny the enforceability of contracts which required parties to perform an act that is illegal under the law of the state of the place of performance.[195] He adds that this is now possible under Article 9(3) of the Rome I

[189] *Ispahani v Bank Melli Iran* (1997) *Times*, 29 December, [1997] Lexis Citation 4800, [1997] All ER (D) 124.

[190] ibid (Robert Walker LJ).

[191] ibid (Robert Walker LJ).

[192] Harris (n 102) 300.

[193] Harris (n 102) 305–06.

[194] Michael McParland, *The Rome I Regulation on the Law Applicable to Contractual Obligations* (Oxford University Press, 2015) 711.

[195] Stone (n 110) 336.

Regulation, but nothing rules out having equal recourse to Article 21 of the Rome I Regulation as was previously the case under the equivalent provision of the Rome Convention.[196]

In relation to the Rome Convention, the question of whether the reservation made by the UK to Article 7(1) may be 'circumvented' by having recourse to Article 7(2) to ensure the application of *Ralli Bros* has already arisen. Hartley noted with some regret that the tailor-made rule of Article 7(1) of the Rome Convention could not apply to situations such as *Regazzoni v Sethia* due to the UK reservation made to this provision,[197] but adds that the application of Article 7(2) of the Rome Convention, embodying the internationally mandatory provisions of the forum, would have had the same result[198] even before the entry into force of the Rome I Regulation. It may be doubted whether Article 7(2) was correct to apply the foreign overriding mandatory norms of the place of performance as the overriding mandatory rules of the forum. It should be noted that Article 16 Rome Convention and Article 21 Rome I Regulation simply authorise the non-application of the otherwise governing law if such application is manifestly incompatible with the public policy (*ordre public*) of the forum, but does not provide instead for the application of the overriding mandatory provisions of a third country, even if it is a friendly foreign state. Harris disapproves of giving effect to the law of foreign states that do not fall within the scope of Article 9(3) via Article 21 of the Rome I Regulation.[199] This is deduced from the legislative intention and also by the arguments of the UK in the legislative procedure to give room to foreign overriding mandatory provisions only exceptionally, as set out by Article 9(3), in favour of the promotion of legal certainty and not to allow the introduction of other foreign overriding mandatory provisions through the public policy reservation.

It must also be stressed that Article 9 of the Rome I Regulation is limited to the overriding mandatory provisions of the forum and those of the place of performance, and does not cover foreign rules, the application of which would be simply justified on the grounds of the preservation of friendly relations with the issuing country as part of the comity. It is another question that the need to maintain friendly relations with other states may be taken into account under Article 9(3) when considering the consequences of the application or non-application of the economic sanction. If interpreting the concept of place of performance in the Rome I Regulation narrowly and limiting it to the ultimate place of performance, as Harris argues, *Foster v Driscoll* and *Regazzoni v Sethia* would not survive the Rome I Regulation.[200] In *Regazzoni v Sethia*, the place of performance of the

[196] ibid 336 and 341.

[197] Trevor C Hartley, 'Mandatory Rules in International Contracts: The Common Law Approach' in *Collected Courses of the Hague Academy of International Law, vol 266 – 1997* (Martinus Nijhoff, 1998) 337, 403.

[198] ibid 403; Hartley (n 110) 241, 243.

[199] Harris (n 102) 333.

[200] ibid 319.

contract between the parties was not South Africa, but Genoa, and in *Foster v Driscoll* the contract could have been performed outside the US. The parties were simply aware that the ultimate destination of the goods was another country. He therefore contends that the rule stemming from *Foster v Driscoll* and *Regazzoni v Sethia* thus could not be maintained under Article 9(3).[201]

F. The Impact of Brexit on the Application of Economic Sanctions

The question is what will happen after Brexit. The precise impact of Brexit on the application of economic sanctions is dependent, of course, upon the content of the agreements on Brexit made between the EU and the UK, which is unknown at present.

From a foreign policy point of view, it is not expected that EU and UK foreign policy will differ in terms of applying economic sanctions.[202] Strong political ties will probably be maintained and some formal cooperation will remain between the EU and the UK even after Brexit as far as the application of economic sanctions is concerned. The House of Lords Report on UK–EU relations after Brexit confirms that the British government, the European Council and the European Parliament all envisage cooperation and coordination in the future concerning sanctions.[203] The Report considers the possibility of a separate agreement between the UK and the EU 'to facilitate cooperation on external affairs and defence, including but not limited to continuing UK participation in EU sanctions regimes'.[204] A formal consultation mechanism on foreign policy, including economic sanctions, is equally envisaged by the EU.[205]

The economic sanctions imposed by the UNSC must be implemented by both the EU and the UK. Beyond the UN sanctions, both the EU and the UK may adopt autonomous sanctions. However, the foreign policy interests of the EU and the UK against the target countries will mostly coincide. However, differences may occur. These may concern sanctions which cover certain sectors, such as the financial sector, where the UK may tend to expose its banks less to economic sanctions.[206]

[201] ibid.

[202] Richard Nephew and David Mortlock, 'Brexit's Implications for UK and European Sanctions Policy' Columbia University Academic Commons, Center on Global Energy Policy Reports (October 2016) 1, 19, https://academiccommons.columbia.edu/catalog/ac:206466.

[203] House of Lords, European Union Committee, 17th Report Session 2017–19, 'UK–EU Relations after Brexit', 8 June 2018, 12, https://publications.parliament.uk/pa/ld201719/ldselect/ldeucom/149/149.pdf.

[204] ibid 33.

[205] European Commission, Task Force for the Preparation and Conduct of the Negotiations with the United Kingdom under Article 50 TEU, 'Foreign, Security and Defence Policy (Slides)', 15 June 2018, TF50 (2018) 50 – Commission to EU 27, 7, https://ec.europa.eu/commission/sites/beta-political/files/slides_on_foreign_security_defence_policy.pdf.

[206] Nephew and Mortlock (n 200) 20.

Differences may also take place in designating persons subject to asset freezes or travel bans. Furthermore, the UK may adopt blocking measures (under the Protection of Trading Interests Act or on a different legal basis) independently of the EU in order to exclude the non-desirable effects of economic sanctions imposed by other states, such as the US.

The UK will qualify as a third country from an EU perspective in the case of a 'hard Brexit'. Before the court of a Member State, a UK sanction may appear as part of the governing law, the law of the place of performance or another law. In deciding whether to apply a differing UK sanction, the courts of the Member States have to turn to the rules of the Rome I Regulation and, more specifically, Article 9(3). It is questionable what happens if the UK sanction is part of the *lex causae* and it will be dependent on the governing law whether a UK sanction may be given effect through substantive law.

At the moment, it is more difficult to assess the outcome when the question arises before an English tribunal after Brexit of whether to apply an EU sanction that is not identical to a UK one – for instance, if an EU sanction regulation goes beyond the restrictions imposed by UK law. It is not easy either to predict how conflict-of-laws rules will develop in England after Brexit. The Rome I Regulation, as a directly applicable EU regulation, has not been implemented by the UK and therefore it will cease to apply in the UK after Brexit. If UK legislation does not adopt specific provisions on the law governing contracts for the time following the Brexit, by virtue of the Contracts (Applicable Law) Act 1990, the Rome Convention remains applicable in the UK. However, as has been noted, the UK made a reservation to Article 7(1) of the Rome Convention. UK legislation has the option to retain in some way the Rome I Regulation or adopt an equivalent solution in line with Article 9 of the Rome I Regulation. Alternatively, English courts may turn back to their case law dating back to before the Rome Convention. Yet, as discussed before, this line of case law has been burdened by several uncertainties. If this happens, these uncertainties may reappear concerning the application of foreign (including EU) economic sanctions.

However, in a policy paper, the British government indicated that its intention is to incorporate the Rome I Regulation into domestic law.[207] The continued application of the rules of the Rome I Regulation may raise problems of interpretation. According to the European Union (Withdrawal) Act 2018, the retained EU law must be interpreted in line with the CJEU case law in most UK courts, even after Brexit.[208] Additionally, UK courts may take the decisions of the CJEU rendered after Brexit into consideration, but they are not bound to do so.[209] This implies

[207] HM Government, *Providing a Cross-Border Civil Judicial Cooperation Framework – A Future Partnership Paper* (22 August 2017) 1, 6, https://assets.publishing.service.gov.uk/government/uploads/system/uploads/attachment_data/file/639271/Providing_a_cross-border_civil_judicial_cooperation_framework.pdf.

[208] European Union (Withdrawal) Act 2018, s 6(3).

[209] ibid s 6(2).

that even if the UK does not cease to apply the rules of the Rome I Regulation, UK courts may deviate from its interpretation given by the CJEU after Brexit.

G. Conclusion

Under English private international law before the Rome Convention and the Rome I Regulation, public policy allowed English courts to disregard the otherwise applicable foreign law or apply the overriding rules of English law. Foreign overriding mandatory norms could also be applied provided they constituted part of the proper law of the contract. The court practice also recognised that the law of the place of performance which renders performance illegal may be taken into account in the case of supervening illegality (*Ralli Bros*) or when the parties' intention was to enter into an illegal contract from the outset. It was debated whether this was a rule of conflict-of-laws or substantive law. In the former case, it could be applied irrespective of the governing law. If it is considered as a substantive rule, then, whenever the conflict-of-laws analysis has the outcome that English law applies, a contract illegal according to the law of the place of performance will not be enforceable before an English court. Accordingly, the *Ralli Bros* rule applies as a rule of English contract law on discharge or suspension of contractual obligations as a result of supervening illegality.

Based on the previous common law practice, under certain circumstances, economic sanctions of a foreign state could also be taken into consideration where the contract had to be performed there. In deciding cases involving economic sanctions, English courts sometimes had recourse to foreign policy considerations (*Regazzoni v Sethia*) and gave effect to the sanction of a foreign friendly state, while on other occasions foreign policy arguments were fully excluded and a foreign economic sanction not pertaining to the *lex causae* was not given effect (the *Libyan Arab Foreign Bank* cases). When the courts gave effect to the rules of the country of the place of performance, they also referred to comity based on public policy. The application of foreign norms on the grounds of public policy used to be linked by English courts to the idea of comity between the UK and friendly foreign states. This sometimes resulted in giving effect to a foreign overriding mandatory norm through the public policy of the forum. It should be noted that the pertinence of this approach and whether comity can indeed justify taking a third country law into account was called into question.[210] It was stressed that it was rather the self-interest of the state of the forum in maintaining friendly relations with other nations that necessitated the acceptance of foreign overriding mandatory norms.[211]

[210] Andrew Dickinson, 'Third-Country Mandatory Rules in the Law Applicable to Contractual Obligations: So Long, Farewell, Auf Wiedersehen, Adieu?' (2007) 3 *Journal of Private International Law* 53, 76–77; Harris (n 102) 279.

[211] Harris (n 102) 279.

The wording of the Rome I Regulation took English common law practice largely into account in order to ensure the participation of the UK in the application of the regulation and put the application of overriding mandatory provisions on a legislative basis. UK courts may continue to give effect to the overriding mandatory provisions of the state of the place of performance when this law renders performance unlawful. When deciding whether to give effect to foreign overriding mandatory provisions within the framework of Article 9(3), English courts can have regard to the maintenance of friendly relations with foreign states, ie, foreign policy considerations, as they did before. If the British government decides to transpose the rules of the Rome I Regulation after Brexit, the approach of UK courts can be predicted not to differ significantly from those of the Member States, though the future judgments of the CJEU rendered after Brexit will no longer be binding on UK courts.

IV. Assessment of the Judicial Practice of the Member States

Economic sanctions necessarily involve uncertainties for private parties. It is not possible to predict the duration of the application of an economic sanction and thus the period of the interruption of the contractual relationship of the parties and their overall impact on the future of their business relations. These uncertainties are often added to the pre-existing uncertainties related to the country subject to the economic sanction: the lack of the rule of law, political upheaval and social tensions. The legal treatment of economic sanctions may even escalate uncertainties for the parties and it seems that the treatment of economic sanctions in private international law does not ease the situation.

In private international law, uncertainties stem from two sources. The first is legislation and in particular the flexible wording used by the Rome I Regulation as demonstrated in Chapter 5. The second source of uncertainties is the judicial practice of the Member States.

As Professor d'Avout has rightly described, although the notion of overriding mandatory provision has been domesticated in EU law, the national factor plays a pre-eminent role in the application of overriding mandatory norms.[212] This statement fits into the above examination of the application of economic sanctions as overriding mandatory provisions by the courts of the Member States. The EU exercises its own competence when it adopts economic sanctions. Regarding EU sanctions, uniformity may be realised by the application of EU sanction regulations as part of the law of the forum. EU foreign policy objectives are thus uniformly enforced. However, the courts of the Member States do not follow a uniform view concerning foreign economic sanctions.

[212] D'Avout (n 52) 2168.

In the absence of a common EU approach towards the sanctions of third countries, the decision on the application of foreign economic sanctions has been left to the Member States. There may be differences as to the application of the overriding mandatory provisions of the *lex causae* and the national judicial practice is divergent regarding the extent to which overriding mandatory provisions of the state of the place of performance may be taken into consideration under Article 9(3) of the Rome I Regulation. This is still aggravated by the method of giving effect to foreign economic sanctions through the governing substantive law outside the Rome I Regulation. Member States have recourse to various techniques and rely either on Article 9 of the Rome I Regulation or include economic sanctions in the substantive law assessment of the case.

The conflict-of-laws approach and the substantive law approach stand beside each other as alternatives.[213] This is made clear by the *Nikiforidis* judgment of the CJEU. This alternative is optional from the point of view of the courts. They are not obliged to give effect to a foreign overriding mandatory norm under Article 9(3) or through substantive contract law.

If the law of the forum permits this, economic sanctions of other states may also be taken into account at the level of substantive law. This option again depends largely on the considerations of the court seised. The *Giti* judgment demonstrates that French judicial practice was reluctant to have recourse to this method, while German courts broadly use substantive law to open the way for foreign economic sanctions. In fact, the substantive law approach is applied if the governing law is the law of the forum. German courts used the substantive law approach only when German law was the governing law.[214] In this case, the forum builds foreign overriding mandatory norms into the analysis of the case at the level of its own substantive law. This process involves the examination of interests and values of the forum and those behind the foreign overriding mandatory provision. If the applicable law is a foreign law, substantive law consideration is possible only if it is allowed by the rules of the governing foreign law. It is more difficult to decide on the interests and values represented by the governing law and the overriding mandatory provision of a third state when the applicable law is a foreign law.

The advantages of the substantive law consideration are clear when, for example, goods are seized by authorities and thus the performance of the contract becomes impossible. However, its applicability is questionable when the foreign economic sanction has not yet been enforced, but there is a probability that it will be. Some authors argue that the exposure to and the probability of imposing penalties on the person concerned and the seriousness of the penalties must be taken into account.[215] Kuckein asserts that exposure to criminal penalties suffices to establish hindrance of performance, provided that the imposing state actually enforces the sanctions and the person concerned is threatened by the criminal

[213] Zimmer (n 59) 66.
[214] Behr (n 69) 105.
[215] Kuckein (n 122) 112–13.

penalty in the given case.[216] A further circumstance is whether the parties can circumvent the import or export prohibition. If the economic sanction can factually hinder performance (eg, by the seizure of goods), the economic sanction, as an overriding mandatory norm, should be given effect as a necessity, otherwise it is difficult to predict whether a court will give effect to an economic sanction.

The application of the formal approach by some courts and the application of economic sanctions at a substantive level may lead to a lopsided and inconsistent application of foreign economic sanctions. The application of the economic sanctions of the forum and the uncertainties related to giving effect to foreign economic sanctions may lead to forum and law shopping.[217] The choice of forum triggers the application of the economic sanctions imposed by the forum state as well as (depending on the discretion of the court) potentially those of the place of performance.

These differences in applying foreign economic sanctions go against the objectives of EU private international law and more specifically those of the Rome I Regulation, of predictability, legal certainty, decisional harmony, preventing forum shopping and avoiding conflicting judgments. Cases may be decided differently depending on the location of the forum. Differences in court practice particularly arise in relation to US sanctions. The US applies severe criminal and administrative sanctions to compel business actors to comply with its economic sanctions. In particular, the withdrawal of export and import or operating licences implies a serious threat for companies; these compel them to observe US sanctions.

It has been demonstrated that the courts of the Member States do not have a consistent approach towards these sanctions: sometimes they are given effect, but not on other occasions. Although some of the reasons for these decisions may be revealed, sometimes the outcome depends on the circumstances of the case; there is no consistent line in the case law on when to give effect to a foreign economic sanction. Within the framework of the Rome I Regulation, as well as the consideration of economic sanctions at the level of substantive contract law, court decisions are influenced by several factors, such as the existence of a close connection between the foreign law and the situation, the factual impossibility of performance, and the examination of the interests and values underlying the sanction. Due to the flexibility of these factors, the judicial practice of the Member States is not free from oscillations between the conflict-of-laws and the substantive law approach, as well as between accepting or ignoring certain interests and values in a given case. Generally speaking, foreign economic sanctions are given effect where: (1) the imposing state can effectively enforce the sanction and can physically exercise control over the goods; or (2) the interests and values of the imposing state and the forum state coincide in terms of the application of the economic sanction.[218]

[216] ibid 113.
[217] Mankowski (n 33) 487.
[218] Großfeld and Junker (n 55) 128–29.

Courts can justify the rejection of the application of a foreign economic sanction by the formal adherence to Article 9 of the Rome I Regulation, but rejection may take place even at the level of substantive contract law, eg, stating that the sanction does not constitute a ground for *force majeure* under the *lex causae*.

Brummer describes the EU's sanctions policy as oscillating 'uneasily between interests, norms and values'.[219] Although the courts of the Member States apply the sanctions imposed by the EU uniformly, Brummer's statement undoubtedly holds when courts decide whether to take non-EU sanctions into account. Considering interests and values can lead to the inclusion of foreign policy considerations in the judicial decision. Foreign policy arguments are often given a legal formulation and appear as legal arguments. Even so, private international law cases involving economic sanctions cannot always escape foreign policy assessment. This is why the next section briefly addresses the foreign policy rhetoric of the courts of the Member States.

V. The Outcome: A Changeable European Judicial Foreign Policy

International political conflicts may be addressed in the easiest way by political means, in particular by diplomacy. If this is not successful, international political disputes are legalised by channelling them into the sphere of law. In this sphere, a court or tribunal renders a decision primarily on a purely legal basis. However, we can notice that the court judgments examined in this book could be easily turned into political statements. Cases may be interpreted so that they expose some political interests: *Massardy*, *Sensor* or *Giti* could be construed as the rejection of US foreign policy interests. Nevertheless, it is the case that courts sometimes take foreign policy considerations into account and reveal them expressly in their decision making. This happened in *Regazzoni v Sethia* and in the *Borax* and *Borsäure* cases. In so proceeding, courts may appear as agents or instruments in the foreign policy battle of states. In particular, when they give effect to economic sanctions, they are forced into the role of 'punisher' for the state(s) imposing the economic sanction.[220] Article 9(3), as well as the substantive law consideration of economic sanctions, lets courts take foreign policy evaluation into account and thereby the judge steps to a certain extent into the shoes of the state organs responsible for foreign policy.

The need for courts to distance themselves from political questions is stressed by several authors generally and in particular concerning private international law. In an article, US Court of Appeals Judge Cabranes stressed that courts should

[219] Klaus Brummer, 'Imposing Sanctions: The Not So "Normative Power Europe"' (2009) 14 *European Foreign Affairs Review* 191, 207.

[220] Gianviti (n 13) 279.

render decisions by exclusively considering the facts of the given case from a myopic perspective, and usually they do not and cannot have regard to the broader foreign policy consequences of the case.[221] In the long term, this may give rise to judicial decisions that are inconsistent with other court decisions and the acts of other branches. Courts lack the required expertise and information to balance foreign policy considerations adequately. Cabranes underlined the point that judges can interpret the law, but not the law's effects on foreign policy.

Regarding the analysis of the interests to be carried out by the courts, when deciding on giving effect to foreign economic sanctions, Schurig argues that the exclusion of a foreign embargo should be decided by political instances and not by the courts.[222] Vischer doubts whether civil courts should give effect to foreign economic sanctions, because otherwise they would substitute the foreign policy power of the executive.[223] He puts it clearly: 'Joining in a foreign embargo, for instance, is in the first line a political decision incumbent on the executive and not on the judiciary branch.'[224] In the absence of clear guidance on the part of the executive power, courts should refrain from taking foreign economic sanctions into account and thereby assisting the extraterritorial enforcement of the foreign policy interests and objectives of a foreign country.[225] Vischer also points out that the immersion of courts in foreign politics may lead to the potential discrepancies between the conduct of the courts and that of the administrative authorities. In the *borax* case, the German BGH declared the parties' conduct to be immoral even if forwarding the goods to Poland had been approved by the central bank of Hessen.[226] Vischer acknowledges at the same time that this is of course not to say that economic sanctions should not be considered where the interests of the forum state and the issuing state coincide, in particular in the case of sanctions imposed by the broader international community, such as the sanctions imposed by the UNSC.[227]

Presupposing the apolitical nature of private international law, courts should keep away from political questions when deciding international private law disputes and they should simply rely on the automatism of private international law rules. Accordingly, courts should not interfere with political issues in order to avoid the pretence that their decision reflects any political position accepting or rejecting an economic sanction, and thereby supporting or punishing a foreign state.[228]

[221] José A Cabranes, 'Withholding Judgment – Why US Courts Shouldn't Make Foreign Policy' (2015) 94 *Foreign Affairs* 125, 130.
[222] Klaus Schurig, 'Zwingendes Recht, "Eingriffsnormen" und neues IPR' (1990) 54 *RabelsZ* 217, 239–40.
[223] Frank Vischer, *General Course on Private International Law, Collected Courses of the Hague Academy of International Law*, vol 232 (Brill, 1992) 175.
[224] ibid 174.
[225] ibid 175.
[226] ibid.
[227] ibid.
[228] Gianviti (n 13) 302.

Economic sanctions as overriding mandatory norms belong to the most important political interests of a country: they are norms of foreign policy. When a court does not take the foreign overriding mandatory norms of the state imposing economic sanctions into account, this can be interpreted by another state as an attack on its vital political interests. This requires some justification. One possibility is the recourse to the *ordre public* exception if the foreign law containing the economic sanctions should have been applicable. When the question is whether to give effect to a foreign economic sanction, the court balances the interests concerned and often supports its conclusion with foreign policy arguments.

As explained above, under English law, a contract is unenforceable if it breaches English public policy, including the relations between the British government and other states with which the British government has friendly relations. Behr asks whether the same standards could be applied by a German court.[229] He rightly points out that the foreign policy interests of the forum constitute an uncertain standard.[230] For private parties, it is challenging to adapt themselves to such a flexible standard. This view is also supported by the constitutional law requirement of the separation of powers. Behr summarises that the German *ordre public* aims at abiding by the law (*Rechtstreue*), whereas English public policy also aims at abiding by politics.[231] However, it must be added that this contraposition is exaggerated. German court decisions are not even free from foreign policy considerations, as demonstrated by the *Borax* and *Borsäure* decisions, which were often cited by German courts later on.

The above analysis demonstrates that courts become a significant player in shaping foreign policy. The inclusion of foreign policy considerations in court decisions in private litigation and thereby taking a stance in foreign policy matters set the ground essentially for a judicial foreign policy. Two forms of judicial foreign policy are distinguished: first, the legal review of foreign policy decisions of the legislature primarily on the grounds of the standards of constitutional law, a corollary of which is the judicialisation of politics; and, second, courts may themselves become immersed in foreign policy by their decisions rendered directly in matters related in some way to foreign policy,[232] which politicise the judiciary to some extent. These cases include, among others, decisions on immunity or the participation of national courts in international judicial cooperation. We can clearly add to this category of cases judicial decisions rendered in matters involving economic sanctions requiring courts to decide the impact of a domestic or a foreign economic sanction as a foreign policy instrument on contracts between private parties. The term 'judicial foreign policy' has appeared in the US legal literature to describe the

[229] Behr (n 69) 124–25.
[230] ibid 124.
[231] ibid 125.
[232] Christopher Whytock, 'From International Law and International Relations to Law and World Politics' Draft, 2 December 2016, 1, 12, www.law.uci.edu/faculty/full-time/whytock/whytock-il-021216b.pdf.

involvement of US courts in shaping foreign policy, and although examinations of judicial foreign policy primarily touched upon the practice of US courts,[233] the cases decided by the courts of the Member States of the EU clearly demonstrate that this is not a uniquely American phenomenon.

Conflict of laws, traditionally considered as an apolitical branch of law, could be seen as a toolbox for preventing or mitigating the collision of the sovereigns' desire to apply their own law and policies to any legal dispute.[234] When deciding on the applicability of foreign economic sanctions, courts enjoy considerable room for manoeuvre; they may rely on a conflict-of-laws or substantive law approach to give effect to or disregard an economic sanction imposed by a third country.

The consideration of foreign economic sanctions at the level of substantive law along with the operation of conflict-of-laws rules leads to the creation of a legal mosaic by the court. Whether the pieces of mosaic are set together only by the conflict-of-laws technique or through substantive law depends on the facts of the case and the assessment of the court. However, both methods imply considerable leeway to take foreign policy considerations into account in rendering a judicial decision, and many times they seem to have been significant factors in decision making. As such, the pieces are assembled quite often by considering foreign policy objectives and interests. This is the politics of piecing together the mosaic and politics in private international law.

This has crucial implications. First, the neutrality of private international law, as well as its resistance to political considerations that are external to the system of private (international) law, is undoubtedly fading. Second, the relative freedom of courts results in the decentralisation of judicial foreign policy in terms of the application of economic sanctions of third countries. Instead of creating a common EU foreign policy position towards such sanctions, foreign policy is multiplying and fluctuating along the divergent approaches of the courts of the Member States. The appearance of foreign policy arguments involves the risk of the politicisation of the courts of the Member States and introduces an element into the judicial practice which is hardly predictable. This results in conflicting solutions. Divergences in the judicial practice of the Member States are sometimes intended to be prevented by the adoption of a blocking regulation through which the EU makes clear that the application of a foreign economic sanction is undesirable. The next chapter therefore deals with blocking legislation.

[233] David Sloss, 'Judicial Foreign Policy: Lessons from the 1970s' (2008) 53 *Saint Louis University Law Journal* 145; Jack I Garvey, 'Judicial Foreign Policy-Making in International Civil Litigation: Ending the Charade of Separation of Powers' (1993) 24 *Law & Policy in International Business* 461; Anne-Marie Slaughter, 'The Real New World Order' (1997) 76 *Foreign Affairs* 183, 186; Thomas M Franck, 'Courts and Foreign Policy' (1991) 83 *Foreign Policy* 66; Noah Feldman, 'When Judges Make Foreign Policy' *New York Times*, 25 September 2008.

[234] Whytock (n 230) 17.

7

Blocking Statutes

I. Blocking Statutes and Private International Law

Economic sanctions are often used extraterritorially. Some countries, most notably the US, determine the personal scope of application of economic sanctions, broadly extending them to foreign entities controlled by natural or legal persons of the issuing state. The territorial scope of application may be equally extensive: a relatively weak territorial link may suffice to apply economic sanctions. Similarly, the subject matter of the transactions restricted may go beyond goods originating from the issuing or the target state and may equally cover technology or licences used for the production or use of those goods.[1] The extraterritorial scope of the national provisions is often justified by the effects doctrine. It is not intended to discuss the issue of the concept, nature and legality of extraterritorial legislation here in detail; this has been done abundantly elsewhere by other authors.[2] The compatibility of extraterritorial sanctions, and in particular US sanctions, with public international law will not be discussed here either. The focus is instead on the private international law aspects of the application of such economic sanctions.

One way to foreclose the far-reaching impact of extraterritorial sanctions may be to deny their applicability on a case-by-case basis, recognising an economic sanction as an overriding mandatory norm of the *lex causae* but excluding its application based on the *ordre public* clause, or exercising the court's discretion under Article 9(3).

[1] Francisco Garcimartín Alférez, 'Embargo' in Jürgen Basedow, Giesela Rühl, Franco Ferrari and Pedro de Miguel Asensio (eds), *Encyclopedia of Private International Law* (Edward Elgar, 2017) 603.

[2] Jean-Michel Jacquet, 'La norme extraterritoriale dans le commerce international' (1985) *Journal du droit international* 327; Andreas F. Lowenfeld, 'Agora: The Cuban Liberty and Democratic Solidarity (Libertad) Act' (1996) 90 *American Journal of International Law* 419, 430–32; Cedric Ryngaert, 'Extraterritorial Export Controls (Secondary Boycotts)' (2008) 7 *Chinese Journal of International Law* 625, 625; Stanley J Marcuss and D Stephen Mathias, 'US Foreign Policy Export Controls: Do They Pass Muster under International Law' (1984) 2 *International Tax & Business Lawyer* 1; David B Adler, *Die Anwendung und Durchetzung US-amerikanischer Handelsbeschräkungen innerhalb der Europäischen Union – Wie schutzlos ist die EU?* (Duncker & Humblot, 2016) 46–61; Brigitte Stern, 'Quelques observations sur les règles internationales relatives à l'application extraterritoriale du droit' (1986) 32 *Annuaire français de droit international* 7; Christian Forwick, *Extraterritoriale US-amerikanische Exportkontrollen. Folgen für die Vertragsgestaltung* (Verlag Recht und Wirtschaft, 1993) 48–88; Jean-Gabriel Castel, *Extraterritoriality in International Trade* (Butterworths, 1988); Werner Meng, *Extraterritoriale Jurisdiktion im öffentlichen Wirtschaftsrecht* (Springer, 1994); François Rigaux, 'Droit économique et conflits de souverainetés' (1988) 52 *RabelsZ* 104.

A further means to thwart the application of a foreign economic sanction is the adoption of a specific norm blocking it. Blocking statutes are most often adopted by the target state, but other states may also adopt such legislation. In addition, blocking statutes may be adopted by a group of states or an organisation. Third countries usually adopt blocking statutes if the application of an economic sanction imposed by a foreign state is not desirable, usually because of its impact on the traders of the state adopting the blocking statute, for example, due to its extraterritorial reach.

Blocking statutes override the impact of economic sanctions. Even if conflict-of-laws rules designate the law containing the economic sanction, or the law of a third country contains the economic sanction, this will be ignored due to the blocking statute of the forum state. In this case, the blocking statute is a specific expression of the domestic *ordre public*. Blocking statutes are overriding mandatory provisions[3] and, as such, the forum will enforce its own blocking statute against the economic sanctions of the target state.

In this sense, some authors call them negative conflict-of-laws norms[4] as well as negative overriding mandatory norms.[5] The latter is a more correct denomination than the former, as the norms contained in a blocking statute are not conflict-of-laws norms, but substantive law rules.

Moreover, foreign blocking statutes may also be taken into account when a neutral forum decides on the application of a foreign economic sanction not targeting the forum state. If a foreign economic sanction should be applied or could be taken into account by the court pursuant to the conflict-of-laws rules, it may be set aside in light of a foreign blocking statute.

Typically, US economic sanctions not only reach the target state, but other countries and their economic operators are also required to respect US sanctions. In this way, the US requires other states to align their foreign policy with US foreign policy objectives.[6] In practice, an economic operator has to decide whether to comply with the economic sanction or the blocking statute, which exposes it to conflicting obligations.

Several countries have passed blocking statutes as an answer to the extraterritorial application of US law (in antitrust law as well as economic sanctions).[7]

[3] Jürgen Basedow, 'Blocking Statutes' in Jürgen Basedow, Giesela Rühl, Franco Ferrari and Pedro de Miguel Asensio (eds), *Encyclopedia of Private International Law*, vol 1 (Edward Elgar, 2017) 209, 212; Peter Mankowski, 'Drittstaatliche Embargonormen, Außenpolitik im IPR, Berücksichtigung von Fakten statt Normen: Art. 9 Abs. 3 Rom I-VO im praktischen Fall (zu Cour d'appel de Paris, 25.2.2015 – 12/23757)' (2016) 36 *IPRax* 485, 489.

[4] Martin Gebauer, 'Kollisionsrechtliche Auswirkungen der US-amerikanischen Helms-Burton-Gesetzgebung' (1998) 18 *IPRax* 145, 153, Mankowski (n 3) 489; see also Michael Cremer, 'Embargovorschriften als Eingriffsnormen' (2016) 10 *Bucerius Law Journal* 18, 23.

[5] Mankowski (n 3) 493.

[6] Aurore Marchand, 'Note – Cass com, 16 mars 2010, no 08-21.511' (2011) 138 *Journal du droit international* 99, 106.

[7] PCF Pettit and CJD Styles, 'The International Response to Extraterritorial Application of United States Antitrust Laws' (1982) 37 *Business Lawyer* 697.

The UK thus adopted the Protection of Trading Interests Act 1980,[8] although this did not expressly mention the US.[9] This was followed by the Protection of Trading Interests (US Re-export Control) Order 1982, which specifically concerned certain restrictive trade measures introduced by the US.

The US enacted trade sanctions against Cuba, Iran and Libya, and these sanctions had an impact even on natural and legal persons under the jurisdiction of the EC Member States. This provoked strong reactions by some of the Member States and the EC itself. As an economic sanction against the Cuban regime, the US adopted the Cuban Democracy Act 1992. This prohibited certain exports and imports to and from Cuba for persons controlled by US persons. As an answer, Canada adopted the Foreign Extraterritorial Measures Act and the UK had recourse to the previously mentioned Protection of Trading Interests Act 1980.[10] In 1996, the Cuban Liberty and Democratic Solidarity (Libertad) Act, also known as the US Helms-Burton Act, held liable any person trafficking US property confiscated by the Cuban government, ie, it extended the application of the act to persons and their acts outside US jurisdiction.[11] This provoked opposition on the part of several countries and the EU.[12] Again, the UK and Canada had recourse to their aforementioned blocking statutes and Mexico also adopted such a statute.[13] This was followed by the Iran and Libya Sanctions Act, the so-called D'Amato Act, in the same year.[14]

The EC protested against the extraterritorial application of these US sanctions. A WTO panel was established to settle the dispute between the parties,[15] but the panel proceedings were suspended.[16] Therefore, the EC adopted a blocking regulation, Council Regulation 2271/96/EC, as a countermeasure against

[8] Lawrence Collins, 'Blocking and Clawback Statutes: The United Kingdom Approach-I' (1986) *Journal of Business Law* 372; Lawrence Collins, 'Blocking and Clawback Statutes: The United Kingdom Approach-II' (1986) *Journal of Business Law* 452; Michael J Danaher, 'Anti-antitrust Law: The Clawback and Other Features of the United Kingdom Protection of Trading Interests Act, 1980' (1980) 12 *Law and Policy in International Business* 947.

[9] AV Lowe, 'Blocking Extraterritorial Jurisdiction: The British Protection of Trading Act, 1980' (1981) 75 *American Journal of International Law* 257, 257; Josef Brinkhaus, *Das britische Abwehrgesetz von 1980* (Peter Lang, 1989) 45.

[10] Werner Meng, *Streitigkeiten über Wirtschaftssanktionen zwischen EU und USA* (Zentrum für Europäisches Wirtschaftsrecht, Rheinische Friedrich-Wilhelms-Universität Bonn, 1997) 3.

[11] Cuban Liberty and Democratic Solidarity (Libertad) Act of 1996 (Helms–Burton Act, PubL 104–14, 110 Stat 785, 22 USC §§ 6021–91, Title III, s 302. See also Werner Meng, 'Extraterritoriale Jurisdiktion in der US-amerikanischen Sanktionsgesetzgebung' (1997) 8 *EuZW* 423; Gebauer (n 4) 145.

[12] See Christopher R Seppala, 'La pratique américaine récente: Les lois Helms-Burton et d'Amato-Kennedy' in Habib Gherari and Sandra Szurek (eds), *Sanctions unilatérales, mondialisation du commerce et ordre juridique international* (Montchrestien, 1998) 83.

[13] Meng (n 10) 9.

[14] See Seppala (n 12) 90.

[15] WTO, United States – The Cuban Liberty and Democratic Solidarity Act, Constitution of the Panel Established at the Request of the European Communities, Communication by the DSB Chairman, WT/DS38/3, 20 February 1997 (97-0694).

[16] WTO, United States – The Cuban Liberty and Democratic Solidarity Act, Communication from the Chairman of the Panel, WT/DS38/5, 25 April 1997 (97-1791).

US economic sanctions.[17] The EC Blocking Regulation intends to counter the effects of laws enacted by third countries which are deemed to violate international law due to their extraterritorial reach and to be contrary to the interests of the EC.[18] The targeted measures are listed in the annex attached to the EC Blocking Regulation. Although the EC Blocking Regulation envisages any extraterritorial measure issued by any state as contrary to the interests of the EU, at present it contains exclusively certain pieces of US sanctions legislation. It prohibits any person from complying with the laws specified in its annex (except in the case of granting an authorisation to this effect)[19] and rules out the recognition and enforcement of judgments, arbitral awards and administrative decisions which give effect to those laws.[20] By virtue of the clawback provision contained in the EC Blocking Regulation, any trader resident or incorporated in the EU may recover any damage caused due to the application of the targeted foreign laws before the courts of the Member States having jurisdiction under the Brussels Convention (currently the Brussels I Regulation).[21] Clawback provisions are to be considered as overriding mandatory norms to be applied irrespective of the governing law.[22]

To prevent conflicts with other states and the EU, the US President has been empowered to waive sanctions.[23] However, the Iran sanctions programme was prolonged and broadened by the Comprehensive Iran Sanctions, Accountability and Divestment Act of 2010 (CISADA), with a broad extraterritorial scope of application.[24] More recently, the Commission conducted a review of the EC Blocking Regulation and proposed a recast regulation.[25] However, the proposed regulation has not yet been adopted. As a reaction to President Trump's decision announced in May 2018 to withdraw the US from the Joint Comprehensive Plan of Action, also known as the Iran nuclear deal, and to reinstate those nuclear-related sanctions previously imposed against Iran that had been lifted or waived as a result of the agreement,[26] the European Commission expressed its intention to have recourse and update the EC Blocking Regulation so as to prevent the negative

[17] Council Regulation (EC) No 2271/96 of 22 November 1996 protecting against the effects of the extra-territorial application of legislation adopted by a third country, and actions based thereon or resulting therefrom [1996] OJ L309/1. On the EC Blocking Regulation, see in particular Gebauer (n 4) 152–55.

[18] EC Blocking Regulation, Preamble.

[19] ibid art 5.

[20] ibid art 4.

[21] ibid art 6; 1968 Brussels Convention on jurisdiction and the enforcement of judgments in civil and commercial matters [1972] OJ L299/32.

[22] Basedow (n 3) 213; Jürgen Basedow, *The Law of Open Societies: Private Ordering and Public Regulation of International Relations – General Course on Private International Law, Collected Courses of the Hague Academy of International Law*, vol 360 (Martinus Nijhoff, 2013) 340.

[23] Matthias Herdegen, *Principles of International Economic Law* (Oxford University Press, 2013) 79.

[24] ibid.

[25] Proposal for a Regulation of the European Parliament and of the Council protecting against the effects of the extra-territorial application of legislation adopted by a third country and actions based thereon or resulting therefrom (recast) Brussels, 6.2.2015 COM(2015) 48 final.

[26] See also Executive Order Reimposing Certain Sanctions with Respect to Iran, 6 August 2018.

effects of the US sanctions against Iran on European companies.[27] Accordingly, the EC Blocking Regulation has been amended to supplement it with the extraterritorial US sanctions re-imposed against Iran.[28] In the meantime, the EU, the UK, France and Germany asked in a letter to grant exemptions from these sanctions to European companies, with the expectation that the US sanctions against Iran will not be enforced extraterritorially against European natural and legal persons.[29] However, this European request was rejected by the US. It is also worth mentioning that Iran reacted to the renewal of US sanctions by bringing a claim before the ICJ on the grounds that the re-imposition of the sanctions breaches the Treaty of Amity, Economic Relations and Consular Rights entered into between the US and Iran in 1955.[30]

The existence of the EU Blocking Regulation and US sanctions regimes poses a challenge for companies, which have to decide with which regime to comply. Since they do not want to lose the possibility to trade in the US and due to the threat of US enforcement measures, they often undertake to observe the stricter US sanctions, despite the EC Blocking Regulation.[31]

Other examples may be found for blocking statutes. The Arab League's boycott of Israel was condemned by several states, including Germany[32] and the US,[33] which adopted acts to counter the effects of the boycott.[34] Although these acts were drawn up in a general way, they were motivated by the boycott of the Arab League that also addressed companies in these states.

Iraq adopted Act No 57 of 1990 to exclude the effects of the UN economic sanctions imposed for the invasion of Kuwait.[35] The Act considered foreign laws

[27] European Commission 'European Commission Acts to Protect the Interests of EU Companies Investing in Iran as Part of the EU's Continued Commitment to the Joint Comprehensive Plan of Action', press release, Brussels, 18 May 2018, IP/18/3861.

[28] Commission Delegated Regulation (EU) 2018/1100 of 6 June 2018 amending the Annex to Council Regulation (EC) No 2271/96 protecting against the effects of extra-territorial application of legislation adopted by a third country, and actions based thereon or resulting therefrom [2018] OJ L1991/1.

[29] Joint E3 letter to Steven Mnuchin and Mike Pompeo on JCPOA, https://assets.publishing.service.gov.uk/government/uploads/system/uploads/attachment_data/file/714262/Joint_E3_letter_on_JCPoA.pdf.

[30] Alleged violations of the 1955 Treaty of Amity, Economic Relations, and Consular Rights (*Islamic Republic of Iran v United States of America*), Application instituting proceedings, 16 July 2018.

[31] Marc Blessing, *Impact of the Extraterritorial Application of Mandatory Rules of Law on International Contracts* (Helbing & Lichtenhahn, 1999) 24–25.

[32] § 4a Außenwirtschaftsverordnung (AWVO) vom 2. August 2013 (BGBl I S 2865).

[33] Export Administration Act (EAA) of 1979 (PL 96-72), ss 3(5) and 8.

[34] Andreas Behr, *Deutsche Unternehmen und der Israel-Boykott* (Verlag Recht und Wissenschaft, 1994) 159–236.

[35] Act No 57/1990. The text of the Act is reproduced and commented on in German by Hilmar Krüger, 'Das irakische Antiboykottgesetz 1990' (1990) *Recht der Internationalen Wirtschaft* 934. See also Bernard Grelon and Charles-Etienne Gudin, 'Contrats et crise du Golfe' (1991) 118 *Journal du droit international* 633, 661–62; Laurence Landy-Osman, 'L'embargo des Nations Unies contre l'Irak et l'exécution des contrats internationaux' (1991) 17 *Droit et Pratique du Commerce International* 597, 626; Geneviève Burdeau, 'Les conséquences de la crise sur les relations économiques privées' in Brigitte Stern (ed), *Les aspects juridiques de la crise et de la guerre du Golfe* (Monthcrestien, 1991) 452–53.

and decisions freezing Iraqi assets as inapplicable. It exempted Iraqi entities from liability regarding any damage resulting from the delay of foreign parties due to the observance of foreign embargo provisions. Moreover, it also provided for the seizure of assets of states which adopted coercive measures against Iraq, as well as organisations, companies and banks from such states. Any court or arbitral tribunal seated in Iraq was prohibited from hearing any claim against the Iraqi state or state entity or any other Iraqi natural or legal person brought in breach of the provisions of the Act. It also excluded the recognition of any foreign judgment or arbitral award rendered in contravention of the Act. Finally, it declared that any domestic or foreign law, regulation or judgment issued contrary to the Act may not be recognised.

Before the court of a state which applied the UNSC sanction, the UNSC resolution and the implementing EEC regulation must have been applied as overriding mandatory provisions.[36] Moreover, since the UNSC sanction represented a decision of the international community, it is evident that the Iraqi blocking statute could not be applied in UN Member States as it would violate the *ordre public*.[37] This is in essence a conflict between the international and a local public policy, where the former triumphs.[38]

In theory, the same effect could be achieved by the application of the *ordre public* exception. However, through blocking statutes, the legislation makes clear its intention to ignore a specific foreign economic sanction.

Although blocking statutes have primarily political significance and their practical use seems to be rather marginal,[39] there are cases where the courts of the Member States had to decide whether to apply a foreign – generally US – sanction or an EU or national blocking measure. This is in fact a conflict between overriding mandatory provisions, as will be discussed in the next section.

II. A Conflict of Overriding Mandatory Provisions

Blocking statutes qualify as overriding mandatory provisions. If a unilateral or multilateral economic sanction comes into conflict with a blocking statute, this is in fact a collision between divergent overriding mandatory provisions.

It may happen that different states adopt conflicting overriding mandatory norms concerning the same situation. This results in the conflict of overriding mandatory norms. As Batiffol and Lagarde note, for this reason the identification of a norm as having overriding mandatory nature is not sufficient in itself

[36] Landy-Osman (n 35) 626.
[37] Grelon and Gudin (n 35) 661–62; Landy-Osman (n 35) 626.
[38] Aurore Marchand, *L'embargo en droit du commerce international* (Larcier, 2012) 107.
[39] Basedow (n 3) 213–14.

to render it applicable, but the choice between the conflicting norms is left to the court seised, which has considerable leeway in this respect.[40] Mayer and Heuzé described this as the concurrence of divergent laws rather than a conflict in private law litigation.[41] Most often, the interests of states are not directly involved in private law disputes and the objective of conflict-of-laws regulation is simply to subsume the legal dispute to the law which best suits it. However, the collision of overriding mandatory norms is indeed a conflict and not only between the parties, but also the states intending to enforce their interests through the overriding mandatory provisions.[42]

The conflict of overriding mandatory norms may be false or real. A false conflict emerges when the domestic and foreign overriding mandatory provisions, or two seemingly conflicting foreign overriding norms, refer to the same interests and values, and the application of either of them leads to the same outcome. As such, there is no difference in relation to whether the domestic or the other foreign mandatory norm is applied.[43]

However, real conflicts are also conceivable, where the outcome reached is different depending on the overriding mandatory norm applied. A conflict between an economic sanction and a blocking statute is certainly a real conflict. If the overriding mandatory provision of the forum collides with an overriding mandatory norm of a foreign state (which may be either in the *lex causae* or in the law of any other state), the court will most probably give priority to the overriding mandatory provision of the forum.[44] Certain authors claim that there is always precedence for the overriding mandatory norms of the forum.[45] In the EU, this follows from Article 9(2) of the Rome I Regulation.

However, Magnus expresses an opposing view.[46] Accordingly, the overriding mandatory norm of the forum is not to be preferred a priori; instead, the court enjoys discretion as laid down by Article 9(3), even if a foreign overriding mandatory norm is in conflict with an overriding mandatory rule of the forum. The balancing of the respective regulatory interests concerned is required and this

[40] Henri Batiffol and Paul Lagarde, *Traité de droit international privé*, vol 1, 8th edn (LGDJ, 1993) 429.

[41] Pierre Mayer and Vincent Heuzé, *Droit international privé*, 11th edn (LGDJ, 2014)106.

[42] ibid 106.

[43] Laurence Idot, 'Les conflits de lois en droit de la concurrence' (1995) 122 *Journal du droit international* 320, 337.

[44] ibid 338; Mayer and Heuzé (n 41) 106; Pierre Mayer, 'Les lois de police étrangères' (1981) 108 *Journal du droit international* 277, 329; Ansgar Staudinger, 'Art. 9 Eingriffsnormen' in Franco Ferrari, Peter Mankowski, Eva-Maria Kieninger, Karsten Otte, Ingo Saenger, Götz Schulze and Ansgar Staudinger (eds), *Internationales Vertragsrecht* (Beck, 2012) 263; Karsten Thorn, 'Artikel 9: Eingriffsnormen' in Thomas Rauscher (ed), *Europäisches Zivilprozess- und Kollisionsrecht*, vol 3 (Otto Schmidt, 2016) 470.

[45] Ivana Kunda, *International Mandatory Rules of a Third Country in European Contract Conflict of Laws: The Rome Convention and the Proposed Rome I Regulation* (Rijeka Law Faculty, 2007) 195.

[46] Ulrich Magnus, 'Art 9 Rom I-VO Eingriffsnormen' in Ulrich Magnus (ed), *J. von Staudingers Kommentar zum Bürgerlichen Gesetzbuch mit Einführungsgesetz und Nebengesetzen* (Sellier/De Gruyter, 2011) 679–80.

might even lead to the preference of the overriding mandatory provisions of the third state.[47] However, even he admits that the overriding mandatory provisions of the forum enjoy a certain factual precedence.[48]

The court will apply the blocking statute instead of the economic sanction if the blocking statute was adopted by the state of the forum or by the EU (in the case of a court of a Member State). Accordingly, a court in an EU Member State will apply the EC Blocking Regulation, disregarding the US economic sanctions targeted by it.

However, if the conflict exists between the overriding mandatory rules of two foreign states, the court is free to decide whether to apply any of them or give effect to it. If it decides to do so, it is compelled to choose one of those overriding mandatory norms. It is immaterial whether the overriding mandatory provisions claim application by the operation of conflict-of-laws rules or through considering them at the level of substantive law.

Different solutions were suggested for the choice between such conflicting norms. It is often asserted that the closeness of the connection between the norm and the case is decisive. The overriding mandatory norm of whichever state the situation is more closely connected to shall be applied.[49] Busse argues that a foreign overriding mandatory norm that can actually be enforced by the issuing state is to be preferred,[50] but most likely the forum will ultimately choose a solution which it expects will correspond to its own interests instead.

If a blocking statute adopted by the target state intends to hinder the operation of an economic sanction emanating from the UNSC, the UNSC sanction, or more precisely the national or regional law transposing it, will prevail.[51] When it is about conflicting unilateral measures, the situation is more complicated. Concerning the choice between a foreign economic sanction and a foreign measure blocking it, the court has to assess and make a judgment on the foreign policy of two different foreign states. It may be questioned whether a court should assume the role of the adjudicator of foreign policies of foreign states.[52] This requires the examination of their purposes, the values and interests behind them,[53] the consequences of their application and non-application. For EU courts, this examination takes place in accordance with Article 9(3) of the Rome I Regulation.

If an overriding mandatory norm of an EU Member State collides with a rule of a third state, it has been argued that EU loyalty requires being granted priority

[47] ibid.

[48] ibid 679.

[49] Daniel Busse, 'Die Berücksichtigung ausländischer "Eingriffsnormen" durch die deutsche Rechtsprechung' (1996) 95 *ZVgRWiss* 386, 412; Idot (n 43) 340.

[50] Busse (n 49) 412.

[51] Mercédeh Azeredo da Silveira, *Trade Sanctions and International Sales* (Kluwer, 2014) 150.

[52] Andrew Dickinson, 'Third-Country Mandatory Rules in the Law Applicable to Contractual Obligations: So Long, Farewell, Auf Wiedersehen, Adieu?' (2007) 3 *Journal of Private International Law* 53, 68–69.

[53] B Audit and L d'Avout, *Droit international privé*, 7th edn (Economica 2013) 171.

over the law of the Member State.[54] However, this is not relevant in the case of economic sanctions and blocking measures adopted at the EU level because, as regulations, they apply in all the Member States with identical content.

Conflict of overriding mandatory provisions is often provoked by the extraterritorial claim of one of the legislations concerned. Overriding mandatory provisions express in themselves a certain imperialism.[55] In the context of economic sanctions, conflicts arise in particular regarding the extensive US sanctions often claiming extraterritorial application. The imperialism of US economic sanctions as overriding mandatory provisions together with an effective enforcement mechanism result in the legal imperialism of the US.[56] The extraterritorial claim of sanctions affects not only the target state, but also the countries allied with the US.[57] Regarding the EU, the EC Blocking Regulation intending to prevent the extraterritorial effects of US embargoes deserves particular attention.

For instance, PayPal intended to enforce the US embargo against Cuba, and more specifically the provisions of the Helms-Burton Act (Cuban Liberty and Democratic Solidarity (Libertad) Act).[58] To use its payment method, PayPal required its partners to refrain from selling Cuban goods and provide services related to Cuba. In the event of breaching the embargo, PayPal froze the account of the trader concerned. PayPal's conduct fully complied with US law, but infringed the EC Blocking Regulation excluding the application of US sanctions.[59] In German legal practice, the question arose as to whether PayPal was entitled to freeze the accounts of online shops selling Cuban rum, Cohiba cigars or even tickets to a Cuban music concert. The case on the sale of Cuban products ended in a settlement between the parties,[60] but concerning the concert tickets, the regional court of Dortmund ordered PayPal to refrain from restricting the accounts of its clients.[61] The court based its decision on the fact that the EC Blocking Regulation ruled out the application of the extraterritorial US embargo.[62]

Even in the absence of blocking statutes, foreign economic sanctions contrary to the foreign policy considerations of the EU Member States could be disregarded

[54] Thorn (n 44) 471.

[55] Yvon Loussouarn, 'Cours général de droit international privé' in *Collected Courses of the Hague Academy of International Law*, vol 139 (Nijhoff, 1973) 269, 333.

[56] In relation to the US sanctions regime, the notion of legal imperalism is used by Sandra Szurek, 'Le recours aux sanctions' in Gherari and Szurek (n 12) 19, 21, referring to Brigitte Stern, 'Les Etats-Unis et le droit imperialiste' *Le Monde*, 12 September 1996, 12; and Jean-Baptiste Racine, 'L'arbitrage commercial international et les mesures d'embargo. À propos de l'arrêt de la Cour d'appel du Québec du 31 mars 2003' (2004) 134 *Journal du droit international* 89, 105.

[57] Marchand (n 38) 43.

[58] Cuban Liberty and Democratic Solidarity (Libertad) Act of 1996 (Helms–Burton Act, PubL 104–114, 110 Stat. 785, 22 USC §§ 6021–91). See Herdegen (n 23) 78–79.

[59] Herdegen (n 23) 79.

[60] Harald Neuber, 'Kuba-Blockade: Paypal hebt Kontosperrung auf', *Nachrichtenblog Amerika21*, 1 November 2011, https://amerika21.de/nachrichten/2011/11/41542/paypal-kuba.

[61] LG Dortmund, Urteil v. 15.1.2016 – 3 O 610/15.

[62] LG Dortmund, Urteil v. 15.1.2016 – 3 O 610/15, Rn 20.

to the extent that they violate the *ordre public* of the forum state. Undoubtedly, the interest in the non-application of the foreign economic sanction is more unequivocally expressed by a blocking statute. Blocking statutes give precise guidance to the forum by prohibiting the application of a foreign economic sanction and thereby promote legal certainty. However, they are exceptional. In the remaining cases, there is no such guidance for the courts. It is not expected that the legislature will react to all non-desired economic sanctions by a blocking measure, making the condemnation of the economic sanction concerned clear for domestic courts. This also holds for the EU. Therefore, even if the position of the EU could be made unequivocal by blocking regulations regarding the non-desired effects of sanctions imposed by third countries, the reorientation of the judicial practice of the Member States, as will be discussed later, seems to be a more realistic option.

After the analysis of economic sanctions in terms of the conflict-of-laws rules of the EU, the next chapter will examine whether the economic sanctions of the EU may be 'deactivated' by agreements conferring jurisdiction to a court in a third country or an arbitral tribunal. The principle of legal certainty and the uniform enforcement of the CFSP would require a uniform attitude concerning such agreements. Nonetheless, if we examine the judicial practice of the Member States, as well as the relevant arbitral awards, no uniform approach may be outlined regarding the legal assessment of such clauses. Such a situation does not contribute to the above purposes.

8

'Deactivation' of Economic Sanctions?

Overriding mandatory provisions, including economic sanctions, are certainly applied by the forum of the issuing state, but the same norms are not necessarily taken into consideration by a foreign forum. As long as it is about sanctions imposed by the UNSC, no problem arises, since most countries incorporate and apply these sanctions. However, the question remains significant for EU autonomous sanctions which may potentially be evaded by the choice of the forum in a third country which does not apply a sanction that is analogous to EU law.

A relatively recently described phenomenon in private international law is the setting aside of overriding mandatory norms by transaction planning.[1] The binding force of overriding mandatory norms, including economic sanctions, may be avoided by the parties through an agreement conferring jurisdiction on a court or an arbitral tribunal. Consequently, overriding mandatory norms have been seen as semi-necessary, quasi necessary[2] or semi-imperative.[3] This involves the delocalisation of the legal dispute, based on a choice-of-court or an arbitration clause that moves it from a predetermined jurisdiction of a state court to the jurisdiction of the court of another state or an arbitral tribunal.[4] This phenomenon implies the devaluation[5] or dilution[6] of overriding mandatory provisions and is therefore described as the deactivation of overriding mandatory provisions.[7] The mandatory nature of the norms seems to be relativised due to the autonomy of the parties. A corollary of this is that the shield of national public policy is weakening.[8] As Bureau and Muir Watt rightly noted, this implies the privatisation of the political choice of states.[9] Under this lens, overriding mandatory provisions

[1] Louis d'Avout and Dominique Bureau, 'Lois de police étrangères devant le juge français du contrat international' (2010) 84 *La Semaine Juridique – Entreprise et Affaires* 18, 26.

[2] Luca G Radicati di Brozolo, 'Mondialisation, juridiction, arbitrage: vers des règles d'application semi-nécessaires?' (2003) 92 *Revue critique de droit international privé* 1, 35; Luca G. Radicati di Brozolo, 'Arbitrage commercial international et lois de police' in *Collected Courses of the Hague Academy of International Law, Vol 315 – 2005* (Martinus Nijhoff, 2006) 265, 363–66.

[3] Bureau and Muir Watt, *Droit international privé – Tome I* (PUF, 2010) 597.

[4] D'Avout and Bureau (n 1) 26.

[5] ibid 25–26.

[6] Bureau and Muir Watt (n 3) 598.

[7] Dominique Bureau and Horatia Muir Watt, 'L'impérativité désactivée?' (2009) 98 Revue critique de droit international privé 1.

[8] See Horatia Muir-Watt and Luca G. Radicati di Brozolo, 'Party Autonomy and Mandatory Rules in a Global World' (2004) 4 Global Jurist Advances 1, 1.

[9] Bureau and Muir Watt (n 3) 597.

formerly clearly took precedence over the autonomy of the parties, while it can be suggested that at present, the reverse is true to a large extent.[10]

Parties to international transactions have greater freedom to shape their legal relationship in conformity to their will (for example, to escape the application of certain mandatory norms) in comparison to purely domestic transactions.[11] Agreements conferring jurisdiction on a foreign court or an arbitral tribunal are means that facilitate this.

The deactivation may take place based on the agreement of the parties by moving a (potential or actual) legal dispute to a state court other than the one which would normally have jurisdiction, or to an arbitral tribunal which would be unlikely to apply the non-intended overriding mandatory provision. The same may happen with EU sanctions that are applied by the courts of the Member States, but not necessarily by a court in a third country or an arbitral tribunal.

I. EU Economic Sanctions and Choice-of-Court Agreements

As Rühl explains, the approach to jurisdiction agreements intending to set aside the application of overriding mandatory provisions may be threefold.[12] First, fully separating the issue of jurisdiction and governing law, such choice-of-court agreements may be fully accepted as valid and leave the possibility of review to the stage when the recognition and enforcement of the decision is sought before a domestic forum. The second option is the automatic rejection of the validity of such agreements. The third way is a case-by-case examination based on certain criteria before ascertaining the (in)validity of the choice-of-court agreement.

The effectiveness of agreements conferring jurisdiction on a forum which intended to evade the application of certain overriding mandatory provisions was recognised on both sides of the Atlantic.[13] An often-cited example for this tendency is the *Monster Cable* decision of the French Cour de cassation, where the Cour de cassation, annulling a contrary decision of the Cour d'appel de Paris, recognised the possibility of avoiding French overriding mandatory provisions through an agreement conferring jurisdiction on San Francisco courts in a distribution

[10] ibid 597.

[11] Norbert Horn, 'Zwingendes Recht in der internationalen Schiedsgerichtsbarkeit' (2008) *SchiedsVZ* 209, 209.

[12] Giesela Rühl, 'Die Wirksamkeit von Gerichtstands- und Schiedsvereinbarungen im Lichte der Ingmar-Entscheidung des EuGH' (2007) *IPRax* 294, 296.

[13] Concerning the Member States of the EU, see the above-mentioned *Monster Cable* judgment, whereas, concerning the US, see the Lloyd's cases: United States Court of Appeals, Seventh Circuit 3 F 3d 156 62 USLW 2116, Fed Sec L Rep P 97,688 *Bonny v Society of Lloyd's* Nos 92-1662, 92-2771; see also Horatia Muir Watt, 'L'affaire Lloyd's: globalisation des marchés et contentieux contractuel' (2002) 91 *Revue critique de droit international privé* 509.

contract between a French and a US company.[14] The question to be addressed by the Cour de cassation was whether the protection of the interests safeguarded by a French overriding mandatory norm could justify the competence of the French court and the setting aside of the choice-of-court agreement of the parties.[15] The judgment clearly reflects the principle that jurisdiction and applicable law are to be treated distinctly and may not be confused.[16] A more recent judgment of the Cour de cassation in the *Lauterbach* case essentially confirmed the above approach and the fact that jurisdiction and applicable law must be distinguished.[17] In relation to a distribution contract, although the court did not find a valid jurisdiction clause, it stated that the competent jurisdiction must be determined solely in accordance with jurisdictional rules, even if overriding mandatory norms would be applicable to the merits of the case.

It is suggested that distinguishing jurisdiction and applicable law by avoiding a prior examination of the nature of the rules in question in terms of the establishment of the jurisdiction of the court is in line with the practice of the CJEU, according to which a court can decide on its own jurisdiction in relation to a choice-of-court agreement under the EU rules on jurisdiction without examining the merits of the case at all.[18] Indeed, in the *Benincasa* judgment, the CJEU interpreting the Brussels Convention delimited the rules applicable to the jurisdiction clause under the Brussels Convention and the substantive rules governing the contract that are designated by private international law.[19] It remarked that the aim of legal certainty requires 'that the court seised should be able readily to decide whether it has jurisdiction on the basis of the rules of the [Brussels] Convention, without having to consider the substance of the case'.[20] In *Trasporti Casteletti*, the CJEU considered the potential limits of a choice-of-court agreement under the Brussels Convention and stated that the Brussels Convention is limited to establishing rules of jurisdiction and does not affect substantive law.[21] The national court seised has to ascertain whether it has jurisdiction based on the rules

[14] Cour de cassation (1re Ch civ) – 22 October 2008, (2009) Revue critique de droit international privé 69; Fabienne Jault-Seseke, 'L'applicabilité d'une loi de police n'entrave pas le jeu de la clause attributive de juridiction' (2009) 3 *Dalloz* 200; Louis d'Avout, 'La clause attributive de juridiction résiste aux lois de police' (2008) 82 *La Semaine Juridique – Edition générale* 47; André Huet, 'Clause attributive de juridiction à un tribunal étranger et loi française de police et de sûreté (étude du droit commun)' (2009) *Receuil Dalloz* 684; Nicolas Mathey, 'Application d'une clause attributive de compétence en cas d'abus de dépendance' (2008) 82 *La Semaine Juridique – Entreprise et Affaires* 51–52.

[15] Jault-Seseke (n 14) 201.

[16] ibid 201; Huet (n 14) 685.

[17] Cour de cassation, Chambre commerciale, 24 novembre 2015, N° de pourvoi: 14-14924. Xavier Delpech, 'Rupture d'une relation commerciale établie: exclusion de clause d'élection de for' (2015) *Dalloz Actualité*, 11 December.

[18] Jault-Seseke (n 14) 202; Eckart Gottschalk and Steffen Breßler, 'Missbrauchskontrolle von Gerichtsstandsvereinbarungen im europäischen Zivilprozessrecht' (2007) *ZEuP* 56, 68–70.

[19] Case C-269/95 *Francesco Benincasa v Dentalkit* Srl [1997] ECR I-3767, para 25.

[20] ibid para 27.

[21] Case C-159/97 *Trasporti Castelletti Spedizioni Internazionali SpA v Hugo Trumpy SpA* [1999] ECR I-1597, para 47.

of the Brussels Convention, without having to consider the substance of the case.[22] A choice-of-forum clause must be assessed exclusively in light of the requirements specified in Article 17 of the Brussels Convention (the predecessor of current Article 25 of the Brussels Ia Regulation). The CJEU concluded that 'any further review of the validity of the clause and of the intention of the party which inserted it must be excluded and substantive rules of liability applicable in the chosen court must not affect the validity of the jurisdiction clause'.[23] However, it should be noted that both the *Benincasa* and *Trasporti Casteletti* judgments addressed cases where a court in a Member States was designated, and the disputes did not involve the application of overriding mandatory norms.

The view, according to which a choice-of-court agreement is admissible even if it results in setting aside an overriding mandatory norm, holds that the state can still exercise control by denying the recognition and enforcement of the foreign judgment on the grounds of public policy of the state where recognition and enforcement is sought.[24] As a court in a third country is usually stipulated, domestic private international law rules on recognition are of interest in this respect; these usually allow the denial of the recognition and enforcement on the grounds of public policy as an exception to the prohibition of *révision au fond*.[25] The question is how to interpret public policy for the purposes of recognition of foreign decisions. Public policy (*ordre public*) for conflict-of-laws and international civil procedure law purposes is differentiated. In international civil procedure law, it is not examined whether the foreign decision itself violates the public policy of the forum, but instead whether the result of its recognition breaches it.[26] Therefore, the subject of the review is not how the law was applied in the given case, but the effects of the potential recognition of the decision in terms of the *ordre public* of the forum. It is often asserted that the standard of scrutiny is more relaxed in the case of recognition of foreign decisions (*effet atténué de ordre public*) in comparison to the *ordre public* of conflict of laws. According to a more permissive view, public policy does not comprise all overriding mandatory provisions, and ignoring an overriding mandatory rule does not necessarily mean a violation of the *ordre public*, because the latter concerns only the 'hard core' of the societal system or the foundations of the legal system of the forum.[27] Ignoring an overriding mandatory provision does not necessarily imply that the judgment could not be recognised or enforced. This could also apply to economic sanctions. Another way to preserve the enforcement of the rules of the state would be the

[22] ibid para 48.

[23] ibid para 51.

[24] Jault-Seseke (n 14) 201–02; d'Avout (n 14) 26.

[25] For example, § 328(1)(4) ZPO in Germany.

[26] Dieter Martiny, 'Anerkennung ausländischer Entscheidungen nach autonomem Recht' in Dieter Martiny (ed) *Handbuch des internationalen Zivilverfahrensrechts*, vol III/1 (Mohr Siebeck, 1984) 445–46.

[27] Radicati di Brozolo (n 2) 21–24; Helena Charlotte Laugwitz, *Die Anerkennung und Vollstreckung drittstaatlicher Entscheidungen in Zivil- und Handelssachen* (Mohr Siebeck, 2015) 249.

establishment of exclusive jurisdiction for the matter in question.[28] However, for overriding mandatory provisions, or more specifically for economic sanctions, the jurisdiction of the courts of the Member States is not exclusive.

English court practice shows some hesitation in this question. In *Morviken*, the British House of Lords found an exclusive jurisdiction clause of a bill of lading to be void due to which the chosen foreign court would have not applied the Hague-Visby Rules implemented by British law, thus reducing the standards of liability of the carrier.[29] Yet, English courts were more inclined to accept the parties' autonomy when a jurisdiction clause did not have the result of avoiding an English law, but a foreign law instead. In *Akai Pty Ltd v People Insurance Co Ltd*,[30] the High Court of Australia considered a jurisdiction clause in favour of English courts in an insurance policy issued by a Singapore insurer to an Australian company to be void because, due to this jurisdiction clause and a choice-of-law clause, English courts would have applied English law, disregarding the application of the Australian Insurance Act, which prohibited the contracting-out of its provisions. The English Queen's Bench, on the contrary, established that the freely negotiated jurisdiction and choice-of-law clause in favour of English courts and English law respectively must be given effect and this may not be overridden on the grounds of comity, taking the Australian decision into account. The court noted that English law did not recognise equivalent restrictions on the parties' choice of law; the case turned upon the potential application of Australian public policy based on an Australian statute.

German court practice and a part of the legal literature took a position contrary to the general admissibility of jurisdiction clauses adopted at the expense of the application of overriding mandatory provisions. Accordingly, a jurisdictional agreement escaping the application of overriding mandatory norms of EU or domestic origin may be considered invalid. This view takes as a point of departure that if a choice of law is not possible within the scope of overriding mandatory norms of the forum, a choice of forum must also be prohibited when it aims at or results in avoiding the application of those overriding mandatory provisions.[31] Additionally, it is asserted that foreign decisions ignoring such norms should not be recognised and enforced, in order to impede the circumvention of an overriding mandatory provision by a choice-of-forum agreement.[32] The recognition and enforcement of foreign decisions disregarding an overriding mandatory norm of the state where recognition is sought may be denied on the grounds of

[28] Jault-Seseke (n 14) 201.

[29] *The 'Morviken'*, HL [1983] 1 Lloyd's Rep 1.

[30] *Akai Pty Ltd v People Insurance Co Ltd*, QB (Comm Ct) [1998] 1 Lloyd's Rep 90.

[31] See Jan Kropholler, 'Internationale Zuständigkeit' in Hans Joachim Herrmann, Jürgen Basedow and Jan Kropholler (eds), *Handbuch des internationalen Zivilverfahrensrechts*, vol 1 (Mohr Siebeck, 1982) 197, 409–10; Gottschalk and Breßler (n 18) 61.

[32] Michael Becker, 'Zwingendes Eingriffsrecht in der Urteilsanerkennung' (1996) 60 *RabelsZ* 691, 705; Martiny (n 26) 458.

the public policy exception.[33] This equally holds for disregarding the economic sanctions of the state of recognition.[34] The standards of the *ordre public* clause and the public policy exception for the purpose of recognition and enforcement cannot be different in this respect.[35] This also follows from the fact that conflict-of-laws and international procedural rules perform similar functions, as even the latter indirectly have an impact on the designation of the applicable law. The presence of an overriding mandatory norm rules out an attenuated public policy control (*ordre public atténué*) in international procedural law.[36] The prohibition of the *révision au fond* does not apply to the extent that the result of the foreign decision may not be extended to the forum state.[37] Although it may also be noted that French judicial practice also allows the denial of recognition and enforcement of third-country judgments in cases of fraud (*fraude à la loi*),[38] French courts have not taken position in a case concerning the disregard of a French overriding mandatory provision, and in particular an economic sanction by a foreign court, from the point of view of fraud. We can therefore see that even in relation to the question of recognition and enforcement of decisions disregarding overriding mandatory norms, there are differences in judicial practice and scholarly views.

It must be added that, under German law, jurisdiction clauses ignoring overriding mandatory provisions are not automatically invalid. Instead, a case-by-case approach seems to be followed by German courts.[39] However, it is not clear under what preconditions a choice of forum is invalid. Mathäß suggests that invalidity is the legal consequence provided that: (1) the domestic mandatory provision is of such fundamental and vast significance that it excludes foreign regulations that deviate from it; and (2) the foreign decision must jeopardise the practical enforcement of the domestic mandatory rule.[40] In the context of securities legislation, the BGH established that the validity of a choice-of-forum agreement may not be recognised if it – together with the choice of law of the parties – has the effect that an overriding mandatory provision based on national law will not apply.[41] It has been added that foreign judgments ignoring such overriding mandatory provisions may not be recognised and enforced.[42] From this, it was inferred that

[33] Anton K Schnyder, '"Gegenmassnahmen" im Internationalen Privat- und Zivilverfahrensrecht' in Wilfried Fiedler, Eckart Klein and Anton K Schnyder, *Gegenmassnahmen – Berichte der Deutschen Gesellschaft für Völkerrecht*, vol 37 (CF Müller Verlag, 1998) 73, 102.

[34] Martiny (n 26) 487.

[35] Becker (n 32) 707.

[36] ibid 708.

[37] ibid 718.

[38] Cour de cassation, civile, Chambre civile 1, 20 février 2007, 05-14.082; Cour de cassation, Chambre civile 1, 7 janvier 1964.

[39] Rühl (n 12) 296.

[40] Sophie Mathäß, *Die Auswirkungen staaten- und personenbezogener Embargomaßnahmen auf Privatrechtsverhältnisse* (Nomos, 2016) 59–60.

[41] BGH, Urteil vom 12.3.1984 – II ZR 10/83, NJW 1984, 2037.

[42] ibid.

an agreement conferring jurisdiction may be deemed to be invalid if the resulting judgment could not be recognised in Germany.[43]

It should be noted that economic sanctions are based on EU regulations; they are EU-level overriding mandatory norms, as opposed to overriding mandatory norms rooted in national law, and this may have crucial implications on the evaluation of agreements conferring jurisdiction. Not only the application of domestic overriding mandatory provisions but also those having an EU origin may render a choice-of-court agreement invalid under the German judicial practice. This was confirmed in relation to the German provisions implementing the rules of the Commercial Agents Directive providing a right of compensation for the agent in the event of the termination of the agency agreement by the principal.[44] A judgment of the OLG Munich did not permit setting aside the protection provided for agents by the German provisions implementing the rules of the Commercial Agents Directive.[45] It laid down that those overriding mandatory provisions may not be derogated from – in addition to a choice in favour of the law of California – by an agreement conferring exclusive jurisdiction on American courts if the law of the selected forum does not acknowledge an equivalent claim for compensation for the agent. Such a derogation of jurisdiction is invalid insofar as there is an obvious danger that the court in a third country – following its own legal approach – does not enforce the overriding mandatory provisions of German law. The same conclusion was essentially confirmed by a decision of the BGH in relation to a claim for a request for preliminary ruling in a matter where the protective rules of the Commercial Agents Directive could not be enforced due to a jurisdiction agreement in favour of the courts of Virginia.[46] Rejecting the claim for a preliminary ruling, the BGH declared that there is no doubt at all that the provisions of the Commercial Agents Directive granting a compensation claim for the agent do not hinder the refusal of the recognition of a jurisdiction agreement in favour of a court in a third country, when the law chosen by the parties (the law of Virginia) does not recognise a mandatory compensation claim for the agent in the case of the termination of the agency contract and the court of the third state will not apply the overriding mandatory provisions of EU law and national law, and the claim for compensation will thus be rejected. It may be questionable whether such an interpretation is limited to the EU Commercial Agents Directive or the same approach prevails with regard to any agreement conferring jurisdiction on a foreign court. Concerning economic sanctions, it is argued that the same applies, since economic sanctions as overriding mandatory norms would fall under this category of rules and therefore cannot be avoided by a choice-of-forum clause.[47]

[43] Rühl (n 12) 297.

[44] Council Directive 86/653/EEC of 18 December 1986 on the coordination of the laws of the Member States relating to self-employed commercial agents [1986] OJ L382/17.

[45] OLG Munich, 17 May 2006–7 U 1781/06, IPRax 2007, 322.

[46] Beschluss BGH 5 September 2012 – VII ZR 25/12.

[47] Mathäß (n 40) 60.

Here, the question is whether the principle of effectiveness of EU law requires giving priority to overriding mandatory provisions of EU origin as opposed to jurisdictional rules permitting the choice of the court of a third country.[48] Rühl argues that the *effet utile* of overriding mandatory norms of EU law, such as those contained in the Commercial Agents Directive, would require the invalidity of choice-of-law clauses as well as – under certain circumstances – of choice-of-court agreements.[49]

Neither the Rome I Regulation nor the Brussels Ia Regulation settles this issue. The above approach has been subject to criticism even in Germany. First of all, the *Ingmar* judgment of the CJEU was limited to the validity of a choice of law agreement and the CJEU did not address agreements conferring jurisdiction to foreign courts or arbitral tribunals at all.[50] Following the view of the above German court practice, parties would be required to anticipate whether a foreign forum will apply the overriding mandatory norm, such as an economic sanction, or whether there is a danger that it will not.[51] However, it is not exactly predictable what kinds of rules would be applied by the forum.[52] Therefore, as Geimer contends, it is pertinent to wait for the foreign decision and, if it breaches the German *ordre public* (because it disregards an overriding mandatory norm to be enforced from a German point of view), this may be sanctioned by non-recognition by domestic courts.[53]

Taking the above into account, two different questions may be posed regarding jurisdiction clauses: first, the court of which country is selected by the agreement; and, second, which is the origin of the overriding mandatory provision.

If the court of a Member State is selected, the Brussels Ia Regulation applies. In light of the interpretation of the CJEU in respect of the Brussels Convention, jurisdiction and substantive law must be distinguished and a jurisdiction agreement under the Brussels Ia Regulation enjoys priority over overriding mandatory norms having an origin in the law of the Member States. Consequently, economic sanctions adopted unilaterally or implemented independently by the law of the Member States and not through EU regulations (eg, arms embargoes or travel restrictions) probably do not bar the choice of the court of another Member State. Within the scope of application of the Brussels Ia Regulation, the courts of the Member States cannot control jurisdiction agreements made in favour of the courts of other Member States.[54] The same holds true within the regime of the Lugano Convention.[55]

[48] Rühl (n 12) 298.

[49] ibid 299.

[50] David Quinke, 'Schiedsvereinbarungen und Eingriffsnormen – Zugleich Anmerkung zu OLG Munich, Urt. v. 17. Mai 2006, Az. 7 U 1781/06–' (2007) *SchiedsVZ* 246, 252.

[51] See Karsten Thorn, 'Artikel 9: Eingriffsnormen' in Thomas Rauscher (ed), *Europäisches Zivilprozess- und Kollisionsrecht*, vol 3 (Otto Schmidt, 2016) 449.

[52] Reinhold Geimer, *Internationales Zivilprozessrecht*, 7th edn (Otto Schmidt, 2015) 654.

[53] ibid 654.

[54] Thorn (n 51) 449.

[55] Convention on jurisdiction and the recognition and enforcement of judgments in civil and commercial matters [2007] OJ L339/3.

If the court of a third country is selected, the Brussels Ia Regulation and the Lugano Convention do not apply, but the Hague Convention on Choice of Court Agreements does or national jurisdictional rules do. The Hague Convention on Choice of Court Agreements is applicable provided that the court(s) of a contracting state is stipulated. Public policy is laid down as a ground for refusal, both in the Hague Convention on Choice of Court Agreements[56] and in national laws. The EU is a member of the Hague Convention. It should be noted that, under Article 21 of the Hague Convention, any member may declare that it has a strong interest not to apply the convention to a specific matter. Neither the EU nor its Member States made a declaration which would exclude overriding mandatory provisions or economic sanctions from the scope of the Convention. The EU declared only 'that it may, at a later stage in the light of the experience acquired in the application of the Convention, reassess the need to maintain its declaration under Article 21 of the Convention'. If the Hague Convention on Choice of Court Agreements does not apply and the overriding mandatory norm has its origin in national law, an agreement conferring jurisdiction may be deemed to be invalid under the domestic law of the forum seised in order to ensure the application of domestic overriding mandatory provisions and the recognition and enforcement of a foreign judgment ignoring the overriding mandatory norm may be refused on the grounds of public policy. This is a question for national law.

The assessment of both situations may differ if the application of an overriding mandatory norm stemming from EU law is at stake. As was demonstrated earlier, it may be argued that the *effet utile* of EU law may require the application of overriding mandatory norms of EU law against choice-of-forum agreements in favour of a court of a Member State, as well as that of a third state. The question is difficult, as it involves a choice between the legal certainty and predictability related to jurisdiction agreements and the need for the enforcement of the overriding mandatory provisions of EU law, including economic sanctions. Concerning EU economic sanctions, the choice of the court of a Member State does not cause any complication because any court in the EU will apply EU sanction regulations. The assessment of the jurisdiction of a court in a third country is more difficult. Here, a judgment by the CJEU could disperse uncertainty. The OLG Munich would have had the possibility to request a preliminary ruling from the CJEU regarding the effect of overriding mandatory norms of EU origin on jurisdiction agreements based on national law.[57] Concerning the impact of overriding mandatory norms of the Commercial Agent Directive on an agreement conferring jurisdiction on the court of a third state, the BGH[58] as well as the OLG Munich gave away the opportunity. An interpretation by the CJEU could also have helped the application of economic sanctions as overriding mandatory provisions.

[56] Hague Conference on Private International Law, Convention of 30 June 2005 on Choice of Court Agreements, art 9e).

[57] Rühl (n 12) 298–300.

[58] BGH 5 September 2012 – VII ZR 25/12.

This situation undoubtedly gives rise to uncertainty. Economic operators cannot foresee with certainty whether their agreement conferring jurisdiction to the court of a third country will be valid and the prospects of the recognition and enforcement of such a foreign judgment in an EU Member State. Certain blocking statutes explicitly provide that the decisions applying the sanction concerned cannot be recognised and enforced. We find such a solution most notably in the EC Blocking Regulation.

As the courts of the EU Member States are all bound to apply the economic sanctions imposed by the EU as part of the law of the forum, the remaining possibility to evade a unilateral EU sanction is to stipulate the jurisdiction of the court of a non-EU Member State to escape from EU sanction provisions. Agreements conferring jurisdiction on the courts of a third state with the intention of avoiding the application of an EU sanction require very careful transaction planning. A jurisdiction must be selected, the law of which does not contain the same or a similar economic sanction; the conflict-of-laws rules cannot designate a law containing the economic sanction as applicable law; this may be easily solved by a choice-of-law clause in favour of the law of the selected jurisdiction or another law which does not provide for equivalent sanctions; and the law of the forum should not even give effect to overriding mandatory provisions, such as economic sanctions, of a third country (from the perspective of the forum, EU Member States may qualify as third countries) through substantive law rules. Taking the above factors into account, it is not easy to predict the attitude of the court in a third country regarding the (non-)application of an economic sanction imposed by the EU. A further question is whether the recognition and enforcement of a foreign judicial decision avoiding EU sanctions will be denied in the EU as contrary to the public policy of the Member States.

The other way of deactivating economic sanctions is to confer jurisdiction on an arbitral tribunal. This leads us to examine the applicability of economic sanctions in arbitral proceedings and to analyse whether referring a case to arbitration endangers the application of EU economic sanctions and the enforcement of the foreign policy interests of the EU and its Member States.

II. EU Economic Sanctions and Arbitration Agreements

A. Introduction

The diverse impact of economic sanctions on arbitration has been widely discussed in the literature. This section addresses only those sanctions unilaterally imposed by the EU. The question that we will attempt to answer here is to what extent unilateral EU sanctions are applied or given effect uniformly in international commercial arbitration.

Sanctions imposed by the UNSC and implemented by the EU are not discussed here in detail. The reason for this is that multilateral economic sanctions adopted by the UNSC are generally considered as part of international or transnational public policy and they are applied by arbitral tribunals irrespective of the governing law.[59] Although an arbitral tribunal does not have a forum and is thus not bound to protect the public policy of any state, UN sanctions cannot be ignored by an arbitral tribunal, since most of the states are members of the UN.[60] If UNSC resolutions were not applied by arbitral tribunals, then it would undermine the legitimacy and acceptance of arbitration.[61] Furthermore, if they were ignored by a tribunal, there is a risk that the resulting award will not be enforced in a country which is a member of the UN. Therefore, UNSC sanctions are given effect in arbitration proceedings.

Economic sanctions qualify as overriding mandatory provisions in a private international law sense. The courts of the Member States apply EU sanction regulations as overriding mandatory provisions of the forum under Article 9(2) of the Rome I Regulation, irrespective of the governing law. They even have the option of giving effect to economic sanctions imposed by third states on the basis of Article 9(3) of the Rome I Regulation.

But what is the situation when the economic sanction does not intervene in court proceedings, but in the procedure of an arbitral tribunal? It may be part of the parties' transaction planning that they stipulate arbitration to avoid the application of EU sanctions. Unlike the courts of the Member States, arbitral tribunals are not bound by the Rome I Regulation.

The deactivation of overriding mandatory provisions, including economic sanctions, may take place by an agreement of the parties to confer jurisdiction on an arbitral tribunal, which does not apply the sanction in question. The same may

[59] Pierre Lalive, 'Transnational (or Truly International) Public Policy and International Arbitration' in Pieter Sanders (ed), *Comparative Arbitration Practice and Public Policy in Arbitration, ICCA Congress Series, 1986 New York*, vol 3 (Kluwer, 1987) 258; Geneviève Burdeau, 'Les effets juridiques des résolutions du Conseil de sécurité sur les contrats privé' in Vera Gowlland-Debbas (ed), *United Nations Sanctions and International Law* (Kluwer, 2001) 267, 268; Laurence Landy-Osman, 'L'embargo des Nations Unies contre l'Irak et l'exécution des contrats internationaux' (1991) 17 *Droit et Pratique du Commerce International* 597, 609; Hans van Houtte, 'Les effets des sanctions économiques sur les contrats transnationaux' in Association européenne pour le droit bancaire et financier, *L'embargo* (Bruylant, 1996) 199; Jean-Baptiste Racine, 'L'arbitrage commercial international et les mesures d'embargo. À propos de l'arrêt de la Cour d'appel du Québec du 31 mars 2003' (2004) 134 *Journal du droit international* 89, 101–02; Mathias Audit, 'L'effet des sanctions économiques internationales sur l'arbitrage international' in Eric Loquin and Sébastien Manciaux (eds), *L'ordre public et l'arbitrage, Actes du colloque des 15 et 16 mars 2013 (Dijon)* (LexisNexis, 2014) 143, 144; Matthias Scherer, 'Corruption, Embargos and Sanctions as a Bar to the Enforcement of Contracts in International Arbitration' (2014) 6 *International Journal of Arab Arbitration* 64, 64; Lambert Matray, 'L'embargo national et international dans l'arbitrage' (1997) 74 *Revue de droit international et de droit comparé* 7, 12; Bernardo Cortese, 'International Economic Sanctions as a Component of Public Policy for Conflict-of-Laws Purposes' in Laura Picchio Forlati and Linos-Alexander Sicilianos (eds), *Economic Sanctions in International Law/ Les sanctions économiques en droit international, Hague Academy of International Law, The Law Books of the Academy*, vol 23 (Nijhoff, 2004) 741–42; Aurore Marchand, *L'embargo en droit du commerce international* (Larcier, 2012) 104.

[60] Landy-Osman (n 59) 611.

[61] Audit (n 59) 154.

happen with EU sanctions that are applied by the courts of the Member States, but not necessarily by an arbitral tribunal.

In addition to opting for arbitration, the parties' freedom extends to the choice of the arbitration venue. Sometimes it happens that, in terms of careful transaction planning, the parties select an arbitration venue outside the EU to avoid the undesired impact of EU sanctions on their contractual relationship. Concerning the sanctions imposed by the EU against Russia, commentators often drew attention to an actual or potential move from traditional European arbitration venues to other places, including Hong Kong and Singapore, to escape the application of the EU sanctions in matters involving Russian parties or a Russian place of performance. Various authors have attributed the EU sanctions against Russia as having differing degrees of impact on the choice of the arbitration venue. Some authors have pointed to a boost in the Far East arbitration market due to the Russian sanctions,[62] while other studies have demonstrated relatively constant preferences as far as arbitration venues are concerned.[63]

It will be examined here whether the choice of arbitration and a particular venue for arbitration may in reality result in disregarding EU sanctions and the claim of these sanctions to be applied uniformly. It will be argued here that the choice of arbitration and the location of arbitration to be outside the EU may not rule out a priori giving effect to EU sanctions, but renders their application in a given case less predictable. This undoubtedly risks the uniform application of EU sanctions.

If the legal dispute concerns an economic sanction, additional questions arise regarding arbitration proceedings. These include the constitution of the tribunal, the arbitrability of the dispute, the application of or giving effect to the economic sanction (in particular when it is not part of the *lex contractus*), and the recognition and enforcement of arbitral awards. Additionally, the impact of Brexit on arbitration cases involving economic sanctions will be discussed briefly.

B. Formation of the Tribunal

In accordance with the principle of competence-competence, an arbitral tribunal is empowered to decide on its own jurisdiction. However, to take a decision on its own competence presupposes the formation of the arbitral tribunal.

Sometimes the question arises as to whether an arbitral tribunal may be formed under an arbitration clause and whether a party may take part in the formation of

[62] Olga Boltenko, 'Hong Kong Emerges as Russia's Refuge While the EU's Sanctions Cripple Major Russian Businesses', http://arbitrationblog.kluwerarbitration.com/2014/11/24/hong-kong-emerges-as-russias-refuge-while-the-eus-sanctions-cripple-major-russian-businesses.

[63] Russian Arbitration Association, '2016: Russian Arbitration Association Survey: The Impact of Sanctions on Commercial Arbitration', http://arbitrations.ru/upload/medialibrary/e1e/2016-raa-survey-on-sanctions-and-arbitration.pdf, 5 and 11.

the tribunal by appointing an arbitrator, in particular when a sanction prohibits instituting proceedings to enforce claims or to satisfy claims relating to contracts affected by economic sanctions. The UNSC sanctions imposed against Iraq,[64] Yugoslavia[65] and Libya[66] contained such a prohibition, using the words 'no claim shall lie' in the English version.

The much-discussed *Air France v Libyan Airlines* case gives guidance on how to address this concern. Air France and Libyan Arab Airlines (LAA) entered into a contract, pursuant to which Air France undertook the obligation to maintain the aircraft of LAA and provide flight crew and special air transport services.[67] The agreement provided for arbitration in accordance with the Arbitration Rules of the International Air Transport Association (IATA). Following the Lockerbie and Ténéré bombings, the UN imposed sanctions against Libya implemented by the EU and Canada. The sanctions not only prohibited furnishing maintenance and other services in relation to Libyan aircraft, but also excluded claims initiated by Libyan entities in relation to contracts affected by the UN sanctions. LAA initiated arbitration proceedings for the non-performance of the contract by Air France before the IATA. Air France argued that it was not possible for it to appoint an arbitrator by virtue of the UN sanctions. Instead of Air France, the Director General of the IATA appointed an arbitrator on behalf of the former, in accordance with IATA Arbitration Rules, and the tribunal was thus formed with an arbitrator appointed by LAA and a president elected by the two arbitrators. The seat of arbitration was Montreal and the parties selected French law to govern the substance of the case. Air France, however, maintained that the UN sanctions foreclosed its participation in any proceedings initiated by a Libyan undertaking. The Cour d'appel declared that the UN resolutions did not prohibit the appointment of an arbitrator by Air France because it would have been illogical to prohibit the parties from triggering the arbitration proceedings, even if their purpose was to establish the applicability of the restrictive measures in question. The arbitral tribunal has competence to ascertain whether the matter may be brought before it and whether the dispute is arbitrable.

EU sanction measures often prohibit the satisfaction[68] or granting[69] of claims affected by the sanctions rather than filing claims or instituting proceedings. For this reason, a request for arbitration is not barred by these regulations.[70]

[64] UNSC Resolution 687 (1991), art 29.

[65] UNSC Resolution 757 (1992), art 8.

[66] UNSC Resolution 883 (1993), art 8.

[67] *Air France v Libyan Airlines*, Cour d'appel du Québec, Judgment of 31 March 2003, Revue de l'arbitrage 1365 (2003), with a note by Alain Prujiner.

[68] See Council Regulation (EU) 2015/1755 of 1 October 2015 concerning restrictive measures in view of the situation in Burundi [2015] OJ L257/1, art 10; Council Regulation 833/2014, art 11.

[69] Council Decision (CFSP) 2015/1333 of 31 July 2015 concerning restrictive measures in view of the situation in Libya, and repealing Decision 2011/137/CFSP [2015] OJ L206/34, art 11.

[70] Irina Moutaye and Elena Billebro, 'Choice of Arbitration Venue in Light of Sanctions against Russia', http://www.sccinstitute.com/media/76670/choice-of-arbitration-venue-in-light-of-the-sanctions-against-russia.pdf, 1, 4–6.

Another problem concerns the participation of arbitration institutions, arbitrators and lawyers in the arbitration proceedings. It is not only the contractual relationship between the parties that had resort to arbitration which may be affected by economic sanctions; arbitrators and arbitral institutions have to take economic sanctions in their relationships with the parties into account just as much, for example, when receiving or transferring funds from or to a party subject to an economic sanction.[71] Economic sanctions often freeze the assets of a party and prohibit the transfer of funds.[72] It may happen that the sanction rules affect the transfer of the amount necessary to institute arbitration or to pay the arbitration fee.[73] The violation of such rules may be prohibited, not only for the party transferring the funds, but also for the arbitrator(s) or arbitration institution benefiting from them.[74] Similarly, providing technical assistance to the transactions covered by the sanction is sometimes also prohibited by the sanctions regime. Interpreting it broadly, technical assistance may even involve the activity of arbitration institutions, arbitrators and lawyers, who undertake to represent clients subject to sanctions. Although such a broad interpretation is open to debate, it has been suggested that doubts may be dispersed by requesting a licence from the competent authorities.[75] It should be noted that EU sanction regulations sometimes permit the release of frozen funds by administrative authorisation if it is necessary 'for payment of reasonable professional fees or reimbursement of incurred expenses associated with the provision of legal services'.[76] These costs may include expenditure on legal advice and the activity of an arbitral tribunal. The CJEU has stated that national authorities do not have an absolute discretion when deciding on the release of frozen funds, and they have to observe the right of the person concerned to an effective judicial remedy, which provides everyone with the possibility of being advised, defended and represented.[77] However, the competent national authority may verify that the release of funds is intended exclusively for payment of reasonable professional fees and reimbursement of incurred expenses associated with the provision of legal services. It may also set certain conditions (allowing bank transfers instead of cash payments) in order to guarantee that the objective of the sanction is not frustrated and the derogation granted is not abused.

[71] Elliott Geisinger, Philippe Bärtsch, Julie Raneda and Solomon Ebere, 'Les conséquences des sanctions économiques sur les obligations contractuelles et sur l'arbitrage commercial international' (2012) *Revue de droit des affaires internationales/International Business Law Journal* 405, 431–32.

[72] Audit (n 59) 146–47.

[73] ibid.

[74] ibid.

[75] Moutaye and Billebro (n 70) 6–7.

[76] Council Regulation (EU) 269/2014, art 4(1)(b). John Beechey, Jacomijn van Haersolte-van Hof and Annette Magnusson, 'The Potential Impact of the EU Sanctions against Russia on International Arbitration Administered by EU-Based Institutions', http://www.sccinstitute.com/media/80988/legal-insight-icc_lcia_scc-on-sanctions_17-june-2015.pdf, 1, 3 and 6; see Eric de Brabandere and David Holloway, 'Sanctions and International Arbitration' in Larissa van den Herik (ed), *Research Handbook on UN Sanctions and International Law* (Edward Elgar, 2017) 304, 322–24.

[77] Case C-314/13 *Užsienio reikalų ministerija and Finansinių nusikaltimų tyrimo tarnyba v Vladimir Peftiev et al* ECLI:EU:C:2014:1645.

C. Arbitrability of the Dispute

Once the parties have appointed the arbitrators and the tribunal is set up, the tribunal can decide on its own competence, including ruling on the arbitrability of the dispute.[78] It must be examined whether cases involving economic sanctions may be subject to arbitration.

In the legal literature, the dominant view is that a dispute is not inarbitrable simply because the case involves the issue of applying overriding mandatory provisions.[79] The fact that the legal dispute involves the question of applying an economic sanction, by virtue of which the contract may be null and void, does not affect the validity of the arbitration clause due to the principle of separability.[80] This approach finds confirmation in both judicial and arbitral practice. Indeed, in the famous *Mitsubishi v Soler* case, the US Supreme Court made clear, regarding an arbitration clause related to a distribution agreement, that the application of antitrust rules qualifying as overriding mandatory provisions did not exclude the arbitrability of a case.[81] This view gained clear confirmation in the arbitration practice in relation to a variety of overriding mandatory provisions having a national or EU origin,[82] including economic sanctions. It has been asserted that public policy may ultimately be relied on regarding the recognition and enforcement of the award if the outcome is unacceptable for the state where recognition and enforcement is sought. The force of this safeguard is weakened by the fact that, as we will see later, public policy is narrowly construed under the Convention on the Recognition and Enforcement of Foreign Arbitral Awards (hereinafter the New York Convention). With regard to the potential application of economic sanctions, several decisions affirm that cases involving economic sanctions are arbitrable, and thus the tribunal has jurisdiction to proceed on the merits of the case and examine whether the economic sanction is applicable in the given case.

In the *Fincantieri* case, the Swiss Federal Tribunal found a case involving economic sanctions to be arbitrable.[83] Here, Fincantieri-Cantieri and Melara, two Italian companies, mandated an agent to sell ships and other military equipment to the Iraqi state. Both the contract entered into with the Iraqi state and the agency

[78] Audit (n 59) 146.

[79] Racine (n 59) 92 and 95–101; Geneviève Bastid-Burdeau, 'Les embargos multilatéraux et unilatéraux et leur incidence sur l'arbitrage commercial international' (2003) *Revue de l'arbitrage* 753, 758–59; Marc Blessing, *Impact of the Extraterritorial Application of Mandatory Rules of Law on International Contracts* (Helbing & Lichtenhahn, 1999) 58–59.

[80] Geisinger et al (n 71) 426.

[81] *Mitsubishi Motors Co v Soler Chrysler-Plymouth*, 473 US 614 (1985).

[82] Chambre de commerce internationale, Sentence rendue dans l'affaire n° 4604 en 1984, (1985) 112 JDI 973, with the case note of Yves Derains (1985) 112 JDI 980; *Société Labinal v Société Mors et Société Westland Aerospace Ltd*, Cour d'appel de Paris, Chambre 1, section A, 19 mai 1993, (1993) 120 JDI 957, with the case note of Laurence Idot (1993) 120 JDI 979, 980; (1993) Revue de l'arbitrage 645, with the case note of Charles Jarrosson (1993) Revue de l'arbitrage 653.

[83] *Fincantieri-Cantieri Navali v M*, Tribunal fédéral suisse (1re Cour civile), Judgment of 23 June 1992 (1993) Revue de l'arbitrage 691.

contract were duly performed until 1987, when the competent Iraqi authority suspended payments. The agent claimed the agency fee from the principals before the ICC Court of Arbitration. The defendants objected to the jurisdiction of the tribunal on the grounds that the dispute was not arbitrable because sanctions had been imposed by the UN against Iraq, and these sanctions had been implemented in Italian and Swiss law. The arbitral tribunal seated in Geneva asserted its competence in the case. The defendants requested the annulment of the award from the Swiss Federal Tribunal. This was rejected, since Article 177(1) of the Swiss Private International Law Act permitted any dispute involving an economic interest to be submitted to arbitration. Claiming the agency fee from the principals qualified as a dispute involving an economic interest. The fact that the economic sanctions imposed against Iraq might have raised the question of the validity of the contract or the impossibility of performance did not automatically lead to the conclusion that the dispute was not arbitrable. The Federal Tribunal did not see any fundamental legal principle that would have established a state monopoly on settling disputes influenced by public law rules.

A further question has been whether the arbitrability of a legal dispute is excluded if the sanctioning measure specifically bars the enforcement of claims related to contracts or transactions affected by the sanction. In *Air France v Libyan Airlines*, the Cour d'appel du Québec established that a UN sanction against Libya did not hinder the arbitrability of the dispute. Additionally, the Cour d'appel noted that the arbitral tribunal did not violate international public policy by declaring itself competent to adjudicate the dispute.

The presence of an overriding mandatory provision, including an economic sanction, does not foreclose the arbitrability of the dispute.[84] An appropriately formed arbitral tribunal has competence to decide whether the case falls within the scope of application of the economic sanction.[85] Simply raising the argument by a party that a claim may not be brought before a court or an arbitral tribunal due to the presence of an economic sanction does not suffice to foreclose arbitration.[86] The sanctioning provisions prohibiting the enforcement of claims affected by the economic sanction concern the admissibility of the claims and not their arbitrability.[87] The fact that the arbitrability of overriding mandatory provisions is not excluded does not bar state control for good, but it delays it until the annulment or the recognition and enforcement of the award arises.[88] The question of arbitrability may still emerge regarding the recognition and enforcement of arbitral awards under Article V (2)(a) of the New York Convention, according

[84] Racine (n 59) 101.

[85] Eric Loquin, 'Les effets des lois d'embargo sur la mise en oeuvre des clauses compromissoires' (2001) *Revue trimestrielle de droit commercial et de droit économique* 66.

[86] ibid.

[87] Garima Shahani, 'Impact of Sanctions under the CISG' (2015) 33 *ASA Bulletin* 849, 854.

[88] See Pierre Mayer, 'L'étendue du contrôle, par le juge étatique, de la conformité des sentences arbitrales aux lois de police' in Tristan Azzi (ed), *Vers de nouveaux équilibres entre ordres juridiques – Liber amicorum Hélène Gaudemet-Tallon* (Dalloz, 2008) 460, 462.

to which recognition and enforcement of an arbitral award may be refused if the court in the country where recognition and enforcement is sought finds that the subject matter of the difference between the parties is not capable of settlement by arbitration under the law of the forum.

The above cases clearly confirm the arbitrability of cases involving an economic sanction. Some authors even write about a general principle of international arbitration law, according to which the public policy nature of the norms applicable in the proceedings does not render the latter inarbitrable.[89] In the context of economic sanctions, it has even been asserted that the issue of arbitrability is no longer a topic of real discussion[90] and is not doubted.[91]

In spite of considering the arbitrability of cases involving public law norms as a 'general principle' and despite stating that the arbitrability of sanction cases is no longer debated, courts in several Member States rejected the arbitrability of legal disputes involving the application of overriding mandatory provisions in general and economic sanctions in particular.

German courts considered agreements conferring jurisdiction to the court of another state invalid if the choice of forum resulted in escape from the application of overriding mandatory provisions of domestic or EU law origin. This also holds true for arbitration agreements. If there is a risk that the tribunal will not apply the overriding mandatory provision, the invalidity of the arbitration agreement may be established.[92] In a judgment, the BGH referred back explicitly to its former judgment on the non-recognition of the validity of a choice-of-court clause to avoid the application of overriding mandatory provisions of German securities law,[93] and held the same for arbitration agreements.[94] The already-mentioned judgment of the OLG Munich did not permit the protection provided for agents by the German provisions implementing the rules of the Commercial Agents Directive to be set aside not only by a choice-of-court agreement but also by an arbitration agreement.[95] It laid down that those overriding mandatory provisions could not be derogated from (in addition to a choice in favour of the law of California) by an agreement conferring exclusive jurisdiction to a court in California if the law of the selected forum did not acknowledge an equivalent claim for compensation for the agent. Such a derogation of jurisdiction was invalid insofar as there is an obvious danger that the court in a third country, following its own legal approach, does not enforce the overriding mandatory provisions of German law. The OLG Munich found that the same applies to an arbitration agreement. In a similar case,[96] the

[89] Racine (n 59) 96.

[90] Audit (n 59) 147 and 150.

[91] Nathalie Voser, 'Mandatory Rules of Law as a Limitation on the Law Applicable in International Commercial Arbitration' (1996) 7 *American Review of International Arbitration* 319, 330.

[92] Mathäß (n 40) 60–61.

[93] BGH, Urteil vom 12.3.1984 – II ZR 10/83.

[94] BGH, Urteil vom 15.6.1987 – Az. II ZR 124/86.

[95] OLG Munich, 17.5.2006 – 7 U 1781/06, IPRax 322 (2007). See Quinke (n 50) 246.

[96] OGH, Beschluss vom 1.3.2017 – 5 Ob 72/16y.

Austrian Oberster Gerichsthof (OGH) found that an arbitration agreement related to an agency agreement entered into between a US principal and an Austrian agent is invalid when it aims at disregarding overriding mandatory provisions. In the given case, the agent could not have enforced a claim for compensation in the case of the termination of the agency contract under the Austrian provisions implementing the Commercial Agents Directive. The OGH noted that US law does not provide for an equivalent protection for agents and that the rejection of the recognition of the arbitration clause is the sole possibility for ensuring the application of the overriding mandatory provisions of the Commercial Agents Directive. As has already been discussed, it is questionable whether the *effet utile* of the overriding mandatory norms of EU law requires (under certain circumstances) the invalidity of choice-of-law clauses as well as of choice-of-court agreements. An interest in the *effet utile* of EU law is clearly present with regard to EU sanctions that claim a uniform application.

More specifically, with regard to economic sanctions, Italian courts rejected the arbitrability of disputes if they involved the application of economic sanctions, though on different grounds. In a decision, the Court of Appeal of Genoa rejected the arbitrability of a contractual dispute concerning the supply of corvettes by Italian shipbuilders to the Iraqi Navy due to the intervention of the sanctions imposed by the UN and the EU during the Gulf War.[97] This was explained by the provision of the Italian Code of Civil Procedure permitting cases to be submitted to arbitration unless the parties may not freely dispose of their rights. The Court of Appeal argued that the arbitrability of the case must be determined in accordance with Italian law, the law of the forum, since the court seised may deny its jurisdiction on the basis of the rules of its own legal system. When concluding the contracts, the dispute could have been the subject of arbitration because the parties were free to dispose of their rights deriving from the contracts, but the parties could no longer dispose freely of their rights due to the supervening embargo. The EU embargo regulation, Council Regulation (EEC) 3541/92, rendered the arbitral clause null and void and the dispute inarbitrable.[98] As the economic sanction impeded the parties from freely disposing of their rights, recourse to arbitration was not possible. The judgment of the Court of Appeal of Genoa suggests that the assessment of the arbitrability of the dispute ultimately depends on the national provisions determining the matters which may be subject to arbitration. Interestingly, this case, like the decision of the Swiss Federal Supreme Court, concerned Fincantieri and Oto Melara, but here their claim was enforced directly against the Iraqi Ministry of Defence and not an intermediary.[99]

[97] *Fincantieri – Cantieri Navali Italiani SpA & Oto Melara SpA v Ministry of Defence, Armament & Supply Directorate of Iraq et al*, Italy No. 138, Corte di Appello, Genoa, Judgment of 7 May 1994, cited in Albert Jan van den Berg (ed), *XXI Yearbook of Commercial Arbitration 1996* (Kluwer, 1996) 594.

[98] Council Regulation (EEC) 3541/92, art 2(1)(a).

[99] Matray (n 59) 16.

As an intriguing continuation of the case, 10 years later, the recognition and enforcement of the award was sought in France based on the Brussels Convention. The Cour d'appel de Paris rejected the request due to the arbitration exception of Article 1(4) of the Brussels Convention[100] and found that the Court of Appeal of Genoa limited itself to the establishment of the invalidity of the arbitration agreement without deciding on the merits of the case. As, in the presence of an arbitration agreement, priority must be given to arbitration, then unless the arbitration clause is manifestly void or inapplicable, the decision had been rendered by a court of instance with no competence to hear it, so the judgment could not be recognised in France.

More recently, the Corte Suprema di Cassazione of Italy found an arbitration clause null and void and a dispute involving economic sanctions inarbitrable.[101] Regarding a contract for the sale of helicopters between an Italian seller and the Iraqi government and the Ministry of Defence, delivery was suspended by the seller, who brought an action for damages for non-performance of the contract by the other party before an Italian court, in spite of an arbitration clause in the contract. While suspending delivery, the UNSC and the EU imposed sanctions against Iraq for the invasion of Kuwait. The Corte Suprema di Cassazione held that an Italian court was entitled to assert jurisdiction in this case, since the embargo had a supranational character and thus the validity of the arbitration clause could be determined only by state courts and not by 'private judges', ie, an arbitral tribunal. The reasoning of the court corresponded to the aforementioned judgment of the Court of Appeal of Genoa. Under Italian law, only disputes over rights of which the parties may freely dispose may be the subject of arbitration. Due to the intervention of economic sanctions, the originally valid arbitration clause became null and void because the parties lost their ability to dispose freely of their rights in relation to the subject matter of the dispute. The court found support in Article II(1) and (3) of the New York Convention. Since the embargo was later lifted, the question arose as to whether the dispute became arbitrable retrospectively. The court rejected this argument, establishing that Italian law recognised the supervening invalidity of acts and transactions, but not their supervening validity.

The above analysis demonstrates that while most authors and arbitral awards, as well as court decisions, find matters involving economic sanctions to be arbitrable, the court practice of other countries represents a different position on the basis of either the requirement of *effet utile* of EU law or national provisions circumscribing the disputes which may be subject to arbitration. Finding a case to be non-arbitrable has the consequence that a court in a Member State that certainly applies EU sanctions will assert jurisdiction. However, the fact that the dispute

[100] *Legal Department du Ministère de la Justice de la République d'Irak v Sociétés Fincantieri Cantieri Navali Italiani, Finmeccanica et Armamementi e Aerospazio*, Cour d'appel de Paris (1re Ch C), Judgment of 15 June 2006, (2007) 1 Revue de l'Arbitrage 87.

[101] *Government and Ministries of the Republic of Iraq v Armamenti e Aerospazio SpA et al*, Italy No 189, Supreme Court of Cassation of Italy, Case No 23893, 24 November 2015, cited in Albert Jan van den Berg (ed), *XLI Yearbook of Commercial Arbitration 2016* (Kluwer, 2016) 503.

involving the application of an economic sanction imposed by the EU is arbitrable does not mean that the sanction will not be applied. This depends on the arbitral tribunal that determines the law governing the merits of the dispute.

D. Applicable Law and Economic Sanctions in Arbitration

Once it has been established that the arbitral tribunal has competence to proceed and the dispute is arbitrable, the tribunal has to determine the governing law and a related question is the application of overriding mandatory provisions. The conflict-of-laws norms of the Rome I Regulation, and more specifically Article 9, do not bind arbitral tribunals as they do the courts of the Member States. The law applicable to the substance of the dispute is established primarily in accordance with the parties' choice. In the absence of this, the governing law may be ascertained following various techniques. The applicable law may be determined either directly, applying the law deemed to be appropriate by the tribunal (for example, on the basis of a close connection), or indirectly, having recourse to the conflict-of-laws rules that it considers applicable. Accordingly, arbitral tribunals have considerable leeway on whether to apply EU sanctions. However, this also implies that there is no assurance that autonomous EU sanctions will be given effect in arbitration.

It has been debated whether overriding mandatory provisions should be taken into consideration at all in arbitration. Some authors supported this,[102] while others found that recourse to public policy sufficed. From the fact that, unlike state courts, arbitral tribunals gain their competence from the parties' autonomy and not from a sovereign state, it may be inferred that arbitral tribunals are not bound by any overriding mandatory provision not envisaged by the parties.[103] The latter approach views the application of overriding mandatory provisions that are alien to the *lex contractus* as an abuse of the competence of the arbitral tribunal, especially in the case of a choice of law by the parties that may risk the annulment of the award.

The question of whether overriding mandatory norms, including economic sanctions, are applied by arbitral tribunals is crucial because ignoring them may encourage private parties to escape these overriding mandatory provisions.[104] Moreover, it is often warned that, by ignoring an economic sanction, arbitrators assume the risk that their award will be annulled by the competent national court or that the recognition and enforcement of the award will be denied.[105] This is

[102] Laurence Idot, 'Les conflits de lois en droit de la concurrence' (1995) 122 *Journal du droit international* 320, 329; Yves Derains, 'Les normes d'application immédiate dans la jurisprudence arbitrale' in Philippe Fouchard, Philippe Kahn and Antoine Lyon-Caen (eds), *Mélanges offerts à Berthold Goldman* (Litec, 1982) 29.

[103] Thorn (n 51) 471.

[104] Mayer (n 88) 467.

[105] See Cortese (n 59) 741; Idot (n 101) 335.

an incentive to observe the economic sanctions imposed by the state that has the competence to annul the arbitral award and by the state where recognition and enforcement may be sought.[106] Reference is often made to the general rule of the ICC Arbitration Rules that 'the arbitral tribunal ... shall make every effort to make sure that the award is enforceable at law'.[107] This may be seen as a reflection of the parties' legitimate expectation that the tribunal will take reasonable steps to render an enforceable award.[108] The UNIDROIT Principles of International Commercial Contracts 2016 (hereinafter the UNIDROIT Principles) as a manifestation of the *lex mercatoria* provide that: 'Nothing in these Principles shall restrict the application of mandatory rules, whether of national, international or supranational origin, which are applicable in accordance with the relevant rules of private international law.'[109] The comments to the UNIDROIT Principles reveal that the term 'mandatory rules' is used here in the sense of 'overriding' mandatory norms applied irrespective of the governing law.[110] For a decision as to whether to take an overriding mandatory provision of the forum or any other state into consideration, even the comments refer explicitly to the ICC Arbitration Rules. In addition to rules belonging to the transnational public policy or the international *ordre public*, the tribunal has to consider these overriding mandatory rules to the extent that they show a significant connection to the case, and the arbitral tribunal has to bear in mind its task to ensure the enforceability of its award.[111]

However, where the enforcement of the award will be sought is not always predictable for an arbitral tribunal and hence the overriding mandatory norms of which country should be considered are not always unequivocal.[112] It is also asserted that the claim for ensuring the enforceability of the award may not override the claim for a legally correct award.[113] The primary obligation of arbitrators is to render a legally correct award and not to render an award that is certainly enforceable.[114] This approach is further supported by the fact that in most cases, the arbitral awards are voluntarily complied with and there is no need for their enforcement.[115] Accordingly, in the *Fincantieri* case, the Swiss Federal Tribunal established that the material precondition for arbitrability related to the nature of the dispute (matters involving economic interest) does not exclude the possibility that the arbitral awards rendered in Switzerland will not be enforced in other states. It is left to the parties to assess the risk of the non-recognition

[106] Cortese (n 59) 741; Voser (n 91) 333–35.

[107] ICC Arbitration Rules 2017, art 42.

[108] Andrew Barraclough and Jeff Waincymer, 'Mandatory Rules of Law in International Commercial Arbitration' (2005) 6 *Melbourne Journal of International Law* 205, 216.

[109] UNIDROIT Principles of International Commercial Contracts 2016, art 1(4).

[110] ibid, Comment to art 1(4), point 3.

[111] ibid, Comment to art 1(4), point 4.

[112] Idot (n 102) 336; Voser (n 91) 335.

[113] Blessing (n 79) 60.

[114] ibid 61.

[115] ibid 61 fn 65.

and non-enforcement of the award in another country. Consequently, it may be inferred that the assessment of the risk is not the task of the arbitral tribunal.

Some authors have proposed a pragmatic approach concerning this issue.[116] Accordingly, if all the available assets are located in a single state, the overriding mandatory provisions of that state may not be ignored to ensure enforcement. On the contrary, if sufficient assets are located in various countries, it is not necessary to take the overriding mandatory provision imposed by only one of them into account.

Economic sanctions may be found in the law of the state of the seat of the arbitral tribunal, in the *lex contractus* and in the law of a third country. These cases will be analysed below.

i. Economic Sanctions of the Lex Contractus

Like state courts, arbitral tribunals respect the law chosen by the parties. However, in the absence of choice of law, the governing law is determined by the arbitrators. In both cases, the question arises as to whether the governing law embraces economic sanctions.

Most authors find it evident that the law found applicable to the contract by the arbitrators includes overriding mandatory provisions,[117] including economic sanctions,[118] because the designated law is to be applied in its entirety. The public law nature or the overriding mandatory characteristic of the norms does not exclude their application as part of the *lex contractus*.[119] This view was accepted in arbitration practice concerning export controls.[120]

Others reject a blanket application of the overriding mandatory provisions of the *lex contractus*. Mandatory provisions of the applicable law that are of a private law nature may well be applied as part of the *lex contractus*. However, in German and Swiss literature, many authors claim that the application of foreign overriding mandatory provisions having a public law origin must be based on a special connection (*Sonderanknüpfung*).[121] This special connection is required irrespective of whether the overriding mandatory provision is in the *lex contractus*, the law

[116] Barraclough and Waincymer (n 108) 216.

[117] Idot (n 102) 335; Christian Forwick, *Extraterritoriale US-amerikanische Exportkontrollen. Folgen für die Vertragsgestaltung* (Verlag Recht und Wirtschaft, 1993) 134; Bastid-Burdeau (n 79) 770; Matray (n 59) 30; Chambre de commerce internationale, *L'apport de la jurisprudence arbitrale* (CCI Institut, 1986) 43; Ulrich Drobnig, 'Internationale Schiedsgerichtsbarkeit und wirtschaftliche Eingriffsnormen' in Hans-Joachim Musielak and Klaus Schurig, *Festschrift für Gerhard Kegel* (Kohlhammer, 1987) 95, 106.

[118] Landy-Osman (n 59) 612; Mercédeh Azeredo da Silveira, *Trade Sanctions and International Sales* (Kluwer, 2014) 111–12; Audit (n 59) 151.

[119] Landy-Osman (n 59) 612–13.

[120] ICC Award of 1982, No. 2930, reproduced in Pieter Sanders (ed), *IX Yearbook of Commercial Arbitration 1984* (Kluwer, 1984) 105, 107.

[121] Anton K Schnyder, 'Anwendung ausländischer Eingriffsnormen durch Schiedsgerichte' (1995) 59 *RabelsZ* 293; Horn (n 11) 213; Voser (n 91) 339–40 and 345–54.

of the state where the arbitral tribunal is seated or the law of a third country. There is no difference in this respect, although due to the presence of a close connection, the application of the overriding mandatory provisions of the *lex contractus* is more probable than foreign provisions.[122] It is argued that when parties choose a neutral seat for arbitration and select the law of this state as applicable, this does not necessarily imply that they desire the application of the overriding mandatory provisions of this state.[123]

The argument that the application of overriding mandatory provisions to the legal dispute is contrary to the legitimate expectation of the parties is not convincing.[124] Neither the parties nor the tribunal can cherry-pick the norms of the governing law and exclude the non-desired overriding mandatory norms, including economic sanctions. In the case of choice of law, the parties select the applicable law as a whole and, similarly, in the absence of choice by the parties, the governing law applies in its entirety. Overriding mandatory provisions protecting public or private interests may not be avoided through the legitimate expectation of the parties.

If the *lex contractus* is the law of a Member State, EU sanctions will most probably apply. UN sanctions are implemented by the EU and national legislation, but the implementing measures often go beyond the restrictions imposed by the UN. In *Government & Ministries of the Republic of Iraq v Armamenti e Aerospazio SpA et al*, the Corte Suprema di Cassazione of Italy qualified the UN and EU sanctions as acts pertaining to international public policy that prevailed over French law, which otherwise governed the contract, and held that their effects had to be assessed in accordance with the *lex fori*. It is not at all surprising to qualify the UNSC sanction resolutions as constituting international public policy, but the implementing regulations referred to in the decision (Regulation (EEC) 2340/1990 and Regulation (EEC) 3155/1990) went beyond the UNSC resolution and extended the sanctions to non-financial services.[125] This difference seems to have been overlooked by the Corte Suprema di Cassazione and thus more extensive EU sanctions were deemed to be part of the international public policy. However, in practical terms, this was not significant in the given case because the governing French law included EU sanctions in any case.

By an award, a sole arbitrator of the Chamber of Arbitration of Milan applied Council Regulation (EEC) 2340/90 of 8 August 1990 preventing trade by the Community as regards Iraq and Kuwait, implementing the UNSC resolution against Iraq, as well as Italian embargo legislation, even in the legal relationship between

[122] Horn (n 11) 213.

[123] Schnyder (n 121) 303.

[124] Landy-Osman (n 59) 611–12.

[125] Council Regulation (EEC) 2340/90 of 8 August 1990 preventing trade by the Community as regards Iraq and Kuwait [1990] OJ L213/1; Council Regulation (EEC) 3155/90 of 29 October 1990 extending and amending Regulation (EEC) 2340/90 preventing trade by the Community as regards Iraq and Kuwait [1990] OJ L304/1.

a subcontractor and a main contractor for the supply of parts for a building of a plant in Iraq by the main contractor, due to the economic and functional interconnections between the main contract and the subcontract.[126] The arbitrator could do so as part of the applicable Italian law, while noting that EC and national sanctions legislation must have necessarily been applied in the EC, irrespective of the law applicable to the contract, considering their purpose and public law character.

It should be noted that even economic sanctions ordered by the *lex contractus* may be set aside if they violate the international or transnational public policy.[127] This is certainly the case when a unilateral sanction imposed by the *lex contractus* is condemned by the international community, for example, by a UN General Assembly resolution,[128] as happened regarding the US Helms-Burton Act. This is crucial for the EU, which intended to exclude the extraterritorial application of the US embargo against Iran, Cuba and Libya through the EC Blocking Regulation.

Like EU competition law, the economic sanctions imposed by the EU must be applied as part of the public policy of the Member States. In the *Eco Swiss* judgment, the CJEU pointed out that Article 81 of the EC Treaty prohibiting anti-competitive agreements constitutes a fundamental provision in terms of the functioning of the internal market.[129] If the law of a Member State permits the annulment of an arbitral award on the grounds of public policy, the arbitral award must be annulled if it fails to observe Article 81 EC.[130] UN sanctions implemented by the EU, as well as economic sanctions imposed unilaterally by the EU, are both to be considered as the expression of public policy, since they represent the fundamental policy objectives and values of the EU. Consequently, disregarding an EU sanction may result in the annulment of an arbitration award. However, this is only the case when a court of a Member State proceeds with the request for annulment. Annulment is not necessarily available if the court competent for the annulment is located outside the EU.

As such, the Swiss Federal Court rejected the public policy qualification of the EC competition rules in the absence of general international recognition.[131] Two Italian companies concluded a contract which agreed to make a joint offer in a tender concerning the building of two bridges along the high-speed railway

[126] CAM Case No 1491, Award of the Chamber of Arbitration of Milan, 20 July 1992, reproduced in Albert Jan van den Berg (ed), *XVIII Yearbook of Commercial Arbitration 1993* (Kluwer, 1993) 80.

[127] Matray (n 59) 31–36; Shahani (n 87) 855.

[128] UN General Assembly Resolution 68/8, 29 October 2013. See Mercédeh Azeredo da Silveira, 'Economic Sanctions, Exchange Control Regulations and the Like: Black Sheep among the Provisions of the *Lex Contractus*?', http://arbitrationblog.kluwerarbitration.com/2014/09/26/brussels-sanctions-against-russia-and-moscows-retaliatory-measures-through-the-eyes-of-the-arbitrator.

[129] Case C-126/97 *Eco Swiss China Time Ltd v Benetton International NV* [1999] ECR I-3055, para 36. See Olivier van der Haegen, 'European Public Policy in Commercial Arbitration: Bridge over Troubled Water?' (2009) 16 *Maastricht Journal of European and Comparative Law* 449.

[130] *Eco Swiss* (n 129) paras 37 and 41; see also Case C-168/05 *Elisa María Mostaza Claro v Centro Móvil Milenium SL* [2006] ECR I-10421, paras 34–39 in the same sense.

[131] Tribunal fédéral 4P.278/2005, Judgment of 8 March 2006, Ire Cour civile; Marcel Meinhardt and Jan-Michael Ahrens, 'Wettbewerbsrecht und Schiedsgerichtsbarkeit in der Schweiz – Eine Würdigung des Entscheids des Bundesgerichts vom 8. März 2006–' (2006) *SchiedsVZ* 182; Horn (n 11) 211.

line between Milan and Naples. The contract contained an arbitration clause for an arbitral tribunal in Lausanne under the ICC Rules and provided for the application of Italian law. Despite the agreement, one of the parties submitted an offer jointly with other companies and won the tender. The other party claimed damages before an arbitral tribunal for the violation of the contract. The party that won the work disputed the claim on the grounds that the contract had been null and void pursuant to EC and Italian competition rules. The arbitral tribunal decided in favour of the claimant. The defendant company sought the annulment of the award before the Swiss Federal Court on the grounds that the award violated public policy under Article 190 (2)(e) of the Swiss Private International Law Act, as it did not observe EC and Italian competition rules. In the view of the court, an award violates public policy if it is incompatible with the principles of the system of values to be followed, ideally by all countries from a Swiss perspective, ie, if it ignores the essential and widely recognised values which, in accordance with the concept prevailing in Switzerland, should constitute the basis of all legal orders. The Swiss Federal Court found that EC competition rules do not correspond to this notion of public policy, because competition rules are based on various economic models which may differ from the one prevailing in Switzerland or the EC. These systems could not be labelled immoral or contrary to the fundamental principles of law by the sole fact that they set aside the Swiss model. Differences in competition rules do not make it possible to deduce any transnational rule or a rule of international public policy. This conclusion is not altered by the fact that the CJEU attaches Article 81 of the EC Treaty to the public policy of the Member States. Taking all the above into consideration, the Swiss Federal Court decided that competition rules are not among the rules that represent essential and widely recognised values, which, in accordance with the concept prevailing in Switzerland, should constitute the fundament of all legal orders. Therefore, the breach of competition rules did not fall under Article 190(2)(e) of the Swiss Private International Law Act and the Swiss Federal Court rejected the request for annulment without examining how competition rules were applied in the given case. The Federal Court also noted that in this way, it could evade the difficulties connected to the application of EC law by a Swiss court that was not in a position to request a preliminary ruling from the CJEU on the correct interpretation of EC law.

This reasoning may also apply to the unilateral sanctions of the EU. In the above case, the law governing the contract was Italian (the law of an EU Member State) and the parties' conduct had effects primarily in Italy: close connection to EU law was present. Nevertheless, courts in non-EU countries do not necessarily share the same objectives and pursue the same values in foreign policy as the EU. A court outside the EU may find that a unilateral EU sanction is not to be followed and the non-observance of an EU unilateral sanction does not necessarily result in the annulment of an arbitral award on the grounds of public policy as conceived by the forum, though they undoubtedly constitute part of EU public policy.

ii. *Economic Sanctions Imposed by the Law of a Third State*

It may happen that the economic sanction may be found in the law of a state other than the state of the *lex contractus* and the tribunal has to decide whether to take it into account. The question posed is whether third-country sanctions should be applied as a legal norm or whether they should be taken into consideration at the level of substantive law. Several authors opine that third-country overriding mandatory norms may not be applied directly, but should simply be taken into consideration.[132] Indeed, arbitral tribunals often have recourse to this technique. When arbitral tribunals give effect to economic sanctions not constituting part of the *lex contractus* at the level of substantive law, this may take place in various ways. The tribunal may treat the economic sanction as a fact which is considered as a ground for *force majeure* that exonerates the parties from performance.[133] The general clauses of contract law prohibiting illegality or immorality may equally serve as a legal basis to take foreign economic sanctions into consideration.[134]

The criteria to decide whether to apply an economic sanction not belonging to the *lex contractus* are formulated in different ways. Most authors require a close connection between the case and the state imposing an overriding mandatory requirement[135] or the overriding mandatory norm itself.[136] Arbitration practice also suggests that overriding mandatory provisions of a third state may be given effect if a close link exists between the case and that state.[137] Other criteria include shared values behind the norm and universally recognised values,[138] the motives of the issuing state,[139] the purpose of the legislation[140] and the consequences of the application or non-application of (giving effect or not to) the norm.[141] Derains and Matray advocate giving effect to or applying foreign overriding mandatory norms if these meet the legitimate expectations of the parties.[142] The extent to which the parties could expect the application of norms, such as economic sanctions, under the circumstances of the case must therefore be examined.[143] Matray adds that the subjectivity of this test may be reduced by the application of the close connection criterion.[144] Interestingly, in the case of the *Amsterdam Grain Trade Association*, in relation to the contracts between an Austrian and a Dutch

[132] Derains 38.
[133] Racine (n 59) 103; Bastid-Burdeau (n 79) 771; Chambre de commerce internationale (n 117) 43–44.
[134] Bastid-Burdeau (n 79) 772.
[135] Blessing (n 79) 64; Voser (n 91) 345.
[136] Bastid-Burdeau (n 79) 772; Matray (n 59) 37; Forwick (n 117) 134.
[137] Amsterdam Grain Trade Association, Award of 11 January 1982, reproduced in Pieter Sanders (ed), *VII Yearbook of Commercial Arbitration 1983* (Kluwer, 1983) 158, 160.
[138] Blessing (n 79) 64.
[139] Shahani (n 87) 854.
[140] ibid 854.
[141] ibid 855; Blessing (n 79) 64; Idot (n 102) 336.
[142] Derains (n 102) 55; Matray (n 59) 41.
[143] Forwick (n 117) 134.
[144] Matray (n 59) 41.

company for the sale of various grain products, the tribunal noted that, even in the case of a close connection existing between the contracts governed by Dutch law and Austria, no effect could have been given to the Austrian mandatory currency provisions because it would have potentially resulted in the nullity of the contract, which could have endangered the interests of the Netherlands in the 'preservation of the normal course of legal relations regarding normal international commercial transactions'.[145] This implies that, beyond the interests and expectations of the parties, the tribunal considered the interests of a state concerned by the transaction. This may also happen regarding the application of EU economic sanctions, where the interests of the EU may easily be revealed. However, the extent to which such an approach may be in accordance with the neutral position of arbitrators is questionable.

Of course, arbitral tribunals have the possibility, but not the obligation, to take overriding mandatory provisions not belonging to the *lex contractus* into account, considering the consequences of their application and non-application.[146] Applying the close connection criterion may enable arbitral tribunals to set aside extraterritorial measures, such as some of the US sanctions, in the absence of the presence of a sufficiently close connection between the case and the issuing state.[147] However, giving effect to such extraterritorial sanctions may prove necessary if the sanction factually excludes performance by the party, even though the extensive sanctions legislation does not pertain to the *lex contractus*.

In the *Götaverken* case, Götaverken, a Swedish shipyard, entered into three contracts with the Libyan General Maritime Transport Organization for the construction and delivery of three oil tankers.[148] Each contract contained an arbitration clause for arbitration in Paris in accordance with the ICC Rules of Arbitration and Conciliation. However, the contracts did not specify the governing law. The Libyan party refused to accept delivery and pay the full agreed price on the grounds that Götaverken breached the Libyan law and regulations on the boycott of Israel, as well as due to some technical deficiencies. The Swedish company started arbitration, claiming the remaining purchase price and damages. The arbitral tribunal held that the parties could not agree on the applicable law, including the application of the Libyan boycott against Israel, and therefore intentionally did not specify it in the contracts. The arbitrators found that Swedish law had to be applied to the contracts and concluded that, in the absence of a special reference in the contract to the compliance with the boycott legislation, the Libyan boycott legislation could not be applied. It was established that the Swedish party had assumed the obligation to refrain from using material or equipment made or

[145] Amsterdam Grain Trade Association, Award of 11 January 1982, 160.

[146] Idot (n 102) 336.

[147] Matray (n 59) 38.

[148] ICC Award made in Case nos. 2977, 2978 and 3033 in 1978, reproduced by Sigvard Jarvin and Yves Derains (eds), *Collection of ICC Arbitral Awards 1974–1985* (ICC Publishing/Kluwer, 1998) 58; Pieter Sanders (ed), *VI Yearbook of Commercial Arbitration 1981* (Kluwer, 1981).

supplied by Israel and to furnish a certificate on that. The tribunal, having recourse to the principle of restrictive interpretation of exceptional clauses, inferred that this requirement would have been redundant if the general boycott law of Libya should have had to be applied. From all the above, the tribunal drew the conclusion that the Libyan buyer could not have refused to take delivery of the vessels due to the Libyan boycott law. Despite this restrictive interpretation, it has been pointed out that in the given case, the limited boycott obligation to provide a certificate of origin was not found to be contrary to international public policy.[149]

Similarly, in *National Oil Corporation v Libyan Sun Oil Company*, the tribunal rejected the allusion to the *force majeure* clause contained in the contract by which Sun Oil, a company incorporated in Delaware, undertook to conduct and finance an oil exploration programme in Libya.[150] The contract was governed by Libyan law and provided for ICC arbitration. Sun Oil suspended its performance under the contract after the US government first prohibited entry to Libya with US passports and, at a second stage, the importation of Libyan oil to the US, and made the export of goods and technical information subject to a licence that was denied to Sun Oil. Subsequently, the other party, National Oil Corporation, a Libyan state undertaking, started ICC arbitration proceedings. The arbitrators found that, based on the *force majeure* clause of the contract, *force majeure* presupposed impossibility of performance, which was lacking in the given case. Hence, the concept of *force majeure* was interpreted within the scope of the applicable Libyan law and the specific clause in the contract, and the US sanctions were not given effect through substantive contract law. We will return to this case regarding the recognition of the arbitral awards involving economic sanctions, but it should be noted here that in a similar case, the object of which was also the US sanctions imposed against Libya regarding the provision of consultancy services by a US company for a Libyan company in relation to construction works, an ICC arbitral tribunal accepted the US sanction as a ground for *force majeure* within the applicable Libyan law, but without a conflict-of-law analysis of the intervention of the economic sanction as an overriding mandatory provision.[151]

iii. Economic Sanctions of the State of the Seat of the Arbitral Tribunal

Overriding mandatory provisions of the state of the seat of the arbitral tribunal are not applied automatically. Unlike national courts, arbitral tribunals are not the

[149] Jean-Hubert Moitry, 'L'arbitre international et l'obligation de boycottage imposée par un Etat' (1991) *Journal du droit international* 349, 354.

[150] *National Oil Corporation v Libyan Sun Oil Company*, First Award on Force Majeure and Final Award, ICC Case No 4462, 31 May 1985 and 23 February 1987, reproduced in Albert Jan van den Berg (ed), *XVI Yearbook of Commercial Arbitration 1991* (Kluwer, 1991) 54.

[151] Chambre de commerce internationale, Sentence rendue dans l'affaire n° 5864 en 1989, (1997) 124 JDI 1073 with the comments of Yves Derains (1997) 124 JDI 1077.

organ of the state and accordingly do not have a forum and are not linked to the legal order of the state of the seat of arbitration. For them, all overriding mandatory norms are foreign.[152]

Some authors still argue that, like courts, arbitral tribunals should apply the overriding mandatory provisions of the law of the state of the seat of the arbitration.[153] This theory, according to which the legal dispute has a close connection to the law of the state where the tribunal is seated and therefore is applicable, has been contradicted in the legal literature and the rules of arbitration institutions. Consequently, the tribunal is not obliged to apply the overriding mandatory provisions of the law of the state of its seat.[154] They may be applied as part of the *lex contractus* or as any third country law deemed applicable by the tribunal. From this, it can be inferred that an arbitral tribunal ignoring the overriding mandatory norms of the *lex arbitri* is not itself a ground for the annulment of the arbitral award.[155] Some authors still argue that the arbitral tribunal cannot ignore economic sanctions of the state of the seat of the tribunal.[156] To observe economic sanctions of the forum may be crucial to prevent the possibility of the annulment of the award by a court of the country of the seat of the tribunal. It is even considered as the arbitrators' obligation to render an award which may not be challenged before the courts of the seat of the tribunal on public policy grounds.[157] It may happen that EU sanctions are not applied by a tribunal in a Member State, in particular if the governing law is not the law of a Member State. However, if the arbitral tribunal does so, it risks its award being annulled by a court in that Member State. Annulment is ensured only if the court of a Member State is competent to annul the award because of the non-application of an EU sanction. As we have seen concerning the judgment of the Swiss Federal Court ignoring EC competition rules, if the court competent for the annulment is located outside the EU, there is no guarantee that disregarding EU rules having a public policy nature, including economic sanctions, results in the annulment of the award.

E. Conflict of Economic Sanctions in Arbitration

Like in litigation, a conflict between overriding mandatory norms may arise equally before arbitral tribunals. If the conflict arises in arbitral proceedings, false conflicts do not pose problems. In the case of real conflicts, certain differences exist compared with state adjudication. The arbitral tribunal does not have a forum

[152] Thorn (n 51) 471; Voser (n 91) 330 and 338.
[153] Shahani (n 87) 854.
[154] Blessing (n 79) 13.
[155] Dietmar Czernich, 'Die Rom I-VO als Grundlage für die Anwendung von Eingriffsnormen durch Schiedsgerichte' (2016) 62 *Recht der Internationalen Wirtschaft* 702.
[156] Geisinger et al (n 71) 423–24.
[157] De Brabandere and Holloway (n 76) 325.

the interests and values of which would involve guidance for it.[158] In the case of conflicting overriding mandatory provisions, including the collision of economic sanctions, the situation of the arbitrators is more challenging than that of judges because their neutrality excludes, in principle, any recourse to locally bound values, interests and policy objectives, when deciding on the conflict. Regarding economic sanctions, such a conflict may arise in particular when an economic sanction and a blocking statute may equally claim application. As has been seen before, such a situation may arise in particular with extensive US sanctions.

Arbitrators may use the international public policy not only to justify the application of certain measures, but also to disregard them.[159] By way of example, a sanction based on a UNSC resolution will be applied as part of the international public policy, while a blocking statute issued by the target state, even if it expresses local public policy, may be disregarded by virtue of the higher-level international public policy.[160]

When none of the sanctions is based on a UNSC resolution, the tribunal has to ascertain whether any of the sanctions perhaps expresses international or transnational public policy. If this is the case (as a rare instance), this sanction applies. If no such coincidence is found, which state's public policy is to be applied is debatable. It is widely recognised that the *ordre public* of the *lex contractus* constitutes the standards. In such a case, the tribunal most probably applies the sanction located in the *lex contractus*, setting aside the sanction found in the law of the third country.[161] In the case of conflicting overriding mandatory norms not constituting part of the *lex contractus*, the tribunal has to examine which overriding mandatory norm is most closely connected to the situation and the consequences of the application or non-application of the overriding mandatory norm, primarily in the context of prospects of enforcement and reducing the chance of the annulment of the award.[162] If the sanction and the blocking measure do not pertain to the international public policy and both are outside the *lex contractus*, the arbitral tribunal may apply or give effect to the measure to which the situation has the closest connection. However, giving preference to one of the sanctions implies that the arbitral award will not be recognised and enforced in the country whose sanction was disregarded.[163] In the context of EU law, it should be noted that in any case, the EC Blocking Regulation rules out the recognition and enforcement of judgments of tribunals giving effect to certain US sanctions.[164]

[158] Idot (n 102) 341.
[159] Racine (n 59) 103.
[160] ibid 104.
[161] Forwick argues giving preference to the sanction which has a closer connection to the case that is probably of the *lex causae*; Forwick (n 117) 135.
[162] Idot (n 102) 341.
[163] See Racine (n 59) 106.
[164] EC Blocking Regulation, art 4.

F. Recognition and Enforcement of Arbitral Awards

Article V(2) of the New York Convention enables the court in the country where recognition and enforcement is sought to refuse the recognition and enforcement of an arbitral award if, among other things, the subject matter of the dispute is not arbitrable under its own law or if the recognition or enforcement of the award would be contrary to the public policy of that country. This begs the question of whether the forum can deny the recognition and enforcement of an award if an overriding mandatory provision of the forum, including an economic sanction, was not applied by the arbitral tribunal.

The public policy exception is to be construed narrowly under the New York Convention.[165] Interestingly, this is also the case with the US, which uses economic sanctions extensively[166] and even tries to compel its partners to observe those sanctions. Public policy, within the meaning of the New York Convention, has often been relied on to inhibit the recognition and enforcement of foreign arbitral awards against US companies which claimed the application of economic sanctions imposed by the US. However, US courts are in general reluctant to accept the public policy defence of the New York Convention and this also holds true for cases involving economic sanctions. In *Parsons & Whittemore v RAKTA*, the US Court of Appeals limited the concept of 'public policy' within the meaning of the New York Convention to the protection of the 'most basic notions of morality and justice' of the forum state.[167] It established that public policy is not a parochial device to serve national political interests and does not include 'the vagaries of international politics'. To put this statement in the context of the application of economic sanctions, if public policy is given a supranational sense as accorded by the Court of Appeals, disregarding a sanction other than the one imposed by the UNSC is not a ground for the denial of the recognition and enforcement of a foreign arbitral award, even if such disregard implies setting aside domestic foreign policy interests and objectives. *Parsons & Whittemore* was followed in other instances.

A narrow concept of public policy was taken over from the New York Convention by US District Court for the Southern District of New York in *Antco v Sidermar* when deciding on the enforceability of a contract between an Italian shipowner and a Bahamian charterer for the carriage of crude oil from Mediterranean ports to Caribbean or American ports.[168] Due to the alleged breach of contract by Antco,

[165] In the US, see *Parsons & Whittemore Overseas Co, Inc. v Société Generale de l'Industrie du Papier (RAKTA)*, 508 F 2d 969 (2d Cir 1974); *Fotochrome, Inc v Copal Co, Ltd.*, 517 F 2d 512 (2d Cir 1975); *Waterside Ocean Navigation Co, Inc v International Navigation Ltd*, 737 F 2d 150 (2d Cir 1984); in Switzerland, see *Inter Maritime Management SA v Russin & Vecchi*, Tribunal fédéral, Judgment of 9 January 1995.

[166] Geisinger et al (n 71) 429.

[167] *Parsons & Whittemore Overseas Co, Inc v Société Generale de l'Industrie du Papier* (n 164) 100.

[168] *Antco Shipping Co, Ltd v Sidermar SPA*, 417 F Supp 207 (SDNY 1976).

the charterer, Sidermar (the shipowner) demanded arbitration. Antco requested before the US court a stay of the arbitration proceedings because, in its view, the contract, including the arbitration clause, infringed US public policy as it excluded Israeli ports from Mediterranean loading ports in compliance with the Arab boycott against Israel in breach of the US prohibition on boycotts against countries friendly to the US. The District Court rejected the reliance on public policy to declare the contract unenforceable. Separating public policy and changing political interests and considerations, it stated that: 'The nation speaks in different tongues and at different times; cases arise where the determination of "public policy" must be a distillation of several governmental utterances.' It found that the New York Convention was applicable to the case and the case was to be referred to arbitration. The exception contained in Article II(3) of the New York Convention, based on which a court may assert jurisdiction provided that the arbitration agreement is null and void, could not be applied. It found the non-enforcement of an arbitral award under Article V(2)(b) on public policy grounds and the unenforceability of the arbitration agreement are comparable, both requiring a narrow construction limited to the forum state's most basic notions of morality and justice. Referring back to *Parsons & Whittemore*, it held that the enforcement of the arbitration agreement did not violate US public policy. A similar position was taken by the US District Court, Southern District of New York in *Belship Navigation v Sealift*.[169] The court found that a contractual dispute is to be referred to arbitration based on the arbitration clause contained in the charter agreement of the parties, notwithstanding the applicability of the US sanctions against Cuba to the contract. The court noted that the national policy prohibiting dealing with Cuba may not be equated with the public policy under the New York Convention, which is to be construed narrowly. Instead, the public policy is best served by the promotion of the enforcement of arbitral awards in accordance with the purpose of the New York Convention. An arbitration agreement may not be refused, even if a US court would decide the case otherwise than the arbitrator.

In the *National Oil Corporation v Libyan Sun Oil Company* case analysed above, the recognition and enforcement of the arbitral award was objected by Sun Oil on public policy grounds.[170] Sun Oil put forward several arguments to support the violation of public policy in the event of recognition and enforcement of the award: first, the recognition and enforcement of the arbitral award would have resulted in penalising the US company for complying with the foreign policy objectives of its government, which would affect the credibility of the US sanctions regimes; and, second, the confirmation of the award would have been inconsistent with the US and international antiterrorism policy.

In this case, the District Court made a very significant statement. It found Sun Oil's arguments to be flawed because '"public policy" and "foreign policy" are not

[169] *Belship Navigation v Sealift*, 95 Civ 2748 (RPP).

[170] *National Oil Corporation v Libyan Sun Oil Co*, 733 F Supp 800 (D Del 1990), 15 March 1990.

synonymous'. It referred back to *Parsons & Whittemore* and elucidated that public policy within the meaning of the New York Convention may not be a device to further national political interests. The court did not dispute the reprehensible character of the Gaddafi government and the fact that, in the reverse situation, Libyan courts would not recognise and enforce a foreign arbitral award against National Oil Corporation. However, it noted that 'Libya's terrorist tactics and opportunistic attitude towards international commercial arbitration are simply *beside the point*'. Moreover, in a footnote, the court remarked that the arguments of Sun Oil were insincere, since already at the time of entering into an agreement with National Oil Corporation, the Gaddafi regime's attitude towards the US had been hostile. The District Court concluded that it could not be established that the confirmation of the award would violate the most basic notions of morality and justice. The recognition and enforcement of the award may give rise potentially to a transfer of funds to the Libyan regime, but the US President had been empowered to prevent such transfers if necessary. Although the District Court commenced its judgment by stating that the case and the arguments brought forward by the parties put it 'in the unenviable and precarious position of having to place labels on the foreign policy maneuvers of the Bush administration' regarding the public policy exception set out by the New York Convention, it presented an interpretation free from any political colour. It did not examine the content of the arbitral award in terms of the realisation of US foreign policy.

In *Ministry of Defense and Support for the Armed Forces of the Islamic Republic of Iran v Cubic Defense Systems Inc*, the US Court of Appeals, Ninth Circuit rejected the denial of the confirmation of a foreign arbitral award rendered on the legal dispute between Cubic, a US company, and the Ministry of War of Iran on the sale of military equipment against the US party for its non-performance related to the Iranian revolution.[171] The Court of Appeals held that the recognition and enforcement of the award did not violate US public policy under the New York Convention. Cubic argued that the recognition and enforcement of the award would have violated US public policy against trade and financial transactions with Iran as evidenced by the economic sanctions imposed by the US against this country. The company also pointed out that the sanctions would have prohibited payment based on the award to the Iranian party. The Court of Appeals stated that Cubic could not demonstrate any public policy interest that could have overcome the policy favouring the recognition and enforcement of foreign arbitral awards under the New York Convention. The sanctions imposed by the US did not exclude the recognition and enforcement of the award. Confirmation and payment on the basis of the award were distinguished, since confirmation itself does not involve the transfer of funds to Iran. Furthermore, even payment was not altogether prohibited, but was subject to licence. In this case, the Court of Appeals

[171] *Ministry of Defense and Support for the Armed Forces of the Islamic Republic of Iran v Cubic Defense Systems Inc*, Nos 99-56380, 99-56444, 15 December 2011.

gave weight to the *amicus curiae* submission of the US government, in which it was concluded that confirmation does not violate US public policy.

In other cases, US courts fully detached the legal dispute concerned from the effects of the economic sanctions and foreign policy considerations. In *Karen v Omar*, the US District Court, Eastern District of New York rejected the denial of the recognition and enforcement of an arbitral award concerning a charterparty on the transport of wheat from Canada to Syria in which Karen, the shipowner, warranted that the vessel was not Israeli-owned or controlled and that it did not call at Israeli ports.[172] Regarding a dispute between the parties, the arbitral tribunal in London decided in favour of Karen. When Karen sought the enforcement of the arbitral award in the US, Omar opposed the enforcement on the public policy grounds under Article V(2)(b) of the New York Convention in light of US law prohibiting the compliance with the Arab boycott against Israel. The Court acknowledged that it faced the difficult 'duty of reconciling the strong judicial policy in favour of the recognition of foreign arbitral awards with the equally strong executive and legislatives policies in opposition to the Arab boycott of Israel'. It found that the contractual dispute between the parties concerned Omar's refusal to pay in full for the use of the ship of Karen and not the Arab boycott against Israel. It also remarked that Omar simply intended to avoid the consequences of the award against it based on a contractual clause it wanted to be included in the contract and which was not objected by it at the time of the conclusion of the contract on legal, moral or patriotic grounds. In *MGM Productions Group v Aeroflot Russian Airlines*, a US company entered into a consultancy agreement with Aeroflot to advise the latter regarding the leasing of aircraft to Iran Air. Following a dispute between the parties, arbitration was initiated in accordance with the contract, in which Aeroflot stated that the consultancy agreement was null and void because it violated the US embargo against Iran. The arbitrators upheld the validity of the agreement. They found no violation of the embargo, since the transactions between the parties were not related to goods or services originating in Iran or owned or controlled by the Iranian government. Later, the enforcement of the award was sought before a US court, which was granted despite the allegation by Aeroflot that the enforcement would have violated the public policy as the agreement infringed the US embargo.[173] The District Court noted that public policy arguments must be treated with caution to avoid discouraging the enforcement of foreign arbitral awards in the US and found that the agreement did not breach the most fundamental notions of morality and justice prevailing in the US. The US Court of Appeals, Second Circuit affirmed this decision, showing deference to the position of the arbitral tribunal that the consultation agreement

[172] US No 487, *Karen Maritime Ltd (Liberia) v Omar International Incorporated (US)*, United States District Court, Eastern District of New York, CV-03-6120, 23 April 2004.

[173] US No 442, *MGM Productions Group, Inc. (US) v Aeroflot Russian Airlines (Russian Federation)*, United States District Court, Southern District of New York, 14 May 2003, reproduced in Jan van den Berg (ed), *XXVIII Yearbook of Commercial Arbitration 2003* (Kluwer, 2003) 1271.

covered only transactions between the US company and Aeroflot and thus did not violate US sanctions, and rejected Aeroflot's reliance on the public policy.[174]

US case law demonstrates that foreign policy objectives do not suffice to deny the recognition and enforcement of a foreign arbitral award, even if the award is not necessarily in accordance with the US foreign policy and in particular the US sanctions programme.[175]

It may be doubted whether the courts of the EU Member States would follow such a generous view if an arbitral award ignored EU sanctions. This is because EU sanctions constitute part of EU public policy. This may be deduced from the *Eco Swiss* judgment of the CJEU. In *Eco Swiss*, the CJEU pointed out that Article 81 of the EC Treaty (Article 101 TFEU) prohibiting anti-competitive agreements constitutes a fundamental provision in terms of the functioning of the internal market.[176] If the law of a Member State permits the annulment of an arbitral award on the grounds of public policy, the arbitral award must be annulled if it fails to observe Article 81 of the EC Treaty.[177] Moreover, it was stated that Article 81 of the EC Treaty must be regarded as a matter of public policy within the meaning of the New York Convention, which constitutes a ground for the denial of the recognition and enforcement of an arbitration award.[178] UN sanctions implemented by the EU, as well as economic sanctions imposed unilaterally by the EU, are to be equally considered as the expression of public policy, since they represent the fundamental policy objectives and values of the EU. Consequently, the disregard of an EU sanction results in the annulment of an arbitration award and, when this is sought, the denial of the recognition and enforcement of the award in the Member States. This obviously implies an incentive for arbitral tribunals seated in the EU to observe economic sanctions imposed by the EU to avoid later annulment or, irrespective of the location of arbitration, to ensure the recognition and enforcement of the award in the territory of the EU. The *Eco Swiss* judgment has been so interpreted that the courts of the Member States have to apply the overriding mandatory provisions of EU law *ex officio* when ruling on the annulment or recognition and enforcement of arbitral awards, even if the parties to the dispute did not raise their application.[179]

To consider EU sanctions as part of the public policy that makes it possible to deny recognition and enforcement under the New York Convention has the impact of arbitral tribunals being induced to take EU sanctions into account if the parties have assets in the EU. In such a case, recourse to arbitration outside the EU does not provide a solution. If enforcement within the territory of the EU is not

[174] US No 478, *MGM Productions Group, Inc. (US) v Aeroflot Russian Airlines (Russian Federation)*, United States Court of Appeals, Second Circuit, 03-7561, 9 February 2004.

[175] Da Silveira (n 118) 122.

[176] *Eco Swiss* (n 129) para 36.

[177] ibid paras 37 and 41.

[178] ibid paras 38–39.

[179] Ivana Kunda, *International Mandatory Rules of a Third Country in European Contract Conflict of Laws: The Rome Convention and the Proposed Rome I Regulation* (Rijeka Law Faculty, 2007) 257–61.

feasible because there are no available assets in the EU, ignoring EU sanctions by an arbitral tribunal outside the EU will not have any further consequences. It is generally accepted that the public policy of the forum may be a basis for the annulment, as well as for the denial of the recognition and enforcement of an arbitral award. However, a control is missing as far as the public policy of countries other than the forum is concerned.[180] If recognition and enforcement is sought outside the EU, the public policy exception will probably not be used on the grounds that EU sanctions were disregarded.

G. The Impact of Brexit on Arbitration Involving Economic Sanctions

After Brexit, the question of how an arbitral tribunal seated in London or elsewhere in the UK will treat cases involving EU sanctions will arise. London may be an attractive place outside the EU for arbitration. The recourse to an arbitral tribunal seated in the UK may be motivated by the objective that the arbitral tribunal will not necessarily apply an EU sanction. For the validity of arbitration clauses stipulating an arbitral tribunal in the UK in order to prevent the application of EU sanctions and for the recognition and enforcement of such awards, our previous conclusions apply, as the UK will amount to a third state following Brexit. The uncertainties mentioned before will also appear in such cases.

How UK arbitration law treats local or domestic arbitration awards disregarding EU sanctions requires further examination. First, UK arbitration provides for the possibility of challenging an arbitral award before a UK court by a party. Pursuant to section 68(1) of the UK Arbitration Act 1996, a party to arbitral proceedings may apply to the court challenging an award in the proceedings on the ground of serious irregularity affecting the award. Serious irregularity includes cases when the award was procured in a way that is contrary to public policy and this has caused or will cause substantial injustice to the applicant.[181] It is therefore questionable whether an award of an arbitral tribunal seated in London or elsewhere in the UK could be successfully challenged on the grounds that it disregarded an EU sanction. If the EU sanction corresponds to a UK sanction, this seems probable, but otherwise the answer will be doubtful.

Second, it needs to be examined whether the recognition and enforcement of a foreign arbitral award may be denied on the grounds that it ignored a sanction imposed by the EU. Section 103(3) of the English Arbitration Act 1996 implements the rule of the New York Convention, pursuant to which the recognition or enforcement of a foreign award may be refused if the award is contrary to public policy.[182] Public policy is narrowly construed by UK courts as regards the enforcement of

[180] See Mayer (n 88) 471.
[181] UK Arbitration Act 1996, s 6 (2)(g).
[182] ibid s 103(3).

arbitral awards.[183] The fact that the award did not apply the law correctly or that it is different in its result from the judgment of an English court does not suffice.[184] Finally, public policy further appears as a means to refuse the recognition and enforcement of foreign awards in accordance with common law rules outside the framework of the New York Convention.[185] It is therefore questionable whether the non-observance of UK or EU sanctions may establish the refusal of the recognition or enforcement of a foreign award. However, in *Soleimany v Soleimany*, the Court of Appeal denied the enforcement of the award of the Beth Din in London in the legal dispute between a father and son smuggling carpets from Iran to the UK by breaching Iranian law on the grounds of public policy.[186] Accordingly, an English court will not enforce an arbitration award on an underlying contract governed by English law, or to be performed in England, that is illegal under English domestic law. Additionally, the enforcement of a foreign award is to be denied when the underlying contract is governed by the law of a foreign and friendly state, or which requires performance in such a country, if performance is illegal according to the law of that country. Transferring this statement to the context of economic sanctions would allow the conclusion that a foreign award ignoring a UK sanction would not be recognised and enforced in the UK, and such a consequence would also be likely in the case of disregarding sanctions imposed by the EU because of the friendly relations between the EU, its Member States and the UK.

H. Conclusion

The EU implements the sanctions of the UNSC and adopts sanctions unilaterally. Sanctions imposed by the UNSC are applied by arbitral tribunals as part of international or transnational public policy. However, the question is whether unilateral EU sanctions adopted outside the UN framework are applied uniformly in arbitral proceedings.

EU sanctions do not bar the formation of the tribunal or the involvement of arbitrators or legal counsels in arbitral proceedings. Uncertainties arise as far as the arbitrability of disputes involving EU sanctions is concerned. A considerable part of the legal literature and arbitral awards find cases involving economic sanctions to be arbitrable. However, German and Austrian court practice has held arbitration agreements to be null and void if they present a risk of avoiding the application of overriding mandatory provisions. The rationale behind this approach is to ensure the *effet utile* of EU law. A corollary of this practice is that an arbitration agreement may be considered null and void if it poses the risk that the application of

[183] Craig Tevendale and Andrew Cannon, 'Enforcement of Awards' in Julian DM Lew, Harris Bor, Gregory Fullelove and Joanne Greenaway (eds), *Arbitration in England* (Kluwer, 2013) 563, 579–80.
[184] Robert Merkin, *Arbitration Law* (LLP, 2004) 835.
[185] English Arbitration Act 1996, s 81(1)(c).
[186] *Soleimany v Soleimany* [1999] QB 785.

EU sanctions will be avoided. However, the legal soundness of this approach has not yet been tested by the CJEU. Italian court practice also calls into question the arbitrability of such legal disputes, but on the basis of national law.

Arbitral tribunals are not bound by preset norms when addressing the application of overriding mandatory provisions and thus have a wide freedom to apply sanctions, which involves some uncertainty as to the application of the sanctions imposed by the EU. When implementing UN sanctions, the EU often goes beyond their provisions. The 'hard core' of the sanctions stemming from the UNSC will certainly be applied by arbitral tribunals, but this is not necessarily the case with those sanction provisions through which the EU goes beyond the restrictions imposed by the UNSC. Similar uncertainties arise regarding unilateral sanctions adopted independently of the UN sanctions regime. EU sanctions are probably applied when they constitute part of the *lex contractus*. If an EU sanction is external to the *lex contractus*, it may be given effect provided that a close connection to the case can be shown.

The fact itself that the venue of the arbitration is in an EU Member State is not decisive from the point of view of the application of EU sanctions. This is because an arbitral tribunal does not give priority to the law of the state of its seat. However, it must be acknowledged that in the case of ignoring an EU sanction, the annulment of the award by the courts of the Member States is more probable, since EU sanctions constitute the public policy of the Member States. Similarly, even if the seat of arbitration is located outside the EU, when recognition and enforcement is sought in the EU, this fact probably also increases the chances of giving effect to EU sanctions, because arbitrators may take this factor into account.

This implies that, in spite of the relative freedom enjoyed by arbitral tribunals in giving effect to economic sanctions, the potential for denying the effects of an award disregarding EU sanctions may be a motive for giving effect to them by arbitral tribunals. This may weaken endeavours to choose arbitral proceedings and arbitration venues outside the EU in order to avoid the application of economic sanctions imposed unilaterally by the EU.

9

Possible Solutions and Conclusions

It has been demonstrated that there is no problem with the uniform application of the economic sanctions of the EU, but a consistent approach is missing as to those imposed by third states. The inconsistency of their application by the courts of the Member States does not promote either legal certainty and predictability or a common EU foreign policy approach. The question of how the problems outlined may be overcome cannot be avoided. There are two possible ways to do this: the public and private ordering of contractual relations affected by economic sanctions.

I. Public Ordering of Contractual Relations Affected by Economic Sanctions

Public intervention includes diplomacy and the promotion of international cooperation legislation in the field of economic sanctions. The frequent frictions between the US and EU sanctions regimes could be mitigated by diplomatic means. Political compromises may be effective to end the overly extensive application of economic sanctions. Such a solution would help to lead national courts back to the apolitical world of private international law and would largely relieve them of their foreign policy function. As most of the decisions where inconsistencies were revealed were rendered in relation to US sanctions, the fine-tuning of sanctions policies would equally promote a more consistent EU approach towards the economic sanctions of third countries. However, until such a compromise is made, the uncertainty is borne by business actors.[1]

Legislation can contribute to a more consistent approach towards foreign sanctions. As an antithesis of international cooperation, another public law option is the adoption of blocking statutes in each case where the application of a foreign economic sanction is not desired. The advantage of the adoption of blocking statutes is that it makes the intention of the legislature not to apply a given sanction clear. However, it places a burden on the legislation to issue blocking measures, even if the blocking state or organisation is not the target of the sanction, but

[1] Michael Cremer, 'Embargovorschriften als Eingriffsnormen' (2016) 10 *Bucerius Law Journal* 18, 23.

the economic sanction is opposed because of its unlawfulness or because it has harmful consequences for the traders established there, or simply because of the friendly diplomatic relations with the targeted third country. In practice, it is hardly conceivable that any sanction adopted by any country that is disapproved of is consistently followed by blocking statutes.

States can compensate companies established in that state for losses suffered due to the application of extensive foreign economic sanctions, the effects of which are intended to be excluded. Blocking statutes sometimes contain clawback provisions, which permit claiming damages suffered due to the application of an economic sanction. This may encourage commercial relations to a certain extent, notwithstanding the risk of economic sanctions. Furthermore, there are instances where the performance of a contract was ordered by a governmental or legislative act in spite of the existence of the economic sanction.[2] In the pipeline case, the French government obliged the French subsidiary of American Dresser Industries to perform its contract, notwithstanding the US embargo.

II. Private Ordering of Contractual Relations Affected by Economic Sanctions

The role of private international law is limited to the designation of the applicable law. Conflict-of-laws rules decide on whether a particular economic sanction applies to the parties' contractual relation or not. Nevertheless, conflict-of-laws norms themselves do not determine the legal consequences of applying economic sanctions.

The impact of economic sanctions on the contractual relationships of the parties has been broadly discussed under both national law[3] and the CISG.[4] As the enquiry of this book is limited to the role of private international law in the application of economic sanctions, it does not deal in detail with substantive

[2] Hans van Houtte, 'Les effets des sanctions économiques sur les contrats transnationaux' in Association européenne pour le droit bancaire et financier, *L'embargo* (Bruylant, 1996) 189, 205.

[3] See, eg, Aurore Marchand, *L'embargo en droit du commerce international* (Larcier, 2012) 245–417; Jean Virole, 'Incidence des mesures d'embargo sur les contrats internationaux' (1981) 7 *Droit et pratique du commerce international* 311; G Burdeau, 'Les effets juridiques des résolutions du Conseil de sécurité sur les contrats privé' in V Gowlland-Debbas (ed), *United Nations Sanctions and International Law* (Kluwer, 2001) 267; Laurence Landy-Osman, 'L'embargo des Nations Unies contre l'Irak et l'exécution des contrats internationaux' (1991) 17 *Droit et Pratique du Commerce International* 597, 618–33; Christian Forwick, *Extraterritoriale US-amerikanische Exportkontrollen. Folgen für die Vertragsgestaltung* (Verlag Recht und Wirtschaft, 1993) 137–53; Sophie Mathäß, *Die Auswirkungen staaten- und personenbezogener Embargomaßnahmen auf Privatrechtsverhältnisse* (Nomos, 2016); Mercédeh Azeredo da Silveira, *Trade Sanctions and International Sales* (Kluwer, 2014) 199–351.

[4] Garima Shahani, 'Impact of Sanctions under the CISG' (2015) 33 *ASA Bulletin* 849, 856–58; Forwick (n 3) 153–56.

law consequences, although this is not to deny that their examination is undoubtedly necessary in assessing the impact of economic sanctions on the contractual relationship of the parties.

In economic sanction cases, in the absence of any contractual stipulation by the parties, the court has to have regard first to the rules providing for the economic sanction. However, these rules do not determine the precise legal consequences of the economic sanction on contracts in most cases or do so only partially. Hence, the substantive law consequences may be determined on the basis of the general contract law provisions of the *lex causae*.

The impact of the existence or intervention of an economic sanction on the contract may be diverse. Economic sanctions may trigger the invalidity of the contract or the termination of the contract automatically by virtue of the economic sanction or by one of the parties, or the contract may be modified following the intervention of the economic sanction by the agreement of the parties or by a court decision.

Obviously, in the case of the intervention of an economic sanction, the most crucial question is whether a party assuming an obligation will be exonerated from its performance. Article 12 of the Rome I Regulation does not explicitly mention the exoneration of parties among the questions covered by the applicable law, but the list in Article 12 includes 'the consequences of a total or partial breach of obligations' and 'the various ways of extinguishing obligations' are mentioned. It is a non-exhaustive list, so the issue of exoneration is certainly covered by the governing law.

Whether a party is exempted from its obligations due to the economic sanction is therefore determined by the applicable law. Sometimes, the legal source imposing the economic sanction determines its legal consequences or the legal consequences may be inferred from that. In the absence of this, the applicable national contract law decides the legal consequences of the economic sanction.

Regarding the substantive law treatment of economic sanctions, two cases must be distinguished. The first is when a supervening economic sanction affects an already existing contract. Second, the case must be treated differently, when the economic sanctions precede the conclusion of the contract.

Concerning economic sanctions supervening subsequent to the conclusion of the contract, the validity of pre-existing contracts depends on the sanctioning norm, but as a main rule it is not affected.[5] This follows from the lack of retroactive effect of economic sanctions. However, the performance of pre-existing contracts is without doubt affected by the economic sanction. The consequences of an obstacle to the performance are determined by the governing law. Usually, when a party is impeded in performance by an economic sanction, the economic sanction qualifies as a ground for impossibility of performance (*Unmöglichkeit*) or a frustration of purpose (*Wegfall der Geschäftsgrundlage*) in German law, *force majeure* (*fait du prince*) using the French or frustration (act of state) in

[5] Burdeau (n 3) 273.

the English terminology. The terminology and the preconditions depend on the concepts and rules of the governing national law. The consequences, again depending on the governing national law, may range from the suspension of the performance for the duration of the economic sanction to the termination of the contract immediately or after the expiry of a period of suspension.[6] If performance is not impossible but is rendered more burdensome due to the economic sanction, some national laws provide for the adaptation of the contract to the changed circumstances.[7] This is feasible when the contract does not provide for the supply of specific products and the goods may be procured from a country not affected by the economic sanction. It is conceivable that even a serious threat of sanctions for the case of the violation of the economic sanction may be considered to be a ground for exemption.[8]

As to the conclusion of new contracts after having adopted an economic sanction, first the legal rule imposing the sanction, then the applicable national contract law will decide on their validity. Economic sanctions may prohibit the conclusion of a contract or may simply prohibit the performance of contracts. In the former case, the contracts concerned are usually seen as null and void due to their unlawful object or cause, the violation of the public policy of the forum, breaching good morals or fraud.[9] In the latter case, the parties may have the possibility to enter into a contract with a suspensive condition that delivery takes place only after the termination of the economic sanction.[10]

It is also a question of substantive contract law whether an economic sanction hindering the performance of the main contract excludes the performance of related contracts, such as subcontracts or finance contracts.[11] Generally speaking, the contracts are to be treated separately and the interference of the economic sanction with the main contract does not affect a related contract. However, the answer always depends on the circumstances of the case. In judicial and arbitral practice, we find cases where the impact of the economic sanction was extended to the related contracts as well. In a case from French judicial practice, the French seller and the Kuwaiti buyer terminated their contract on the sale of sunflower oil

[6] See Saber Salama, 'Le sort des contrats conclus avec des opératuers irakiens à la suite de la levée de l'embargo' (2003) *Revue de droit des affaires internationales/International Business Law Journal* 887.

[7] Forwick (n 3) 139–40.

[8] Lambert Matray, 'L'embargo national et international dans l'arbitrage' (1997) 74 *Revue de droit international et de droit comparé* 7, 46–47.

[9] Geneviève Burdeau, 'Les conséquences de la crise sur les relations économiques privées' in Brigitte Stern (ed), *Les aspects juridiques de la crise et de la guerre du Golfe* (Monthcrestien, 1991) 415, 456; Elliott Geisinger, Philippe Bärtsch, Julie Raneda and Solomon Ebere, 'Les conséquences des sanctions économiques sur les obligations contractuelles et sur l'arbitrage commercial international' (2012) *Revue de droit des affaires internationales/International Business Law Journal* 405, 410–15; Mathias Audit, 'L'effet des sanctions économiques internationales sur l'arbitrage international' in Eric Loquin and Sébastien Manciaux (eds), *L'ordre public et l'arbitrage, Actes du colloque des 15 et 16 mars 2013 (Dijon)* (LexisNexis, 2014) 143, 152.

[10] Burdeau (n 3) 276–78; Mathäß (n 3) 81.

[11] Burdeau (n 3) 283; Landy-Osman (n 3) 632–33; J Périlleux, 'L'embargo et le droit des obligations' in Association européenne pour le droit bancaire et financier, *L'embargo* (Bruylant, 1996) 167, 174; Burdeau (n 9) 457.

by agreement, taking the UNSC embargo against Iraq and Kuwait into account.[12] The commercial court of Nanterre ordered at the seller's request the restitution of the goods located in Dubai from the carrier, as the buyer did not pay for the products and declared the bill of lading null and void. The decision thus gave effect to the economic sanction of the forum in the contractual relationship between the seller and the carrier. The same question had to be addressed by the arbitral tribunal in the *Fincantieri* case. The arbitrator of the Chamber of Arbitration of Milan extended the effect of the impossibility to perform under the EC regulation imposing sanctions against Iraq to the relationship between a subcontractor and a main contractor because of the economic and functional interconnection of the contracts. The subcontractor undertook to supply specifically developed parts to the main contractor, which aimed at enabling it to build a plant in Iraq and the subcontractor was aware of the destination of the products.[13]

Recognising the autonomy of parties, national contract laws generally allow the parties to prevent *ex ante* the uncertainties surrounding economic sanctions by including a clause in their contract providing for intervening events, such as economic sanctions. The parties may stipulate for the legal consequences of the intervention of economic sanctions in their contract, provided that such a clause is not invalid or contrary to general principles. Private prevention as the private ordering of commercial relations in particular involves inserting a general or a more specific clause by the parties into their contract determining their rights and obligations in the event of the intervention of an economic sanction. Such clauses may provide for the possibility to deny performance due to the intervention of an economic sanction and to be exempted from liability in such a case. In addition, even after the emergence of the economic sanction, the parties can *ex post* renegotiate and rearrange their contractual relationship by agreement.

The parties often make conditional the performance of the contract 'subject to licence'.[14] This means that the party has to perform only if an export or import licence has been granted. To be exempted from liability, the party who relies on the clause may be expected to prove that he has done everything that may be generally expected of him to obtain the licence.

General *force majeure*[15] and hardship clauses may cover economic sanctions. However, it is not always clear whether general exoneration grounds cover a specific economic sanction. The interpretation of the general clauses depends on the national law applicable to the contract.

The parties can insert into their contract a more specific clause referring explicitly to economic sanctions, which makes it clear that any intervening economic sanction

[12] Tribunal de commerce Nanterre, 31 October 1990, *SA Lesieur International c/ Sté Norasia Line*, 380 Les Petites Affiches 156, 28 December 1990, 21.

[13] Chamber of Arbitration of Milan, 20 July 1992, CAM Case No 1491.

[14] Forwick (n 3) 160–61.

[15] Mathäß (n 3) 194–200.

amounts to a ground for *force majeure*. These may qualify an economic sanction as *force majeure* or frustration even if the economic sanction did not constitute a ground therefor under general contract law. It is also possible for the parties to determine the legal consequences of economic sanctions, including:[16] the exoneration from or limitation of liability in the event of non-performance; extension of the deadline for performance with the duration of the application of the economic sanction either automatically or by the agreement of the parties; modification of the contract otherwise by the agreement of the parties or by a court decision; the automatic termination of the contract due to the intervention of the economic sanction or the possibility of the termination of the contract for the buyer or for both parties. The default rules on *force majeure* or frustration of the governing national law will apply as necessary in the case of uncertainty concerning the interpretation of the clause inserted by the parties.

The parties' contract may also contain a general or a more specific hardship clause.[17] Contrary to a *force majeure* clause, hardship clauses provide for cases where the performance does not become impossible, but is rendered more difficult after the conclusion of the contract. A hardship clause may refer to the change in the circumstances generally or may specify events which qualify as a ground of hardship, such as an economic sanction. Hardship clauses usually require the parties to adapt their contract to the changed circumstances; if they fail to make an agreement, a court or arbitral tribunal usually decides the case based on a choice-of-forum clause or the general rules of jurisdiction.

To sum up, the legal effects of an economic sanction depends primarily on the sanctioning legislation. If this does not contain specific provisions on the effects of the sanction on contracts, these are determined by the contract law rules of the *lex causae*. In order to reduce the risk inherent in the intervention of economic sanctions, the parties can use more general or specific contractual clauses by which they can determine in advance the legal consequences of an economic sanction on the contractual relationship of the parties.

Another means of reducing risks related to economic sanctions is taking out an insurance policy. In many countries, exporters may take out export insurance with an insurance company, such as COFACE or Euler Hermes, covering commercial as well as political risks. Internationally active companies are often urged to launch a compliance programme to identify transactions falling within the scope of economic sanctions.[18]

[16] Bernard Grelon and Charles-Etienne Gudin, 'Contrats et crise du Golfe' (1991) 118 *Journal du droit international* 633, 657; Nabil Ferjani and Véronique Huet, 'L'impact de la décision onusienne d'embargo sur l'exécution des contrats internationaux' (2010) *Journal du droit international* 737, 759.

[17] Marchand (n 3) 327–33; Forwick (n 3) 166–68.

[18] Meredith Rathbone, Peter Jeydel and Amy Lentz, 'Sanctions, Sanctions Everywhere: Forging a Path through Complex Transnational Sanctions Laws' (2013) 44 *Georgetown Journal of International Law* 1055, 1123–26.

Finally, private prevention may also include cases where the parties concerned simply contact authorities, including the US authorities if they are involved, in a proactive way, provide them with the necessary information and ask for their assessment before conducting a transaction. This course of proceedings contributes to preventing potential penalties.

III. The Role of Private International Law

Private international law can equally contribute to mitigating the divergences in the national court practice. Such an effect may be achieved by the amendment of private international law rules or by a fine-tuned interpretation of the existing private international law rules by the CJEU or the courts of the Member States. These techniques require public intervention on the part of legislature or courts.

First, the uncertainties related to the application of the overriding mandatory norms, including economic sanctions, of the *lex causae* could be eliminated by amending the Rome I Regulation as suggested by the Proposal of the Max Planck Institute on the Conversion of the Rome Convention into a Community Instrument. Such an amendment should make it unequivocal whether such overriding mandatory norms, in particular those having a public law origin, are to be applied at all and, if so, automatically, or if they meet the requirements of Article 9(3).

Second, the approximation of the judicial practice of the Member States by the CJEU could reduce inconsistencies in court practice. The CJEU could give guidance in certain crucial questions, such as the application of the overriding mandatory provisions, and thus economic sanctions, of the *lex causae* or the circumstances to be examined under Article 9(3) of the Rome I Regulation; for instance, when a national court has to decide on giving effect to an extraterritorial US sanction which is not part of the governing law. A ruling of the CJEU may give guidance on the permissibility of jurisdiction and arbitration clauses (often coupled with choice-of-law clauses) which have the effect of escaping from the application of the economic sanctions imposed by the EU. However, the preliminary ruling procedure has its own limits. The CJEU cannot decide directly whether an economic sanction has to be applied in the given case; its role is the interpretation of EU law. In the distribution of functions between the CJEU and the national courts, the ultimate decision on the application of an economic sanction is left to the referring national court. Furthermore, this option is dependent on the preliminary ruling request by the courts of the Member States made by their own motion or at the request of the parties.

Third, consistency could be promoted by the refinement of the judicial practice of the Member States. The differences in the approaches of the courts of the

Member States may lead to inconsistencies. This is contrary to the objective of the promotion of coherence between EU foreign policy and private international law and the principle of legal certainty.

As discussed before, the economic sanctions of the EU and third countries, in particular the US, could be coordinated in a more efficient way. Coordination is crucial to reducing divergence, though it seems illusory that national sanction policies of countries will be identical due to the differences in national foreign policy and commercial interests. Legislative intervention has its own limits. More realistic is the refinement of the judicial practice of the courts of the Member States on foreign economic sanctions to achieve a more consistent approach by placing the emphasis on common European interests and values when applying Article 9(3) or when a court otherwise gives effect to a foreign economic sanction. An analogous solution has been proposed by Köhler more generally to decide when to give effect to a foreign overriding mandatory rule.

Following Köhler, the interest in giving effect to a foreign overriding mandatory norm is to be assessed autonomously from an EU point of view and not from a national perspective, due to the fact that the Rome I Regulation involves the application of an EU legal source.[19] Accordingly, one can take as a point of departure that, following the adoption of the Rome I Regulation, the Member States lost their competence to independently determine the factors to be taken into account when deciding whether to give effect to foreign overriding mandatory provisions. The Member States can no longer decide for themselves on the interest in applying a foreign overriding mandatory norm. Setting criteria at the national level deprives the Rome I Regulation of an autonomous EU law interpretation. Although the interests of the EU in giving effect to a foreign overriding mandatory norm may coincide with national interests, the interests of the EU and those of the Member State may also differ. Leaving the courts of the Member States to take diverging national interests into account, instead of the common European interests, would imply that cases could be decided differently in the EU depending on the forum.[20] As a consequence, a foreign overriding mandatory norm should be applied if its application would correspond to the substantive values of the legal systems of all Member States.[21] In this sense, the assessment of the interests from a European point of view would not be torn away from the national interests; instead, it embodies the lowest common denominator of the interests and values of the Member States.[22]

[19] A Köhler, *Eingriffsnormen – Der 'unfertige Teil' des europäischen IPR (Mohr Siebeck, 2013)* 246. It should be noted that Köhler speaks about the 'application' of foreign overriding mandatory norms.

[20] ibid 251.

[21] ibid 252.

[22] ibid 252–53.

This approach may be equally applied to economic sanctions imposed by third countries. The criteria for giving effect to foreign economic sanctions should not be decided accordingly on the basis of various national interests and foreign policy considerations, but on the grounds of common EU-level interests. Köhler argues that this follows from the transfer of the competence on sanctions policy from the Member States to the EU as part of the CFSP by virtue of Article 215 TFEU.[23] Here, a qualification must be made. Article 215 TFEU authorises the EU to impose sanctions, but it does not say anything about the sanctions imposed by third countries. Instead, it follows from the consistent and coherent application of the CFSP, as well as the principle of legal certainty, that foreign economic sanctions must be treated in accordance with a common European approach. Apart from the EC Blocking Regulation, a normative statement towards the application of the economic sanctions of third countries is missing. Therefore, courts have recourse to the method suggested by Köhler for cases where there is no EU-level legal norm that unequivocally orientates judicial practice, ie, a court in a Member State has to examine, in light of a comparative analysis, whether the purpose of the foreign law is shared by all Member States.[24] Köhler also explains the pertinence of giving effect to a foreign overriding norm, provided that it expresses common European values, by the fact that giving effect to a foreign overriding mandatory norm also affects the interests of private parties.[25] Therefore, it does not suffice if giving effect to the foreign overriding mandatory norm is simply not contrary to the interests and values of the forum state.

Such a proposal is not flawless either. The observance of European interests and values may only be reviewed with difficulty by a higher court or interpreted by the CJEU in a preliminary ruling. Furthermore, focusing on European interests and values does not necessarily relieve courts of foreign policy considerations. However, paying heed to common interests and values undoubtedly results in a comparable yardstick for the courts that can orientate judicial practice across the EU. The *borax* and *Borsäure* cases, where it was held that the US embargo not only served the interests of the US but also those of the Western world (including, of course, Europe), and as part thereof German interests, may be considered to be precursors. The more recent decisions of the LG Hamburg and the OLG Frankfurt am Main, which rejected giving effect to US sanctions partly based on EU policy objectives, point to an approach that could be followed by the courts of the Member States. The reorientation of the judicial practice of the courts of the Member States in this direction could strengthen the consistency of court decisions and thereby promote a common EU approach towards the sanctions imposed by third countries. Such a change would clearly further the coherence between private international law and the foreign policy of the EU.

[23] ibid 254.
[24] ibid 255.
[25] ibid 257.

IV. Conclusions

The consistent application of economic sanctions in private law litigation is required in order to guarantee legal certainty for the contracting parties as well as a uniform, foreign policy approach at the EU level.

In private international law, economic sanctions qualify as overriding mandatory provisions. Article 9 of the Rome I Regulation is limited to the application of the overriding mandatory provisions of the forum and potentially giving effect to the overriding mandatory rules of the place of performance, provided they render the performance of the contract unlawful.

Under Article 9(2) of the Rome I Regulation, nothing restricts the application of the overriding mandatory norms of the law of the forum. This provision provides for a legal basis for the application of the economic sanctions imposed by the EU and these are applied uniformly as overriding mandatory norms of the law of the forum. By applying the rules of the forum, the relevant foreign policy objectives of the EU are enforced.

Several uncertainties arise regarding overriding mandatory provisions, and thus economic sanctions, of foreign states that may be largely traced back to the formulation of Article 9 of the Rome I Regulation. First, it is not clear whether the overriding mandatory provisions, such as economic sanctions, of the *lex causae* must be applied by the court seised. Second, based on Article 9(3) of the Rome I Regulation, effect may be given to the overriding mandatory rules of the state of the place of performance, but the factors (the nature and purpose of the overriding mandatory norm, and the consequences of its application or non-application) referred to in that paragraph leave the courts of the Member States with considerable leeway on when to do so. Third, some authors and the judicial practice of some Member States followed a restrictive interpretation of the question as to whether overriding mandatory norms other than those referred to by Article 9 can be given effect. In French judicial practice, the consideration of other economic sanctions was excluded, as demonstrated by the *Giti* judgment of the Cour d'appel de Paris. However, in the *Nikiforidis* judgment, the CJEU made it clear that national courts are free to consider a foreign overriding mandatory norm through the provisions of substantive contract law, even if the foreign provision could not be given effect under Article 9 of the Rome I Regulation. This decision confirms the previous judicial practice of some Member States, such as Germany, where economic sanctions were often considered at the level of substantive contract law. In this way, private international law rules can be overridden through substantive law that extends the circle of the economic sanctions which may be considered.

Economic sanctions belong to the inventory of foreign policy. Private international law and private law cannot entirely exclude foreign policy arguments in legal disputes concerning economic sanctions. The consideration, as well as the rejection of the consideration of foreign economic sanctions, may be justified by foreign policy arguments in a given case. The discretion granted by Article 9(3) of the Rome I Regulation permits the courts to consider the foreign policy interests of the forum as well and, in the case of considering a foreign economic sanction, to require the correspondence of the interests of the forum and the issuing state. The same applies for the consideration of foreign economic sanctions at the level of substantive contract law. This calls into question the apolitical character of private international law.

The effect of the above-mentioned uncertainties is that the courts of the Member States approach economic sanctions imposed by third countries differently. This results in a decentralised judicial foreign policy in the EU that may be contrasted with the demand for coherence between private international law and EU foreign policy.

Parties to a contract may endeavour to 'deactivate' the application of the economic sanctions imposed by the EU by a choice-of-court or arbitration clause. The admissibility of agreements conferring jurisdiction on a court or an arbitral tribunal in a third country is assessed differently in the Member States, where these result in escaping from the application of overriding mandatory provisions. In some Member States, the courts accept such agreements, while in other Member States, they are deemed to be invalid, in particular if the overriding mandatory norm is of EU origin, because any derogation violates the *effet utile* of EU law.

Arbitral tribunals do not have a forum; therefore, even if an arbitral tribunal is seated in an EU Member State, it is not bound to apply the sanctions imposed by the EU. However, it is probable that an arbitral tribunal in an EU Member State will apply or give effect to the EU sanction, constituting the public policy of the Member States, in order to avoid the annulment of the award by the courts of the Member States. Similarly, even if the venue of arbitration is outside of the EU, when recognition and enforcement is sought in the EU, this induces arbitrators to take a sanction imposed by the EU into account.

As a consequence, it is not always predictable whether an economic sanction may be applied or considered through substantive law in a given case, particularly when it concerns a sanction imposed by a third state. Complications often arise in relation to the extensive US sanctions. These uncertainties stem first from the flexible wording of Article 9 of the Rome I Regulation and second from the differences in the judicial practice of the courts of the Member States. Uncertainties are aggravated by the divergent assessment of agreements conferring jurisdiction on a court or an arbitral tribunal in a third country. This situation promotes neither legal certainty nor a uniform EU approach concerning economic sanctions imposed by third countries.

These uncertainties may be prevented or mitigated by the intervention of public organs. This includes eliminating the divergences among sanction regimes by diplomatic means promoting international cooperation. Uncertainties stemming from the interpretation of Article 9 of the Rome I Regulation, such as the question of the application of the overriding mandatory provisions of the *lex causae*, could be partly solved by legislative intervention. Judicial practice should be reoriented in order to achieve a more consistent case law. In certain questions, we can again refer to the application of the overriding mandatory provisions of the *lex causae*, the CJEU could provide guidance following a request for preliminary ruling. A change in the focus of national courts – shifting from purely national interests and values towards common European interests, values and policy objectives – could more comprehensively contribute to achieving a more coherent relationship between private international law and EU foreign policy. Private parties are equally in possession of certain means of reducing risks related to the intervention of economic sanctions, most notably the stipulation of contractual clauses settling the legal relationship of the parties in the event of a supervening sanction, taking out a special insurance policy or proactive cooperation with the relevant authorities of the sanctioning state.

BIBLIOGRAPHY

Adler, DB, *Die Anwendung und Durchetzung US-amerikanischer Handelsbeschräkungen innerhalb der Europäischen Union – Wie schutzlos ist die EU?* (Duncker & Humblot, 2016).

Ahmetaj, H, 'Legal Certainty and Legitimate Expectations in the EU Law' (2014) 1 *Interdisciplinary Journal of Research and Development* 20.

Aladyev, I, 'Die EU-autonomen "smart sanctions" gegen die Russische Föderation – Rechtsgrundlage, Rechtsmäßigkeit und Rechtsschutz' (2015) 56 *Jahrbuch für Ostrecht* 21.

Alexander, K, *Economic Sanctions: Law and Public Policy* (Palgrave Macmillan, 2009).

Anderegg, K, *Ausländische Eingriffsnormen im internationalen Vertragsrecht* (Mohr Siebeck, 1989).

Askari, HG, Forrer, J, Teegen, H and Yang, J, *Economic Sanctions* (Praeger, 2003).

Audit, B, 'Extra-territorialité et commerce international. L'affaire du gazoduc sibérien' (1983) 72 *Revue critique de droit international privé* 401.

Audit, B and d'Avout, L, *Droit international privé*, 7th edn (Economica, 2013).

Audit, M, 'L'effet des sanctions économiques internationales sur l'arbitrage international' in E Loquin and S Manciaux (eds), *L'ordre public et l'arbitrage, Actes du colloque des 15 et 16 mars 2013 (Dijon)* (LexisNexis, 2014) 143.

——. 'Application extraterritoriale du droit américain : un enjeu pour les entreprises françaises' (2015) 104 *Echanges internationaux, Magazine du Comité Français de la Chambre de Commerce Internationale* 9.

Audit, M, Bismuth, R and Mignon-Colombet, A, 'Sanctions et extraterritorialité du droit américain : quelles réponses pour les entreprises françaises ?' (2015) 89 *La Semaine Juridique – Édition générale* 1–2, 12 January 2015, 64.

Ayhan, T, 'The Principle of Legal Certainty in EU Case Law' (2010) 4 *TODAIE's Review of Public Administration* 149.

Bariatti, S, 'Bilateral Agreements with Non-Member States after the *Lugano* Opinion: Some Procedural Issues' in A Malatesta, S Bariatti and F Pocar (eds), *The External Dimension of EC Private International Law in Family and Succession Matters* (CEDAM, 2008) 77.

Barraclough, A and Waincymer, J, 'Mandatory Rules of Law in International Commercial Arbitration' (2005) 6 *Melbourne Journal of International Law* 205.

Basedow, J., 'Entscheidung – Das Amerikanische Pipeline-Embargo vor Gericht. Niederlande: Pres. Rb. Den Haag 17. 9. 1982. (Fall Sensor)' (1983) 47 *RabelsZ* 141.

——. 'Private Law Effects of Foreign Export Controls' (1984) 27 *German Yearbook of International Law* 109.

——. 'Wirtschaftskollisionsrecht' (1988) 52 *RabelsZ* 8.

——. *The Law of Open Societies: Private Ordering and Public Regulation of International Relations – General Course on Private International Law, Collected Courses of the Hague Academy of International Law*, vol 360 (Martinus Nijhoff, 2013).

——. 'Blocking Statutes' in Basedow, J, Rühl, G, Ferrari, F. and de Miguel Asensio, P (eds), *Encyclopedia of Private International Law*, vol 1 (Edward Elgar, 2017) 209.

Bastid-Burdeau, G, 'Les embargos multilatéraux et unilatéraux et leur incidence sur l'arbitrage commercial international' (2003) *Revue de l'arbitrage* 753.

Batiffol, H and Lagarde, P, *Traité de droit international privé*, vol 1, 8th edn (LGDJ, 1993).

Baum, H, 'Anmerkung: Faktische und potentielle Eingriffsnormen' (1989) 53 *RabelsZ* 152.

Becker, M, 'Zwingendes Eingriffsrecht in der Urteilsanerkennung' (1996) 60 *RabelsZ* 691.

Beckers, Y and Demigneux, N, 'Les mesures d'embargo américaines édictées par l'OFAC sont-elles des lois de police étrangère applicables en France?' (2015) 141 *Actes pratiques et ingénierie sociétaire* 1.

Behr, A, *Deutsche Unternehmen und der Israel-Boykott* (Verlag Recht und Wissenschaft, 1994).

Benedettelli, MV, 'Sull' applicazione extraterritoriale delle misure di embargo degli stati uniti relative al "gasodotto siberiano"' (1984) 67 *Rivista di diritto internazionale* 529.

Beulker, J, *Die Eingriffsnormenproblematik in internationalen Schiedsverfahren* (Mohr Siebeck, 2005).

Bismuth, J-L, *Le boycottage dans les échanges économiques internationaux au regard du droit* (Economica, 1980).

Blair, HO, 'Toward a Workable System of Controls on the Export of Technology – Export Controls on Non-military Goods and Technology: Are We Penalizing the Soviets or Ourselves?' (1986) 21 *Texas International Law Journal* 363.

Blessing, M, *Impact of the Extraterritorial Application of Mandatory Rules of Law on International Contracts* (Helbing & Lichtenhahn, 1999).

Bockslaff, K, 'The Pipeline Affair of 1981/82: A Case History' in J Delbrück, R Hofmann and A Zimmermann (eds), *German Yearbook of International Law, Vol 27 – 1984* (Duncker & Humblot, 1985) 28.

Bollée, S, 'Conflits des lois en matière de contrats' in L d'Avout and S Bollée, 'Panorama – Droit du commerce international (septembre 2009–août 2010)' (2010) 186 *Recueil Dalloz*, 2323.

Bonomi, A, 'Quelques observations sur le règlement Rome I sur la loi applicable aux obligations contractuelles' in *Regards comparatistes sur le phénomène contractuel* (PUAM, 2009) 225.

Briggs, A, 'Public Policy in the Conflict of Laws: A Sword and a Shield?' (2002) 6 *Singapore Journal of International & Comparative Law* 953.

——. 'When in Rome, Choose as the Romans Choose' (2009) 125 *Law Quarterly Review* 191.

Briggs, A, *The Conflict of Laws* (3rd edn, Oxford University Press, 2013).

——. *Private International Law in English Courts* (Oxford University Press, 2014).

Brinkhaus, J, *Das britische Abwehrgesetz von 1980* (Peter Lang, 1989).

Brummer, K, 'Imposing Sanctions: The Not So 'Normative Power Europe'' (2009) 14 *European Foreign Affairs Review* 191.

Bueb, J and Geffrault, M, 'Un colosse chez les géants. Splendeur et déclin de la stratégie économique américaine' in Frédéric Charillon and Célia Belin (eds), *Les États-Unis dans le monde* (CNRS, 2016) 83.

Burdeau, G, 'Les conséquences de la crise sur les relations économiques privées' in B Stern (ed), *Les aspects juridiques de la crise et de la guerre du Golfe* (Monthcrestien, 1991) 415.

——. 'Le gel d'avoirs étrangers' (1997) 124 *Journal du droit international* 5.

——. 'Les effets juridiques des résolutions du Conseil de sécurité sur les contrats privé' in V Gowlland-Debbas (ed), *United Nations Sanctions and International Law* (Kluwer, 2001) 267.

Bureau, D and Muir Watt, H, *Droit international privé – Tome 1* (PUF, 2010).

Bureau, D and Muir Watt, H, 'L'impérativité désactivée ?' (2009) 98 *Revue critique de droit international privé* 1.

Burián, L, 'A jogi személyek honossága különös tekintettel az amerikai embargó extraterritoriális hatályára' (1984) *Jogtudományi Közlöny* 199.

Busse, D, 'Die Berücksichtigung ausländischer "Eingriffsnormen" durch die deutsche Rechtsprechung' (1996) 95 *ZVglRWiss* 386.

Bydlinski, F, 'Anmerkung zur Entscheidung des OGH. 24. Juni 1959, 6 Ob 204/59' (1961) 2 *Zeitschrift für Rechtsvergleichung* 18.

Cabranes, JA, 'Withholding Judgment – Why US Courts Shouldn't Make Foreign Policy' (2015) *Foreign Affairs* 125.

Carter, BE, 'Economic Sanctions' in Wolfrum, R, *The Max Planck Encyclopedia of Public International Law*, vol 3 (Max-Planck-Gesellschaft/Oxford University Press, 2012) 323.

Carter, PB, 'Rejection of Foreign Law: Some Private International Law Inhibitions' (1984) 55 *British Yearbook of International Law* 111.

——. 'The Rôle of Public Policy in English Private International Law' (1993) 42 *International & Comparative Law Quarterly* 1.

Castel, J-G, *Extraterritoriality in International Trade* (Butterworths, 1988).

Cavaré, L, 'L'idée de sanction et sa mise en oeuvre en droit international public' (1937) 44 *Revue générale de droit international public* 385.

Chambre de commerce internationale, *L'apport de la jurisprudence arbitrale* (CCI Institut, 1986).

Charvin, R, 'Les mesures d'embargo : La part du droit' (1996) 29 *Revue belge de droit international* 5.

Chemain, R, 'Sanctions économiques : contre-mesures, boycott, embargo, blocus' in *Encyclopédie Dalloz du droit international, Répertoire de droit international* (Dalloz, 2017).

Chong, A, 'The Public Policy and Mandatory Rules of Third Countries in International Contracts' (2006) 2 *Journal of Private International Law* 27.

Coester-Waltjen, D, '"Totgesagte leben länger" – gilt auch für das klassische internationale Privatrecht? –' in SL Gössl (ed), *Politik und Internationales Privatrecht* (Mohr Siebeck, 2017) 1.

Collins, L, 'Blocking and Clawback Statutes: The United Kingdom Approach – I' (1986) *Journal of Business Law* 372.

——. 'Blocking and Clawback Statutes: The United Kingdom Approach – II' (1986) *Journal of Business Law* 452.

——. (ed), *Dicey, Morris & Collins on the Conflict of Laws*, 15th edn (Sweet & Maxwell, 2012).

Cortese, B, 'International Economic Sanctions as a Component of Public Policy for Conflict-of-Laws Purposes' in LP Forlati and LA Sicilianos (eds), *Economic Sanctions in International Law/Les sanctions économiques en droit international, Hague Academy of International Law, The Law Books of the Academy*, vol 23 (Nijhoff, 2004) 717.

Craig, P, *EU Administrative Law* (Oxford University Press, 2012).

Craig, WL, 'Application of the Trading with the Enemy Act to Foreign Corporations Owned by Americans: Reflections on *Fruehauf v Massardy*' (1969–70) 83 *Harvard Law Review* 579.

Cranston, R, 'The Libyan Arab Foreign Bank Case' (1987) *Journal of Business Law* 499.

——. 'The Libyan Assets Case: Limits to Extraterritorial Claims' (1987) 3 *Journal of International Banking Law* 177.

Cremer, M, 'Embargovorschriften als Eingriffsnormen' (2016) 10 *Bucerius Law Journal* 18.

Cremona, M, 'A Triple Braid – Interactions between International Law, EU Law, and Private Law' in M Cremona and H-W Micklitz (eds), *Private Law in the External Relations of the EU* (Oxford University Press, 2016) 33.

Cremona, M and Micklitz, H-W, 'Introduction' in M Cremona and H-W Micklitz (eds), *Private Law in the External Relations of the EU* (Oxford University Press, 2016) 1.

Currie, B, 'On the Displacement of the Law of the Forum' in *Selected Essays on the Conflict of Laws* (Duke University Press, 1963) 3.

Czernich, D, 'Die Rom I-VO als Grundlage für die Anwendung von Eingriffsnormen durch Schiedsgerichte' (2016) 62 *Recht der Internationalen Wirtschaft* 701.

Danaher, MJ, 'Anti-antitrust Law: The Clawback and Other Features of the United Kingdom Protection of Trading Interests Act, 1980' (1980) 12 *Law and Policy in International Business* 947.

Da Silveira, MA, *Trade Sanctions and International Sales* (Kluwer, 2014).

——. 'Economic Sanctions and Contractual Disputes between Private Operators' in L van den Herik (ed), *Research Handbook on UN Sanctions and International Law* (Edward Elgar, 2017) 330.

D'Avout, L, 'Case Note on Cour de cassation (Ch. soc.) – 24 février 2004' (2005) 94 *Revue critique de droit international privé* 62.

——. 'La clause attributive de juridiction résiste aux lois de police' (2008) 82 *La Semaine Juridique*, Edition générale 47, 19 November 2008, 25.

——. 'Le sort des règles impératives dans le règlement Rome I' (2008) 184 *Recueil Dalloz*, 2165.

——. 'Sources – Entreprises mondiales, régulation locale' in L d'Avout and S Bollée (eds), 'Panorama – Droit du commerce international août – juillet 2014' (2014) 190 *Recueil Dalloz* 1967.

——. 'Opérations – L'extraterritorialité contrariée par la théorie des lois de police ?' in L d'Avout and S Bollée (eds), 'Panorama – Droit du commerce international, août 2014 – juillet 2015' (2015) 191 *Recueil Dalloz* 2031.

D'Avout, L and Bureau, D, 'Lois de police étrangères devant le juge français du contrat international' (2010) 84 La *Semaine Juridique – Entreprise et Affaires* 18–19.

De Boer, TM, 'Living Apart Together: The Relationship Between Public and Private International Law' (2010) 57 *Netherlands International Law Review* 183.

De Boer, TM and Kotting, R, 'Der niederländische Richter und das US-Gasröhren-Embargo' (1984) *IPRax* 108.

De Brabandere, E and Holloway, D, 'Sanctions and International Arbitration' in L van den Herik (ed), *Research Handbook on UN Sanctions and International Law* (Edward Elgar, 2017) 304.

De Vauplane, H, 'Une nouvelle géopolitique de la norme', in A Garapon and P Servan-Schreiber (eds), *Deals de justice* (PUF, 2013) 23.

De Vries, AW and Hazelzet, H, 'The EU as a New Actor on the Sanctions Scene' in Wallensteen, P. and Staibano, C. (eds), *International Sanctions - Between Words and Wars in the Global System* (Frank Cass 2005) 95.

Deelen, JEJT, 'Carriage of Goods by Sea. Party Autonomy - Supreme Court, May 13, 1966, NJ 1967, no 3 ("Alnati"-Case)' (1968) 15 *Netherlands International Law Review* 82.

Defalque, L and Luff, D, 'L'embargo et l'Union européenne' in *L'embargo, International Symposium, European Society for Banking and Financial Law* (Bruylant, 1996) 87.

Deinert, O, *Internationales Arbeitsrecht* (Mohr Siebeck, 2013).

Delebecque, P, 'L'acceuil des lois de police étrangères' (2010) *Revue de droit des transports* 15.

——. 'Transport maritime. Loi de police étrangère. Qualification. Effet (oui)' (2010) *Revue trimestrielle de droit commercial et de droit économique* 457.

Delpech, X, 'Rupture d'une relation commerciale établie : exclusion de clause d'élection de for' (2015) *Dalloz Actualité*, 11 December.

Derains, Y, 'Les normes d'application immédiate dans la jurisprudence arbitrale' in P Fouchard, P Kahn and A Lyon-Caen (eds), *Mélanges offerts à Berthold Goldman* (Litec, 1982) 29.

Deumier, P, Racine, J-B and Treppoz, E, 'La loi de police étrangère : une possibilité que le juge a l'obligation d'envisager' (2010) *Revue des contrats* 1385.

Dewost, J-L, 'La Communauté, les Dix et les "sanctions" contre l'Argentine - De la crise iranienne à la crise des Malouines' (1982) 28 *Annuaire français de droit international* 215.

Dickinson, A, 'Third-Country Mandatory Rules in the Law Applicable to Contractual Obligations: So Long, Farewell, auf Wiedersehen, Adieu?' (2007) 3 *Journal of Private International Law* 53.

Dieux, X, 'Questions relatives aux effets de la contrainte étatique sur les contrats économiques internationaux - un point de vue belge' (1987) 20 *Revue belge de droit international* 184.

Drobnig, U, 'Die Beachtung von ausländischen Eingriffsgesetzen - eine Interessenanalyse' in W Barfuß, B Dutoit, H Forkel, U Immenga and F Majoros (eds), *Festschrift für Karl H Neumayer* (Nomos, 1985) 159.

——. 'Internationale Schiedsgerichtsbarkeit und wirtschaftliche Eingriffsnormen' in H-J Musielak and K Schurig, *Festschrift für Gerhard Kegel* (Kohlhammer, 1987) 95.

Dubouis, L, 'L'embargo dans la pratique contemporaine' (1967) 13 *Annuaire français de droit international* 99.

Dutson, S, 'The Law Applicable to Contracts - Amendments to Undermine Common Sense and the Attractiveness of European Courts' (2006) 7 *Journal of International Banking and Financial Law* 300.

Eckes, C, 'Controlling the Most Dangerous Branch from Afar: Multilayered Counter-terrorist Policies and the European Judiciary' (2011) 2 *European Journal of Risk Regulation* 505.

Eeckhout, P, *External Relations of the European Union* (Oxford University Press, 2011).

Ehrenzweig, AA, 'Local and Moral Data in the Conflict of Laws: Terra Incognita' (1966) 16 *Buffalo Law Review* 55.

——. *Private International Law - General Part* (Sijthoff, 1967).

Ehrenzweig, AA and Jayme, E, *Private International Law Vol III - Special Part* (Sijthoff, 1967).

Ellicot, JL, 'Trends in Export Regulation' (1983) 38 *Business Lawyer* 533.

Emenegger, S, 'Extraterritorial Economic Sanctions and their Foundation in International Law' (2016) 33 *Arizona Journal of International & Comparative Law* 631.

Enonchong, N, 'Public Policy in the Conflict of Laws: A Chinese Wall around Little England?' (1996) 45 *International & Comparative Law Quarterly* 633.

Fawcett, JJ, 'Evasion of Law and Mandatory Rules in Private International Law' (1990) 49 *Cambridge Law Journal* 44.

Feldman, N, 'When Judges Make Foreign Policy' *New York Times*, 25 September 2008.

Ferjani, N and Huet, V, 'L'impact de la décision onusienne d'embargo sur l'exécution des contrats internationaux' (2010) 137 *Journal du droit international* 737.

Forwick, C, *Extraterritoriale US-amerikanische Exportkontrollen. Folgen für die Vertragsgestaltung* (Verlag Recht und Wirtschaft, 1993).

Francescakis, P, 'Quelques précisions sur les 'lois d'application immédiate' et leurs rapports avec les règles sur les conflits de lois' (1966) 55 *Revue critique de droit international privé* 1.

Franck, TM, 'Courts and Foreign Policy' (1991) 83 *Foreign Policy* 66.

Francq, S, 'The External Dimension of Rome I and Rome II – Neutrality or Schizophrenia?' in M Cremona and H-W Micklitz (eds), *Private Law in the External Relations of the EU* (Oxford University Press, 2016) 71.

Freitag, R, 'Einfach und international zwingende Normen' in S Leible (ed), *Das Grünbuch zum Internationalen Vertragsrecht* (Sellier, 2004) 167.

——. 'Die kollisionsrechtliche Behandlung ausländischer Eingriffsnormen nach Art. 9 Abs. 3 Rom I-VO' (2009) 29 *IPRax* 109.

——. 'Eingriffsnormen (international zwingende Bestimmungen), Berücksichtigung ausländischer Devisenvorschriften, Formvorschriften' in C Reithmann and D Martiny (eds), *Internationales Vertragsrecht*, 8th edn (Otto Schmidt, 2015) 349.

Fohrer-Dedeurwaerder, E, *La prise en considération des normes étrangères* (LGDJ, 2008).

Fuchs, A, 'Freigabe libyschen Vermögens in England trotz US-Einfrierungsbeschluß' (1990) 10 *IPRax* 260.

Garapon, A and Servan-Schreiben, P, 'Un changement de paradigme' in A Garapon and P Servan-Schreiben (eds), *Deals* de *justice* (PUF, 2013) 1.

Garcimartín Alférez, FJ, 'Medidas adoptadas por España ante la invasión iraquí' (1990) 42 *Revista española de derecho internacional* 693.

——. *Contratación internacional y medidas de coerción económica* (Beramar, 1993).

——. 'Embargo' in J Basedow, G Rühl, F Ferrari and P de Miguel Asensio (eds), *Encyclopedia of Private International Law* (Edward Elgar, 2017) 599.

Garvey, JI, 'Judicial Foreign Policy-Making in International Civil Litigation: Ending the Charade of Separation of Powers' (1993) 24 *Law & Policy in International Business* 461.

Gatti, M, *European External Action Service: Promoting Coherence through Autonomy and Coordination* (Martinus Nijhoff, 2016).

Gauttier, P, 'Horizontal Coherence and the External Competences of the European Union' (2004) 10 *European Law Journal* 23.

Gavalda, C, 'L'efficacité juridique en France de l'executive order du président Carter "gelant" les avoirs officiels iraniens?' (1979) *Gazette du Palais*, 18 December 1979, 645.

——. 'Tribunal de grande instance de Paris 21 décembre 1979 and 21 janvier 1980' (1980) 100 Gazette du Palais, 13 March 1980, vol I, 154.

Gebauer, M, 'Kollisionsrechtliche Auswirkungen der US-amerikanischen Helms-Burton-Gesetzgebung' (1998) 18 *IPRax* 145.

Gebhard, C, 'Coherence' in C Hill and M Smith, *International Relations and the European Union*, 2nd edn (Oxford University Press, 2011) 101.

Geimer, R, *Internationales Zivilprozessrecht*, 7th edn (Otto Schmidt, 2015).

Geisinger, E, Bärtsch, P, Raneda, J and Ebere, S, 'Les conséquences des sanctions économiques sur les obligations contractuelles et sur l'arbitrage commercial international' (2012) *Revue de droit des affaires internationales/International Business Law Journal* 405.

Georgieff, A, *Kollisonen durch extraterritoriale staatliche Regelungen im internationalen Wirtschaftsrecht* (Carl Heymanns Verlag, 1989).

Geurts, M, 'Rechtsfragen der Embargo-Maßnahmen durch die EU am Beispiel des Konfliktes mit der Russischen Föderation' (2015) 61 *Recht der Internationalen Wirtschaft* 32.

Gherari, H, 'La mise en oeuvre des sanctions' in Habib Gherari and Sandra Szurek (eds), *Sanctions unilatérales, mondialisation du commerce et ordre juridique international* (Montchrestien, 1998) 53.
Gianviti, F, 'Le blocage des avoirs officiels iraniens par les Etats-Unis (executive order du 14 novembre 1979)' (1980) 69 *Revue critique de droit international privé* 279.
Gold, J, *The Fund Agreement in the Courts*, vol 4 (IMF, 1989).
Gottschalk, E and Breßler, S, 'Missbrauchskontrolle von Gerichtsstandsvereinbarungen im europäischen Zivilprozessrecht' (2007) 15 *ZEuP* 56.
Göthel, S, 'Grenzüberschreitende Reichweite ausländischen Kapitalmarktrechts' (2001) 21 *IPRax* 411.
Graveson, RH, *Conflict of Laws*, 7th edn (Sweet & Maxwell, 1974).
Grelon, B and Gudin, C-E, 'Contrats et crise du Golfe' (1991) 118 *Journal du droit international* 633.
Großfeld, B and Junker, A, *Das CoCom im internationalen Wirtschaftsrecht* (Mohr Siebeck, 1991).
Grossfeld, B and Rogers, CP, 'A Shared Value Approach to Jurisditional Conflicts in International Economic Law' (1983) 32 *International & Comparative Law Quarterly* 931.
Gurson, M, 'The U.S. Jurisdiction over Transfers of U.S. Dollars between Foreigners and over Ownership of U.S. Dollar Accounts in Foreign Banks' (2004) *Columbia Business Law Review* 721.
Harris, J, 'Mandatory Rules and Public Policy under the Rome I Regulation' in F Ferrari and S Leible (eds), *Rome I Regulation* (Sellier, 2009) 269.
Hartley, TC, 'Mandatory Rules in International Contracts: The Common Law Approach' in *Collected Courses of the Hague Academy of International Law, Vol 266 – 1997* (Martinus Nijhoff, 1998) 337.
——. 'The Modern Approach to Private International Law: International Litigation and Transactions from a Common-Law Perspective' in *Collected Courses of the Hague Academy of International Law*, vol 319 (Martinus Nijhoff, 2006) 9.
Hauser, P, *Eingriffsnormen in der Rom I-Verordnung* (Mohr Siebeck, 2012).
Heini, A, 'Ausländische Staatsinteressen und internationales Privatrecht' (1981) 100 *Zeitschrift für Schweizerisches Recht* 65.
——. 'Die Anwendung wirtschaftlicher Zwangsmaßnahmen im internationalen Privatrecht' in WA Kewenig and A Heini, *Die Anwendung wirtschaftlicher Zwangsmaßnahmen im Völkerrecht und im internationalen Privatrecht* (CF Müller, 1982) 43.
Heiss, H, 'Party Autonomy' in F Ferrari and S Leible (eds), *Rome I Regulation* (Sellier, 2009).
Heiz, R, *Das fremde öffentliche Recht im internationalen Kollisionsrecht* (Polygraphischer Verlag, 1959).
Hellner, M, 'Third Country Overriding Mandatory Rules in the Rome I Regulation: Old Wine in New Bottles?' (2009) 5 *Journal of Private International Law* 447.
Herdegen, M, *Principles of International Economic Law* (Oxford University Press, 2013).
Hessler, H-J, 'Datum-Theorie und Zweistufigkeit des internationalen Privatrechts' in R Serick, H Niederländer and E Jayme (eds), *Albert A Ehrenzweig und das internationale Privatrecht* (Carl Winter/Universitätsverlag, 1986) 137.
Hillion, C, 'Tous pour un, un pour tous! Coherence in the External Relations of the European Union' in M Cremona (ed), *Developments in EU External Relations Law* (Oxford University Press, 2008) 10.
Horn, N, 'Zwingendes Recht in der internationalen Schiedsgerichtsbarkeit' (2008) 6 *SchiedsVZ* 209.
Horváthy, B, 'Az Európai Unió Oroszországi Föderációval szemben bevezetett gazdasági szankciói és a Kereskedelmi Világszervezet joga' (2015) 59 *Külgazdaság* 172.
Huet, A, 'Clause attributive de juridiction à un tribunal étranger et loi française de police et de sûreté (étude du droit commun)' (2009) 185 *Recueil Dalloz* 684.
Hufbauer, GC, Schott, JJ and Elliott, KA, *Economic Sanctions Reconsidered: History and Current Policy* (Institute for International Economics, 1985).
Idot, L, 'Les conflits de lois en droit de la concurrence' (1995) 122 *Journal du droit international* 320.
Jackson, D, 'Mandatory Rules and Rules of "Ordre Public"' in PM North (ed), *Contract Conflicts* (North-Holland Publishing Company, 1982) 59.
Jacquet, J-M, 'La norme extraterritoriale dans le commerce international' (1985) 112 *Journal du droit international* 327.
Jaffey, AJE, *Introduction to the Conflict of Laws* (Butterworths, 1988).
James, S, 'Rome I: Shall We Dance?' (2008) 2 *Law and Financial Markets Review* 113.

Jault-Seseke, F, 'L'applicabilité d'une loi de police n'entrave pas le jeu de la clause attributive de juridiction' (2009) 185 *Recueil Dalloz*, 200.

——. 'Panorama – Droit internal privé (février 2010–février 2011)' (2011) 187 *Recueil Dalloz* 1374.

Jayme, E, 'Ausländische Rechtsregeln und Tatbestand inländischer Sachnormen – Betrachtungen zu Ehrenzweigs Datum-Theorie' in E Jayme and G Kegel (eds), *Gedächtnisschrift für Albert Ehrenzweig* (CF Müller, 1976) 35.

Johnston, A, 'Other Exception Clauses' in P Oliver (ed), *Oliver on Free Movement of Goods in the European Union*, 5th edn (Hart Publishing, 2010) 370.

Joyce, A, '*Libyan Arab Foreign Bank v Bankers Trust*: Common Law Meets its Limits?' (1988) 29 *Harvard International Law Journal* 451.

Junker, A, 'Schadensersatzpflicht bei einem Verstoß gegen ein ausländisches Embargo – Zugleich eine Besprechung der Entscheidung des BGH vom 20. 11. 1990' (1991) 46 *JuristenZeitung* 699.

Kessedjian, C, *Droit du commerce international* (Thémis, 2013).

Keyes, M, 'Statutes, Choice of Law, and the Role of Forum Choice' (2008) 4 *Journal of Private International Law* 1.

Kinsch, P, *Le fait du prince étranger* (LGDJ, 1994).

Knöfel, S, 'Mandatory Rules and Choice of Law: A Comparative Approach to Article 7(2) of the Rome Convention' (1999) *Journal of Business Law* 239.

Knüppel, N, 'Zwingendes materielles Recht und internationale Schuldverträge' (PhD thesis, Rheinische Friedrich-Wilhelms-Universität Bonn, 1988).

Koutrakos, P, 'Is Article 297 EC a "Reserve of Sovereignty"?' (2000) 37 *Common Market Law Review* 1339.

——. *Trade, Foreign Policy and Defence under the Law of the EU* (Hart Publishing, 2001).

Koutrakos, P, *EU International Relations Law* (Hart 2006).

Köhler, A, 'Die Berücksichtigung ausländischer Eingriffsnormen im Europäischen Internationalen Vertragsrecht' in K Binder and F Eichel (eds), *Internationale Dimensionen des Wirtschaftsrechts* (Nomos, 2013) 199.

——. *Eingriffsnormen – Der 'unfertige Teil' des europäischen IPR* (Mohr Siebeck, 2013).

Kreuzer, KF, 'Parteiautonomie und fremdes Außenwirtschaftsrecht' in P Schlechtriem and HG Leser (eds), *Zum Deutschen und Internationalen Schuldrecht* (Mohr Siebeck, 1983) 89.

——. *Ausländisches Wirtschaftsrecht vor deutschen Gerichten* (CF Müller 1986).

Kropholler, J, 'Internationale Zuständigkeit' in HJ Herrmann, J Basedow and J Kropholler (eds), *Handbuch des internationalen Zivilverfahrensrechts* (Mohr Siebeck, 1982) 197.

Krüger, H, 'Das irakische Antiboykottgesetz 1990' (1990) 36 *Recht der Internationalen Wirtschaft* 934.

Kuckein, M, *Die ‚Berücksichtigung' von Eingriffsnormen im deutschen und englischen internationalen Vertragsrecht* (Mohr Siebeck, 2008).

Kühne, G, 'Methodeneinheit und Methodenvielfalt im internationalen Privatrecht – Eine Generation nach "Kollisionsnorm und Sahrecht"' in R Michaels and D Solomon (eds), *Liber Amicorum Klaus Schurig* (Sellier, 2012) 129.

Kunda, I, *International Mandatory Rules of a Third Country in European Contract Conflict of Laws: The Rome Convention and the Proposed Rome I Regulation* (Rijeka Law Faculty, 2007).

Kuyper, PJ, 'The European Community and the US Pipeline Embargo: Comments on Comments' in J Delbrück, R Hofmann and A Zimmermann (eds), *German Yearbook of International Law, Vol 27 – 1984* (Duncker & Humblot, 1985) 72.

Laferrière, J, 'Le boycott et le droit international' (1910) 17 *Revue générale de droit international public* 288.

Lagarde, P and Tenenbaum, A, 'De la convention du Rome au règlement Rome I' 2008 (97) *Revue critique de droit international privé* 727.

Lalive, P, 'Transnational (or Truly International) Public Policy and International Arbitration' in P Sanders (ed), *Comparative Arbitration Practice and Public Policy in Arbitration, ICCA Congress Series, 1986 New York*, vol 3 (Kluwer, 1987) 258.

Lando, O, 'Party Autonomy in the EC Convention on the Law Applicable to Contractual Obligations' in F Rigaux (ed), F, *L'influence des Communautés européennes sur le droit international privé des Etats members* (Larcier, 1981) 191.

Lando, O and Nielsen, PA, 'The Rome I Regulation' (2008) *Common Market Law Review* 1687.

Landy-Osman, L, 'L'embargo des Nations Unies contre l'Irak et l'exécution des contrats internationaux' (1991) 17 *Droit et Pratique du Commerce International* 597.

Laugwitz, HC, *Die Anerkennung und Vollstreckung drittstaatlicher Entscheidungen in Zivil- und Handelssachen* (Mohr Siebeck, 2015).

Laursen, F, *The EU's Lisbon Treaty: Institutional Choices and Implementation* (Ashgate, 2012).

Lehmann, R, *Zwingendes Recht dritter Staaten im internationalen Vertragsrecht* (Peter Lang, 1986).

Leible, S, 'Außenhandel und Rechtssicherheit' (1998) 97 *ZVglRWiss* 286.

Lenaerts, K and de Smijter, E, 'The United Nations and the European Union: Living Apart Together' in Wellens, K, *International Law: Theory and Practice – Essays in Honour of Eric Suy* (Martinus Nijhoff, 1998) 439.

Lindemeyer, B, 'Das Handelsembargo als wirtschaftliches Zwangsmittel der staatlichen Außenpolitik' (1981) 27 *Recht der Internationalen Wirtschaft* 10.

Loquin, E, 'Les effets des lois d'embargo sur la mise en oeuvre des clauses compromissoires' (2001) *Revue trimestrielle de droit commercial et de droit économique* 66.

Loussouarn, Y, 'Cours général de droit international privé' in *Collected Courses of the Hague Academy of International Law*, vol 139 (Martinus Nijhoff, 1973) 269.

Lowe, AV, 'Blocking Extraterritorial Jurisdiction: The British Protection of Trading Act, 1980' (1981) 75 *American Journal of International Law* 257.

——. 'Public International Law and the Conflict of Laws: The European Response to the United States Export Administration Regulations' (1984) 33 *International & Comparative Law Quarterly* 515.

——. 'International Law Issues Arising in the "Pipeline" Dispute: the British Position' in J Delbrück, R Hofmann and A Zimmermann (eds), *German Yearbook of International Law, Vol 27 – 1984* (Duncker & Humblot, 1985) 54.

——. 'Extraterritorial Jurisdiction – British Practice' (1988) 52 *RabelsZ* 157.

——. 'Freezing Foreign Bank Accounts – *Libyan Arab Foreign Bank v Bankers Trust Co*' (1988) *Lloyd's Maritime and Commercial Law Quarterly* 1.

Lowenfeld, AF, 'Agora: The Cuban Liberty and Democratic Solidarity (Libertad) Act' (1996) 90 *American Journal of International Law* 419.

——. *International Economic Law*, 2nd edn (Oxford University Press, 2008).

Lucchini, L, 'Le boycottage in Société française pour le droit international' in P Weil (ed), *Colloque d'Orléans, Aspects du droit international économique* (Pedone, 1972) 67.

Magnus, U, 'Art 9 Rom I-VO Eingriffsnormen', in U Magnus (ed), *J. von Staudingers Kommentar zum Bürgerlichen Gesetzbuch mit Einführungsgesetz und Nebengesetzen* (Sellier/de Gruyter, 2011) 637.

Malatesta, A, 'The *Lugano* Opinion and its Consequences in Family and Succession Matters' in A Malatesta, S Bariatti and F Pocar (eds), *The External Dimension of EC Private International Law in Family and Succession Matters* (CEDAM, 2008) 19.

Mankowski, P, 'Die Rom I-Verordnung – Änderungen im europäischen IPR für Schuldverträge' (2008) 8 *Internationales Handelsrecht* 133.

——. *Interessenpolitik und europäisches Kollisionsrecht* (Nomos, 2011).

——. 'Deutscher Versicherer und das US-Embargo gegen den Iran – ein kleines Lehrstück zu ausländischen Eingriffsnormen' (2015) *Recht der Internationalen Wirtschaft* 405.

——. 'Drittstaatliche Embargonormen, Außenpolitik im IPR, Berücksichtigung von Fakten statt Normen: Art. 9 Abs. 3 Rom I-VO im praktischen Fall (zu Cour d'appel de Paris, 25.2.2015 – 12/23757)' (2016) 36 *IPRax* 485.

Mann, FA, 'Proper Law and Illegality in Private International Law' (1937) 18 *British Yearbook of International Law* 97.

——. 'Illegality and the Conflict of Laws' (1958) 21 *Modern Law Review* 180.

——. Conflict of Laws and Public Law' in *Collected Courses of the Hague Academy of International Law – 1971*, vol 132 (Sijthoff, 1971) 107.

——. 'Eingriffsgesetze und Internationales Privatrecht' in Klaus Müller and Hermann Soell, *Festschrift für Eduard Wahl* (Carl Winter/Universitätsverlag, 1973) 146.

Marchand, A, 'Note – Cass Com, 16 mars 2010, n° 08-21.511' (2011) 138 *Journal du droit international* 99.

——. *L'embargo en droit du commerce international* (Larcier, 2012).

Marcuss, SJ and Mathias, DS, 'US Foreign Policy Export Controls: Do They Pass Muster under International Law' (1984) 2 *International Tax & Business Lawyer* 1.

Martiny, D, 'Anerkennung ausländischer Entscheidungen nach autonomem Recht' in D Martiny (ed), *Handbuch des internationalen Zivilverfahrensrechts*, vol III/1 (Mohr Siebeck, 1984) 1.

Mathäß, S, *Die Auswirkungen staaten- und personenbezogener Embargomaßnahmen auf Privatrechtsverhältnisse* (Nomos, 2016).

Mathey, N, 'Application d'une clause attributive de compétence en cas d'abus de dépendance' (2008) 82 *La Semaine Juridique – Entreprise et Affaires* 51–52, 18 December, 25.

Matray, L, 'L'embargo national et international dans l'arbitrage' (1997) 74 *Revue de droit international et de droit comparé* 7.

Mattout, J-P, 'Opérations internationales' in J-P Mattout and A Prüm, 'Chronique – Droit bancaire, Janvier 2010 – juin 2010 : Clair-obscure' (2010) 195 *Droit & Patrimoine* 100.

Mayer, BR and Albrecht, M, 'Bankvertrag und Finanzsanktionen: Leistungsverweigerungsrecht bei drohendem Verstoß gegen US-Verordnungen?' (2015) 26 *Wirtschafts- und Bankrecht* 1226.

Mayer, P, 'Les lois de police étrangères' (1981) 108 *Journal du droit international* 277.

——. 'Mandatory Rules of Law in International Arbitration' (1986) 2 *Arbitration International* 274.

——. 'Les lois de police' (1988) *Droit international privé : travaux du Comité français de droit international privé* 105.

——. 'L'étendue du contrôle, par le juge étatique, de la conformité des sentences arbitrales aux lois de police' in T Azzi (ed), *Vers de nouveaux équilibres entre ordres juridiques – Liber amicorum Hélène Gaudemet-Tallon* (Dalloz, 2008) 460.

Mayer, P and Heuzé, V, *Droit international privé*, 11th edn (LGDJ, 2014).

McClean, D, 'Bilateral Agreements with Non-Member States after the *Lugano* Opinion' in A Malatesta, S Bariatti and F Pocar (eds), *The External Dimension of EC Private International Law in Family and Succession Matters* (CEDAM, 2008) 55.

McLachlan, C, *Foreign Relations Law* (Cambridge University Press, 2014).

McParland, M, *The Rome I Regulation on the Law Applicable to Contractual Obligations* (Oxford University Press, 2015).

Meessen, KM, 'Extraterritoriality of Export Control: A German Lawyer's Analysis of the Pipeline Case' in J Delbrück, R Hofmann and A Zimmermann (eds), *German Yearbook of International Law, Vol 27 – 1984* (Duncker & Humblot, 1985) 97.

Mehle, B and Mehle, V, 'Die notwendige Einhaltung von EU-Embargo-Regelungen durch Unternehmen mit Sitz in Drittstaaten' (2015) 61 *Recht der Internationalen Wirtschaft* 397.

Meinhardt, M and Ahrens, J-M, 'Wettbewerbsrecht und Schiedsgerichtsbarkeit in der Schweiz – Eine Würdigung des Entscheids des Bundesgerichts vom 8. März 2006–' (2006) 4 *SchiedsVZ* 182.

Meng, W, *Extraterritoriale Jurisdiktion im öffentlichen Wirtschaftsrecht* (Springer, 1994).

——. 'Extraterritoriale Jurisdiktion in der US-amerikanischen Sanktionsgesetzgebung' (1997) 8 *EuZW* 423.

——. *Streitigkeiten über Wirtschaftssanktionen zwischen EU und USA* (Zentrum für Europäisches Wirtschaftsrecht, Rheinische Friedrich-Wilhelms-Universität Bonn, 1997).

Menjucq, M, *Droit international et européen des sociétés*, 4th edn (LGDJ, 2016).

Merkin, R, *Arbitration Law* (LLP, 2004).

Micklitz, H-W, 'The Internal versus the External Dimension of European Private Law: A Conceptual Design and a Research Agenda' in M Cremona and H-W Micklitz (eds), *Private Law in the External Relations of the EU* (Oxford University Press, 2016) 9.

Mills, A, *The Confluence of Public and Private International Law* (Cambridge University Press, 2009).

——. 'Private International Law and EU External Relations: Think Local Act Global, or Think Global Act Local?' (2016) 65 *International & Comparative Law Quarterly* 541.

Moitry, J-H, 'L'arbitre international et l'obligation de boycottage imposée par un Etat' (1991) 118 *Journal du droit international* 349.

Morse, CGJ, 'The EEC Convention on the Law Applicable to Contractual Obligations' in GG Jacobs (ed), *Yearbook of European Law (1982)* (Clarendon, 1983) 107.

Muir Watt, H, 'L'affaire Lloyd's : globalisation des marchés et contentieux contractuel' (2002) 91 *Revue critique de droit international privé* 509.

——. 'Aspects économiques du droit international privé' in *Collected Courses of the Hague Academy of International Law*, vol 307 (Martinus Nijhoff, 2005) 307.

——. 'The Role of Conflict of Laws in European Private Law' in C Twigg-Flesner (ed), *The Cambridge Companion to European Union Private Law* (Cambridge University Press, 2010) 44.

Muir-Watt, H and Radicati di Brozolo, L. G, 'Party Autonomy and Mandatory Rules in a Global World' (2004) 4 *Global Jurist Advances* 1.

Mülbert, PO, 'Ausländische Eingriffsnormen als Datum' (1986) 6 *IPRax* 140.

Neumann, NC, *Internationale Handelsembargos und privatrechtliche Verträge* (Nomos, 2000).

Neuss, JJ, *Handelsembargos zwischen Völkerrecht und IPR* (VVF, 1989).

Niboyet, M-L and de Geouffre de la Pradelle, G, *Droit international privé*, 5th edn (LGDJ, 2015).

Nourissat, C, 'Lois de police étrangères devant le juge français du contrat international : une première sous l'empire de la Convention de Rome et peut-être pas une dernière sous l'empire du règlement "Rome I"' (2010) 5 *Revue Lamy droit des affaires* 63.

Nygh, P, *Autonomy in International Contracts* (Clarendon, 1999).

Périlleux, J, 'L'embargo et le droit des obligations' in Association européenne pour le droit bancaire et financier, *L'embargo* (Bruylant, 1996) 167.

Pettit, PCF. and Styles, CJD, 'The International Response to Extraterritorial Application of United States Antitrust Laws' (1982) 37 *Business Lawyer* 697.

Pfeiffer, T, 'Datumtheorie un "local data" in der Rom II-VO – am Beispiel von Straßenverkehrsunfällen' in R Michaels and D Solomon (eds), *Liber Amicorum Klaus Schurig* (Sellier, 2012) 229.

Philip, A, 'Mandatory Rules, Public Law (Political Rules) and Choice of Law in the EEC Convention on the Law Applicable to Contractual Obligations' in PM North (ed), *Contract Conflicts* (North-Holland Publishing Company, 1982) 81.

Portela, C, *European Union Sanctions and Foreign Policy* (Routledge, 2010).

Prieß, H-J and Schaper, M, 'Erfüllung oder Nichterfüllung – Zur Durchsetzbarkeit vertraglicher Ansprüche bei entgegenstehendem ausländischen Embargorecht' in D Ehlers and H-M Wolffgang (eds), *Recht der Exportkontrolle: Bestandsaufnahme und Perspektiven; Handbuch zum Exportkontrollrecht – Festschrift für Dr. Arnold Wallraff* (Fachmedien Recht & Wirtschaft, 2015) 267.

Quinke, D, 'Schiedsvereinbarungen und Eingriffsnormen – Zugleich Anmerkung zu OLG München, Urt. v. 17. Mai 2006, Az. 7 U 1781/06–' (2007) 5 *SchiedsVZ* 246, 252.

Racine, J-B, 'L'arbitrage commercial international et les mesures d'embargo. À propos de l'arrêt de la Cour d'appel du Québec du 31 mars 2003' (2004) 134 *Journal du droit international* 89.

Radicati di Brozolo, LG, 'Mondialisation, juridiction, arbitrage : vers des règles d'application semi-nécessaires?' (2003) 92 *Revue critique de droit international privé* 1.

——. 'Arbitrage commercial international et lois de police' in *Collected Courses of the Hague Academy of International Law, Vol 315 – 2005* (Martinus Nijhoff, 2006) 265.

Radtke, RC, 'Schuldstatut und Eingriffsrecht' (1985) 84 *ZVglRWiss* 325.

Raitio, J, 'Legal Certainty, Non-retroactivity and Periods of Limitation in EU Law' (2008) 2 *Legisprudence* 1.

——. 'The Expectation of Legal Certainty and Horizontal Effect of EU Law' in U Bernitz, X Groussot and F Schulyok (eds), *General Principles of EU Law and European Private Law* (Kluwer, 2013) 199.

Rathbone, M, Jeydel, P and Lentz, A, 'Sanctions, Sanctions Everywhere: Forging a Path Through Complex Transnational Sanctions Laws' (2013) 44 *Georgetown Journal of International Law* 1055.

Remien, O, 'Außenwirtschaftsrecht in kollisionsrechtlicher Sicht' (1990) 54 *RabelsZ* 431.

——. 'Art 9 ROM I' in H Prütting, G Wegen and G Weinreich (eds), *BGB Kommentar*, 11th edn (Luchterhand, 2016) 3324.

Renner, M, 'Article 9 Overriding Mandatory Provisions' in G-P Calliess (ed), *Rome Regulations* (Kluwer, 2011) 195.

Rentsch, B, 'Krisenbewältigung durch konstitutionalisiertes Kollisionsrecht, oder: Eingriffsrecht als integraler Bestandteil des europäischen IPR' in J Bauerschmidt, B Fassbender, MW Müller, A Siehr and C Unseld (eds), *Konstitutionalisierung in Zeiten globaler Krisen* (Nomos, 2015) 255.

Rigaux, F, 'Droit économique et conflits de souverainetés' (1988) 52 *RabelsZ* 104.

Ringe, W-G, 'Art. 9 Rom I-VO Eingriffsnormen' in I Ludwig (ed), *JurisPraxis Kommentar BGB, Band 6, Internationales Privatrecht*, 5th edn (Juris, 2011) 1119.

Roth, W-H, 'Savigny, Eingriffsnormen und die Rom I-Verordnung' in JF Baur, O Sandrock, B Scholtka and A Shapira (eds), *Festsschrift für Gunther Kühne* (Verlag Recht und Wirtschaft, 2009) 859.

——. 'Europäische Kollisionsrechtsvereinheitlichung: Überblick – Kompetenz – Grundfragen' in E-M Kieninger and O Remien (eds), *Europäische Kollisionsrechtsvereinheitlichung* (Nomos, 2012) 11.

——. 'Drittstaatliche Eingriffsnormen und Rom I-Verordnung' (2018) 38 *IPRax* 177.

Rousseau, C, 'Le boycottage dans les rapports internationaux' (1958) 62 *Revue générale de droit international public* 5.

Rutzke, CR, 'The Libyan Asset Freeze and Its Application to Foreign Government Deposits in Overseas Branches of United States Banks: *Libyan Arab Foreign Bank v Bankers Trust Co*' (1988) 3 *American University International Law Review* 241.

Rühl, G, 'Die Wirksamkeit von Gerichtstands- und Schiedsvereinbarungen im Lichte der Ingmar-Entscheidung des EuGH' (2007) 27 *IPRax* 294.

Ryngaert, C, 'Extraterritorial Export Controls (Secondary Boycotts)' (2008) 7 *Chinese Journal of International Law* 625.

Salama, S, 'Le sort des contrats conclus avec des opératuers irakiens à la suite de la levée de l'embargo' (2003) *Revue de droit des affaires internationales/International Business Law Journal* 887.

Sana-Chaille de Nere, S, 'Transport maritime et lois de police étrangères' (2010) 62 *Droit maritime français* 367.

Santini, A, 'The Doctrine of Implied External Powers and Private International Law Concerning Family and Succession Matters' in A Malatesta, S Bariatti and F Pocar (eds), *The External Dimension of EC Private International Law in Family and Succession Matters* (CEDAM, 2008) 31.

Scherer, M, 'Corruption, Embargos and Sanctions as a Bar to the Enforcement of Contracts in International Arbitration' (2014) 6 *International Journal of Arab Arbitration* 64.

Schnyder, AK, 'Anwendung ausländischer Eingriffsnormen durch Schiedsgerichte' (1995) 59 *RabelsZ* 293.

——. '"Gegenmassnahmen" im Internationalen Privat- und Zivilverfahrensrecht' in W Fiedler, E Klein and AK Schnyder, *Gegenmassnahmen – Berichte der Deutschen Gesellschaft für Völkerrecht*, vol 37 (CF Müller Verlag, 1998) 73.

Schultsz, JC, 'Dutch Antecedents and Parallels to Article 7 of the EEC Contracts Convention of 1980' (1983) 47 *RabelsZ* 267.

Schulze, G, 'Datum-Theorie und narrative Norm – Zu einem Privatrecht für die multikulturelle Gesellschaft' in E Jayme (ed), *Kulturelle Identität und Internationales Privatrecht* (CF Müller, 2003) 155.

Schurig, K, *Kollisionsnorm und Sachrecht* (Duncker & Humblot, 1981).

——. 'Zwingendes Recht, "Eingriffsnormen" und neues IPR' (1990) 54 *RabelsZ* 217.

Schütze, R, 'External Union Policies: A Substantive Overview' in R Schütze (ed), *Foreign Affairs and the EU Constitution* (Cambridge University Press, 2014) 407.

——. 'On "Middle Ground": The European Union and Public International Law' in *Foreign Affairs and the EU Constitution* (Cambridge University Press, 2014) 47.

Seppala, CR, 'La pratique américaine récente : Les lois Helms-Burton et d'Amato-Kennedy' in H Gherari and S Szurek (eds), *Sanctions unilatérales, mondialisation du commerce et ordre juridique international* (Montchrestien, 1998) 83.

Shahani, G, 'Impact of Sanctions under the CISG' (2015) 33 *ASA Bulletin* 849.

Siehr, K, 'Ausländische Eingriffsnormen im inländischen Wirtschaftskollisiomsrecht' (1988) 52 *RabelsZ* 41.

Slaughter, A-M, 'The Real New World Order' (1997) 76 *Foreign Affairs* 183.

Sloss, D, 'Judicial Foreign Policy: Lessons from the 1970s' (2008) 53 *Saint Louis University Law Journal* 145.

Sonnenberger, HJ, 'Die Eingriffsnorm: ein internationalprivatrechtliches σκανδαλον? Beobachtungen und Betrachtungen' in B Großfeld, R Sack, TM Möllers, J Drexl and A Heinemann (eds), *Festschrift für Wolfgang Fikentscher* (Mohr Siebeck, 1998) 283.

Sossai, M, 'UN Sanctions and Regional Organizations: An Analytical Framework' in L van den Herik (ed), *Research Handbook on UN Sanctions and International Law* (Edward Elgar, 2017) 395.

Staudinger, A, 'Art. 9 Eingriffsnormen', in F Ferrari, P Mankowski, E-M Kieninger, K Otte, I Saenger, G Schulze and A Staudinger (eds), *Internationales Vertragsrecht* (Beck, 2012) 241.

Stern, B, 'Quelques observations sur les règles internationales relatives à l'application extraterritoriale du droit' (1986) 32 *Annuaire français de droit international* 7.

——. 'Les Etats-Unis et le droit imperialiste' *Le Monde*, 12 September 1996, 12.

Stone, P, *EU Private International Law*, 3rd edn (Edward Elgar, 2014).

Szurek, S, 'Le recours aux sanctions' in H Gherari and S Szurek (eds), *Sanctions unilatérales, mondialisation du commerce et ordre juridique international* (Montchrestien, 1998) 19.

Tevendale, C and Cannon, A, 'Enforcement of Awards' in JDM Lew, H Bor, G Fullelove and J Greenaway (eds), *Arbitration in England* (Kluwer, 2013) 563.

Thomale, C, 'Österreichisches Arbeitsvertragsstatut und deutsches Betriebsverfassungsrecht – intertemporale Dimensionen ausländischer Eingriffsnormen' (2013) 33 *IPRax* 375.

Thompson, EA, *Romans and Barbarians: The Decline of the Western Empire* (University of Wisconsin Press, 2002).

Thorn, K, 'Artikel 9: Eingriffsnormen' in T Rauscher (ed), *Europäisches Zivilprozess- und Kollisionsrecht*, vol 3 (Otto Schmidt, 2016) 432.

Tietje, C, 'The Concept of Coherence in the Treaty on European Union and the Common Foreign and Security Policy' (1997) 2 *European Foreign Affairs Review* 211.

Timmermans, C, 'The Specificity of Private Law in EU External Relations: The Area of Freedom, Security and Justice' in M Cremona and H-W Micklitz (eds), *Private Law in the External Relations of the EU* (Oxford University Press, 2016) 59.

Toubiana, A, *Le domaine de la loi du contrat en droit international privé* (Dalloz, 1972).

Tridimas, T, *The General Principles of EU Law*, 2nd edn (Oxford University Press, 2006).

Urech, D, 'Eurodollar Deposits and Freezing Orders: The Libyan Assets Case Revisited' (1988) 3 *Journal of International Banking Law* 269.

Vagts, DF., 'The Pipeline Controversy: An American Viewpoint' in J Delbrück, R Hofmann and A Zimmermann (eds), *German Yearbook of International Law, Vol 27 – 1984* (Duncker & Humblot, 1985) 38.

Vance, DZ, 'Export Controls-Challenge to the Validity of Department of Commerce Regulations Restricting the Export of Oil and Gas Equipment and Technology to the Soviet Union-Temporary Restraining Order Denied. *Dresser Industries v. Baldridge*, No. 82-2385 (D. D.C. filed Aug. 23, 1982)' (1983) 18 *Texas International Law Journal* 203.

Van der Haegen, O, 'European Public Policy in Commercial Arbitration: Bridge over Troubled Water?' (2009) 16 *Maastricht Journal of European and Comparative Law* 449.

Van Hecke, G, 'Foreign Public Law in the Courts' (1969) 1 *Revue belge de droit international* 63.

Van Houtte, H, 'Treaty Protection against Economic Sanctions' (1984–85) 18 *Revue belge de droit international* 34.

——. 'Les effets des sanctions économiques sur les contrats transnationaux' in Association européenne pour le droit bancaire et financier, *L'embargo* (Bruylant, 1996) 189.

Van Meerbeeck, J, 'The Principle of Legal Certainty in the Case-Law of the European Court of Justice: From Certainty to Trust' (2016) 41 *European Law Review* 275.

Van Vooren, B and Wessel, RA, *EU External Relations Law* (Cambridge University Press, 2014).

Vaucher, M, 'L'évolution récente de la pratique des sanctions communautaires à l'encontre des Etats tiers' (1993) 29 *Revue trimestrielle de droit européen* 39.

Vetter, E, 'Kollisionsrechtliche Fragen bei grenzüberschreitenden Subunternehmensverträgen im Industrieanlagenbau' (1988) 87 *ZVGlRWiss* 248.

Virole, J, 'Incidence des mesures d'embargo sur les contrats internationaux' (1981) 7 *Droit et pratique du commerce international* 311.

Vischer, F, 'Kollisionsrechtliche Parteiautonomie und dirigistische Wirtschaftsgesetzgebung' in Juristische Fakultät der Universität Basel, *Festgabe für Max Gerwig* (Helbing & Lichtenhahn, 1960) 167.

——. *General Course on Private International Law, Collected Courses of the Hague Academy of International Law*, vol 232 (Martinus Nijhoff, 1992) 180.

Von Allwörden, S, *US-Terrorlisten im deutschen Privatrecht: zur kollisions- und sachrechtlichen Problematik drittstaatlicher Sperrlisten mit extraterritorialer Wirkung* (Mohr Siebeck, 2014).

Von Hein, J, 'Einleitung zum IPR' in Säcker, F. J, Rixecker R. and Oetker, H. (eds), *Münchener Kommentar zum Bürgerlichen Gesetzbuch, Band 10, Internationales Privatrecht I*, 6th edn (Beck, 2015) 1.

Von Hein, W, 'Recht und Praxis der Ahndungsvorschriften des US-Export Administration Act' (1986) 32 *Recht der Internationalen Wirtschaft* 496.

Von Savigny, FK, *System des heutigen römischen Rechts*, vol 8 (Scientia, 1974).

Voser, N, 'Mandatory Rules of Law as a Limitation on the Law Applicable in International Commercial Arbitration' (1996) 7 *American Review of International Arbitration* 319.

Weller, M-P, 'Die neue Mobilitätsanknüpfung im Internationalen Familienrecht – Abfederung des Personalstatutenwechsels über die Datumtheorie' (2014) 34 *IPRax* 225.

Wengler, W, 'Die Anknüpfung des zwingenden Schuldrechts im internationalen Privatrecht' (1941) 54 *ZVglRWiss* 168.

Wernert, S, 'Le gel d'avoirs étrangers. Aspects de droit international public et de droit international privé' (dissertation, Université Paris II Panthéon-Assas, 2001).

Wessel, RA, 'The Inside Looking Out: Consistency and Delimitation in EU External Relations' (2000) 37 *Common Market Law Review* 1135.

Wilderspin, M and Rouchaud-Joët, A-M, 'La compétence externe de la Communauté européenne en droit international privé' (2004) 93 *Revue critique de droit international privé* 1.

Williams, R, 'The Impact of Sanctions on Charterparty Operations' (2013) 19 *Journal of International Maritime Law* 290.

Winkler, M and Lacombe, A, 'Mesures à vocation extraterritoriale et lois de police: un revers à l'hégémonie juridique outre-Atlantique?' (2015) 191 *Recueil Dalloz* 1260.

Wortley, BA, *The Interaction of Public and Private International Law, Collected Courses of the Hague Academy of International Law*, vol 85 (Martinus Nijhoff, 1954).

Wöhlert, H-T, 'EU-Verordnungen genießen beim Einfrieren von Geldern gegenüber einer Exekutiv-Order des Präsidenten der USA Anwendungsvorrang' (2011) 3 *Gesellschafts- und Wirtschaftsrecht* 340.

Wyler, E and Papaux, A, 'Extraneité de valeurs et de systèmes en droit international privé et en droit international public' in E Wyler and A Papaux (eds), *L'éxtraneité ou le dépassement de l'ordre juridique étatique* (Pedone, 1999) 239.

Zeigler, AD, 'The Siberian Piepline Dispute and the Export Administration Act: What's Left of Extraterritorial Limits and the Act of State Doctrine?' (1983) 6 *Houston Journal of International Law* 63.

Zeppenfeld, M, *Die allseitige Anknüpfung von Eingriffsnormen im Internationalen Wirtschaftsrecht* (Duncker & Humblot, 2001).

Zimmer, D, 'Ausländisches Wirtschaftsrecht vor deutschen Zivilgerichten: Zur Unterscheidung zwischen einer normativen Berücksichtigung fremder zwingender Normen und einer bloßen Beachtung ihrer tatsächlichen Folgen' (1993) 13 *IPRax* 65.

Zweigert, K, 'Nichterfüllung auf Grund ausländischer Leistungsverbote' (1942) 14 *Zeitschrift für ausländisches und internationales Privatrecht* 283.

INDEX

Note: for further information on individual countries and EU practice, reference should be made to the Tables of Cases and Legislation